THE CONCEPT OF KNIGHTHOOD
IN THE MIDDLE AGES

AMS Studies in the Middle Ages: No. 2
ISSN: 0270-6261

THE CONCEPT OF

Knighthood
in the Middle Ages

By Joachim Bumke

*Translated from the German
by W. T. H. and Erika Jackson*

INTRODUCTION BY W. T. H. JACKSON

AMS PRESS, INC.
NEW YORK, N.Y.

Library of Congress Cataloging in Publication Data

Bumke, Joachim.
    The concept of knighthood in the Middle Ages.

    (AMS studies in the Middle Ages, ISSN 0270-6261; no. 2)
    Translation of: Studien zum Ritterbegriff im 12. und 13. Jahr-
hundert. 2. Aufl.
    Bibliography: p.
    Includes index.
    1. Knights and knighthood. I. Title. II. Series.
CR4513.B813   1982   940.1'7   79-8840
ISBN 0-404-18034-5   AACR2

MANUFACTURED IN THE UNITED STATES
OF AMERICA

Contents

Translators' Preface

This book is a translation of the second edition of Joachim Bumke's *Studien zum Ritterbegriff im 12. und 13. Jahrhundert*. The title immediately calls attention to the problems of translating a work of very wide scope and considerable technical complication. The individual chapters do indeed constitute studies of different aspects of knighthood, but the whole is much more than a sum of its parts and it constitutes a thorough study of all features of knighthood. We have therefore omitted the word "studies" from the title. The word "Begriff" has been translated as "concept" because that is what the book is about. But the same word can also mean "term," and we have so translated it on many occasions where it is the naming of a characteristic of knighthood rather than its nature which is being discussed. Any reader who compares the translation with the German text will see that we have not always used the same English word in translating a German term. An obvious example is *ritterschaft,* which sometimes means "knighthood" and sometimes "chivalry." Technical terms present a special difficulty. Often there is no exact English equivalent of a German term in feudal law, and it has been necessary to improvise.

The book is concerned primarily with knighthood in Germany, and most of the evidence is drawn from German documents and German literature, but there is frequent comparison with knighthood in other countries, particularly in France. The author's object is to establish what contemporaries understood by knighthood in a political, social, and even moral sense; he does not concern himself with the often fanciful ideas of knighthood held by authors of the later Middle Ages and by writers of the late nineteenth and early twentieth centuries. To this end he has drawn heavily on legal documents of the period, but much of the evidence is derived from literary sources. It may be asked whether evidence taken from such diverse sources is strictly comparable, but the author shows conclusively that many aspects of knighthood were strongly influenced if not determined by features developed in literature. Nevertheless, he makes it clear that it is impossible to speak of a concept of knighthood which is applicable to all instances which occur in literature and in social life. When faced by the detailed evidence presented by Professor Bumke, many of the cherished conventions on the nature of knighthood prove to be ill-founded: that knights were always *military* servants; that they were always a superior class of soldier with better arms; that they were noblemen or always became such; and, most important, that there was a knightly class. It is not part of the author's purpose to explore the nature of courtliness, but a great deal of information on this subject emerges from his study.

We have translated all the quotations in the text, whatever the language in which they appear, so that the reader may have a complete English text. We have thought it best, however, to add the original texts, so that the specialist reader may make his own evaluations independently of my translations. This practice sometimes leads to rather cumbrous sentences, but it is difficult to see how it could have been avoided. In the notes, however, we have not translated the texts of quotations, on the assumption that the notes are for specialist readers. The lists of citations at the end of chapters and the bibliography have been left exactly in their German form. Because of the highly complex material contained in the footnotes, appendices, etc., of the original, it has not proved possible to maintain a completely consistent editorial style in the English rendering of these.

This translation makes accessible in English one of the best documented and thorough studies of the nature of knighthood ever written.

THE CONCEPT OF KNIGHTHOOD
IN THE MIDDLE AGES

I. Introduction

T here is scarcely any chapter in German literature in which extraliterary factors have been given such weight as in the classical Middle High German period. Handbooks of literary history usually interrupt their account as they approach the courtly period and give a historico-sociological digression on the shift in class relationships. At this time, they say, a new noble class emerged and was defined, namely the knightly class, which had a determining influence on the rise of literary culture of the last third of the twelfth century. It not only produced the poets who in a very short time brought German literature to heights never before attained but at the same time formed an audience with the capability of understanding and enjoying the highly sophisticated art-form of that poet. Furthermore, the knights mastered the topic "minne and aventiure," to which literature remained indebted for centuries and developed a code of honor which has influenced the forms of social intercourse to the present day.

The Hohenstaufen knight as proponent of the "first lay-culture since classical antiquity" has become an almost mythical figure. Everything produced by the High Middle Ages is connected with this term, whether it concerns life-style or aristocratic outlook. We link the flowering period and the decline of courtly poetry with the rise of knighthood and its early collapse respectively. We feel that we have grasped the essential nature of this literature if we interpret it as the poetic self-representation of this knightly class; an idealistic representation admittedly, but one which nevertheless derives its principal strength from the reality behind it. This chivalric reality is understood not only as an actual social state but as a moral and esthetic actuality in itself, that is, as an aristocratic mode of life which appears in literature intensified and illuminated by its poetic form. Thus *Minnesang* is interpreted as the poetical documentation of an actual experience of love-service[1] and the system of chivalric values is regarded as "an ideal aim for a moral life amid the crudity of every day existence."[2] Thus the main character of the courtly romance, the knight who seeks *aventiure,* is explained by the social conditions of the lesser

3

nobility.[3] Finally the Middle High German literary-language is derived from a spoken aristocratic language, the cultivated colloquial speech of the courts of southwestern Germany.[4]

If the poetry of the classical period thus showed the marks of actual conditions of class situations connected with it, then the question of the relationship of poetry and real life in the chivalric period must be of prime importance for the understanding of that poetry. Its significance has long been recognized, and books by Erich Köhler on the courtly romance[5] and by Friedrich-Wilhelm Wentzlaff-Eggebert on crusading literature[6] have recently brought it back into the forefront of research.[7] Nevertheless we are still far away from a solution of the problem. Hugo Kuhn has put it very clearly. On the "apparently indisputable view that the basis of courtly literature is social fact,"[8] he writes: "What people are so sure they know as fact is, in reality, only a modern scholarly construct, the result of a concept of the relationship between reality and literature which is naive in its presumptions and untested in method." From this there emerges a disturbing picture of the state of research. I see only one way to settle this matter: the "apparently indisputable view" must be subjected point by point to critical examination and even deep rooted concepts and those long regarded as certain must not be spared. And one must be ready to be contradicted, for these questions touch upon the romantic core of our discipline. This work should be understood as a contribution to such a study.

"As is well known, knights were a class of mounted soldiers consisting of the ancient nobility, and including even the king, and of the *ministeriales,* unfree service personnel. Nevertheless, as knights they were all on an equal footing and formed the knightly class." In the twelfth century, Emperor Friedrich I promulgated "the basic laws of knighthood": "thus the class from then on was officially recognized as a class by birth." "There is no doubt that in the Hohenstaufen period the knights provided the leading figures in war, politics, law and literature."[9] Such, briefly, was the result of "the social revolution,"[10] which produced a new nobility and a new literature; in the classical period "all the great German poets were knights"[11] and at that time "knights wrote for knights."[12] This view of the knightly class is one of the oldest assumptions of Germanic research. It is to be found in outline as early as Ludwig Tieck, who writes in the preface to the *Minnelieder aus dem Schwäbischen Zeitalter*: "The knightly class at that time bound together all the nations in Europe. . . . Believers sang of their belief and its miracles, lovers sang of love, knights described knightly deeds and combats and knights who loved and were believers were their select audience."[13] On the basis of the material from the great work on chivalry by Jean Baptiste de la Curne de Sainte-Palaye[14] and endowed with life by the rediscovered ancient German poems, a series of semi-scholarly expositions of chivalry were written which popularized the romantic image.[15] For the authors, knighthood was an institution far off in history but at the same time close to the present. Most of them had been alive at the undistinguished end of the old imperial knighthood in 1806 and the chivalric glory of the imperial era gleamed so much the brighter in the gloomy present. They were trying to adapt the great past of the nation and at the same time to ward off liberal criticism about the meaning and function of the nobility.[16] From this impulse came the chivalric books of Freiherr Karl Heinrich Roth von Schreckenstein,[17] which are still basic today, even though antiquated in many details. Since then there has been no further complete study of the knightly class.[18]

In 1836 there appeared August von Fürth's book on the *ministeriales,*[19] which put research on the lesser nobility on a scholarly basis and started off the discussion of the problem of the *ministeriales* which is still going on today.[20] In the course of this, there were occasional side-glances at the knights[21] but no true historical research into knighthood developed from it. Nor was the total picture changed by publications on problems of detail—girding on the sword or initiation ceremonies.[22] In German literary research, the penetrating investigations of Julius Petersen[23] and Paul Kluckhohn[24] have no successors. The image of the knight of the Romantic period was passed on unblemished into cultural history and transmitted from generation to generation, often enough untouched by the sharp blast of research into sources.[25] In the course of this, the actuality of knighthood paled more and more into an empty construct of concepts pasted all over with pictures of knightly arms and clothing, castles and tournaments. And in the end people were completely satisfied with the "higher reality," with "chivalric idealism."[26] This "cultural image" of knighthood still rules undisputed in handbooks of history and literary history.[27] In 1895 Aloys Schulte gave a clear warning that research in Germanics "even today had not completely freed itself from the thralldom of Romantic conceptions of medieval chivalry,"[28] and his words are as valid today as then. Only very recently have there appeared the beginnings of a change.[29] In 1959 there appeared an article by Arno Borst on "Knighthood in the High Middle Ages," which is intended as a preparatory sketch of a "comprehensive history of medieval knighthood."[30] If the question is asked: "Is it not perhaps the case, in fact, that knighthood altogether is only a name and fantasy, a creation of the artistic imagination without any real basis and form,"[31] then it becomes clear that research into knights must be started all over again from the beginning.

In the field of medieval historiography a modified, indeed a totally new approach has been in process for more than a generation. It is a rebellion of historians against jurists. The old dogmas of constitutional history are being overthrown one after the other. No new construction is rising on their ruins, no new theoretical structure, but gradually there is growing up a picture of state and social life in the Middle Ages which looks quite different from the old theories, many faceted and often awkward but corresponding to medieval reality in a new way.[32] Otto Brunner has shown that in many cases the enormous concept-apparatus, which was taken over from the political theories of the nineteenth century and applied to the Middle Ages, distorted real knowledge; he demands "that the terminology . . . should as far as possible, be taken from the sources themselves."[33] His methodological criticism here merges with the "translation problem," whose significance was first perceived by Philip Heck:[34] the pervasive bilinguality of the Middle Ages, the parallel use of Latin and *lingua vulgaris* makes it necessary to take note of the vernacular documents too, whose importance became greater as the living language of the law in the Middle Ages ceased to be Latin. "It is an obvious requirement for the true understanding of ancient law that one should start from its indigenous, even if often, diffuse and apparently contradictory concepts. But for German law only German legal terms have this key value."[35] Here a wide field is opened to cooperation between historians and Germanists.[36]

Ritter (knight) is a vernacular word, which for several centuries is to be found almost exclusively in poetic texts and, in contrast to other German legal terms such as *gràve* and *dienestman,* never made its way into the Latin of legal documents.[37] If the historians do speak of knights, of knights' properties and knightly birth, they are thinking less of the poetic knights of Middle High German literature than about the term "miles," which, with its derivatives and compounds, was familiar to them from historical sources: *feudum militare, ex genere militiae,* etc. The old Roman word for soldier, *miles,* had a very complicated semantic history in the Middle Ages, which is known only in broad outline. But when, from a definite point of time on, the word is rendered not by "Krieger" or "Lehnsmann" (warrior, liegeman) but by "Ritter" (knight), it may be assumed that a concept or an institution had been formed which could be characterized by the term "knight." That can be demonstrated only when the vernacular word "ritter" appears. Thus it may be justified to start from the poetic texts. There is as yet no history of the word "Ritter,"[38] and the present work cannot be regarded as a substitute for one, for we are not concerned with the totality of the term. About 1200, knighthood had become a program of culture and education, the dominating cultural idea of the courtly period. Nevertheless, the achievement which lies in the esthetic and moral elevation of the word can be fully appreciated only when it is contrasted with the social reality of knighthood during the classical period. For this reason the central question in any investigation must be whether it is possible to distinguish behind the image of the knight in courtly poetry a social class of knights to which the poetic conception of knighthood may be related. A question like this certainly cannot be answered by reference to vernacular evidence alone. Only the investigation of the historical tradition will decide the viability of the results. Throughout my work, I have been unpleasantly conscious of this lack of a final solution, which I am not in a position to remedy. I have tried to make amends by consulting the technical historical literature to the greatest possible extent, so as to check my observations against the historians' results. I have not hesitated sometimes to make further reference to the problems and results of historical research where that appeared necessary in connection with questions on knights. In doing this I am not telling the historian anything new, of course, but in a series of periodicals for students of German literature these pages have perhaps some instructional value, at least bibliographically.

Today the use of poetic texts as sources for legal and social history no longer needs any long methodological justification. It has long been recognized that poetry, as Richard Schröder wrote in 1866, "introduces us with warmth and freshness to the legal life of the Middle Ages."[39] And more recent research has followed Jacob Grimm in confirming the close connection between art and law.[40] Nevertheless the difficulties in evaluating the literary evidence have not become any less in the intervening period. The sensible remarks of Paul Kluckhohn should be read in this connection.[41] These reservations are twice as strong in the case of courtly literature, because the great part of this poetry is adapted from French originals. "It would undoubtedly be methodologically right and desirable to ask about sources in each individual case. But that is impossible."[42] So it is impossible to proceed without some compromise. But the discussion about the knighting ceremony has shown that precisely in the case of knights the courtly poets (who can here be checked against historical reports) observed exactly the conditions prevailing in Germany in their terminology and description. In other respects this work keeps within the framework of philology in its methods: its point of departure is not an institution but a word which is being investigated as to its realistic content.[43]

Middle High German literature is full of knights, but only a few references give any indication of their social rank and position in society. It was my most important task to collect and coordinate this material. I have begun with a few observations on the external history of the word, on its form, its first appearance and relative frequency, and on its place in heroic and warrior terminology in Middle High German. In the second and third sections the knights are sought where they are most frequently in evidence: as soldiers on the battlefield and liegemen at the lord's court.

The next section is devoted to the most important event of the history of the concept of knighthood, namely the transfer of knighthood to the higher nobility and to the formation of an aristocratic ideal of knighthood. In the last section I shall investigate what German texts have to say about the class-concept of knights. Basically I have confined myself, both in collecting and evaluating the evidence, to the period up to the middle of the thirteenth century; I shall observe this limit strictly, however tempting the later evidence may be. At the end of the thirteenth century the texts become more numerous and communicate to us a lively image of the reality of knightly life. Knightly literature does, however, show well enough, how dangerous and confusing it is to apply the late evidence to earlier periods. About 1250 the classical period of literature comes to an end in Germany and that is why I set the limit there. For in the end, even though we are here discussing only one word and its meanings, we are dealing in this work with the historical conditions for literary culture at its peak of perfection and for its understanding as part of the great European cultural movement of the twelfth and thirteenth century.

II.   The Word "Ritter": Its Age and Form

𝕴n Middle High German texts the forms *rîter* and *ritter* are found side by side.[1] Their linguistic relationship is variously explained: the most convincing assumption[2] is that *rîter* is formed on the present stem of the strong verb **rīd-* "to progress," while *ritter* on the other hand is derived from a noun-stem, a Germanic *nomen agentis* **ridjan-*, which appears in the Anglo-Saxon *ridda*.[3] If this is true, then *ritter* could be the older form, since the oldest stratum of forms in **ari* comprises exclusively denominatives. There has, however, been more interest in the historical relationship of the two forms than in etymological explanations. Ernst Martin in 1888 was the first to express the "feeling" that the form *ritter* "as a corporate part of the chivalric cultural language" was borrowed from Flemish.[4] This view has been generally accepted in recent handbooks. Most recently Edmund Wiessner has pointed to medieval Dutch *riddere* "which spread to the language of neighboring areas. The word *ritter* which derived from it now took its place side by side with the native *rîtaere, rîter*."[5] However well such a procedure may fit into the general development ("it might well be surprising if the actual central word for the new status did not show signs of Lower Rhine influence"[6]), we should not fail to mention the reservations which are against it.

First "our native *rîter*." The dictionaries refer to Old High German *rîtari*, which is found in Graff's *Sprachschatz* (II, 477). But if one disentangles the complicated *sigla*, it becomes clear that none of the examples goes back further than the early Middle High German period. A search of the gloss-tradition produces the same result. This cannot be explained by the fact that in the earlier period there was no occasion to use the word.[7] The words *miles* and *eques* are glossed frequently from the very first collections but the gloss *rîter* appears first in manuscripts of the twelfth century. The oldest translations of *miles* are in the copies of the old *Abrogans* from Paris and St. Gallen:

9

militum	milizzo anti (endi K*) hari(heri-* K)*manno* (Pa, K) (I, 80, 26)
serui militum	*scalcho milizzo* (Pa), *scalkha milizzo edho herimanno edho eouuelihhes mannes* (K) (I, 86, 25f.)
multitudo militum	manaki milizzo (Pa), *endi manaki* (K) (I, 90, 26)
multitudo militum	manaki heri (Pa), *herimanno heri* (K) (I, 144, 1f.)

Milizza with the shift of the unvoiced dental looks like an early borrowing, but there are few extant examples.[8] If it was more than an ephemeral formation, we can regard it as an indication that late Germanic lacked a neutral term for warrior. Perhaps Germanic soldiers brought it back after service in the Roman army. In the later manuscripts of the glosses, the translation of *miles* became more picturesque. At the top in age and number are: *degan,* found in manuscripts of the ninth century[9] (IV, 221, 49f.), of the tenth/eleventh centuries (I, 755, 3) and of the twelfth century (III, 428, 28); the collective noun formed on it, *gidigini,* is found in manuscripts of the eleventh century (II, 397, 68, 398, 50. 398, 53. 561, 55. 573, 11). These findings are not unimportant for the medieval understanding of *miles*; they point to a basic form of military levy. Further *miles-* glosses of the eleventh century are *kempfo* (II, 464, 63f. 524, 20. 530, 11. 567, 66) *heri* (II, 464, 48) and *girit* (II, 668, 61), glossed as *equitatus* elsewhere.[10] The picture for the derivatives of *miles* is similar.[11] On the other hand *eques* and its family are glossed in more consistent fashion. The first examples are to be found in the Reichenau glossaries IC and the Oxford copy Jun. 25:

equites   ritante (R, O) (I, 278, 20)
equites   risheri (*heri* O) *kirit* (R, O) (I, 278, 27)

From the tenth century on, *reitman* (mounted man) is the predominant translation of *eques* (I, 704, 63 f. II, 437, 19. 658, 46. III, 235, 19f. 273, 5. 299, 44. 316, 60. 334, 29f.).[12] Are we to believe that the gloss-makers consistently avoided the word *rîter*? The fact that the terminology of warfare is very well represented in the glosses makes this all the more unlikely. We find *strîtari* (soldiers) (II, 395, 24), *fehtari* (fighting man) (I, 56, 35), *wîgman* (warriors) (II, 525, 24, etc.), quite apart from *degan, kempfo* and *wîgant* (all mean "warrior"). In manuscripts of the tenth/eleventh centuries the expression "qui accincti erant balteo" (those girded with a belt) is glossed as *heridegana* (army heroes) (I, 450, 46f. 456, 1f.). The obvious word *rîter* appears nowhere.

The word first appears in manuscripts of the twelfth century and in fairly large numbers, which indicates that the picture of the tradition of its use has not been distorted by chance:

Miles   riter (A), rîter (C), Rieter (B), ritbir (E) (III, 134, 25/53); ABE: 12. Jh., C: 13, jH.

Miles	riddere. Eques idem (III, 382, 14); 13. Jh.
Durziol miles	ritdere (III, 395, 49); 13, Jh.
Cibarius miles	brotriddere (III, 378, 31); 13. Jh.
Ordinarius. l.	
gregarius miles	einscilt rîter (C), enschiltriter (A), einscilte riter (B), einscilterithir (E), ainscilt ritir vel scoldinar (G) (III, 135, iff.); ABE: 12, Jh., CG: 13. Jh.
Ordinarius vel gregarius	einscildicriter vel scoldiner (III, 183, 15f.); 12. Jh.
Millites. l. equites	ritere (III, 183, 14); 12. Jh.
Eques	riter (III, 428, 29); 12. Jh.
Eques	riter (A, B) (III, 638, 9); AB: 12. Jh.

The evidence from the glosses leads to the conclusion that the word "Ritter" in Germany can hardly be older than the oldest examples in manuscripts. This result is bolstered if the literary texts are adduced for comparison. The fact that the early texts are religious in character does not explain the absence of the word, since miles is also a word in the Bible. It can be found in the account of the Passion in the four Gospels as a designation of the men-at-arms, Pilate's Roman soldiers who nailed Christ to the Cross and diced for his cloak. The Passion was put into the vernacular several times in the ninth century and it is interesting to look into the Carolingian expressions for miles. The Fulda translators translate milites presidis as thie kenphon thes grâuen (ed. Sievers 200, 1), and the same translation is found a second time, miles = kempfo (203, 1). Otfrid is remarkably reticent in his Evangelienbuch: he leaves miles untranslated and only once says thie genóza (ed. Erdmann-Wolff IV, 28, 9). The Heliand on the other hand develops a rich terminology for "soldier" in its Passion-scenes: uueros (ed. Behaghel[4] 5496), thia gisî os (5501), heli os (5507), uuîgandos (5543), dere ia man (5544), rincos (5545). The absence of rîter in this connection is all the more remarkable because the milites in the Passion story had actually been called rîter since the twelfth century, as they had for example in the work on Der Wilde Mann (Veronica 428). Not until the second half of the eleventh century is the word found for the first time in a German text,[13] not in the warlike Annolied but in the early Middle High German Bible epic, in the Joseph story of the Wiener Genesis:

> Ioseph sa dar reit,
> mit ime manich rîter gemeit (5060f.).

From here it was taken over by the Millstätter (101, 29) and the Vorauer reworking (819) and at the beginning of the twelfth century the oldest example of rîterschaft is found in the Wiener Exodus (1346). We then meet the word in the *Jüngere Judith* and in the *Speculum ecclesiae*. With Lamprecht's Alexander, the examples become gradually more numerous but a good century goes by after its first appearance before the new word is fully accepted.[14]

The new form *ritter,* borrowed from Lower Franconian appears side by side with the old form "after about 1170."[15] It is well known how difficult it is to make distinctions between them, because the distinction in meaning which used to be assumed (*rîter* = mounted soldier, *ritter* = a member of the knightly class) did not in fact develop until very much later[16] and because the examples in rhyme are spread thin until the second half of the thirteenth century.[17] So there remains no other way than to ask the scribes rather than the poets and to check the manuscript tradition. Unfortunately there are plenty of doubtful factors: the uncertain dating of most manuscripts, the unreliability of many editions, etc.[18] The basis is constituted by the four great early Middle High German manuscript collections. There are certainly differences of opinion about the time they were written but their relative dating seems firm. They are, in succession, Vienna manuscript, Millstatt manuscript, Vorau manuscript, and Strassburg manuscript.[19] A summary of the forms given there follows; the only addition, because of its age,[20] is the Munich manuscript (Cgm. 39) of the *Speculum ecclesiae*:[21]

Wiener Hs.	*rîter-*	(Wien Genesis 5061
	riter-	(Wien. Exodus 1346)
Millstätter Hs.	*riter-*	(Millst. Genesis 77, 7. 101, 29. 137, 18. 139, 12. Hochzeit 304)
	ritter-	(Hochzeit 265)
Vorauer Hs.	*rîter-*	(Vor. Alex. 156. 411. 1242. 1276. 1299. 1446)
	riter-	(Vor. Alex. 213. 925. Vor. Joseph 819. Jg. Judith 153, 9. 163, 27. Kaiserchr. 110. 480. 1140. 4090. 4209. 4309. 4350. 4565. 4572. 4710. 4876. 5765. 8104. 16992)
	ritter-	(Kaiserchr. 6801)
Straßburger Hs.	*rîter-*	(Straßbg. Alex. 174. 182. 243. 430. 482. 1287. 1716. 1718. 1762. 1888. 2211. 4374. 4949. 5958. 6048)
Münchner Hs.[22]	*rîter-*	(Specul. eccl. 41, 7. 41, 20)
	riter-	(Specul. eccl. 141, 24. 141, 27)

The picture is not uniform. The oldest and latest of the manuscript collections have no examples at all of the form *ritter*. In the Millstatt manuscript the two forms appear in the proportion of 1 : 5, in the Vorau manuscript 1 : 25; there is no evidence of progressive increase of the form *ritter*. We can say with certainty that the first evidence of the form with the double dental are to be found in religious manuscripts from Millstatt and Vorau after the middle of the twelfth century.

The second group consists of the manuscripts which research dates at the end of the twelfth century:[23]

Pr.Br. Zingerle	*riter-*	(407, 12. 33. 37. 408, 4)
Pr. Wackernagel	*riter-*	(XII, 53)
Roland., Hs. A	*ritter-*	(4776)
Roland., Hs. P	*riter-*	(287. 4490. 4776. 4898. 4964. 4996. 5577. 5811. 5979. 8006. 8280)
Rother, Hs.H	*riter-*	(131. 155. 203. 1366)
	ritir-	(246)
	ritar-	(239. 278. 301. 490. 745. 791. 1331. 1484. 1515. 1560. 1824. 1870. 2048. 2109. 2156. 2173. 2434. 2487. 2673. 2966. 2989. 3066. 3155. 3212. 3337. 3404)
	rittar-	(1446)
Tr. Silvester	*ritter-*	(395)
Kaiserchr.,		
Wien 13006[24]	*riter-*	(4572)
	ritter-	(4309. 4350. 4565. 16992)
Eilhart, Hs. M[25]	*riter-*	(M 4ᵛ 33)
Priest. Wernher, Hs.D		
	riter-	(1412. 3108)
Eneit, Hs. Me[26]	*riter-*	(205, 20. 241, 2. 242, 19. 25. 40. 243, 9. 21. 23. 25)
Eneit, Münchner		
Fragm.[27]	*ritar-*	(164, 18)
Tagzeitengedicht	*ritt[er]-*	(54)

Four of these have the form *ritter,* either exclusively or predominantly, against eight which write the word always or preferably with a single dental. The proportion of examples is 8 : 62 whereas in the first manuscript group it was 2 : 51.

The picture becomes clearer only when we summarize the manuscripts in a third group which are dated at the turn of the twelfth/thirteenth centuries or at the beginning of the thirteenth century:[28]

Pr. Mone	*ritter-*	(528. 529)
Kaiserchr., Nürnbg. Hs.[29]	*riter-*	(4710)
Gr. Rudolf	*ritter-*	(δ 6)
Heiml. Bote	*riter-*	(11)
Tundalus,	*ridder-*	(90)
Hz. Ernst A, Prager Hs	*ritter-*	(I, 11)

Eneit, Hs. B	*reter-*	(243, 25)
	riter-	(315, 10. 341, 14. 344, 18)
	ritâr-	(248, 6. 311, 1. 339, 32)
	ritter-	(81 times, also *ritte*: 184, 38. 217, 33; *ritten*: 148, 3)
Lucidarius, Hs. M-Sch[30]	*rither-*	(119, 50)
Reinhart Fuchs, Hs. S	*riter-*	(779. 783)
Nibelungenlied, Hs. Z[31]	*ritter-*	(2293, 3. 2303, 2)

To this group may be added the oldest *Iwein* manuscript B which always shows *rîter*,[32] and the *Nibelungen* manuscript C, which, so far as I can see, has the double dental throughout. There would thus be seven manuscripts here with the form *ritter* predominantly or exclusively against five with *rîter*. If we once again compare the proportions in the three groups, the development becomes quite clear:

1. Group: 0 : 5
2. Group: 4 : 8
3. Group: 7 : 5

This means that the form *ritter*, which had previously been only sporadic, suddenly becomes more frequent at the end of the twelfth century. At the turn of the twelfth/thirteenth centuries it becomes as valid as the forms *rîter* and *riter* and at the beginning of the new century gains a slight preponderance. So far as I am able to judge the further developments, the form with a simple dental recedes even further in the following decades without disappearing entirely. The relatively late predominance should not cause the oldest evidence for *ritter* to be forgotten. In the light of the manuscripts the chronological distance between "old" *rîter* and "new" *ritter* is reduced to the few years which lie between the writing down of the Vienna and of the Millstatt manuscript collections.[33] Both forms appear almost at the same time after the middle of the twelfth century, a fact which accords very ill with the assumption that the form *ritter* was borrowed from Middle Dutch.

The finest examples for the very important linguistic influence of Flanders on courtly refined speech in Southern Germany are the words in *-kin*, as well as *dörper* with its derivatives, *wâpen, ors, muoten, tadel* and some others.[34] What distinguishes these words as fashionable words from the Northwest, for us and for contemporary courtly circles, is their Dutch sound and particularly their unshifted stops which are all the more striking in view of the fact that the corresponding shifted forms were still in existence in High German. Thus we find *dörper* side by side with High German *dorf, wâpen* with *wâfen, tadel* with *zadel* and, with a different but equally clear change, *ors* side by side with High German *ros*.[35] It is quite different with *ritter*. If it were borrowed from Flemish, it would be the only word in this group to have given up its specific sound-form.[36] For the form *ridder* is unknown in those parts of the High German area where the shift took place. The word would, so to speak, have deprived itself of its own effect, of the fashionable Flemish sound of unshifted consonants.

There is something else. Evidence for words borrowed from the Northwest does not appear at all in Southern Germany until a generation after the earliest *ritter* forms.[37] The forms in *-kin* appear first in Ulrich von Gutenberg, in Ulrich's *Lanzelet* and in Wolfram; *dörper* is first found in Hartmann's later works, *Iwein* and *Der Arme Heinrich*, *wâpen* first in *Erek* but in rhyming position not before the thirteenth century; *ors* is rhymed for the first time in Ulrich's *Lanzelet; muote* appears first in Hartmann's *Erek; tadel* first in Wolfram like *trecken; gelücke* is first known through Heinrich von Veldeke and so is *blîde*, which is adopted by Ulrich von Zatzikhoven and Wolfram; *baneken* is found in the *Trierer Floyris*, then in *Graf Rudolf* and in Hartmann; *draben* appears first in *Iwein*. The whole group of Dutch loan-words does not go back further than the early works of Hartmann, and the first instances start to appear about 1180 and are all in modern courtly poetry.[38] The form *ritter* on the other hand is at home in religious manuscripts from Millstatt and Vorau.[39] New and stronger arguments are needed to prove the Flemish origin of the word.

The alternation *rîter* and *ritter* exists not only in High German but also in Low German (*rîder/ridder*), in Dutch (*rîjder/riddere*) and Norse (*riðari/riddari*). This cannot be accidental. The generally accepted explanation today states that the form with a double dental is a Dutch neologism, a borrowing modeled on the Old French *chevalier*, which spread from Flanders over the whole Germanic-speaking area and took its place in the various dialects side by side with the native form with a long stem vowel. We have seen that the German tradition scarcely gives support to this view, nor do the Scandinavian examples provide any evidence for it, since in Old Norse *riðari* is as much a continental borrowing as *riddari*.[40] The main argument for the Dutch origin of *ridder/ritter* is allegedly the very early evidence for the form in Flanders: "Middle Dutch *riddere* appears about 1100."[41] But we have no Flemish texts from this time; the connection is made from the one Anglo-Saxon example for "knight," which thus has to carry the main weight of the whole theory of a Dutch neologism. It is cited by Friedrich Kluge: "In the *Sachsenkronik* for the year 1085 it is stated of William the Conqueror 'he dubbade his sunu Henric to riddére' (he dubbed his son Henry knight). *Riddere* here is undoubtedly a Flemish loan-word; it is in this position the earliest evidence for our *Ritter*."[42] Friedrich Kluge gave no source for the Anglo-Saxon quotation, and I do not know where it comes from. The editions of the *Anglo-Saxon Chronicle* have a different reading of the sentence at the crucial point: "he dubbade his sunu Henric to ridere" (I, 216f.) and for the year 1090: "aefter isum he begeat ma castelas innan þam lande, þaer inne his rideras gelogode" (I, 225).[43] This Anglo-Saxon *rídere* naturally corresponds to the Middle High German *rîter*, not the form *ritter*. I have had no more success in verifying the reference given in German dictionaries: "Middle English (shortly after 1100) *riddēre*."[44] Neither the Bosworth and Toller dictionary of Anglo-Saxon nor the Stratmann and Bradley dictionary of Middle English have any knowledge of this form *riddere*. I hesitate to believe that the whole theory of the Flemish origin of the word *ridder/ritter* rests on a false reading but at the moment I have no other explanation.

I can make no final decision about the relationships of the forms of "ritter" in the various Germanic languages. The facts are that the *Wiener Genesis* in the second half of the twelfth century provides the oldest example in the Germanic-speaking area. Half a century later the word appears in England; then follow the next examples from Southern Germany and towards the end of the twelfth century the tradition begins in the Netherlands and Scandinavia. There is no question that the formation is continental, since it reached England and Scandinavia only as a loan-word. It is perfectly possible that the word was newly formed in the tenth century and that the two forms *rîter* and *ritter* were there side by side from the beginning and migrated together. Where the formation took place remains an open question and so does the question of the forces which provided the impulse. Throughout Europe the eleventh century was a period of significant political, religious, and social change. In Germany the group of the most powerful princes and lords emerges from the old aristocratic framework, a group which was later to constitute itself as the "princes of the Empire." There is a parallel development of the unfree men-at-arms class and the division of service personel into classes. At the end of the eleventh century the idea of a Crusade became a political reality. The word *miles* gradually widened its meaning both upwards and downwards and at the same time the new devotion to classical antiquity brought the classical word *eques* back into fashion. About 1100 the word *chevalier*[45] appears in France. The tradition of Old High German glosses had already made it clear that the language needed a neutral form for "warrior." There must have been a large number of forces working together, finally to produce the new word *rîter/ritter*.

Ritter[46] is a prose word, a colorless technical term. Poets use it, of course, as they do *man* and *kneht,* but it produces no glory, the word has no distinctive poetic reverberation. Even in the first century in which it appeared, *ritter* is not an unusual word: from the *Wiener Genesis* to *Herzog Ernst A* I have found a mere 180 instances of it,[47] admittedly the

greater part of them in the last thirty years. But this very respectable total
shrinks to a tiny group when compared with the figures for the following
period. In the seventy years from 1180 to 1250 the term *ritter*, with its
derivatives, is found in 6000 instances. In the thirteenth century there is
scarcely another personal designation of even approximately similar frequency. Hartmann's *Erek*, with almost seventeen instances in every thousand lines starts the enormous upswing in the use of the term "ritter."
Later works go far beyond it. But it is not at all the best poets who use
the word every twenty to thirty lines: Berthold von Holle, Wirnt von
Gravenberg, Ulrich von Zatzikhoven.[48] For the period under consideration
the melancholy record for sheer numbers is held by Ulrich von Lichtenstein with the *Frauendienst*: I counted 739 instances in it of the word
ritter and its derivatives. There is no doubt about it, the quantitative
expansion reflects a qualitative intensification and is the result of applying
aesthetic and moral values to the concept of knighthood. The prose-word
ritter has become *the* poetic noun of courtly poetry. The process is also
reflected in its relation to the old terms for "hero." Edward Schröder
has contrasted the words *recke, wigant, degen* and *helt* as "poetic and
emphatic attributes" with the "purely technical designation rîter."[49] As
long as *ritter* continued to sound prosy, it could make no progress against
the traditional words for hero. In the oldest "secular" epics of the twelfth
century it ranks numerically at the bottom of the list of warrior-desig-
nations and is at best only slightly ahead of the word *recke*.[50] In Veldeke's
Eneit it has already moved up to second place behind *helt*; and in Hartmann's *Erek* the word *ritter* is found four times as often as all the other
words for warrior put together.[51] We shall discuss later what forces
brought about and promoted the upward poetic revaluation of the word
in poetry. Our starting point is the technical knight-concept of the earlier
period.

APPENDIX

1. Evidence of Knighthood from 1060 to 1180[52]

1060/65	Wien. Genesis 5061
1120	Wien. Exodus 1346 [*r.schaft*]
1130	Millst. Genesis 77, 7. 101, 29. 137, 18 [*r.schaft*]. 139, 12
1130/40	Vor. Alex. 156. 213. 411. 925. 1242. 1276. 1299. 1446
1130/50	Vor. Joseph 819
1130/50	Jg. Judith 153, 9. 163, 27
1145	Roland 287 [*r.schaft*]. 4490. 4776. 4898 [*r.liche*]. 4964. 4996 [*r.liche*]. 5577 [*r.lich*]. 5811 [*r.schaft*]. 5979. 8006 [*r.lich*]. 8280 [*r.liche*]
1150/60	Rother 131. 155. 203 [*r.lich*]. 239. 246 [*r.schaft*]. 278. 301. 490. 745. 791. 1331. 1366 [*r.lich*]. 1446. 1484. 1515. 1560. 1824 [*r.lich*]. 1870. 2048. 2109. 2156. 2173. 2434. 2487. 2673. 2966. 2989. 3066. 3155. 3212. 3337. 3404

1150/70	Kürnberg 7, 21. 8, 3. 8, 20. 10, 21
1160	Melk Erin. 289. 342. 344. 354 [r.schaft]. 427
1160	Hochzeit 265. 305
1160	Tr. Silvester 395
1160/65	Kaiserchr. 110 [r.schaft]. 480 [r.schaft]. 1140. 4090. 4209. 4309. 4350 [r.lich]. 4565 [r.schaft]. 4572. 4710. 4876 [r.schaft]. 5765. 6801. 8104. 16992
1160/70	Wild. Mann Veron. 428
1160/80	MSF. Namenlos 6, 5
1160/80	Dietmar 32, 21. 38, 16. 39, 4. 40, 5
1160/80	Regensburg 16, 2. 16, 24
1170	Strassbg. Alex. 174 [r.liche]. 182. 243. 430 [r.lich]. 482. 1287. 1716. 1718. 1729. 1762. 1773. 1888 [r.liche]. 2211. 4374. 4949. 5958. 6048 [r.lich]
1170	Gr. Rudolf δ 6
1170	Eilhart 72 [r.liche]. 149 [r.liche]. 495 [r.schaft]. 527. 561. 1466. 1471. 2873. 2876. 2886. 2902. 2909. 2959. 3001. 3022. 3594. 4235. 4350. 5059. 5453. 5669. 5705 [r.schaft]. 5770 [r.liche]. 5817. 5849. 5866. 5918. 5945. 5947. 5956 [r.liche]. 6158. 6397 [r.schaft]. 6421. 6435. 6904. 7533. 7742. 7754. 7760. 7787. 7796. 7869 [r.schaft]. 8554. 8792. 8828. 8851
1170	Servatius 5277 [r.schaft]. 5580. 5826. 5877
1170/80	Elmendorf 189. 720
1170/80	Maze 41
1170/80	Heiml. Bote 11 [r.schaft]
1170/80	Meinloh 14, 4
1170/90	Kaiser Heinr. 4, 27
1172	Priest. Wernher 1412. 1549 [r.lich]. 3108
1180	Tundalus 90
1180	Tnugdalus 41, 22. 43, 27. 51, 68. 57, 41 [r.schaft]
1180	Hz. Ernst A I, 11. 17 S

2. Frequency for the Word "Knight" (Ritter) in the More Important Epics of The 12th and 13th Centuries

	No. of instances	per 1000 lines	1 instance in every
Ems Barlaam	4	0,2	4041 Verse
	8	0,5	2020 „
Halberstadt[54]	3	0,3	3677 „
	8	0,7	1379 „
Roland	4	0,4	2273 „
	11	1,2	872 „
Kaiserchr.	10	0,6	1728 „
	15	0,9	1152 „
Reinhart Fuchs	2	0,9	1133 „
	2	0,9	1133 „
Otte	6	1,1	898 „
	9	1,7	599 „
Flore	10	1,2	800 „
	13	1,6	616 „
Straßbg. Alex.	13	1,9	522 „
	17	2,5	406 „
Klage[55]	11	2,3	431 „
	12	2,5	395 „
Wolfdietr. A[56]	11	2,7	366 „
	11	2,7	366 „
Gotfrid	64	3,3	305 „
	126	6,4	155 „
Gregorius	14	3,5	286 „
	31	7,7	129 „

	No. of instances	per 1000 lines	1 instance in every
Ems Alex.	76	3,5	285 Verse
	268	12,4	81 „
Eilhart	38	3,9	251 „
	46	4,8	207 „
Stricker Karl	50	4,1	244 „
	87	7,2	140 „
Eneit	59	4.4	246 „
	92	6.9	147 „
Türheim Trist.	18	4,8	207 „
	26	6,9	143 „
Kudrun	70	5,1	195 „
	87	6,4	157 „
Vor. Alex.	8	5,2	192 „
	8	5,2	192 „
Rother	28	5.4	186 „
	32	6,1	162 „
Herbort	111	6,0	166 „
	147	7,9	126 „
Morant	35	6,2	160 „
	36	6,4	155 „
Willehalm	89	6,4	157 „
	173	12,4	81 „
Nibelungenlied[57]	123	6,5	155 „
	142	7,4	134 „
Türheim Renn.	307	8,4	119 „
	402	11,0	91 „
Ems Gerhard	59	8,5	117 „
	104	15,0	67 „
Iwein	83	10,2	98 „
	109	13,5	74 „
Stricker Dan.	91	10,7	93 „
	107	12,6	79 „
Ems Willeh.	200	12,7	78 „
	401	25,5	39 „
Erek	134	13,2	76 „
	169	16,7	60 „
Parzival	372	15,0	66 „
	512	20,6	48 „
Türlin Krone	557	18,5	54 „
	639	21,3	47 „
Lichtenst. Frd.[58]	395	21,3	47 „
	739	39,9	25 „
Lanzelet	208	22,0	45 „
	241	25,5	39 „
Holle Crane	128	26,0	38 „
	130	26,4	38 „
Wigalois	335	28,6	35 „
	444	37,1	26 „
Holle Demant.	446	37,9	26 „
	483	41,1	24 „

3. The Relation to the Old Words for Hero

	ritter	*helt*	*degen*	*wigant*	*recke*	*guoter kneht*
Wien. Genesis	1	5	–	–	1	1[60]
Anno	–	4	–	–	2	2

	ritter	*helt*	*degen*	*wigant*	*recke*	*guoter kneht*
Wien. Exodus	–	1	4	–	–	1[61]
Millst. Genesis	3	7	5	3	2	4[62]
Vor. Moses	–	3	3	2	1	3[63]
Vor. Joseph	1	4	–	–	1	2
Jg. Judith	2	7	–	1	–	2
Vor. Alex.	8	14	4	–	–	2[64]
Roland	4	184	19[65]	19	5	24[66]
Rother	28	99	9[67]	35	27	27[68]
Rittersitte	–	2	1	–	–	–
Melk Erin.	4	–	–	–	–	2
Hochzeit	2	–	1	2	–	7[69]
Kaiserchr.	10	102	3[70]	11	6	23[71]
Straßbg. Alex.[72]	13	65	9[73]	24	10	11[74]
Gr. Rudolf	1	14	13	1	3	2
Eilhart	38	98	62	44	4	20[75]
Elmendorf	2	1	–	–	1	–
Hz. Ernst A[76]	2	14	8[77]	5	1	–
Salman	36	40	65	3	1	–
Orendel	19	35	72	49	1	–
Oswald M.	17	24	17	1	1	–
Oswald W.	3	–	–	–	1	–
Brandan	1	–	4	1	–	–
Priest. Wernher	2	4	1[78]	–	2	–
Servatius	3	2	–	–	–	–
Eneit	59	132	19	39	1	15
Erek	134	1	11	–	–	20
Gregorius	14	1	–	–	–	–
Arm. Heinrich	3	–	–	–	–	–
Iwein	83	4	4	–	–	5
Reinhart Fuchs	2	–	–	–	–	5
Albertus	4	–	1	–	–	–
Obdt. Servatius	2	6	6	–	–	3
Craun	10	3	–	2	–	–
Herbort	113	49	30[79]	1	2	3
Halberstadt	3	2	3	–	4	–[80]
Morant	35	1	1	–	–	1[81]
Lanzelet	208	104[82]	59[83]	47	18	28
Nibelungenlied[84]	170	390	362[85]	2	492	4[86]
Walther	14	4	–	–	–	–
Parzival	372	124[87]	65	19	4	–
Willehalm	89	35[88]	–	2	1	–
Titurel	4	–	–	–	2	–
Gotfrid	64	1	–	–	–	5
Klage	6[89]	72[90]	23[91]	18[92]	17[93]	1[94]
Wigalois	335	69	29	6	1	2[95]
Athis	10	24	2	1	–	–
Hz. Ernst B	17	111	37[96]	70	38	11
Otte	6	20	2	2	1	4[97]
Ebernand	2	3	6	–	–	2[98]
Freidank	3	–	1	–	–	1
Thomasin	75	2	–	–	–	1
Gandersheim	2	3	2	–	–	–
Flore	10	3	1	–	1	2
Walther-Epos	–	4	3	–	8	–
Sächs. Weltchronik[99]	92	3	–	–	–	–
Ems Gerhard	59	4	6[100]	6	–	–[101]
Ems Barlaam	4	–	22	12	–	–
Ems Willehalm	200	61	128[102]	58	–	–[103]
Ems Alexander	76	120	187	91	–	–

	ritter	helt	degen	wigant	recke	guoter kneht
Ems Weltchr.[104]	3	69	295	108	1	1
Stricker Karl	50	43	48[105]	1	–	6
Stricker Daniel	91	23	1[106]	1	–	5
Türlin Krone	557	46	40[107]	10	81[108]	55
Türheim Tristan	18	4	–	–	–	–
Türheim Renn.	307	18	6[109]	3	–	–
Kudrun	72	256	113[110]	1	161	2
Neidhart	17	2	–	–	–	1[111]
Reinbot v. Durne	30	36	11	1	–	–
Wolfdietr. A	11	9	5[112]	–	2	–[113]
Christopherus	9	–	1	–	–	–
Franciskus	5	1	1	1	–	–
Tirol[114]	–	2	–	–	1	–
Tannhäuser[115]	–	5	1	–	1	–
Holle Demant.	446	128	6	–	–	–
Holle Crane	128	13	–	–	–	1
Lichtenst. Frd.	395	3	6	–	–	–

III. The Knight as Soldier

> horse, shield, spear, helmet and
> sword
> these make a good knight's value

Knighthood is originally a military institution. Medieval sources and modern research both agree on that. According to the *Sächsische Weltchronik* the name "knight" originated in ancient Rome, when Romulus founded the city: "de sammede do allerslachte lude unde makede en volk. Darvan scop he hundert an den rat, de het he senatores, dusent an dat orloge, de het he riddere. Inde miles quasi unus ex mille. Dar wart allererst den ridderen de name gegeven" (he collected all sorts of persons and made a people. From them he selected a hundred for the council and called them senators and a thousand for war and called them knights. Hence the name *miles* [soldier], meaning "one from a thousand." And that was the first time that knights got their name) (79, 39–80, 2).[1] Nowadays we look for the origins in Frankish rather than Roman military institutions. "In the Frankish period the role of the mounted soldier developed into a professional one. . . . In the Middle Ages the knightly class developed from these first beginnings of a professional soldiery fighting on horseback."[2] This picture is very neatly confirmed by the dictionaries: "*Ritter* originally designated the heavily armored horseman; later it became a 'class-designation.' "[3]

In Middle High German texts we find large numbers of knights on every battlefield. The heathen Malprimis of Ampelgart leads "aine egesliche scár, zwelf tusent riter" (a horrible band, twelve thousand knights) (*Roland*, 4489f.). Duke Ernst has "tûsent ritter an sîner schar" (a thousand knights in his band) (*Herzog Ernst* B, 1966). Eneas commands "drû tûsent schilde unde ritter alsô vile" (three thousand shields and as many knights) (*Eneit*, 21, 6f.). Diomedes threatens the Trojans " 'Ir sult hie ritterschaft noch sehē. Hūdert tusent vñ noch me' '' (You are going to see some more knights—a hundred thousand or more) (Herbort, 3834f.). Certainly the armies are normally thought of as armored and mounted, but that is not always what the word implies in the poems of the twelfth century. Knights without horses are encountered in several passages. In the Strassburg *Alexander* we hear of Indian war-elephants: they carried in strîte und in sturme berhfriden unde turme und rîter dar inne (in battle and in attack turrets and towers and knights inside them) (4372–74). Veldeke says of the Trojan horse "daz man tete enbinnen ritter funfzich hundert" (that five hundred knights were put in it) (*Eneit*, 41, 32f.).[4] In *König Rother*, soldiers are hidden on the ship of the pedlar: "Seszith ritare lossam. Die solin der inne uerholne sin" (Sixty fine knights. They were to be hidden inside) (3066f.). In Eilhart, "wol hundert ritter" (some hundred knights) (1471) go across the sea with Tristan. Morolf is pursued by "funfzig heidenischer man" (fifty heathen men) in a ship (*Salman*, 302, 2). After they have captured him, two of them bring the news to the court: "zwên ritter gingen hin zu tal" (two knights went down there) (306, 2). These are not dismounted horsemen but ordinary soldiers. It is reported that in the defense of the town of Abdirus "dà wáren rïtere gemeit . . . si beslozzen ir burge und giengen vaste an di were" (there were bold knights. . . . they shut up their castles and prepared to defend themselves strongly) (Strassburg *Alexander*, 2211, 14f.), naturally on foot. At the bridgehead at Belrapeire "stuonden mit helmen ûf gebuonden sehzec ritter oder mêr" (there stood sixty or more knights with their helmets on) (*Parzival, 181, 11–13*). When the Romans conquered Jerusalem, so many men "erslagin dar inne, daz die rittere gingen uf den totin und wuten biz an die knie in dem blute" (were killed there that the knights went up to the dead and waded in blood up to their knees) (Pr. Schönbach I, 120, 24–25).[5] In the appendix to the *Sächsische Weltchronik* the story is told that in the battles for the old Thuringian kingdom the Saxons came to the aid of the Franks "mit negen dusent ridderen to helpe" (with nine thousand knights) (261, 47). These Saxon "knights" are described as savage warriors, with no armor and no horses: "se waren alle enmüdich, unde gecledet mit pellele, se hadden lange sper unde korte schilde unde grote mezzese bi den siden" (they were all alike and dressed in skins, they had long spears and short shields and big knives at their sides) (262, 4–6). In Herbort von Fritzlar we read:

> Swie er dē ritter vant
> Zv rosse oder zv vuzze,

(However he found the knight / On horseback or on foot) (13020f.), and this formula occurs frequently.[6] In the *Rolandslied*, when the pagan Eschermunt, with 12,000 men, comes up against the Christians with only

1,100 and calls out to them " 'der riter nehabet ir nicht wider susgetaner crefte: ia fure ich guter chnechte zwelf tusent man' " (You don't have a large enough force of knights; I am the leader of 12,000 good soldiers) (4776–79), the meaning is hardly the one which Edward Schröder gives in his translation: "you don't have any cavalry at all,"[7] since it is assumed that the 1,100 Christians are on horseback. The pagan means rather: "against my 12,000 men you are just not strong enough, you haven't enough soldiers." And that is the case almost everywhere. Basically no distinction is made in the older texts between mounted and unmounted, lightly-armed and heavily-armed troops, but the word "knight" is simply applied to all of them. Twelve thousand knights means just 12,000 men; they constitute the army, the levy, without any hierarchy. Very occasionally one person emerges from this anonymous mass, like the knight Daclym in the *Vorau Alexander* (1299), saves the life of his lord in battle, and then immediately disappears.

It is not until 1170 that the military differentiation of knights begins in German sources. In the *Strassburg Alexander* it is said of the Persian general Mennes: "stolzer rîter er nam ze sih zehen hundrit ûz sîneme here gesundrit" (he took with him 1,000 proud knights selected from his army) (1718–20). Mennes's knights were mentioned even in the old Vorau version, but there the formula of selection was not yet present, only the simple statement: "ein hundert rîter hâter umbe sich" (he had 100 knights with him) (1242). The new distinction is also to be found in Veldeke: "Enêas zû ime nam ritter funf hundert, die hete her gesundert unde erkoren ûz dem here" (Eneas took 500 knights with him, whom he had selected and chosen from the army) (34, 10–13). It is in the *Eneit*, too, that we find for the first time the terminological distinction of knights from other groups in the army. It is said of Aventinus: "tûsent ritter heter braht sunder schutzen und fûzhere" (he had brought 1,000 knights, not counting bowmen and infantry) (143, 38f., similarly 238, 17f.); and of the Margrave of Pallante: "tûsent ritter sunder sarjante und hundert schutzen brahter dare" (he brought there 1,000 knights not counting men-at-arms and a hundred bowmen) (144, 16f.). Veldeke also knows of *schiltknechte* (infantry) (177, 22. 26. 38), who fight in their own formation on foot.[8] They were obviously not very highly regarded troops, since, when many of them are killed, the poet's comment is: "solde man schiltknehte klagen, sô moht dâ michel jâmer wesen" (if anyone were to mourn infantry, there might well be a great deal of sorrow) (177, 38f.), a remark that throws some light on the much vaunted Hohenstaufen "humanity." After this it becomes normal to distinguish between knights and non-knights by their weapons and manner of fighting. There is evidence for this everywhere in the poetry of the "Blütezeit" (Middle High German classical period); here a few examples must suffice. In Herbort we find "Beide vuzgenge. Ritter vñ knechte" (both on foot, knights and soldiers) (9,000f.). In the *Athis* fragments: "Vor den sarjantin ritin Dusint rittir" (In front of the men-at-arms rode a dozen knights) (A* 140f.). In *Willehalm*, during the attack on Orange there appear "slingaere unt patelierre, sarjande und schützen" (slingers and soldiers, men-at-arms and bowmen) (223, 10f.). And in Rudolf von Ems: "Fúnfhundert ritter braht er (sc. Lehgunt) dar, Turkopel, sarjende genuc" (he [i.e. Lehgunt] brought 500 knights, Turkopel plenty of men-at-arms) (*Willehalm*, 644f.). The knight is now the heavily armored warrior on horseback and a man can be recognized as a knight by his equipment, as in the celebrated definition of a knight in Harmann's *Iwein*: " 'nû sich wie ich gewâfent bin: ich heize ein rîtr . . .' " (now look how I am armed: I am called a knight . . .) (529ff.). The fact that the knight is known by his principles as well as by his arms may be ignored for the moment. How much the visual image of the knight is determined by his horse is shown by the passage in *Parzival* where the naive hero refuses to get off his horse for fear that he would cease to be a knight on foot: " 'mich hiez ein künec ritter sîn: swaz halt drûffe mir geschiht, ine kum von disem orse niht' " (A king told me to be a knight: whatever happens to me as a result, I shall not get off this horse) (163, 22–24).[9]

Nevertheless there are only rarely clear factual differences to correspond to this terminological differentiation. Even in the classical period we still find unarmored knights;[10] we find knights who fight with bow and arrow,[11] and the differentiation of knights from soldiers and men-at-arms is unclear and contradictory. Veldeke, who introduced the French borrowing *sarjant*, seems to think of them as unmounted. In Ulrich von Zatzikhoven they are expressly counted as infantry (*fuozher*) (*Lanzelet*, 1404, 17). In *Wigalois*, on the other hand, they fight on horseback and are distinguished from knights by their lighter weapons (10501ff.). In *Parzival* they are armored and mounted but have no shields (210, 14f., 124, 21ff. 681, 18ff.). But Wolfram also knows of men-at-arms on foot (*sarjande ad piet* [*Parzival*, 386, 12]). And in Rudolf von Ems, too, they are again fighting on foot (*Alexander*, 5148f.). Where knights and men-at-arms are named together, there is in most cases no intention of distinguishing between them; it is rather a formulaic periphrasis for the whole army. The same is true for the coupling of *ritter unde knehte*, of which the first instance is in Hartmann's *Erek* (2975, 3084, 6277) and which there points to conjunction, not distinction: the military retinue of a count is called variously "ritter" (knights) and "knehte" (soldiers) (4103/4244, 6302/09). Herbort von Fritzlar, too, sometimes calls Paris's troops "knights," sometimes "soldiers" (13626/86). In the *Nibelungenlied* we find a precise distinction: the Burgundians set out for the Huns' territory with 1,000 knights and 9,000 "soldiers" (*knehte*), except that here the "soldiers" are not part of the fighting force but of the baggage train. When knights and soldiers ("ritter unde knehte") appear on battlefields in texts of the thirteenth century (*Otte*, 2719. Ems, *Willehalm*, 281. Türheim, *Rennewart*, 31106, etc.), we should not look for any differences in arms and manner of fighting. Throughout the period under consideration, the old use of the word "ritter" persists, side by side with the meaning which makes a military differentiation (*ritter* = heavily-armored horseman). The thousands and hundreds of thousands of knights who are encountered everywhere in the German sources[12] are not a small elite group but the totality of the fighting army. In the literature on the history of warfare there are detailed statements about the association of heavy and light cavalry, about the technical distinction of equipment between knights and squires, and noble cadets.[13] These problems are usually treated much too dogmatically. People talk about "weapon types" and look for a system where none existed. We do not need to go into this, for the attempts to interpret the difference in arms sociologically and to define those who wore heavy cavalry armor as the core of the new knightly nobility have had no success. "We must simply accept that there were many variations in arms and equipment even among knights in the 'knightly' army."[14]

As long as the knights constitute the mass of anonymous soldiers, it is virtually impossible to determine anything about their social standing, their position in society. The meaning can be assessed only in a negative sense: the people who do not matter, in whose fate no one is interested, who are counted in hundreds and thousands, are called knights. When a hero strikes home, a dozen of them die at once. Achilles "Vnder der ritterschaft streit. Zwenzic mit eime slage sneit" (fights with the knights. He cuts down twenty at a stroke) (Herbort, 8851f.). And when the fight is over, the dead knights lie on the battlefield like cattle: "dô lâgin sie recht als daz vê, manch ritter, an dem wale" (there they lay like cattle, many a knight, on the battlefield) (Eilhart, 5946f.). Wolfram calls them a "kumberhaftin diet" (a wretched collection) (*Parzival*, 336, 18), but such sympathy is rare. The knights are the simple soldiers who cannot be distinguished from what is below but only from what is above them, as Herbort testifies in respect of the army of Prothesilaus: "Prothesilaus do gwan. Bi im siben hundert man. Drizzic tusent ritter da mite" (Prothesilaus had seven hundred men with him and thirty thousand knights too) (4279–81). It is only occasionally and by accident that we get any incidental information about the way of life of these lower-class soldiers. Eilhart uses the term "arme rittere" of the two servants who are given the task of killing Brangaene by Queen Isolde (M 1ᵛ 13). The three robbers (*drîe roubaere* [3116]) who lie in wait for Erek in the woods are also called knights (*Erek*, 3186). The crude giant Harpin is called "knight" by Iwein who was very conscious of social stratification (*Iwein*, 5008).[15] The *Sächsische Weltchronik* mentions "werlike rovere, der under ridderes namen alleswar vile was" (warlike robbers of whom there were many everywhere under the name of knights) (196, 41f.), armed bands of robbers, who made the neighborhood unsafe. The *Kaiserchronik* tells of the mad behavior of the emperor Nero: "er hiez rîter wâfen vil, er hiez si mitten in daz fiur gân, si muosen alle ainander slahen" (he had many knights armed and told them to go through fire and they had all to kill one another) (4090–92); these knights were thus gladiators. In Wolfram, knights and merchants appear together as the armed *bovel* (populace) of a city: "hie der ritter, dort der koufman, diu juncfrouwe (sc. Antikonie) erhôrte sân den bovel komen ûz der stat" (here the knight, there the merchant, the demoiselle [i.e. Antikonie] heard the populace coming from the town((*Parzival*, 408, 1–3). In the army of King Oswald we find twelve knights, who "all used to be goldsmiths" (*Oswald* M. 2106), before they became knights (2109) and these smith-knights brought *den wercziuc* (2112), their professional tools, with them on the campaign, as becomes apparent when Oswald needs a smith on the way. In the *Sächsische Weltchronik* we are told that the Emperor Augustus removed 20,000 knights from his army. They were escaped slaves, whom he restored to their masters; anyone who did not wish to go back was hanged: "De riddere waren alte ummatich. De keiser nam de ridderschap af twintich dusent mannen, de van rechte nicht riddere solden sin, unde gaf twintich dusent schalke eren herren weder; ses dusent, de nicht dienen ne wolden, de let he han" (the knights were old and weak. The emperor took 20,000 men from the body of knights who had no right to be knights and gave 2,000 slaves back to their masters. Six thousand, who were unwilling to be servants, he had hanged) (89, 5–7). In sermons the devil's servants are called knights: "der pose geist hat siner riter zwo schar . . . daz sint die ubelere, roubere und prennære und moderere" (the evil spirit had two groups of his knights . . . they are the sinners, robbers, and arsonists and murderers) (Pr. br. I Schönbach 197, 25–28; also Pr. Schönbach I, 331, 26ff.). In another sermon the "volgere" (followers) of the devil are described like this: "bose und unrechte lute und nemeliche rittere und bose gewaldige lute die da machint urluge, rub und brant und andere bosheit" (wicked and evil people and so-called knights and evil violent people who make war, robbery, arson and other wickedness) (Pr. Schönbach I, 109, 28–30). The soldiers of Herod who murder the children in Bethlehem are also described as knights (Pr. Schönbach I, 144, 3). The soldiers of the emperor Maximian who behead Severus are called knights (Pr. br. Jeitteles, 407, 12). We find knights at the execution of St. George (Durne, 3638), at the martyrdom of St. Christopher (*Christoph*, 1787), and of St. Sebastian (Pr. br. I, Schönbach, 188, 10). And finally the soldiers of Pilate who guard the grave of Jesus are knights.[16]

The knights in Heinrich von Melk should also be regarded as soldiers. The significance of his *Des Todes Gehugede* (Memento mori) for cultural history has long been recognized. The reference to *Minnesang* in the scene where the "knight's lady" (de Boor) is brought to her dead husband, aroused particular interest and where the poet makes use of the whole "Vanitas-Pathos" topos in describing the corpse of this "courtly knight" (Ehrismann) who in his lifetime used to sing love songs (612). We never find out directly what social class the dead *Minnesänger* belonged to, but when his son is addressed as "rîcher unt edeler jungelinc" (rich and noble youth) (663), there is no doubt that an aristocratic environment is envisaged. The decisive point for Heinrich von Melk's concept of knighthood is that the word is just not used in this connection. It is true that the poet uses the expression "rîter unt frowen" (knights and ladies) (289, and similarly 427) elsewhere, an expression found here for the first time, and one which clearly points to the courtly sphere. But what is actually said about the knights makes it clear that they belong to a totally different sphere from that of the aristocratic *Minnesänger*. The section on knights (343–72) is a parallel to that on lower-class women (319–42), the *tagewurchen* (daily workers) (320) and *gebiurinne* (peasant-women) (330) who make themselves up and play the courtly lady. This part of the work is concerned with the basic sin of *superbia* (pride), and the poet presents each social class with its particular sins. In the case of knights, he names two variants of *superbia*: "zwêne geverten hât diu ubermuot, die setzent die rîter an die gluot" (there are two companions of pride, which put knights in the fire) (343f.). One is immorality: wherever "diu rîterschaft gesamnet" (knights assemble) (354), their only theme in conversation is "wie manige der unt der behûret habe" (how many girls this man or that has seduced) (356). And when people "der manhäit wirt gidâcht" (think of their virility) (363), then they fall victim to the second sin, they boast of how many men they have killed: "si sprechent 'den mac man in allen landen ze einem guotem chnecht wol haven: der hât sô manigen erslagen' " (they say "you can regard any man as a good soldier in every land who has killed many people") (370-72). Whoring and murder are typical sins of knights. This is directed at a different social level from that in the description of the noble lord, who fritters away his life in courtly games. For Heinrich von Melk, knights are crude fighters, mercenaries, the male counterpart of *tagewurchen*.

There is evidence for the knight as mercenary, as a soldier of inferior origin, all through the classical period. But a sensible alteration set in at the time that the word was reserved, for preference, for the heavy cavalry. From then on the title "knight" takes on a new tone in the military sphere: it becomes the designation for the traditional battle-equipment of nobles, armor and horse. This change does not, however, mean that the old mercenary soldiers had changed in the meantime into distinguished gentlemen. It is a question here of a philological, not a sociological process. We shall treat this process in context later, so that it is sufficient here to state the fact that, after the end of the twelfth century, anybody who fought in armor on horseback could be called "knight," whether the person inside the armor was an emperor or a mercenary soldier.[17] This identity in their appearance as military figures was certainly well suited to bridge gaps in social standing, but it would be just as certainly a mistake to attempt to regard as a nobleman every man who appeared on the battlefield armed as a knight. In Eneas's army we encounter Chores, a priest who was "was doch ritter vile gût" (a very good knight) (*Eneit*, 243, 21). So he was a priest who had put on armor and got on a horse and was fighting as a knight. He must have been a distinguished gentleman, since he commanded his own troops: "grôz was sîn geselleschaft ritter unde schutzen" (his retinue of knights and archers was large) (243, 24f.). Here we see that a lord and part of his people fight in the same way and both are called knights. But we also see that identity of arms does not mean identity of social position. This statement is generally valid: wherever knights in the narrower military sense are encountered in texts of the classical period, no judgments should be made about their social standing from the fact that they are called knights. "Masters and servants meet as companions-in-arms but nobility and service remain . . . politically, legally, and socially sharply distinguished from one another."[18] In Willehalm, for example, the simple soldiers fight just like princes—as knights. Rennewart, however, a king's son, fights on foot with his club and is therefore not a knight but a *knappe* (squire) (315, 12 etc.) and a *sarjant* (man-at-arms) (311, 28 etc.). This *sarjant* is in social standing and family far above the knights.

If no conclusions about the social position of knights can be drawn from their outward appearance, the question can be answered only if it is known under what conditions they were ordered on campaign or, in crassly material terms, where they got their expensive equipment. The literary sources—and they are, incidentally, no different from the historical ones—are not very forthcoming. They do, however, permit us to distinguish in broad outline two different forms of summoning knights. In several passages we hear how a king or prince sent his messengers round the land and ordered the knights to court. In *König Rother*, for example: "Do sante der kuninc constantin. Wide sine mere. Vnde gebot den ritarin (herren E). Hin zo der wertschefte" (Then King Constantin sent his command far and wide and ordered the knights to the levy) (1558–61). The invitation is coupled with the threat that anyone who fails to obey will be hanged (1565ff.). The result is that all the knights appear:

"sich gesellete man wider man, zo sime gelichen. Vnde vazziten sic vlizeliche" (each joined with the other, each to his like, and were properly equipped) (1570–72). This is the classic recruitment of an army of knights: the knights are distributed all over the land and are liable to their lord for military service. Admittedly a great deal remains unclear. It is not stated whether these knights were summoned on the basis of feudal tenure or claim on service, and the last line, "sie vazziten sic" seems to indicate that they did not receive their equipment until they reached the king's court. Other texts have even less to say. It is reported of the order given by Turnus: "dar quam diu mâre ritterschaft, die her besande wîten after lande" (there came the famed knights which he sent for far and wide throughout the land) (*Eneit*, 130, 12–14). The armed invasion of Count Alier is resisted by "die rîter vonme lande unde ir sarjande" (the knights from the land and their men-at-arms) (*Iwein*, 3707f.). Riwalin and Rual "sanden über al ir lant und samenten ir ritterschaft" (sent out throughout all their lands and collected their knights) (Gotfried von Strassburg, 1660f.). "di junghe vorste Dêmantîn di rittere al besande wîte an sîneme lande" (The young prince Demantin summoned all the knights far and wide in his land) (Holle, *Demant*, 4806–08). There are many similar passages.[19] It is assumed in most cases that the knights provide their own equipment but it is expressly stated only once, in *Willehalm*: "an den selben stunden was dâ diu beste rîterschaft über al der Franzeiser kraft, und heten ouch alle harnasch dâ: was ez aber anderswâ, dâ wart balde nâch gesant. die strâzen wurden gar berant von den rîtern selbe und von ir boten" (at that time all the flower of knighthood from the whole of French power was there and all had armor too: any who were not there were speedily summoned. The streets were overrun with the knights themselves and their messengers) (185, 20–27). We are told nothing of the social condition of these knights, but that they own horses and take part in the military life-style of the nobility.

Side by side with the summons to vassals, as we may call it for short, there was a second major method of recruiting, the provision of equipment by the lord. König Rother once again provides a clear picture of it: "Alse die vart wart gelobit. do nam suvert vfe deme houe. ein uil iunger degen. beide sabel vn kelen. ein graue der heiz erevin. Dar mite zireter di riter sin. Die anderen herren daten sam. uil wol uazetin ire man" (When the voyage was approved, a very young warrior took swords at the court, both sabre and staff, and a count called Erwin equipped his knights with them. The other lords did the same. They equipped their men very well) (150–57). These knights are socially at a different level. They own no armor and no horses but are equipped with them by their master. At the end of the campaign they had to take off the expensive equipment and then they became what they were before—servants. Nevertheless there does seem to have been an upper stratum among the dependents who were employed in this way as cavalry. A distinction is made between the knights and non-knights in the "notigen diet" (needy people) whom Rother takes into his service: "Svve dar hate ritaris namen. Die sundirte man dan. Vnde gach en gote rosse. Vnde pelleline rocke, zo den rossin staline ringe . . . Vnde vazzite sie al geliche" (Anyone who had the title "knight" was then set apart and given a good horse and fur cloaks and steel mail in addition to the horses . . . and they were all equipped alike) (1331–35. 40). But then the distinction is eliminated and they are all called Rother's "men" (man) (1380): "Die ime waren vnderdan. Mit dieniste aller tagelich" (who were subject to him for service everyday) (1382f.). Here, too, the knights are dependent on a lord for material goods. The term for knightly equipment for soldiers is "ritter vazzen." Asprian promised a foreign count "driezich rittarc vazen ein jar" (that he will equip thirty knights a year for him) (*Rother*, 1446), that is, that he will put the means at his disposal to maintain thirty armed horsemen for a whole year. Keeping knights about one is thus a preeminently financial problem. The more powerful and rich a lord is, the more knights he can equip. The *Jüngere Judith* tells of "uursten so getan, der zehenzich riter mochte haben" (a prince so great, he could maintain a hundred knights) (153, 8f). There is no doubt that these knights could be of great military significance. They could be kept at court and were in a constant state of readiness; and the lord had a quite different power of disposition over them from the one he had over vassal-knights, who had to be summoned from all over the land and then only with the help of threats and promises.

It is not only in *König Rother* that we find such cavalry soldiers without their own equipment. In a St. Martin's sermon it says: "in des wart ein herevart und gab man den rittern allen heresture, daz ist allis des sie bedorften zu der herevart" (meanwhile there was a campaign and the knights were given all military equipment, that is everything they needed for the campaign) (Pr. Schönbach I, 355, 23–25 and similarly in Pr. br. II Schönbach 249, 20f.). We read in *Kudrum* "die ritter die dâ wâren, helm unde swert brâhte man den helden und manegen schilt guoten" (the knights, they were there: helmets and swords were brought for the heroes and many a good shield) (460, 2f.). It is however perfectly possible that here the reference is to gifts for the knights.[20] An interesting scene is preserved in the *Christopherus*: there the knights are dissatisfied with the king and renounce service to him by taking off their equipment and throwing it at his feet: "si nâmen alle ir beste habe und zugen ouch daz harnasch abe und gâben ez dem künege wider und wurfenz smâhlîch vür in nider" (They took all their best possessions and also stripped off their armor; they gave it back to the king and threw it scornfully down before him) (1323–26). But anyone who had enough horses and equipment found people ready to serve him as knights and then he was probably not particular choosing them. The complaint of Wirnt von Gravenberg is well known: "swer vil kûme wære kneht, der wil nu rîter werden" (people who could hardly be called servants now want to become knights) (*Wigalois*, 2333f.). The reproach is directed less against the people themselves than against the lords: "die dem immer swert gegeben der daz rîterlîche leben niht behalten künne" (who have always given a sword to people who cannot keep up a knightly life) (2340–42).

Closely related to the service-knights are the mercenary knights, whom we encounter several times in the texts of our period. They have in common their economic dependence on their lord and the tie to him which results from it. In most cases we hear only of the fact of knight-service for pay. Thus Hector makes a recruiting speech by saying: " 'Swelich ritter gabe gart. Der kvme albalde vffe solt' " ("Any knight who desires a gift, let him come at once for pay") (Herbort, 2131f.). Gotfrid tells of the expedition of Gurmum, the king's son: he recruited "ritter und sarjande, die er mit sinem guote oder mit höfschlichem muote zuo zime gewinnen kunde" (knights and men-at-arms, whom he could win over to his cause with his wealth or chivalric spirit) (5898–901). That knights did indeed go to war for chivalric spirit alone, without pay, is particularly stressed in *Wigalois*: "dehein rîter nâch solde diente dâ mit sîner wer: im (sc. Wigalois) was sô willic gar daz her durch sîne grôze manheit, daz im ir dienst was bereit mit ganzem willen, âne guot" (No knight served for pay there in his army, because of his great manliness, the army was so attached to him that their service was wholeheartedly at his disposal, without material reward) (10449–54). Alexander sends Prince Kliander to Lycia "mit silber und mit golde dâ mit er werben solde nâch werden soldieren" (with silver and with gold so that he can recruit worthy soldiers) (Rudolf von Ems, *Alex.*, 5021–23). A prince in Berthold von Holle declares: "rittere dorch mîns gûtes gere sîn komen ûz manchem lande here" ("knights have come from many lands desiring my riches") (*Demant*, 9657f.).[21]

There is at least one text from the classical period which provides us with a detailed picture of the way in which a large army was assembled. This is the *Willehalm*, whose value as testimony is all the more valuable because Wolfram gives far more exact and detailed information than his French source. Margrave Willehalm needs a new army to continue the struggle against the pagans who have arrived in Provence. He therefore turns to the "Roman" king Loys, who is at the time holding court in Munleun, and to his relations, whom he meets at the king's court. He gains their support and in three different ways they decide on a new military potential:

1. by the voluntary help of Willehalm's relatives. They are great lords, who make their own decisions about war and assemble their own armies. Their military power is in most instances derived from one domain. His father Heinrich is Count of Narbonne and among his brothers are Duke Bernart of Brubant and Count Arnalt of Gerunde.
2. by the royal summons of the king. Loys declares the war against the pagans to be a matter of state and gives his order to the French princes assembled at Munleun: "diu urteil vor dem rîche wart gesprochen endelîche und gevolget von den hœsten" (the decision was given finally before the assembly and obeyed by the nobles) (185, 11–13). Since the king is prevented from leading the army in person, he hands over the imperial standard and the supreme command over the imperial forces to Willehalm (211, 10ff.).
3. by the recruiting of mercenaries. Willehalm's mother Irmenschart and his sister, the queen, provide financial resources from their private fortunes, and, with the help of this assistance (161, 23), a mercenary army is assembled, which later fights under Willehalm's direct command, while the *sunderher* (special forces) (305, 1) of his relatives remain under their command. Only the disposition of all the forces and the succession of the attack is determined by Willehalm.

Here feudal troops and mercenary troops stand side by side. It would be expected at first that the main impetus of the military force would lie in the imperial levy. Instead of that, the imperial army soon proves to be the least reliable factor. Even the king's summons is not an order but an invitation: " 'swaz ieslîchem sî gelegen, dâ wil ich sînes willen phlegen mit gâb, mit lêhn, mit eigen' " ("whatever suits each person, I shall carry out his decision with gifts, land tenure, and property") (184, 11–13). The king provides money (*gâbe*), and either leases or donates land (*lêhen/eigen*), to provide an incentive for his princes to go campaigning. Some take the money, others undertake the duty without compensation: "etslîche nâmen sînen solt: etslîche wârn im sus sô holt, daz sie die hervart swuoren" (some took his pay, some were so gracious to him that they swore [to undertake] the campaign) (184, 21–23). There is in fact legal pressure on ordinary soldiers (*turkopel sarjande*, and *rîter*) (185, 1/3)—they are simply declared *rehtelos* (outside the law) (185, 7) if they refuse to go on a campaign—but the effect of this measure should not be overlooked. What really counts is only the agreement of the princes, who, just like Willehalm's relatives, assemble their own armies and divisions and take part in the campaign "mit manegem sunderringe grôz" (with many a large separate camp) (214, 4). As soon as the army is face to face with the enemy, it becomes clear how small is the significance of the king's order and his money. The princes declare the undertaking to be too risky, immediately renounce their participation, and the whole imperial army withdraws (321, 1ff.). Willehalm as representative of the *rîch* (empire) has no legal means of holding them back. The fact that in the end they do take part in the battle is entirely due to Rennewart, who uses naked force to turn them back.

The will of the princes is decisive in military matters. We do not find out what their power of command over the troops they have raised is based on. But the assurance with which they can order their soldiers into battle or can withdraw them from the battlefield makes it clear that there is a stronger connection than the vague feudal duty to serve in an armed levy.[21a]

The second decisive factor beside suzerainty over men capable of waging war is money. Mercenaries are subject to immediate command and have no means of avoiding combat: "sîner swestr und sîner muoter her bî dem marcrâven blibn ze wer" (his sister's and his mother's armies stayed with the margrave for his defense) (323, 7f.). The mustering of this mercenary army is the most interesting part of the account of the campaign. Princess Irmenschart could not know that she would meet her son Willehalm at Munleun and that he would need soldiers. And she had naturally not brought all her liquid financial assets with her on her journey. But her banker from Narbonne was in her retinue and she charges this man with the financing of the army: "einen juden von Narbôn liez dâ diu fürstinne Irmenschart: der solte gein der hervart bereiten des marcgrâven diet" (Princess Irmenschart brought a Jew from Narbonne there: he was to equip the margrave's men for the campaign) (195, 12–15). The way in which this happens is that each man "sîn kumber daz geriet" (whose state of poverty makes it advisable) (195, 16)—an indication of the social standing of the mercenaries—reports to the man from Narbonne and receives at once *rîchen solt* (195, 18), a hand-out (advance payment). Furthermore, the banker provides "harnasch ors unt gewant" (armor, horse, and clothing) (195, 24), that is, a complete outfit for each mercenary. Incidentally, we find out an interesting detail of economic history: the capitalist puts the artisans in Munleun, the tailors and smiths, to work on his own account (196, 6ff.) and he is thus able to equip the recruits for the campaign in very short order. In making the selection no questions are asked about rank and social position but only about military capacity. The queen has given her brother Buov the task of calling for recruits throughout the whole Roman Empire: " 'wâ nu soldiere? swaz der in rœmschem rîche sî, den künde, Buov von Kumarzî, der rœmschen küneginne solt' " ("where are there mercenaries? Buov of Kumarzi, announce to any of them there may be in the Roman Empire the payment of the Roman queen") (165, 14–17). Later foreign mercenaries are recruited too: " 'daz sî den vremden ouch benant, er sî rittr od sarjant, turkopel, od swer ze strîte tüge' " ("have it reported to foreigners too,

whether he be knight or man-at-arms, infantryman or anyone fit to fight'')
(170, 17–19). All the recruits: "rîtr und ander soldiere" (knights and
other mercenaries) (201, 19) are divided immediately into troops and
Willehalm assigns a "rotten meister: hie dem rîter, dort dem sarjant der
marcgrâf rotten meister gap" (troop-commander to each section, here to
the knights, there to the men-at-arms the margrave gave a troop commander) (197, 4f.).[22] So strike-formations are produced, organized entirely from the military point of view, which purely because of the
command structure under which they operate are bound to be superior
to a looser feudal levy.

Finally, a special case among the armies of the princes is worth
noting. Willehalm's youngest brother, Heimrich, and King Schilbert appear unexpectedly on the battlefield with an army that cannot be feudal,
since the Schetis owns no land and has no suzerainty: "erne hete der
erden niht sô breit als ein gezelt möht umbehaben" (he did not even have
enough land for a tent to cover) (241, 20f.). The fact is that the two had
assembled the army in the pay of Venice to fight against the Patriarch
of Agley (240, 28ff.). The fact that they have not advanced into southern
France with this army makes it clear that they are not paid generals of
Venetian troops but that they have raised a private army with Venetian
money and, after completing their assignment for Venice, are waging
war on their own account, exactly like the later *condottieri* and leaders
of free companies. It is entirely consistent with this that they have no
baggage train but live off the land and are rewarded by booty: "niht
anderr urbor moht er (sc. Heimrich) haben, wan als der unverzagte an
den vînden bejagte" (he [i.e., Heinrich] could have no other income,
except what the undaunted man extorted from the enemy) (241, 22–24).
That is the ultimate act of independence of mercenary horse soldiers.

Willehalm shows us imperial army, princes' army and mercenary
army side by side. Once the battle has begun it is impossible to distinguish
which soldiers are fighting as vassals, which as liegemen, and which as
mercenaries. All are equipped as knights and all are called knights. But
in the military organization and the command structure the differences
appear clearly and here the epic presentation leaves no doubt about the
superior reliability and usefulness of the knights bound by obligations of
service and pay-agreements as opposed to mere feudal levies. This means
that the military phenomenon of knighthood is not to be explained by
reference to an individual social type, the vassal-warrior. The equipment
common to all knights hides social stratifications which defy any unitary
social interpretation and can be understood only when account is taken
of the various types of military subordination. The picture which has been
obtained from the German sources will now be compared with the results
of historical research.

In historical literature knighthood is regarded almost exclusively from the aspect of feudal law and interpreted as a typical phenomenon of medieval feudalism:[23] "Feudality provided the constitutional bases for the development of the knightly class."[24] Possession of a fief was at the same time "the economic basis of the knightly class,"[25] since "feudality was the only . . . basis on which the support of a mounted professional soldiery was possible in the Middle Ages."[26] There are thousands of recorded instances in the historical sources from the ninth century on of the vassal who performs war service for his fief in heavy equipment, and no further proof is needed that this type of warrior made a significant contribution to our impression of the nature of armed force in the Middle Ages. There is authority for calling him "knight" in the speech-usage of the sources, for in the Latin texts of the tenth to twelfth centuries, and partly beyond, "miles" was the predominant designation for vassals.[27] This serves as a basis for the frequent use of the term "knight" in a more general sense for vassal relationships, so that the connection between a fief as benefice and the vassal relationship is designated from the beginning and fundamentally as a "knight's fief," and even in the Merovingian period people are spoken of as "of the knightly class";[28] to the degree that the historical roots of medieval vassal relationships are seen in Germanic "comitatus" system, the origins of knighthood are sought there too.[29] This verbal usage first gets its characteristic form, however, as a result of the social interpretation of the knight-concept. The *milites* of the eleventh century were "free liegemen," "free vassals";[30] and hence they are called "free knights."[31] If it is determined "that at least in southern Germany there is absolutely no proof of the existence of a class of free knights which . . . did not belong to the nobles or free lords,"[32] then it is possible to equate the vassal-knights with the old aristocracy or nobility.[33] Thus we speak of a "free knightly class,"[34] or more exactly, of a "closed knightly class consisting of free vassals."[35] Later this class took on its specifically Hohenstaufen stamp by "merging" with the "unfree knights," the *ministeriales*.[36]

The theoretical basis for the social interpretation of the concept of knighthood is provided by the legal works of the thirteenth century. "When, in the thirteenth century the system of coats of arms reached the point of theoretical organization, there was a very close connection between the right to a fief and knightly birth."[37] In the *Sachsenspiegel*, this connection is expressed as a principle for the first time and the foundation-stone was thus laid for the conception of the knight in the late Middle Ages: "Papen (unde) wif, dorpere, koplude, unde alle de rechtes darvet oder unecht geboren sint, unde alle de nicht ne sin van riddere art van vader unde van eldervader, de scolen lenrechtes darven" (Priests and women, peasants, merchants and all those outside the law or born illegitimate and all who are not of knightly descent from father and grand-father, all these have no title to a fief) (Lnr., 2 1). In Eike von Repgow, the knight-concept is, in fact, still missing in the list of coats-of-arms (Ldr., I, 3, 2), and der Spiegler leaves the question of the seventh shield unresolved. The later legal works, starting with the *Schwabenspiegel* are the first to complete the system by putting the knight in the last place in the coat-of-arms as a single-shield knight. As a result of this system "feudal law . . . is designated as the social law of knights."[38] However important the statements of the *Spiegel* are as witnesses of legal thinking in the thirteenth century, their value as evidence for knowledge of the legal conditions actually existing in earlier centuries is limited. The theory of the knight's shield (*clipeus militaris*) rests on a lawyer's invention, the separation and individualization of the vassal fief, granted in return for *homagium* (homage) which is clearly separated from all other types of fealty. "As a result of this upgrading of a special (conditioned) case to the normal case, however, feudal law was at one and the same time given dogmatic form and in a certain sense ossified and canonized . . . No axiom about the genetic development in previous centuries can be derived from this."[39] "The ranking of coats-of-arms is not a system of compulsory norms but of instructions for ranking, *leges imperfectae*" (unenforced laws)[40] and "it remained very largely mere theory."[41] Modern research into feudalism has rediscovered the whole breadth of medieval thinking on fiefs which lies behind the dogmatism of the law treatises,[42] thinking which did not recognize class boundaries. Neither the receiving of a fief nor the performance of homage was tied to clear-cut social conditions. "People of the most varied social class and rank were qualified to receive benefices . . . All classes of the population from the unfree retainers to the king had a part in it."[43] As early as the Carolingian period there were *servi* (slaves or serfs) who swore an oath of loyalty to the king and did military service for their fief.[44] And in the later Middle Ages there is good evidence for homage by peasants: "For the oath of loyalty as well as for homage it makes no difference whether the peasant as a person is free or unfree."[45] There are grounds for the assumption "that medieval homage of unfree peasants did not first appear as a late counterpart to the *homagium* of vassals but had had a continuous underground existence since Frankish times."[46] As a result of these observations, Heinrich Mitteis formulated "a fundamental rule of international feudal law: Only legal considerations about real property are . . . taken up in property law. The legal standing of the acquirer as a person is determined by the appropriate social status."[47] Put in layman's language, this means that the fact of receiving a fief says nothing about the social standing of the receiver. A good example is the late medieval parallel of noble "knight-fief" (*Ritterlehen*) and peasant "pocket-fief" (*Beutellehen*).[48] Herbert

Klein has shown from sources in Salzburg, that the difference between the two types is not determined by the fiefs themselves but is governed according to the social circumstances of the holder of the fief: "In Salzburg this system . . . was managed in such a way that every knight-fief which came into bourgeois or peasant hands became a "pocket-fief" and every "pocket-fief" which was acquired by a noble became a nobleman's fief."[49] The consequence is that the social structure in Germany cannot be comprehended by means of categories of feudal law. Unlike the situation in France and England, hierarchic-aristocratic social ranking prevailed in Germany over the feudal system: "Briefly, *Landrecht* (National law) prevailed over *Lehnrecht* (feudal law)."[50] In Germany, unlike the rest of western Europe, "feudal organization did not become the framework of the structure of the state."[51] Today we can see "the deep division between form and content, appearance and reality which run right through feudal law"[52] and the stress is put on "allodialism," that is to say on aristocratic domain independent of kingship and feudal tenure.[53]

The title "miles" has even less claim than the receipt of a fief to be regarded as an indication of social standing. Throughout the whole Middle Ages the basic meaning of the Roman word for "soldier" remained active: *miles* is quite simply "the soldier," independently of his rank or armament. Paul Guilhiermoz has shown how the specialized meaning miles = vassus was able to develop as a result of the shifts in social and military stratification in late antiquity. The whole vocabulary of vassalage originates in low social conditions: vassus itself means nothing more than "servant"[54] and the symbolic gesture of clasping hands continued to recall its origins in serfdom. The words *"miles, militia, militare"* finally came to take on the general senses of servant, service, and serve or obey. "This means that *miles* had acquired the necessary flexibility to act as a translation of words like *vassus* and *vassallus*, which meant at one and the same time servant, private soldier and . . . warrior in the absolute sense."[55] In its meaning "vassal" *miles* means primarily the man who is obligated to a lord for service.[56] Since military service was more frequently performed on horseback and in heavy armor, the word was able to develop the special meaning "armored horseman," which appears for the first time in Richer von St. Remy at the end of the tenth century in the formula *milites peditesque* (cavalry and infantry).[57] There is plenty of evidence after the eleventh century for this limitation to heavy cavalry: "admittedly the word never became a clearly defined and technically unambiguous expression."[58] A diploma from Corvey of the tenth century gives evidence for differences in social standing with vassalage by distinguishing between noble vassals, *vassalli nobiles*, and those of a lower class, *inferioris vero conditionis*.[59] Other sources draw a distinction between *milites* and princes and great lords.[60] From Carolingian times on there were two clearly distinguished groups of vassals, those established on a fief and those who lived at their lord's court. While the former gradually became more and more independent, the second remained socially very close to the household personnel. In France these "soldiers of the household" played an important role;[61] in Germany they were "a definite minority"[62] but there were such landless vassals into the thirteenth century.[63] In Germany their position was very soon assumed by people of low social rank, by unfree persons who swore no homage and were dependent on their lord not in feudal law but court law. There is frequent evidence in Germany for such unfree *milites*:[64] in 992 Otto III grants to Halberstadt a "regalem heribannum super milites liberos et servos ejusdem ecclesiae"[65] (royal power of calling to arms of soldiers both free and unfree of that same church); similarly in 1009 a *privilegium* of Heinrich II for Minden speaks of a "bannus sive heribannus über Francos liberos et aecclesiasticos, litones, maalman vel servos cuiuslibet conditionis seu colonos" (call or mustering of Franks both free and ecclesiastical, daily workers, millers, or unfree men of any condition or peasants).[66] Such evidence makes it clear that in Germany the equation *miles* = free vassal never works out without a remainder.[67] The Latin concept *miles* no more designates a social quality than does the German word *ritter*. The two words have in common the fact that they are not primarily concerned with the type of armament: both can designate fighting-men of any type as well as the special group "armored cavalry." In both cases the stress is laid rather on the personal obligation of the armed man, on the dependence of the warrior on a lord. In Widukind of Corvey a *miles* is "a warrior who is always at the service of his lord . . . and who performs mounted service";[68] and the glosses on *degan* in Old High German already point in the same direction. Among the *milites*/knights there are free and unfree, landed and landless, men of high and low birth. These concepts do not permit of a unified social interpretation. "For the period up to about 1250, therefore, the expression *miles*, even when clearly used as a rank or title, cannot be employed as a criterion for social differentiation."[69]

"By the twelfth century the cavalry arm had achieved superiority . . . this change in the nature of armies made knighthood the actual instrument of armed force."[70] A clear impression of the social composition of this knighthood can be gained only when it is determined who actually went to war in knight's equipment. "The feudal population provided the most distinguished and valuable soldiers."[71] "The army . . . had predominantly the character of a feudal militia."[72] The military importance of the vassals is not in question; but the sources hardly allow us to determine how large the participation of feudal warriors in the levies was. And opinions are sharply divided about the question of the degree to which fiefs were devoted to purely military ends, that is, to the raising of a military force.[73] Historians of war do not give very favorable opinions of the military use of feudalism: "A marked disadvantage in military matters had to be accepted: a part of the mounted soldiery was no longer in a permanent state of military service but lived on the fiefs."[74] Enfiefing almost invariably meant a loosening of the condition of dependence,[75] and the increasing independence of the vassals brought about a lessening of their military employment. The literature of the history of war gives a very negative view of the military qualities of the vassal soldiers.[76] Modern research stresses that there was a highly developed art of war even in the Middle Ages,[77] which is apparently opposed to this view, but it must then be expected that the stress is no longer entirely on the feudal organization of medieval armed forces. "In the area of army organization . . . feudal law, even when feudalism was at its height, was never totally predominant."[78] In Germany, feudal conceptions penetrated the law of military mobilization from the end of the tenth century on[79] and in the twelfth century Friedrich I pulled harder on the reins.[80] But Barbarossa's imperial wars show with great clarity the degree to which the military obligations of vassals were already in decline. The obligation for military service was, in principle, limited to forty days, a limitation "which in practice was bound to make any larger undertaking impossible."[81] The local limitations on military duty had a similarly restricting effect; there were also special privileges for particular parts of the Empire. Finally, since there were no fixed numbers at all for the levies,[82] the German king about 1200 would have had no military power to show which was worthy of serious consideration if he had had to rely only on his feudal levies. Heinrich Mitteis has, however, determined "that in practice . . . no one took the slightest notice of all this theory"[83]—another instance of the haunting will o' the wisp of feudal theory. In the histories of war, it is almost exclusively expeditions to Rome and imperial wars which are treated under the rubric of "assembly of an army," because it is only for such undertakings that lists of levies or specific treaties are preserved. The closer one gets to military normality, internecine wars and feuds of great lords, the less explicit become the descriptions. But it is in these contests that the military actuality of the Middle Ages is most clearly documented. It is therefore of significance for the evaluation of feudal law in the military sphere that a feudal levy in the case of a private feud is not recognized in the theory of fiefs. "The duty of the vassal to take part in them is totally unknown to the statute books."[84] That is to say that the type of war which was by far the most common remained totally unaffected by feudal law.

There was no time at which the military power of a medieval lord was limited to a levy of his vassals. "In practice, there were in every army many, often very many servants armed like knights side by side with the actual knights."[85] The more clumsy and ineffective the feudal levy became, the more the military importance of such knights increased as they were in a closer state of dependence. Lambert von Hersfeld tells how the great feudal lords denied the king an expedition in 1074 and how Heinrich IV thereupon invaded Hungary without the support of the princes, using only his household and private troops (*milites gregarii ac privati*).[86] There is evidence in the service-law of Limburg of 1036 that the abbot of the monastery there picked his knights (*milites*) from the dependent rural population.[87] In the German texts of the classical period the peasant still appears in the army side by side with the knight: "dô hiez man ze sturme gân daz volc gemeinlîche, beide arme und rîche, ritter und gebûre" (then the whole people together was ordered to the attack, both poor and rich, knight and peasant) (*Herzog Ernst* B, 1534–37).[88] "There were at every period mounted peasants,[89] even when their service was less and less called for by economic considerations. The military success of an undertaking was in many cases dependent on the ready availability of the troops for action. Consequently a force trained for war and in the immediate neighborhood of the lord was bound to be superior to any feudal levy. In Hartmann's *Erek*, the story is told that a count equipped nineteen of the servants at court with horses and weapons for the quick pursuit of his opponent (4028ff.); these people are then called sometimes his knights and sometimes his servants.[90] There is evidence for such centralized equipping as early as the Carolingian period. In the *Capitulare Bononiense* of 811, it is laid down "that the spiritual office holders who keep in a church or other sacred place more mail-shirts than are needed for the equipping of their people are required to make a report to the ruler."[91] The fact that this was not an exception but a system practiced everywhere is confirmed by the *Constitutio de expeditione Romana* of the twelfth century, which expressly leaves it to the discretion of the lords, which of their people they decide to equip with heavy weapons.[92] This fighting force also has great military importance as garrisons for the lord's castles. Many sources make it clear how low was the social standing of the occupants of such "castle-fiefs." "In a document of Bishop Thiemos [of Bamberg], of about 1196, mention is made of eight soldiers of the personal household (*milites de propria familia*) of the noble lord Friedrich von Schwelt who received one talent a year and free lodging for guarding (*pro warda*) the Schauerburg";[93] "soldiers of his personal household," "soldiers of his household," "the military household" (*milites de propria familia; milites de sua familia; familia militaris*); these are the usual designations for the fighting retinue of a lord,[94] which, in Germany, was mostly made up of unfree persons. There was a "military household" (*familia militaris*) in all the great domains, spiritual and temporal; it was the basic form of the medieval war-organization. The *familia militaris* is the military manifestation of the old aristocratic structure: the lord gave orders to the fighting men of his household, which was equipped and maintained at his court not as a consequence of delegated rights but on the basis of his original power as head of a family (*Munt*) and over property (*Gewere*).[95] In time of peace they sit at his table or act as servants at court, accompany him on hunts or act as messengers; in war the lord himself marches at their head into a battle or on personal feuds. The bond which held these soldiers together was not their membership of a specific social class but their personal legal dependence on their lord; and "court law was never social law."[96] At the beginning it was the vassals who determined the shape of the *familia*; after they obtained fiefs and the personal ties were relaxed, *ministeriales* often took their place; in the twelfth century the upper *ministeriales* also left the *familia*; new groups of *milites* followed them and now constituted the upper level of dependents at the lords' court.[97] The constituents changed, but the *familia militaris* remained very much alive as an important instrument of medieval seigneural power.

From the eleventh century on there appeared a new type of soldier: the mercenaries, the first truly professional soldiers of the Middle Ages.[98] As early as the wars of Heinrich IV "money played a significant role"[99] and the *ministeriales* very early received special financial compensation from their liege-lords for a campaign.[100] Later there was scarcely one of the great princes and vassals who obeyed the king's call to arms without calling for payment for carrying out his military obligations.[101] By the mid-twelfth century the new type was fully developed: the free companies, the troops and mercenaries[102] from now on played a large part in determining military decisions. Friedrich I used them in Italy, just as the Archbishop of Köln did in his struggle with Heinrich der Löwe (Henry the Lion of Brunswick) and as did the kings of France and England. The wandering bands of mercenaries soon became a plague and even ecclesiastical prohibitions did not succeed in banishing them. It is true that at the beginning of the thirteenth century the free mercenaries declined but "even after that wars were often fought with mercenaries, with hired knights and even hired infantry."[103] It was no longer possible to do without them, since they were militarily superior to the clumsy feudal levies.[104]

"There can be no possible doubt that a professional duty and obligation to bear arms which had once been the function only of a free man by selected servants of unfree origin was bound to upset and shift the primordial social relationships."[105] At the beginning of this section we presented the thesis of the military origin of knighthood, the view that "out of simple mounted soldiery . . . a social class of noble knighthood" developed,[106] so that, in the Hohenstaufen period, those who bore knightly weapons grew into "a unified knightly class, held together by cavalry service."[107] As a result of this conception the "equality of the knightly profession"[108] led to a "position for unfree knights which approached very closely"[109] to the old nobility "from the professional standpoint" and then further to a "professionally closed grouping"[110] of those who fought as knights and to a "professional class of knights."[111] This then developed "from a professional class to a hereditary class."[112] Thus, it is stated, "achievement in warfare produced, in the Middle Ages, a noble class."[113] We must defer judgment on the question of whether it is fair to the ruling function of the upper nobility to regard kings and princes as "professional soldiers;[114] nowadays the professional side of their services is no longer regarded as of primary importance even for the *ministeriales*.[115] What is more important is the fact that definite pronouncements about the sociological effect of association with knightly weapons are hardly possible. In the Middle Ages individual families and whole groups kept ascending in the social scale. It is quite certain that military effectiveness and quality of weapons played a role in this. But these were always no more than the superficial means of upward movement, not the reasons.[116] At one point at least we can see more clearly: we may observe in the case of the mercenaries, who were the first true professional soldiers, that the equipment of the old nobility, horse and armor, did not have any ennobling effect on its users, that professional employment of knightly weapons did not in itself possess any power of creating a social class. The mercenaries who fought as knights did not, as a whole, rise in the social scale nor did any hereditary class evolve from their professional unity.

Military knighthood in the Hohenstaufen period can be reduced to a common sociological denominator. All those who fought in knightly equipment are knights: kings, princes, vassals, mercenaries. But the uniformity of armament never wiped out the differences between lords and servants: "Nothing could be more mistaken than to think that in the Hohenstaufen period there was a leveling out of hereditary distinctions because of the equality within the knightly profession."[117] The sources testify that there was not an "aristocratization of warfare"[118] but only an "aristocratization of weapons." Armor and a horse, once the badge of the noble lord, are part of the equipment of unfree cavalry men and mercenaries around 1200. But the transference of aristocratic weapons to non-nobles is scarcely to be attributed to the social dynamism of the lower orders, for we have seen that the expensive equipment was by no means always the property of the people who wore it. The appearance of servants armed as knights is primarily the result of the massive increase in power, both economic and political, of the highest levels of the nobility, which is now rich and powerful enough to equip its people with armor and horses. Similarly, the appearance of mercenary armies can hardly be sufficiently explained on the grounds that there were so many "landless knightly *ministeriales*" and so many "landless free knights," who could no longer find a livelihood.[119] The decisive reason can rather be found in the fact that the financial strength of the princes had increased so much that they could buy themselves the services of soldiers in large numbers. So the investigation of military knighthood with reference to the creation of a social class leads only to the negative result which Otto von Dungern pronounced half a century ago: "Knighthood did not originate from cavalry soldiers."[120]

APPENDIX

Knights in Large Number[121]

"The astoundingly large number of knights who appear after the eleventh century is in itself ample proof that the individual knight could have had very little political or social significance" (Roth von Schreckenstein, *Ritterwürde*, p. 184).

20 Ritter: Rother 3212. Eneit 24, 3. Herbort 13563. Lanzelet 3139. Gotfr. 8586. Türlin Krone 9006. 18696. 19433. Holle Demant. 9748. 9771. 9806. 9867. 9999. Lichtenst. Frd. 249, 6. 614, 7. 663, 2. 1473, 3
22 Ritter: Lichtenst. Frd. 248, 3
23 Ritter: Lichtenst. Frd. 247, 6
24 Ritter: Parz. 45, 15. Lichtenst. Frd. 1479, 2
25 Ritter: Lichtenst. Frd. 252, 2. 622, 7
26 Ritter: Lichtenst. Frd. 1495, 8
30 Ritter: Rother 1446. 1484. Eilhart 5945. Erek 6855. Herbort 16159f. [*drizzic ... / rittere*]. Gotfr. 4552. 5334. Türheim Renn. 1729. Lichtenst. Frd. 197, 2. 583, 2. 678, 2
36 Ritter: Lichtenst. Frd. 202, 2
40 Ritter: Eilhart 5918. Lanzelet 5555. Sächs. Weltchr. 118, 3. Türheim Renn. 16399. Holle Demant. 4253. Lichtenst. Frd. 247, 4. 249, 2. 606, 6. 907, 5. 1467, 3
46 Ritter: Pr.br. Dieffenbach A IV, 2, 9
50 Ritter: Eneit 337, 7. Ems Weltchr. 2276. 35618. Holle Demant. 4137. Lichtenst. Frd. 251, 2. 286, 1. 806, 1. 834, 2. 969, 6
60 Ritter: Rother 3066. Parz. 181, 13. Sächs. Weltchr. 253, 35. Durne 1461. Ems Willeh. 6217. Lichtenst. Frd. 250, 8. 851, 1
70 Ritter: Kudrun 1495, 1. Lichtenst. Frd. 1538, 2. 1557, 2
80 Ritter: Lichtenst. Frd. 798, 5
100 Ritter: Jg. Judith 153, 8f. [*zehenzich / ritter*]. Vor. Alex. 1242. Eilhart 1471. 5866. Herbort 16768. Morant 2996. Lanzelet 1782. 3132. 3557. 5133. 5454. 5503. 6164. 6422. 7497. 7573. Iwein 1936. Wigalois 10419. 10874. 11288. Gotfr. 5557. 18819f. [*ritter ... / niht minner danne hundert*]. Willeh. 66, 27. Heimesfurt Urst. 112, 50. Sächs. Weltchr. 261, 48. Stricker Karl 8407. Türlin Krone 26647. Kudrun 494, 4. Ems Willeh. 679. 3051. 5787. 8336. Türheim Renn. 26281. Hz. Ernst B 4929. Wolfdietr. A 186, 4. 377, 2. Holle Demant. 2680. 2779. 4706. 4713. 9079. 10485. Lichtenst. Frd. 220, 5. 246, 3. 341, 6. 556, 1. 589, 7. 850, 2. 884, 5. 956, 1f.

103 Ritter: Wigalois 4551f. [*hundert unde drie / was der riter*]
130 Ritter: Lanzelet 3209
200 Ritter: Rother 745. Eilhart 5817. Eneit 251, 9. Lanzelet 3329. Stricker Karl 11099.
               Christoph. 1143. Ems Willeh. 668. 703f. 5925. 14535. 14695. Holle Demant.
               10427. Holle Crane 1161. Lichtenst. Frd. 906, 1
250 Ritter: Lichtenst. Frd. 365, 1. 1013, 5
300 Ritter: Eilhart 8554. Eneit 26, 27. 113, 25. 135, 30. 135, 40. Herbort 4580f. [*ritter .../
               dri hüdert vñ me*]. Lanzelet 5371. Sächs. Weltchr. 230, 16. Ems Willeh. 7250.
               Holle Crane 1183. Lichtenst. Frd. 322, 6
400 Ritter: Wigalois 3712. Gotfr. 18850f. [*ritter ... / vierhundert oder mere*]. Sächs.
               Weltchr. 247, 11. Stricker Karl 4861. Ems Willeh. 661. 697. 917. 7170. 7533.
               8341. Ems Alex. 3422. 5186. Holle Demant. 6798. 8850. 10393
500 Ritter: Eneit 34, 11. Nl. 1182, 2. Klage 502. Parz. 210, 19f. [*ritter kluoc, / fünf hun-
               dert*]. 399, 27. 682, 30. Wigalois 10929. Türlin Krone 9934. Kudrun 549, 3.
               1390, 4. Ems Willeh. 644. 868. 2890. 5710. 8854, 10798. 14920. Ems Alex. 18719.
               Türheim Renn. 3709. 3815. 4373. 8829. Holle Demant. 626. 1442. 9425. Holle
               Crane 1135. Lichtenst. Frd. 533, 2
600 Ritter: Herbort 1479. Athis A* 103f. Sächs. Weltchr. 231, 19. 256, 9. Stricker Karl 2206.
               Ems Willeh. 691. 694. 10748. Ems Alex 20147
700 Ritter: Herbort 4022. Morant 1807f. Ems Willeh. 675
800 Ritter: Sächs. Weltchr. 255, 19. Christoph. 1335. Ems Willeh. 6193. 10743. Holle
               Demant. 5100f. 6216. 10784
900 Ritter: Parz. 214, 19. Flore 401
1000 Ritter: Kaiserchr. 16992. Rother 490. Orendel 298. 306. Eilhart 6904. Straßbg. Alex.
               1718f. [*riter ... / zehen hundrit*]. Eneit 143, 2. 143, 38. 144, 5. 144, 16. 195, 36.
               237, 40. Oswald M. 1155. 1383. Herbort 3032. 3998. 4017. 4024. 6515. 6544. Nl.
               503, 2. 1303, 2. 1472, 3. 1573, 1. 1647, 3. Parz. 47, 19. 106, 10. Wigalois 210.
               10501. 10777. 10789. 10795. 10801. 10824. Lanzelet 8858. Athis A* 141. Stricker
               Karl 4856. Ems Gerh. 5881. Ems Willeh. 8857. 10738. 13247. Ems Alex. 3459.
               4338. 11634. 13402. Sächs. Weltchr. 87, 9. Türheim Renn. 8653. Hz. Ernst B
               1966. Wolfdietr. A 318, 4. 371, 4. Holle Demant. 637. 10971. 11042. 11205.
               Lichtenst. Frd. 41, 5
1500 Ritter: Oswald W. 502. Sächs. Weltchr. 229, 7. 231, 4f.
1700 Ritter: Oswald W. 28
2000 Ritter: Klage 394. Wigalois 10678. Stricker Dan. 3074. 5031. Ems Gerh. 5663. Ems
               Willeh. 708. 5741. 7269. Ems Alex. 5151. 5184. Türheim Renn. 29565. Holle
               Demant. 3662. 10872
2500 Ritter: Ems Willeh. 681f. [*ritter ... / drithalb tusent*]
3000 Ritter: Eneit 21, 6f. [*drû tûsent schilde / unde ritter alsô vile*]. 199, 30. Herbort 2370.
               3993. Lanzelet 2635. 6877. 8062. 8940. Wigalois 1451. 10647. Kudrun 689, 2.
               Ems Willeh. 14777. Ems Alex. 13339. Türheim Renn. 4950
4000 Ritter: Sächs. Weltchr. 84, 18. 87, 4. Holle Demant. 10001. 10769
5000 Ritter: Eneit 41, 33. Holle Demant. 5110. Lichtenst. Frd. 42, 1
6000 Ritter: Lanzelet 3651. Parz. 48, 23. Wigalois 10444. Stricker Karl 5309. Türheim Renn.
               21781
7000 Ritter: Willeh. 142, 27
8000 Ritter: Stricker Dan. 6012
9000 Ritter: Sächs. Weltchr. 261, 47
10 000 Ritter: Eneit 238, 17. Ems Alex. 5147. Türheim Renn. 13290. 20837
12 000 Ritter: Roland 4490. Rother 3404. Stricker Karl 4340
18 000 Ritter: Stricker Karl 3088
20 000 Ritter: Herbort 4789f. Morant 293. Stricker Karl 2838. 3075. 3532. Holle Demant. 8703
30 000 Ritter: Herbort 4281. Wolfdietr. A 485, 2
40 000 Ritter: Sächs. Weltchr. 84, 19. 232, 10
50 000 Ritter: Eneit 47, 8
100 000 Ritter: Stricker Karl 7286
120 000 Ritter: Sächs. Weltchr. 83, 31f.
200 000 Ritter: Stricker Karl 6766

IV. The Knight as Retainer

Ein ritter sô gelêret was
daz er an den buochen las
swaz er dar an geschriben vant:
der was Hartman genant,
dienstman was er zOuwe
(*Arm. Heinr.*, 1–5)

𝕿he beginning of the thirteenth century becomes the classical period of chivalry because the unfree bondservants . . . strain every nerve to attain the dignity of knighthood and carry out its duties worthily . . . He attains hereditary knighthood and very soon, as a result of that, nobility."[1] Should we see evidence for this procedure in the opening lines of *Der arme Heinrich*? "Hartmann belonged to the unfree nobility"[2]; he calls himself "knight" (*ritter*) and "bondservant" (*dienestman*). Was he an unfree *ministerialis*, who had attained aristocratic knightly dignity? Or do the lines celebrate the fact that about 1200 the whole *ministerialis* class was counted as knightly? Hartmann's autobiographical testimony is not a completely isolated phenomenon; there are other people who are knights and bondservants at the same time. In Eilhart, for example: "dô vûren mit Tristrande wol hundert ritter dannen, des koninges dînstmanne" (then full a hundred knights, the king's bondservants, set out with Tristan, (1470–72). And in Rudolf von Ems where "zehen ritter" (ten knights) (*Willehalm*, 3314) are named whom Willehalm assures "das ir mine dienestman sint" (that you are my bondservants) (3372f. similarly 8675/8712). And in Ulrich von Lichtenstein too, where he speaks of his lady: "ich meine die lieben frowen mîn, der ritter ich sol immer sîn und ir getriwer dienestman" (I mean my dear lady, whose knight and faithful bondservant I shall always be) (*Frauendienst*, 1639, 5–7). In none of these passages does the word knight have any particular tone which would

indicate that it designates any newly won nobility for the *ministeriales*.
Rather the reverse. It would seem that the word "dienestman" indicates
a selected group of the knights.

From the beginning we find knights not only on the battlefield as
soldiers but just as frequently at the courts of great lords. The *Wiener
Genesis* tells us that Joseph rode towards his old father Jacob: "Ioseph
sa dar reit. mit ime manich rîter gemeit" (Joseph rode there and with
him many well-made knights) (5060f.). Joseph does not set out with
soldiers to receive his father; but he does not ride alone either. As a
powerful lord, he has men to accompany him, a retinue, and they are
knights.[3] Similarly in the *Hochzeit*: there a lord is mentioned: "der habete
vil chnehte" (who had many servants" (161); when he went to meet his
bride, "dô gewan er vil liute, rittere gemeite" (he took many people,
well-made knights) (264f.) and these knights then accompany the bride
to her lord: "dô riten mit der broute chindische loute, riter gemeite,
hêrlich gereite. hoy, wie si dô sungen, dô si sie heim brungen!" (then
there rode with the bride young nobles, well-made knights, gloriously
mounted. Hey, how they sang as they brought her home!) (303–308).
Having knights about one was a sign of power and greatness. We find
them everywhere when princes appear: "(der) kunig Fôre zu der kirchen
drang, nâch im manig ritter lobesam" (king Fôre went on to the church
and with him many notable knights) (*Salman*, 191, 2; similarly 196, 1f.
202, 2f.); "fur die burg ging (der) kunig Princiân, nâch im manig ritter
lobesam" (in front of the castle went king Princian and after him many
a fine knight) (ibid., 640, 1f.). Eneas "hiez mit ime rîten funfzich ritter
wol getân" (told fifty well-equipped knights to go with him) (*Eneit*, 337,
6f.); "im volgete manich riter gemeit" (and many a well-made knight
followed him) (ibid., 341, 14). When King Rother's wife goes to the
harbor, she is escorted by knights: "Zvenzich ritar lossam. Volgeden der
urowen zo deme kiele" (twenty fine knights followed the lady to the
ship) (3212f.). When Duke Ernst rides to the imperial court "grôziu
kraft, beide ritter und knehte" (a great force, both knights and servants)
follows him (B 148f.). The Emperor Charlemagne has "in syme houe.
Mangen riddere die mit loue. Yem hulpen zu allen stunden" (in his court
many knights who help him at all times) (*Morant*, 101–103). It is said
of King Arthur "rîter unde knehte die giengen mit im" (knights and
servants went with him) (*Wigalois*, 1541f.). In the retinue of the Grey
Knight "gienc dâ rittr und knappen mêr" (there went more knights and
squires) (*Parzival*, 446, 28). A marshall "und sîne rîter" (and his knights)
(ibid., 23, 12) accompany Gahmuret to Queen Belacane. Parzival meets
Gurnemanz at his court: "dô kom der wirt mit triwen kraft: nâch dem
gienc stolziu rîterschaft" (there came the host with his loyal force: after
him went proud knights) (ibid., 168, 21f.). For his journey to Ireland,

Tristan has "uz dem hove lesen des küneges heinlichære, zweinzec ritter gewære" (twenty dependable knights chosen from the king's court by the secretaries) (Gottfried, 8584–86). Rüdiger comes to Gunther's court with a large escort: "dô sach man von den rossen fünfhundert ritter stân" (there five hundred men could be seen dismounting from their horses) (*Nibelungenlied*, 1182, 2). The Saxons assure their duke " 'jo hestu, hertoge, riddere genoch, de di twar mit allen truwen to hulpe stan' " ("Duke, you have enough knights ready to help you in all loyalty") (Gandersheim, 1128f.). The Emperor Tiberius "ret enes dages mit sinen ridderen durch kortewile an en velt" (rode one day with his knights to a field to amuse himself) (*Sächs, Weltchr.*, 92, 6f.). The Archbishop of Köln rides to meet the emperor "mit edeln rittern wol bekleit und ouch der burgære ein teil" (with noble knights well dressed and a part of the citizenry) (Ems, *Gerhard*, 664f.). Walther von der Vogelweide makes jokes at the expense of the activity at the court of Hermann von Thüringen: "und gulte ein fuoder guotes wînes tûsent pfunt, dâ stüende ouch niemer ritters becher lære" (and even if a cask of good wine were worth a thousand pounds, no knight's goblet would stand empty) (20, 14f.). Ulrich von Lichtenstein is received by Herr Wülfing von Stubenberg: "wol drîzic ritter oder mêr ûf orssen mit im gegen mir riten" (a good thirty knights or more rode towards me with him on horseback) (*Frauendienst*, 678, 2f.). For the tournament lords appear with their escort: "von Tûfers Hûc . . . het zweinzic ritter unde drî" (he had twenty-three knights from Tufer's Huc) (ibid., 247, 5f.); "ez het der vogt von Lengebach dâ zwên und zweinzic ritter guot" (the lord of Lengebach had twenty-two good knights) (ibid., 248, 2f.). And Ulrich himself declares: "fünfzic ritter mînen schilt dîze dem turneye müezzen tragen" (fifty knights had to bear my shield to the tournament there) (ibid., 834, 2f.). Wherever a lord's court is mentioned, people think of knights: "von disem hove sagt man ie wie vrume rîter hie wæren" (it is said of this court how fine the knights here were) (*Wigalois*, 1757f.). Thus Reinmar der Zweter's concludes his satire on "hovemünche" (court monks) and "clôsterritter" (cloister knights) with the warning that monks belong in the monastery as knights belong at court: "sô suln des hoves sich ritter underwinden" (thus knights should subject themselves to the court) (129, 12).

Who are these court-knights? The evidence has already shown that they are not the lords at the courts. Everywhere they are in a dependent relationship to the lord of the court, they are part of his retinue, his household. In the *Kaiserchronik* Jupiter demands of the Romans: " 'ûzer allen iweren gesinden ain edelen rîter sult ir mir gewinnen' " ("from all your households you shall obtain for me a noble knight") (1139f.). At King Aron's court, "ritter unde knehte" (knights and servants) (*Oswald M.*, 839), constitute "hofegesinde" (the household at court) (834). "ez wære ritter oder kneht, der ze ir gesinde horte . . . ." (whether it was knights or servants who belonged to their household . . .) (Albertus, 771f.); "her Gâwein zem gesinde gie und sagt in die geschiht dô; des wurden die rîter alle vrô" (Sir Gawain went to the household and told them the story; all the knights were delighted with it) (*Wigalois*, 385–387); "wir vinden undir al desim ingesinde keinen ritter alsô stolt der vechtin wil . . ." (we do not find in all his household any knight proud enough to fight . . .) (Eilhart, 559–562). It is said of King Arthur: "wol tûsent rîter er hêt ze gesinde tägelîche" (he had a good thousand knights in his household every day) (*Wigalois*, 210f.). And Feirefiz testifies: " 'mit schilde bevangen ist zingesinde mir benant manec rîter wert erkant' " (many a well-recognized knight equipped with shield is appointed to my household) (*Parzival*, 768, 20–22). Old Heimrich appears at the king's court "mit grôzme gesinde: . . . siben tûsent ritter oder mêr, die fuorte der alte fürste hêr" (with a large household . . . seven thousand knights or more the old prince led there) (*Willehalm*, 142, 25, 27f.). Marjodoc dreams that a wild boar has come to the king's court: "nu kam geloufen al zehant des hovegesindes michel craft. da lief michel ritterschaft umbe den eber her unde hin" (now there came running at once a great force from the court household. There ran a large group of knights back and forth around the boar) (Gottfried, 13520–23). Wilhelm of Brabant receives a retinue at his knighting ceremony: "Sus was im ze ingesinde erkant Hundert ritter ze aller zit" (and so a hundred knights were allotted to him as a household at all times) (Ems, *Willehalm*, 5786f.). In the *Sächsische Weltchronik* it is stated: "do nam sic ut en riddere van des koninges gesinde . . ." (then he chose himself a knight from the king's household . . .) (214, 13f.). In Türlin's *Krone* a lord says: " 'Under allem dem gesinde mîn Enweiz ich ritter noch kneht . . .' " ("among all my household I don't know knight or servant") (4826f.). Ulrich von Lichtenstein reports about the retinue of the Duke of Austria: "die ritter, die ich hie hân genant, die het der fürst ûz Osterlant . . . ze gesinde alle an sich genomen" (the knights whom I have named here were all taken by the prince from Osterlant into his retinue) (*Frauendienst*, 1488, 1f. 5); and in another passage: "dâ ich ir gesinde vant, ritter und vil manigen kneht" (when I found their escort, knights and many servants) (ibid., 116, 4f.). In a sermon in the *Speculum ecclesiae*, two cities are named: "die habint och zwene herren mislich" (they have also two evil lords) (47, 18f.); each lord has a household (47, 21); in one city they are "die gotis rîter" (God's knights) (47, 22) and in the other "die schâlche des tiefils" (the devil's servants) (47, 23).

Women also belong to the court household. The formula "ritter unde vrouwen" (knights and ladies) properly belongs here. In Hartmann's *Iwein* "von rîtern und von vrouwen ein selch gesinde schouwen daz wol den wirt êrte'' (such a household of knights and ladies can be seen as to do honor to the host) (5933–35). It is asked in *Parzival* "wie der von Norwæge sînes volkes pflæge, der rîter unt der frouwen?'' (how the man from Norway looks after his people, the knights and ladies) (676, 3–5). In Holle's *Demantin* there is found at a count's court "gût gesinde dâr von rittern und von vrouwen'' (a good household of knights and ladies) (2354f.). In Türlin's *Mantel*, when "der künic und diu künigin'' (the king and queen) (326) go to the cathedral, "die frowen und ritter nâch in'' (the ladies and knights) follow after them (327). It is announced to Queen Helena before she rides out that her escort is ready: " 'Wolt ir varen ir hat Ritter vnd frauwe' '' ("If you want to set off, you have knights and ladies) (Herbort, 2482f.). The word *vrouwe* originates in an aristocratic context and at first means "the female ruler'' in Middle High German texts. The combination "hêrren unde vrouwen'' (lords and ladies) proves this (e.g. Strassburg *Alexander*, 7299) and many individual references. In Holle's *Crane* a table-seating is described; sitting together are "ein vorste ind ein vorstinne . . . , ein hêre ind ein vrouwe . . . , ein ritter ind ein juncfrowelîn'' (a prince and a princess . . . , a lord and a lady . . . , a knight and a demoiselle) (2046f. 49). The aristocratic significance of *vrouwe* remains alive right up to the end of the Middle Ages. But parallel with this the word *vrouwe* goes through the same development as *herre*: not only those who really exercise dominion but all those who belong to the domain are designated in the courtly sphere as *herren* and *vrouwen*.[4] It is thus that the ladies come into contact with knights and bondservants. The juxtaposition of "frauwē vñ die dinstman'' (Herbort, 208) provides some evidence of this. Herbort puts *Kinc kvneginne* (kings and queens) in one group (13308), then the top stratum of their dependents: "Ir kint ir furstē ir man'' (their children, their princes, their liegemen-in-chief) (13309); and under them the mass of those, "die sie anders gehortē an. Ritter frowē manic knecht'' (those who belonged elsewhere, knights, ladies and many servants). Similarly, but on a lower level, Count Oringles in Hartmann's *Erek* promises Enit " 'ritter unde knehte, vrouwen, rîche dienestman, sô ir nie grâve mê gewan, die mache ich iu undertân' '' ("knights and servants, ladies, rich bond-servants, of whom no count ever had more, these I will make subject to you'') (6277–80). Here too the ladies, with knights and bond-servants make up the household of the court which is subject to the count.[5]

The sources give only incidental information about the position and duties of the knights at court. In a few passages, however, we do find the knights carrying out the classic courtly offices. In *Salman und Morolf* a chamberlain (*ein kamerer* [193, 1]) is addressed as "ritter lobesam'' (famous knight), first by the disguised Morolf (194, 2), then once again by Queen Salme (212, 1). In Ulrich von Lichtenstein, there is a statement:

"hie kumt der kameræe mîn und wil von mir hie daz amt sîn enpfâhen, als ein ritter sol" (here comes my chamberlain and here wishes to receive his office from me, as a knight should) (*Frauendienst*, 765, 3–5). In Otte's *Heraclius* there appears "ein rîter von dem lande in guotem gewande, des keisers truhsæze er was" (as knight from the country in fine clothing. He was the emperor's seneschal) (735–37). In *Wigalois*, too, we find a knight who is a seneschal (3889/3905). Berthold von Holle names "die drossâten ind die schenken" (the seneschals and butlers" at the king's court and declares: "dat wâren ritter hôchgeborn" (they were high-born knights) (*Crane*, 4275/77). Gawain appoints four knights to his "ambetliuten" (office-holders) (*Parzival*, 667, 10), who are to organize his ceremonial entry into Arthur's court area: "dô nam mîn hêr Gâwân vier werde rîter sunder dan, daz einer kameræerc und der ander schenke wære, und der dritte truhsæze, und daz der vierde niht vergæze, ern wære marschalc" (Then my lord Gawain picked out four worthy knights, one as a chamberlain, the second as a butler, the third seneschal and the fourth was not to forget that he was the marshall) (666, 23–29). Furthermore the knights carry out ceremonial functions at court. They provided escort for their lord[6] and particularly appear on the scene to receive guests: "die rîter giengen vür daz tor und enpfiengen wol die geste" (the knights went out of the gates and received the guests well) (*Wigalois*, 9583f.); "Do kamē sie zv des kvniges houe. Die ritter gegen in gingē. Wol sie sie enphingen" (Then they came to the king's court. The knights went to meet them. They received them well) (Herbort, 516–18); "manig ritter kam gegân . . . und enpfiengen in" (many knights came . . . and received him) (Türlin, *Krone*, 21003/05); "die ritter mich nâch ritters siten enpfiengen ritterlîchen wol" (the knights received me in knightly fashion as is the knight's custom) (Lichtenstein, *Frauendienst*, 340, 2f.).[7] Even after the reception, the guests continue to be looked after by knights; in Munsalvaesche they take Parzival to bed (*Parzival*, 243, 4ff.); in Orange they help in the entertainment of the French princes: "ir muosen werde rîter phlegn" (worthy knights had the duty of looking after them) (*Willehalm*, 263, 27). Similarly in Berthold von Holle: "vumf hundert ritter rîche di dînten dâr di wîl man az" (five hundred rich knights served there while they ate) (*Demant.*, 1442f.).[8]

The relationship of the knights to their lords is expressed by the words "dienest" and "dienen" (service and serve). The obligation to service is expressed clearly by the terms "ritters dienest" (knight's service) (Türheim, *Rennewart*, 31455. Holle, *Crane*, 1704. 3317. Lichtenstein, *Frauendienst*, 1389, 6. Lichtenstein, *Frb.*, 611, 15), "ritterlîcher dienest" (Lichtenstein, *Frd.*, 466, 7), "ritterlîche dienen" (serve like a knight) (*Parzival*, 33, 1; Stricker, *Karl*, 5263. *Kudrun*, 1461, 3; Rudolf von Ems, *Willehalm*, 14758. Lichtenstein, XLII, 5, 1. Lichtenstein, *Frd.*,

424, 4. 755, 6. 835, 1. 902, 4. 1652, 2. Lichtenstein, *Frb.*, 610, 19.
617, 18. 658, 19). There is frequent mention of the knights' service
elsewhere too: "ritter unde knehte die dienten ime gar rehte" (knights
and servants they served him really well) (*Oswald* M, 17f.); "man sach
dâr manchen ritter vromen sich zu dînste bîten dâr" (there one saw many
fine knights offering their service) (Holle, *Demant.*, 2752f.); "in diente
von ir landen vil stolziu ritterschaft" (many proud knights from their
lands served them) (*Nib.*, 6, 2); "ouch was der ritter dienest niht der
küneginne leit" (nor did the queen dislike the service of the knights)
(ibid., 1306, 4); "die rittershaft vil dienstes bot Willehalme dem markîse"
(Türheim, *Rennewart*, 3068f.); "Want er wolte ritters kraft An dienest
und an ritterschaft Uben ze allen stunden" (Since he wanted knights to
practice service and knighthood at all times" (Ems, *Willehalm*, 15239–41).
Veldeke tells of a knight from Brabant who repented of his violent life:
"der riddere dinde immer sint sente Servase al sin leven. te eigen hadde'r
sich ergeven" (the knight afterwards served St. Servatius all his life; he
had made himself his bondsman) (*Servatius*, 5826–28). In Holle's *Demantin* there are directions about how a lord should behave towards his
knights: "swer rittere wil zu dînste hân, sîn hûs daz sal on ophen stân:
he sal sî vrôlîchin untfân: sô mag he sî zu dînste hân, swenn he or darf
zu der nôt" (he who wants to have knights serve should keep his house
open he should receive them joyfully; then he may have them in his
service when any need should arise) (7259–63). One passage in the
Nibelungenlied is particularly informative; where Brünhild justifies the
presumed demand for Siegfried's act of service with the question: " 'swiu
sold' ich verkiesen sô maniges ritters lîp, der uns mit dem degene
dienstlîch ist undertân?' " ("Why should I do without so many knights
who are bound to us in service like this warrior") (823, 2f.). A knight
is a man who is "dienstlîch undertân" (subject to service to a lord).[9]

Occasionally we find out how the knights were rewarded for their
service. In the Vorau *Alexander* it is stated: "nû vernemt, wie sich
Alexander vur nam: swâ sô ein frumich rîter zu zim chom, dem bôt er
lîp und gût" (now hear how Alexander dealt with this; whenever a noble
knight came to him, he offered him board and pay) (155–57). The knights
received *lîp* and *guot* board, clothing, and pay. This "dienen umbe guot"
(service for gain) seems to have been the normal form of service obligation. It is thus that Gahmuret enters the service of Belacane: "er bôt
sîn dienest umbe guot, als noch vil dicke ein rîter tuot" (he offered his
service for pay, as a knight very often does) (*Parzival*, 17, 11f.). Ulrich
von Lichtenstein tells of his encounter with the wicked Rapot of Val-
kenberg: "doch riten dâ dem übeln mite niwn ritter ritterlîch gemuot: die
dienten im dâ umb sîn guot" (nine knights of knightly spirit rode with
him: they served him there for gain) (*Frauendienst*, 1493, 6–8). In Rudolf

von Ems it is stated: "Och ist alhie mit frecher ger Ritter vil umb únser gut" (There are plenty of knights about here eager for our goods) (*Willehalm*, 802f.). In Holle's *Crane* the marshal, Assundin, states that he paid the knights on behalf of the king: " 'hîr quam nî ritter an daz rîche gereden durch sîn heil, im inworde mînes gûtes deil: des gunte mir die hêre mîn' " ("no knight ever came riding to the empire for his salvation without receiving part of my goods: my lord granted me that") (850–53). Orgeluse, too, has such service knights in her retinue: "der herzoginne von Lôgroys dient manc rîter kurtoys, beidiu nâch minne und umb ir solt" (the duchess of Lôgrois was served by many courtly knights, both for love and for pay) (*Parzival*, 632, 15–17). Tristan, in exile, is equipped by Kaedin's father "mit phärit unt mit kleiden" (with horse and clothing) (Türheim, *Tristan*, 516, 31); he expresses his thanks with the words: " 'nie herre ez rittern baz gebôt danne ir uns, herre, habet getân' " (never did a lord make a better offer to knights than you, my lord, have made to us) (516, 38f.). King Comandeon tells how he assembled his knightly household: " 'swâr mir wart ritter î bekant di mîner grôze gerte, mîn hant on gewerte. dorch daz hab ich gesindes vil" (wherever there were knights known to me who were eager for my greatness, I laid my hands on them. Therefore I have a large household) (Holle, *Demunt.*, 7432-35). When Ulrich von Lichtenstein says of the knights of the Duke of Austria: they were "gekleidet und georsset wol, als fürsten gesinde von rehte sol" (well dressed and mounted, as a prince's household should be) (*Frauendienst*, 1488, 7f), it is highly probable that the knights got their clothes and horses from the prince. There is evidence for this elsewhere too.[10]

Because of the service relationship, the lord possesses almost unlimited power of command and disposal over his knights. The boasting of Duke Falsaron gives some indication of this: " 'ich bin sô rîche des libes und des muotes, beidiu ritter unde guotes' " (I am so rich in person and mind, both in knights and property) (Stricker, *Karl*, 4368–70). The prince has the same powers of disposition over his knightly household as he has over his material possessions. Thus the pagan king Terramer can make over to his grandson Malfer any given number of knights: "der kunc Terramer im liez zehen tusent ritter er hiez im dienen gar fur eigen" (King Terramer left him ten thousand knights and told them to serve him as bondsmen) (Türheim, *Rennewart*, 13289–91). And the Emperor Charlemagne lends a faithful man a hundred knights as *rente* (pension): " 'Vr rente sal syn gemert. Iairgeltz vierhundert marke. Ind hundert riddere wal starke. Sult ir zo dienste hain' " ("Your pension shall be increased four hundred marks a year and a hundred strong knights shall serve you") (*Morant*, 2994–97). In Ulrich von Türheim, knights are given as presents, like clothes and horses: " 'wild du es noh, es ist gereht, ors chlaider ritter chneht, der nim swelhes dir gevall' " ("if you want anything more, it is fair, take whatever horses, clothes, knights or servants you like'') (*Clig.*, 16–18). Admittedly the lord is obliged to treat his knights well. Otherwise he suffers the fate of King Pant: ''er was ze grimme an sînen siten, dâ von wâren im entriten die ritter alle gemeine'' (he was too severe in his behavior and so all his knights rode away from him at once) (*Lanzelet*, 133–35).

There is no clear answer to the question of the social position and rank of these service knights or of their place in society. We find ''rich knights'' and ''poor knights'' and their standing is to a large extent dependent on how high is the position of the lord whom they serve. At a king's court, for example, that of King Arthur, the knights are powerful lords: ''wol tûsent rîter er hêt ze gesinde tägelîche; der iegelîcher was sô rîche an rossen und an gewande, an bürgen und an lande, daz im nihtes gebrast'' (he had some 1000 knights daily in his household; each was so rich in horses and clothes, castles and land, that he lacked for nothing) (*Wigalois*, 210–215). We have seen that even Gahmuret, a king's son, made a contract as a mercenary knight and that Tristan, a king's son, had himself dressed as a knight. Such great lords are called knights only in so far as they do not exercise the role to which their birthright entitles them but enter the service of other lords: Gahmuret moves out into the world without any inheritance and Tristan comes to Duke Jovelin as an exile.[11] But since serving—quite apart from the family status of the person serving—is always opposed to ruling, it is always possible to make a clear distinction between the lord on the one side and anybody called ''knight'' on the other. This opposition often appears in the sources: ''Wol zwênzic ritter vant er dâ Und einen herren'' (He found some twenty knights there and a lord) (Türlin, *Krone*, 18696f.); ''zwei hundert herren wâren dâr, veir tûsent rittere mit in'' (two hundred lords were there and four thousand knights with them) (Holle, *Demant.*, 10000f.); ''die ritter taten als in ir herre gibot'' (the knights did as their lords told them) (Pass. Zacher, 279, 24f.); ''dô saher engegen ime gân rîter unde knehte . . . als in ir herre gebôt'' (then he saw knights and servants approaching him . . . as their lord ordered them) (*Iwein*, 5592f. 98); ''nie herre ez rittern baz gebôt'' (never did a lord give better orders to knights) (Türlin, *Trist.*, 516, 38); ''sîn rîter vüert der tœrsche herre dicke undr die vînde verre'' (the foolish lord frequently leads his knights far among the enemy) (Thomasin, 6657f.); ''iclîch herre sal ûz lesen zwênzig rittere di bî om wesen'' (Every lord shall pick out twenty knights to be with him) (Holle, *Demant.*, 9747f., similarly 9805ff.); ''die ritter die dâ genâren und bî ir herren wâren'' (the knights who lived there and were with their lord) (*Erek*, 4244f., similarly 3084ff.); ''ein ieslîch armer rîter truoc hêrrn od mâge ûz dem wal'' (each poor knight took a lord or relative in the selection) (*Willehalm*, 72, 4f.); ''hundert ritter ûz erwelt die heten under in gesworn und in (sc. den Grafen Ritschart) ze herren erkorn'' (a hundred choice knights had made a sworn pact and had chosen him [Count Ritschart] as their lord) (*Lanzelet*, 3132-34); "des soltu, rîter, volgen mir, swie du wil daz dîn herr mit dir lebe, alsô lebe du'' (therefore, knight, you should follow me and as you wish your lord to live with you, live yourself in the same way) (Thomasin, 7835-37); "swaz den rîter lastert gar, dâ wirt der herre niht von gêrt, wan swaz des rîters ist unwert, daz kumt niht dem herren wol, und swaz den herren zieren sol, daz muoz gezierde dem rîter sîn'' (what disgraces the knight will not honor the lord, since whatever is not worthy of the knight will not be good for the lord and whatever should glorify the lord must be a glory to the knight) (ibid., 2006-11, similarly 1999ff.). When Jesus comes to Capernaum, a "rich lord'' has him informed: "ich . . . han auch ritter die mir undertan sint. swaz ich den gebeut, des sint si mir undertan'' (I have also knights who are subject to me. Whatever I tell them to do, they are subject to me'' (Pr. Schönbach II, 40, 12. 22-24). The value of the testimony of these passages[12] can hardly be called in question by the fact that, on the other hand, knights are quite often given the title "lord.'' Where the social rank of a person has to be designated, the word "herre'' long remained a mark of nobility; but in personal address it soon began to ossify into a mere formula of politeness and in such cases gives no evidence of equality of rank.[13] The same is true, incidentally, for the corresponding Latin concept "dominus.''[14] I will refer only to the scene in Hartmann von Aue, where the three robbers (*Erek*, 3116) lie in wait for Erek in the forest and who are called "ritter'' by Enite (3186) and who address one another as "herre'' (3202).

König Rother offers an interesting piece of evidence for the distinction between "lords'' and "knights.'' There appears in that work "ein ritare. De geweldich was ze bare'' (a knight who had attained power and reputation in the royal town of Bari) (3155f.). His children are sick and he is determined to ask the queen to buy ointments for them from the deceitful pedlar. When he goes to make his petition, he takes "sine uronde'' (his friends) with him: these are "scszen coufman'' (six merchants) (3171); and when he comes to the queen, "Do infienc in die riche. Harde gunsteliche. In allen den gebere. Alser ein herre were'' (then the rich lady received him very graciously in every respect as if he were a lord) (3173-76). The knight is not a lord but he is treated by the queen as if he were. Herbort von Fritzlar emphasizes the same point, except that he does so with much more scorn for the knights. He tells of the death of Agamemnon and of the relationship between Clytemnestra and Aegistheus: "Sie hette bosliche. Mit eime ritter getan. Den wolde sie zv adel han'' (she had acted wickedly with a knight whom she wanted to treat as a nobleman) (17255-57). So far as the poet is concerned, the queen's desire to raise a knight to her sphere of nobility flies in the face of the laws of her social status. Herbort is annoyed, "Daz ein frowe irn genoz. Durch einē bosen verkos" (that a lady chose her relationship with a wicked man) (17271f.) and in his eyes it is a scandal "Daz ein kvnic wol geborn. Vō svlchme ritter was verlorn" (that a king well born was destroyed by such a knight) (17268f.). Here it may be seen how high was the barrier which separated the knight from the nobility about 1200. Even around the middle of the thirteenth century the distinction was still very much alive. This is proved by the very well known *Spruch* of Reinmar von Zweter:

> Ein herre von gebürte vrî
> ob der rittr unt kneht, dienestman unt
>   eigen sî,
> wie daz geschehen müge, des sol
>   niht wunder nemen man noch wîp.
> Ein vrî geburt niht irren kan,
> ein hêrre ensî wol vrî unt doch der
>   Eren dienestman,
> ein ritter sîner tât, der milte ein
>   kneht, der zühte ein eigen lîp.
> Swelch hêrre alsus undersniten wære,
> der dûhte mich ein hübscher
>   wunderære:
> hie vrî, dort dienestman, hie eigen,
> ûf jenez ein rittr, ûf diz ein kneht,
> wære er ze disen vünven reht,
> ein künigîn solt im ir houbet neigen.
>   (56, 1–12).[15]

> (A lord of free birth
> whether he be knight or servant,
>   bondservant or serf,
> neither man nor woman should be
>   surprised how that
> comes about.
> A free birth cannot go astray
> if a lord is indeed free and yet the
>   bondservant
> of honor,
> a knight of his deeds, the servant of
>   generosity, a
> serf of good behavior.

Any lord who fell below these
  standards
would seem to me a pretty and
  remarkable figure
free here, a bond servant there, here
  a serf
in that respect a knight, in this a
  servant,
a queen should bow her head to
  him.)

In the hundred years from *König Rother* to Reinmar von Zweter the
position of the knight has not fundamentally changed. The concepts
knight, servant, bondservant and serf (ritter, kneht, dienestman, eigen)
are related and are sharply separated from lord, free, and noble (herre,
vrî, adel).[16]

We have encountered kings' sons and unfree mercenaries among the
knights. A single legal or social characteristic distinguishing knights as
such which would enable us to constitute them into a knight class (*Ritterstand*) was not to be found. The only thing common to all knights is
their belonging to a domain, their service-dependence on a lord. There
obviously is the core of the concept of knighthood. That is true not only
for the service-knights of this chapter; it was also true for the soldier-
knights of the previous one. The knights on the battlefield and the knights
at the lord's court must be regarded in the same way; it is the same people
who serve their lord in war with weapons and in peace as court-knights.
The knight is characterized neither by his employment as a soldier nor
by his activity at court but by what is common to both manifestations:
service to his lord.[17] Such an explanation, however, inevitably conflicts
with the original meaning of *rîter* and *ritter*. Why exactly was a man
who was "subject to the service" (*dienestlîch undertân*) of a lord designated as "a rider?" Would it be possible to conjecture that the connection of the knight with a horse, apparently so obvious, is in fact the
result of a secondary development? We have encountered plenty of
knights without horses both at court and in battle. Perhaps it should be
recalled that the basic meaning of Old High German *rîtan* is not "to sit
on a horse" but "to move oneself, to travel," and only in a secondary
sense "to move on a horse, to ride"; the English verb "ride" even today
has only an incidental connection with the horse. Basic cognates of "rei-
ten" are German "Reise" and English "road."[18] Among the Germanic
"designations for men in royal service," who almost all "rose from
humble circumstances,"[19] there are some whose basic meaning is precisely that of "movement." The best known is Old High German

"gisind" (the man on the road), derived from "sind" = way. Also related is Old Saxon "segg," old Norse "seggr," cognate with Latin "socius" and "sequi"; further the verbs "folgen" and "leisten," "whose basic meaning was accompany or escort."[20] "Ritter" too may very well have belonged to this group originally.[21]

This limitation of the concept "knight" brings us back to the word "dienestman," from which we started. "Dienestman" is the most prosaic but also the most precise designation for people in a lord's service. Because of the labors of Walther Kotzenberg and Paul Kluckhohn we are far better informed on the history of the word than we are about the concept "knight." Paul Kluckhohn has established that in earlier times the word meant "any person in service,"[22] not a particular kind of service. This stays the same for several centuries. In the literary texts of the ninth century the word "dienestman" is rare. In Otfried[23] it occurs once only, for Joseph, who takes care of his wife and child in the flight to Egypt: "Jóseph io thes sínthes er húatta thes kíndes; was thíonostman gúater, bisuórgata ouh thia múater" (On the journey Joseph looked after the child; he was a good servant, he also looked after the mother) (I, 19, 1f.). At the turn of the eleventh century Notker[24] used *dienestman* as the equivalent of *famulus* (ed. Piper, I, 765, 29) and of *minister* (II, 205, 2; 222, 3; 436, 18; 446, 22). The word does not appear in the glossary collections before the tenth century.[25] In the oldest manuscripts it stands for *pedissequus* (Steinmeyer-Sievers, I, 441, 20ff.), a word that reproduces very well the character of the bondservant: he lives close to his lord and is always to be found in his vicinity.[26] The connection with the court is made clear in the gloss on *curialis* (III, 134, 38ff. 183, 10).[27] The personal dependence of the bondservant is reflected in the glosses on *serviens* (II, 77, 59) and *cliens* (III, 396, 64; 663, 1), while its frequent use as a translation of *apparitor* (I, 402, 21f.; III, 135, 42ff.; 266, 40f.; 294, 22; IV, 266, 26), as well as of *apparitor vel minister* (III, 183, 38f.) points to activity in the service of a lord, which is to be regarded primarily as administrative service or service at court, certainly not particularly service in war. To this degree Paul Kluckhohn's statement "that the word *dienestman* never means an official, only a person engaged in service generally and particularly one who fulfills his service in war" needs a twofold modification.[28] The early Middle High German texts are the first to provide a more exact picture. In the *Wiener Genesis* the word occurs once: Potiphar buys the young Joseph and takes him into his service: "Durch sine lussame nam er ín ze dienest man" (because of his charm he was taken into service) (3679f.). We are not told what kind of service Joseph performs, but the humble position of the bondservant is clear: only when Joseph has proved himself does he ascend and become an "ambtman" (official) (3692); his office at court gives him influence and dignity. A passage in the *Lob Salomons* also illustrates the fact that the concept of bondservant does not point to a particular activity of the person performing the service. The conduct of the king's court is there described: Salomon is surrounded by people who wait on him at table (166ff.) and who act as armed sentinels when he sleeps (176ff.); all of them alike are called *dî dînistmin* (229 and similarly 171). Service at court and in arms are two sides of one and the same thing.[29] From the middle of the twelfth century "dienestman" becomes a "clear cut designation of the class of *ministeriales*."[30] The significance of the word for the formation of legal concepts is revealed most clearly by the fact that the word "dienestman" was taken into the Latin of legal documents.[31] It is undisputed and perfectly clear, on the other hand that "the social words *ministerialis* and *minister* are merely translations of the German 'Dienstmann.'"[32] The word is astonishingly rare in the German texts of the Middle High German classical period. There is not a single instance in the Vorau *Alexander*, the Strassburg *Alexander, König Rother*, Veldeke's *Eneit*, the *Nibelungenlied, Kudrun*, Konrad Fleck's *Flore*, Stricker's *Karl*, or Tûrheim's *Tristan* and there is not even an example in the *Minnesang* before Walther von der Vogelweide.[33] The remaining texts, for the most part, offer only a few instances.[34] This can certainly not be explained by the social circumstances of the Middle High German poets;[35] and hardly from "the use of French sources";[36] for it is precisely the heroic epic, which does not derive from French sources, which most consistently avoids the word.[37] The reason is rather to be sought in the fact that the word *dienestman* is by its very nature an extremely unpoetic word; and as soon as it became the legal term for the class of *ministeriales* it must have seemed even more colorless and dry from the poetical point of view. Nevertheless it remains remarkable that courtly literature which is supposed to have been composed preponderantly by *ministeriales* should have had so little idea how to deal with the central concept of service knighthood (*Ministerialität*). Often the poets use the word metaphorically, in a religious[38] or courtly sense.[39] Where it refers directly to people in a lord's service, it preserves a certain flexibility throughout the classical period. In the *Kaiserchronik*, the wicked administrator in the *Crescentia* story is variously named "des herzogen man" (the duke's liegeman) (12313), "dienestman" (bond-servant) (12467), "viztuom" (deputy) (12245), and "kneht" (servant) (12360). Even later the words *man* and *dienestman* are interchangeable.[40] In *Herzog Ernst* B we find *dienestman* (1716), as the garrison of imperial castles; in the *Kaiserchronik* the "duke's bond-servants" (*herzogen dienestman*) (12417) are designated as "burgære" (castle-dwellers) (12415). Castles and bond-servants are the typical attributes of a domain: " 'Ich gebe iv no hute. Allez daz ich ie gwan. Lant burge dinstman . . .' " ("I give you now protection.

Everything that I ever won, lands, castles, bond-servants . . .'') (Herbort, 2694–96). The listing of bond-servants with "land" is also testified in *Wigalois*: " 'als ich dir ê hân gesaget, dir wirt daz lant und diu maget, dar zuo rîche dienstman . . .' " ("as I said to you before, you will have the land and the maid and rich retainers too") (4827–29). Similarly in *Der gute Gerhard*, at the founding of the archbishopric of Magdeburg: "sî gâben dran eigen, dar zuo dienstman stete bürge unde lant" (they handed over as possessions bond-servants, towns, castles, and land) (179–81). As well as this, bond-servants appear in association with great lords, with counts (*Erek*, 6332; 6361. *Wigalois*, 8615; 8713 etc.), dukes (*Kaiserchronik*, 6768; 6786; 6826. *Herzog Ernst* B, 1993 etc.), kings (*Kaiserchronik*, 15416. *Erek*, 9762. Gotfried, 3375. *Willehalm*, 211, 18 etc.). It is doubtful whether we should be thinking here of *ministeriales* in the technical sense. Even the formula *man unde dienestman* (*Kaiserchronik*, 15324. Herbort 3947. Gotfried, 5808 etc.) does not definitely point to a precise distinction between vassals and *ministeriales*; for the terms "mâge unde man" (relations and liegeman) (*Nibelungenlied*, 163, 4, etc.), "mâge unde dienstman" (*Salman*, 478, 1 etc.), "mâge man und dienstman" (relations, liegemen, and retainers) (*Gregorius*, 201),[41] are to a large degree synonymous with them. The "concept of rank" becomes most clearly evident where the *dienestman* (retainers) are clearly separated from the *vrîen* (free men)[42] and in rank-series of the type "fursten herren dienestman" (princes, lords, retainers) to which we shall return later.

As a result of this survey we are able to determine that the core of the meaning of *dienestman* is closely related to that of the word *ritter*: it is of the character of both that there is dependence on a lord. We still have to determine their relation to one another. In this regard it is important that in only one of the supporting quotations in this chapter were *dienestman* and *ritter* named together in such a way that different persons could be understood by the two terms. That was the passage in Hartmann's *Erek* in which Count Oringles wooed Enite: " 'ritter unde knehte, vrouwen, rîche dienestman, . . . die mache ich iu undertân' " (6277f. 80). There is no recognizable order of rank here. In all other passages where *dienestman* and *ritter* are juxtaposed they refer to one and the same person or group of persons—that was our starting point. This means that the two words correspond to a considerable degree in their field of usage. There is the difference, however, that *ritter* is the broader and vaguer, *dienestman* the narrower and more precise designation. This, in fact, contradicts the conclusion of Walther Kotzenberg: "In all the records of the Middle High German period, in whatever region they may originate, rank-listings of the type 'fürsten, grâven, frîen, dienestman, ritter' appear throughout."[43] It is made clear here how important an exact chronological distinction is for investigations of this sort, for the texts on which Kotzenberg bases his pronouncement do not begin, for the most part, until the second half of the thirteenth century, with Seifrid Helbling, Berthold von Regensburg, *Ludwigs Kreuzfahrt*, etc.[44] On the other hand it is significant that in the classical period ca. 1200 the knights have not yet found a fixed place in the pyramid of social precedence. It is not until the last decades of our period that we find two pieces of evidence which do not indeed express the rank-listing set up by Walther Kotzenberg exactly but do foreshadow it and prepare for it. One is in Bruder Wernher's ''Spruch'' on Duke Friedrich of Austria: ''sîn reinez herze sich nie vergaz gegen grâven, vrîen, dienestman, die ritter unde knehte wurden alle bî im rîch'' (his pure heart never forgot counts, free men, retainers; knights and servants all became rich at his court) (48, 4–6); the other is in Lichtenstein's *Frauendienst*, in the description of the marriage of Duke Leopold the Glorious of Austria: ''grâven, vrîen, dienestman, wol tûsent rittern oder mêr, den gab der edel fürste hêr silber, golt, ros unde kleit'' (to the counts, free men, and retainers, a good thousand knights or more, the noble glorious prince gave silver, gold, horses, and clothing) (41, 4–7).[45] In both instances the knights are strangely isolated and tacked on to the actual series of social precedence in such a way that they rank below the retainers. It is not so much a degradation of the concept ''knighthood'' which is reflected here as an amelioration of the concept ''retainer'': ''At this point the feeling of baseness associated with the name *dienestman* vanished.''[46] It is no accident that the earliest evidence comes from Austria: it was here that the new order of precedence first became established and then gained more general significance after the middle of the thirteenth century.[47]

The relationship between the corresponding Latin concepts *ministerialis* and *miles* points in the same direction. Roughly the following picture emerges from the results of historical investigations[48]—''if we ignore the unavoidable doubts and difficulties which result from the fluctuating meanings of the words *ministeriales* and *milites*''[49]—from the Carolingian period on, the term *ministerialis* means an official without distinction of high or low, spiritual or temporal. There was still no ''class'' of *ministeriales* for ''when count and customs-collector are so called, there can be no question of a 'class.' ''[50] The first clear-cut evidence for a ''ministerialis'' class in the high Middle Ages as a separate group of persons living according to its own law within a *familia* of spiritual and, later, of temporal domains is to be found in the earliest service laws from Worms, Limburg, and Bamberg in the eleventh century. But these new *ministeriales* (officials) are only occasionally called by the Latin term *ministeriales* in the tenth and eleventh centuries; the normal designations are *servientes, ministri, servitores, famuli*, etc. In the common formula

milites et servientes a distinction is made between the people who are the
dependents of a domain according to feudal law and service law, that is
to say, between vassals and *ministeriales*. Only toward the end of the
eleventh and at the beginning of the twelfth centuries—even later in some
places; there are regional differences—does the name *ministeriales* become completely accepted for this long since clearly defined group. At
about the same time or a little later—and there are regional differences
here too—the word *miles* appears in documents as a designation for
ministeriales. This use increases in the second half of the twelfth century
and in the first half of the thirteenth century it is the predominant designation for *ministeriales* in many areas.[51] But as early as the twelfth
century there is documentary evidence for *milites* who are not identical
with *ministeriales* but dependent on them.[52] From the beginning of the
thirteenth century, an occasional distinction is made in individual domains
between *ministeriales* and *milites* and in such a way that it is clear that
the *ministeriales* rank more highly than the *milites*. Gradually "*miles*
developed as a special term for the lowest class of knights,"[53] and after
the middle of the century the new classification is frequently documented
by the formula *ministeriales* and *milites*. However incomplete such a
survey must remain at the moment, the parallel nature of the German and
Latin terminology is nevertheless unmistakable. In very general terms it
may be stated that in the century of the classical period, between 1150
and 1250, the terms *dienestman* and *ritter*, just like the corresponding
terms *ministerialis* and *miles* are to some degree interchangeable and
applicable to one and the same group of people and that after this time
they gradually separate into designations of a hierarchy of rank, in which
the *ministerialis-dienestman* ranks higher than the *miles-ritter*.

The question of what the name *miles* means for the *ministeriales*
leads on to the relationship between the position of the *ministerialis* and
that of the knight, the relationship which, in our context, is the most
important problem and one which has not excited any particular interest
in the voluminous literature on the question of the *ministeriales*. Usually
any *ministerialis* who was called *miles* was quite simply promoted to
knight. If a man with the title "miles et ministerialis" appears in a
document, it may be concluded "that the man in question who belongs
to the unfree class of knights has indeed been *dubbed* knight."[54] And
"when in a list of witnesses the *milites* are kept separate from the *ministeriales*, the easiest explanation is usually that the *milites* are those who
have been dubbed knight and the others are squires."[55] Only "where the
milites are obviously part of the *ministeriales*" must it be admitted that
"these explanations do not suffice."[56] While the differentiation of the
ministerialis concept has long been the common property of research, the
opinion is still widely held on the subject of *miles* that wherever the word

clearly refers to a *ministerialis* "it is naturally to be interpreted as 'knight,' "[57] and there is apparently not the slightest doubt that these "milites," as they are called in the records, were "real knights."[58] This conviction leads to the sentence: "With the entry of the *ministeriales* into the knightly class, the title *miles* was added to the name."[59] In fact, the reverse is true; it was only the title *miles* which ensured entry into the knightly class. The *ministerialis* laws provide a clearer picture than the laconic series of witnesses in the records. In the older service-law of Köln,[60] for example, the word *miles* occasionally appears side by side with the predominant designation *ministerialis* for the retainer, particularly in para. 4, where the subject is the military service obligations of the *ministeriales*.[61] But *miles* applies not only to military service; the *ministeriales* in service at court were also called *milites*: in para. 11 the Archbishop announces his intention "XXX milites de familia sua de novo vestire" (to reclothe thirty knights of his household) on three holy days of the year.[62] Paragraph 12, finally, is particularly interesting for the terminology. It lays down that the oldest son of a *ministerialis* shall at all times inherit the *beneficium*, the rights and duties of his father. Then there follows: "Quicumque frater suus miles fuerit nec adeo dives quin servire eum oporteat" (any brother of his who was a knight and not rich enough to make it unfitting for him to serve) shall come to the Archbishop's court on horseback and armed with shield and lance and there standing before his lord shall declare himself to be the knight and *ministerialis* of Saint Peter and shall offer his loyalty and service to his lord ("ibique coram domino suo stans se militem esse et ministerialem beati Petri profitebitur atque fidelitatem et servitium suum domino suo offeret"[63]). For the young man who declares himself to be the *miles* and the *ministerialis* of the Archbishop, the two words have the same meaning.[64] The most that could be said is that here the word *miles* has a special emphasis in so far as it designates a *ministerialis* of military age who has not yet been entrusted with any office.[65] This *miles* may be designated as "*Ritter*" (knight), in conformity with the usage of Middle High German texts but it is necessary to keep completely clear of the idea that such a man "had been dubbed knight" or "had entered the knightly class."

The creation of the class of *ministeriales* was legally completed in two large stages: distinction within the aristocratic household (completed in the eleventh century) and its rise into the landed so-called "lesser" nobility (completed in the fourteenth-fifteenth century). It has long been recognized, however, that a purely juridical way of looking at the phenomenon of the medieval *ministeriales* cannot do justice to it, for the simple reason that the unified and self-contained character which it assumes has proved to be a fiction.[66] Throughout the twelfth and thirteenth centuries the *ministerialis* class was open upwards and downwards; serfs and dependents were "freed" into the *ministeriales*, free men and noblemen renounced their nobility and freedom and became retainers.[67] (*nobilitati et liberalitati renuncians*). Furthermore, "the regional and domain differentiations in service-law in Germany"[68] make it impossible to speak of a unified class: the "*ius ministerialium . . .* varies according to the individual *familia*, the individual *dominus*."[69] This was already known by Eike von Repgow, who therefore explained in the *Sachsenspiegel*: "Nu ne latet uch nicht wunderen, dat dit buk so luttel seget van denstlude rechte; went it is so manichvolt, dat is neman to ende komen ne kan" (Don't be surprised that this book says so little about retainers; it varies so much that no one can get to the end of it) (*Landreht*, III, 42, para. 2). A comparison of the *ministerialis* laws which have been preserved leads to the same result.[70] Finally, there were so many fundamental stratifications that it is hardly possible to continue to believe in a *ministerialis* class which was an entity in law.[71] On the basis of these observations Eberhard F. Otto and Friedrich von Klocke both rejected almost simultaneously the thesis of the equality of status of the *ministeriales*.[72] "There is no *ministerialis* class, just the legal form of a service-relationship specifically formulated."[73]

Nowadays the sociological approach has been replaced by that of the "genealogical-history of a property" (Karl Bosl), and it is not so much the institution in law as the social development of the *ministeriales* and their function in medieval state structure which is the center of interest. In this the question of the unified nature of the *ministeriales* is no longer of significance for there can be even less question of its existence in a social connection than in a legal one. In power, property, and social influence there is a world of difference between the great imperial *ministeriales* under Heinrich VI and a *magister coquine* (master of the kitchen) in a small religious foundation, who was also a *ministerialis,* or even from the peasant retainers of the late Middle Ages.[74] The rise of the *ministeriales*, which even Hans Naumann still regarded as "a social revolution of the greatest magnitude"[75] is nowadays regarded rather as "a slow evolution."[76] It is true that the view is still widely held that the *ministeriales* rose from servitude to nobility; and therein lies a still unresolved remainder of the old ministerialis problem.[77] But the contrast between free and unfree has lost its sharpness since the frequently conditional nature of both concepts in the Middle Ages has been recognized.[78] The search for the genealogical roots of the *ministeriales* in a thin and "particularly qualified upper stratum of the unfree"[79] long since led to the charge of "making up "a nobility composed of camp-followers."[80] No noble family of *ministeriales* in the late Middle Ages can be traced back to a founder who fed the horses as a stable boy in the tenth or

eleventh centuries. If it is commonly assumed that the retainers developed
from a household, that is to say, that all ministeriales originally obtained
board and lodging at their lord's court,[81] then the result is a picture of
logical development which, however, cannot possibly have corresponded
in every case with the genealogical development. The rise of the *ministeriales* shows remarkable parallels with the building up of the administration of landed domain.[82] Very early, and in some domains from the
very start, the famous families of *ministeriales* were already in possession
of fiefs and ownership.[83]

The old dispute about whether it was military service, court service,
or administrative service which elevated the *ministeriales* has now been
laid to rest. It has been agreed that it is not the type of service but "service
in itself"[84] which contributed to their rise in society. It would perhaps
be better to say "their specialized use in feudal service";[85] for many
served but only a few rose in rank. The famous rise of the *ministeriales*
has only too often been seen in isolation. Even as early as Tacitus there
is evidence that unfree men or freedmen rose high in royal service or,
in more general terms, in the service of lords, even over the heads of
"free men and nobles" (*Germania*, chap 25); sources from the Merovingian and Carolingian periods provide numerous examples of the
process.[86] The *ministeriales* were one link in a long chain; behind them
we can already see the rise of the next stratum, the unfree *milites*, who,
at least in South Germany, did succeed in attaining "noble" status.[87] In
the second place, the rise of the *ministeriales* cannot be regarded as a
unified occurrence. A phenomenon like Werner II of Bolanden, who, at
the end of the twelfth century, had fiefs from forty-three princes and was
himself liegelord of almost 140 vassals,[88] can hardly be regarded as a
typical example but rather as an extraordinary exception. Only a very few
ministeriales succeeded in crossing the definite dividing line between the
great aristocratic families and the remaining "gentlemen" (*Herren*), the
Reuss, for example. Very few indeed, like the Schönburgs, built up great
land-holdings. The number of *ministeriales* among the gentry of the late
Middle Ages has yet to be clearly determined; it is obvious that there
were significant regional differences. In any case, a large number of
retainers moved up into the landed knights of the late Middle Ages.[89] It
may well be doubted whether this was always a "rise."[90]

It is virtually impossible to grasp the unique historical quality of the
class of *ministeriales* from the *ministeriales* as individuals. Its significance
can be understood only when account is taken of the historical force
which formed the retainer class and of which they made use. The class
of *ministeriales* was a function of aristocratic government, its soil was
immunity, both spiritual and secular. The sociological "dynamism" of
the *ministeriales*[91] was certainly not the decisive force. "Corporate fed-

eration, a drive for power from below and similar factors were certainly not enough to raise retainers to what they became: there must have been the additional factor of support by interested parties from above."[92] It is quite certain that the *ministeriales* took over rights of domain when they had the chance. But that is a general phenomenon: in the Middle Ages, domain and state were not institutions which functioned on their own. They needed individuals to ensure unbroken operation. Only where domain was not exercised in person was it possible for parts of the power of domain to be "usurped" from below. The first to be affected were the smaller clerical foundations and convents,[93] and it is from these circles that we hear the loudest complaints about the insubordination of the *ministeriales*.[94] But that was only one side of the phenomenon, the dark side. The other side was more important: the increase in power of the great clerical and secular princes from the eleventh century on called for the formation of new instruments of rule. In the competition for landed domains, the *ministeriales* became the most important and effective instrument of the princes, closely bound as they were to their lords by their service relationship. In his work on the imperial *ministerialis* class, Karl Bosl has shown how first the Salian emperors and then the Hohenstaufen deliberately employed their *ministeriales* to reshape the whole structure of the state. The same is true for the clerical and secular lords who, unlike the emperors, did succeed in creating a closed state organization with the help of their retainers.[95] The princes promoted their *ministeriales* by involving them in large and important undertakings and distinguishing and rewarding them accordingly for their services. The rise of the *ministeriales* is primarily a reflection and result of the reorganization of the state in the course of which the princes of the Empire became territorial lords.

What is the position of the knightly class in this development? In Middle High German texts, as we have seen, the retainers are called "knights." But the title "knight" does not indicate any distinction for them: it may be used not only for the *ministeriales* but also for "ordinary soldiers" (*simplices milites*) and for all those who are "obligated for service" (*dienstlîch undertân*) to a lord. The word "retainer" (*dienestman*), on the other hand, soon became a clear-cut concept for a small privileged group among the dependents. The gradation of the concepts comes out clearly in the enumeration of ranks from the middle of the thirteenth century on, in which "retainer" is higher than "knight." But when, in research on the *ministeriales*, mention is made of "the entry of the *ministeriales* into the knightly class,"[96] of their "rise into the knightly class,"[97] and of the "upward thrust of lower class people into the knightly class,"[98] it is obvious that a different concept of knighthood is intended. "Knightly class" and "knighthood" here mean the same as "nobility," and the word is frequently used in this sense.[99] Roth von

Schreckenstein, however, warned us long ago that "nothing is more confusing for our understanding of medieval social relationships than counting knights as nobility without further ado.[100] The time at which the *ministeriales* began to be counted as nobility is an academic question which was of interest to research only so long as the *ministeriales* class was treated as a closed unit.[101] Even before 1200 the most important imperial *ministeriales* can no longer be distinguished from the upper nobility in their public behavior or way of life. Half a century later the same is true of the great families of ducal retainers in Austria. But this does not permit us to make up a noble "class" of *ministeriales*: not in a social sense, since the enormous social differences within the *ministerialis* class were not leveled out by the rise of individual families but rather became more perceptible; nor in a legal sense, since the basic legal distinction between *nobiles* and *ministeriales* remained in force until the end of the thirteenth century and beyond.[102] It was only then, long after the period with which we are concerned here, that a large part of the *ministeriales* belonged to the "knightly class," which gradually came to be regarded as "noble." "There is confusion here. Two phenomena, retainership and lower nobility, which in social law do not come together before the fourteenth century, are ascribed to the twelfth and thirteenth."[103] The century of the classical period of medieval literature, from 1150 to 1250, was politically an age of great transformations, in which the domain state of the early Middle Ages developed towards the state of social classes of the late Middle Ages. In this process the *ministeriales* played a significant role, not as independent personages but as tools in the hands of the new territorial lords. Because of the greatness of their duties and achievements the old service obligation under court law was gradually forgotten. The most important of them lived like great lords, even though they were still "unfree." It was precisely at this time that great divisions appeared between social and socio-legal actuality. There is no place here for a "unified knightly class."[104]

APPENDIX

1. The Knight as a Dependant[105]

The following is a list of expressions found in literature which indicate the state of dependence:

min(e) ritter	Strassbg. Alex. 4949. Herbort 9183. 12831. Parz. 77, 8. 358, 2. 396, 6. 414, 25. 618, 28. Craun 602. Heimesfurt Urst. 113, 10. Türlin Krone 17838. 17911. Ems Willeh. 5155. 5161. 6313. 7591. Holle Demant. 1560. 4762. 7447. 7941. 9044. 10398. 11484. Holle Crane 746. 1260
	miniu ritterschaft: Willeh. 89, 27. Stricker Karl 4471. Ems Alex. 4630

unser(e) ritter   Holle Crane 2313
                       unseriu ritterschaft: Ems Willeh. 6567. Ems Alex. 18136
din(e) ritter   Parz. 353, 29. Franciskus 4261. Holle Crane 397
                       dîniu ritterschaft: Orendel 719
iuwer(e) ritter   Iwein 7531. Stricker Dan. 2322. Holle Crane 2363. Lichtenst. Frd. 148,
                       2. Lichtenst. Frd. 3. Büchl. 163. 230
                       iuweriu ritterschaft: Gotfr. 6411. Ems Willeh. 819
sin(e) ritter   Jg. Judith 163, 27. Vor. Alex. 1446. Rother 155. 239. Strassbg. Alex.
                       [538]. 1729. Oswald M. 1481. Eneit 200, 13. Herbort 4580. 6204. 12507.
                       12669. 12875. 13255. 13626. 16865. 17774. 17790. 18113. Lanzelet 3248.
                       Parz. 23, 12. Thomasin 2001. 2011. 6657. Prosa-Lanz. A I, 6. Sächs.
                       Weltchr. 92, 7. 99, 8f. 109, 12. [*van sines selves ridderen*]. 112, 20
                       [dito]. 115, 35. 127, 18. 177, 22. 177, 23. Stricker Karl 6017. Hz. Ernst
                       B 5576. Kudrun 806, 2. Christoph. 1110. Ems Willeh. 858. Ems Weltchr.
                       33094. Holle Demant. 1730. 4145. 5168. 5187. 5416. 6767. 6771. 8839.
                       9422. 10369. 11404. Holle Crane 381. 1563. 3790. 4227. Lichtenst. Frd.
                       816, 5. Pr. Schönbach I, 331, 26. 332, 1. II, 53, 1. Pass. Zacher 279, 24.
                       Pr.br. Dieffenbach A IV, 2, 9. Pr.br. Jeitteles 172, 26. Pr.br. I Schönbach
                       197, 26
                       siniu ritterschaft: Herbort 6239. 8039. 10221. 10920. 16723. 17850. Parz.
                       787, 8. Gotfr. 356. Sächs. Weltchr. 113, 1. Stricker Karl 4792. Hz. Ernst
                       B 2398. Ems Willeh. 639. 949. 1161. 6087. 11859. Ems Alex. 211. 2819.
                       3750. 3962. 4676. 4731. 4776. 5127. 5353. 5862. 5876. 5899. 6278. 11757.
                       12116. 14430. 20705. 21338. Ems Weltchr. 8469. 11347. 28318. 29990.
                       32076. Lichtenst. Frd. 298, 6. 599, 3
ir(e) ritter[106]   Herbort 3735. Parz. 78, 19. 98, 4. 305, 17. Willeh. 153, 19. Ems Gerh.
                       1756. Türlin Krone 759. Holle Demant. 4319. 8758. Lichtenst. Frd. 65,
                       5. 390, 2. Lichtenst. Frd. 1. Büchl. 64. 69. Pr. Jeitteles 79, 16
                       iriu ritterschaft: Eneit 60, 38. Herbort 4002. Parz. 674, 15. Gotfr. 1661.
                       5327. 5500. 18917. Ems Willeh. 764. 845. 10719. 12066. Ems Alex. 278.
                       6154. 6845. 10145. 11705. 11998. 12420. 12531. 13360
jemandes *ritter*[107] *Alexanders ritter* (Ems Alex. 7501)
                       Julius ritter (Sächs. Weltchr. 87, 3)
                       Constantines ritter (Sächs. Weltchr. 117, 35)
                       des chûniges Herodes ritter (Pr. Schönbach II, 169, 28)
                       ritter des keiseres (Sächs. Weltchr. 130, 34)
                       ritter des koninges (Sächs. Weltchr. 261, 1)
                       der kuneginne ritter (Ems Willeh. 11293)
                       des hertogen ritter (Sächs. Weltchr. 212, 35)
                       der herzoginne ritter (Parz. 676, 13. 699, 17)
                       sines broder ritter (Sächs. Weltchr. 79, 34)
                       ir swester ritter (Türlin Krone 18613)
                       des wirtes ritter (Parz. 174, 29)
                       Arofels ritterschaft (Willeh. 33, 28)
                       Nöupatrîses ritterschaft (Willeh. 267, 3)
                       Jofrides ritterschaft (Ems Willeh. 860)
                       Amilotes ritterschaft (Ems Willeh. 12060)
                       Alanes ritterschaft (Ems Willeh. 12109)
                       Alexanders ritterschaft (Ems Alex. 2349. 4499. 5030. 5613. 7124. 7300.
                           7318. 8951. 9466. 10489. 12635. 20321)
                       Madrianes ritterschaft (Ems Weltchr. 18522)
                       des fürsten Liupoldes ritterschaft (Lichtenst. Frd. 284, 1)
                       des bâruckes ritterschaft (Parz. 105, 27)
                       des küniges ritterschaft (Hz. Ernst B 5384)
                       der vier kunege ritterschaft (Ems Weltchr. 4159)
                       des herzogen ritterschaft (Gregorius 2149)
                       des grâven ritterschaft (Lichtenst. Frd. 273, 1)
                       mînes vater ritterschaft (Willeh. 234, 26)

2. Knights in Society[108]

The following is a list of expressions found in literature which refer to the social status of knights.

ritter unde vrouwen   Kaiserchr. 4209. 5765. Melk Erin. 289. Strassbg. Alex. 5958. Orendel
1280. Eilhart 8851. Eneit 79, 18. Erek 651. 1390. 5254. Gregorius 2113.
Iwein 4384. Herbort 1173. 2437. 2483. 9156. 16207. Morant 2129, 5569.
Lanzelet 1836. 2165. 2622. 2744. 5175. 6174. 6337. 8979. Nl. 766, 2.
1668, 2. 1671, 2. 2379, 2. Klage 2570 (B). Craun 759. Walther 25, 2.
106, 25. Singenberg 32, 9. Parz. 387, 16. 669, 12. 705, 3. 773, 11. 776, 11.
Titurel 11, 1. Wigalois 2903. 5676. 11485. Gotfr. 18682. Thomasin 403.
12320. Flore 162. Ems Gerh. 4975. Ems Willeh. 10095. Stricker Dan.
4893. 8198. Türlin Krone 1156. 16729. 21779. 23475. 24966. 29439.
Kudrun 47, 1. 297, 4. Durne 271. 5835. Türheim Trist. 507, 7. Türheim
Renn. 7233. 7862. 36213. Holle Crane 3844
ein ritter und ein vrouwe: Parz. 592, 23. Thomasin 978. Türlin Krone
29302. Holle Crane 2264
die ritter und die vrouwen: Parz. 644, 10. 676, 5. 726, 3. 763, 10. Ems
Gerh. 2374. 2544. Stricker Ehre D 487. Türlin Krone 26488. Türheim
Renn. 14917. 32207. Holle Crane 2175. 2239
ir ritter und ir vrouwen: Wigalois 5788
an rittern und an vrouwen: Türlin Krone 23171. 24848
durch ritter und durch vrouwen: Flore 1407
mit rittern und mit vrouwen: Parz. 151, 9. 611, 3. 698, 19. 761, 13. 765,
5. Thomasin 12241. Ems Barl. 293, 7. Holle Crane 4034
mit rittern und vrouwen: Lanzelet 6318
under rittern und vrouwen: Türlin Krone 13718
von rittern und von vrouwen: Rother 278. Maze 41. Erek 5278. 10078.
Iwein 5933. Morant 3374. 4814. Lanzelet 79. 2421. Nl. 1036, 2. Parz.
654, 19. Wigalois 9783. 11402. Gotfr. 12553. Otte 1835. Thomasin
1170. Ems Gerh. 2152. 4555. 4890. Ems Willeh. 10067. Stricker Dan.
7403. Türlin Krone 634. 11524. 29183. Türheim Renn. 25337. Holle
Demant. 2355. Holle Crane 4214
von rittern, vrouwen: Parz. 277, 2
zen rittern und zen vrouwen: Parz. 331, 5
zuo den rittern und den vrouwen: Holle Crane 579
manec ritter und vrouwe: Parz. 655, 6
werde ritter und vrouwen: Türheim Renn. 35082
werde ritter und werde vrouwen: Parz. 309, 27
vrume ritter und goute vrouwen: Thomasin 14695
vrouwen unde ritter: Melk Erin. 427. Parz. 764, 22. Stricker Ehre 1532.
Ems Willeh. 10031f. Türlin Krone 24198. Holle Crane 3652
vrouwen noch ritter: Thomasin 12260
vrouwen unde ritterschaft: Herbort 2753. Parz. 187, 7. Wigalois 11612.
Türlin Mant. 145
die vrouwen und ritter: Türlin Mant. 327
die vrouwen und die ritter: Holle Demant. 1560. Holle Crane 1354
die vrouwen und die ritterschaft: Parz. 637, 17. Wigalois 11513. Türlin
Krone 25686
mit vrouwen, mit ritterschaft: Athis F 78
von vrouwen und von ritterschaft: Türlin Krone 29266
ritter, vrouwen und meide: Türlin Krone 25572
vrouwen, ritter und meide: Türlin Krone 17853
magede unde vrouwen und ouch ritter guot: Kudrun 969, 2
stolze megde, ritter unde vrouwen: Neidhart [LVI, 10]
vrouwe maget ritter kneht: Herbort 10457
ritter vrouwen manic kneht: Herbort 13311
vrouwen, ritter noch kneht: Wigalois 7621

ritter unde magede   Kudrun 927, 1
ritter unde maget: Nl. 581, 4. 583, 2
ritter oder maget: Parz. 795, 8
der ritter und diu maget: Türlin Krone 9602. 16155
der ritter und daz megedin: Holle Demant. 175
magede unde ritter: Parz. 789, 12
ritter und magede und ouch schœne vrouwen: Kudrun 620, 3
ritter, magede unde wîp: Parz. 718, 17
ritter maget noch wîp: Holle Demant. 3672

ritter unde knehte   Oswald M. 17. 89. 107. 147. 839. 1481. 1523. 2252. Oswald W. 314. Erek
2975. 3084. 6277. Iwein 5593. Herbort 6068. 9001. 9846. 10179. 12970.
Morant 3949. Nl. 133, 2. 807, 2. 1952, 4. Klage 852. Wigalois 682. 1142.
1541. 3973. Hz. Ernst B 149. Türlin Krone 17045. Kudrun 282, 2. 369,
4. 1148, 3. Stricker Dan. 1433. Ems Willeh. 3652. Türheim Renn. 3834.
Br. Wernher 48, 6. Holle Demant. 40. 7022
ritter unde kneht: Nl. 75, 1. 701, 1. 1587, 1. 1649, 1. 1722, 2. Zweter 56,
2. Türheim Renn. 19816. 32072
der ritter und der kneht: Parz. 473, 2. Ems Barl. 343, 24. Wolfdietr. A
335, 3. Türheim Renn. 8678
ritter und vil maniger kneht: Lichtenst. Frd. 116, 5
die ritter und ir knehte: Türheim Renn. 2356
die ritter, dar zuo die knehte: Türheim Renn. 31577
der ritter als der kneht: Ems Alex. 1528
ir ritter und ir knehte: Pr. Jeitteles 79, 16
iuwer ritter und iuwer kneht: Iwein 7531. Stricker Dan. 2322
mit rittern und mit knehten: Oswald M. 448
ritter oder kneht: Morant 2714. 4346. Klage 60 (C). Parz. 523, 30. Gotfr.
10769. 14781. Otte 2719. Ems Gerh. 5786. Ems Willeh. 281. 3072.
8712. Türlin Krone 5259. Kudrun 984, 2. Albertus 771. Holle Demant. 6692
ritter oder der kneht: Türheim Renn. 13842. 31106
der ritter oder der kneht: Türheim Renn. 13744
ritter noch kneht: Herbort 18313. Parz. 162, 26. Türlin Krone 4827
die ritter noch die knehte: Klage 2855
weder ritter noch der kneht: Wolfdietr. A 192, 4
ors cleider ritter kneht: Türheim Clig. 17

ritter unde knappen   Parz. 446, 28. Lichtenst. Frd. 133, 3
ritter, knappen: Durne 4603
mit rittern und mit knappen: Morant 1059. Ems Gerh. 2542
von rittern und von knappen: Türheim Renn. 30973
knappen unde ritter: Türlin Krone 22701

ritter und sarjande   Gotfr. 5898
ritter, sarjande: Parz. 646, 29. Willeh. 116, 25. 186, 16. 225, 30
hie der ritter, dort der sarjant: Willeh. 197, 4. 304, 25
sarjande, ritter: Parz. 816, 18
sarjande unde ritterschaft: Willeh. 18, 13
manec sarjant, edeliu ritterschaft: Parz. 558, 21
ritter oder sarjant, turkopel: Willeh. 170, 18f.
ritter . . ., sarjande, burgære: Parz. 581, 14f.
sarjande, ritter, vrouwen: Parz. 666, 11

ritter unde schützen   Eneit 243, 25
schützen, ritter: Ems Alex. 11747
schützen vrech und ritter wert: Ems Alex. 11670
ritter schutzen und sarjande: Christoph. 1787

ritter unde künege   *künege unde ritter*: Türheim Renn. 24122
künege oder ritter: Türheim Renn. 24106
der künec und der ritter: Pr.br. Jeitteles 174, 18

ritter unde vürsten   Ems Willeh. 1060
vürsten unde ritter: Holle Crane 1817

	die vürsten und diu ritterschaft: Ems Alex. 9646
	vürsten ritter knehte: Ems Alex. 19566
ritter und barûne	Gotfr. 11075. 11187. 11370
	von rittern und barûnen: Gotfr. 4052
	barûne und arme ritter: Parz. 785, 7
ritter unde herren	Eneit 320, 25
	ritter oder herren: Ems Willeh. 6202
	die ritter und die herren: Ems Willeh. 6533
	herre unde ritter: Sächs. Weltchr. 255, 6f.
	herren unde ritter: Lichtenst. Frd. 201, 1
	ritter, herren, knehte: Ems Willeh. 9083
	herre ritter oder kneht: Ems Alex. 20173
	juncherren, ritter, knehte: Ems Willeh. 3489. 5505
ritter unde man	*mit rittern und mannen*: Herbort 13697
	mîne ritter und mîne man: Herbort 9183
ritter und gebûre	Tnugdalus 51, 68. Eneit 248, 6. Hz. Ernst B 1462. 1537
	ritter noch gebûre: Klage 3078 (B)
	ritter und ouch gebûren: Orendel 2358
ritter unde koufman	*ritter oder koufman* Parz. 142, 7
	hie der ritter, dort der koufman: Parz. 408, 1
ritter und burgære	Morant 5447
	ritter noch burgære: Flore 6510
	die burgære und die ritter: Flore 7634
	ritter burger und knappen: Türheim Renn. 10480
ritter unde pfaffen	*ritter unde pfaffe*: Türlin Krone 2076
	pfaffen unde ritter: Sachsensp. Ldr. II 27 § 2
	pfaffen unde ritterschaft: Gotfr. 15635
	die pfaffen und diu ritterschaft: Türheim Renn. 9257
	pfafliche ritter, ritterliche pfaffen: Walther 80, 21
	pfaffen ritter burgære: Morant 5139
	pfaffen ritter unde vrouwen: Christoph. 83
	pfaffen ritter werdiu wîp: Ems Gerh. 3490

V. The Noble Knights

We find a king there,
who is a fearless knight

It was not only vassals and *ministeriales* who were candidates for the order of knighthood; it was held in such honor that even emperors, as well as high-ranking princes, felt themselves honored by it.''[1] That is the turning-point in the history of the concept of knighthood: at the end of the twelfth century the word acquires a new content which soon pushes the old usage into the background. It is transferred to the lower and upper nobility and becomes a proud distinction for emperors and kings. And further: the noble title ''knight'' now becomes the central concept of a whole culture, the keyword in a new system of ethics and esthetics, the program of a new idea of man. In the literary works of the classical courtly period, this new use of the word was so dominant that it was accepted without further consideration as the core of the medieval conception of knighthood and everything else was dismissed as subsidiary or as an early or transitional stage. Even today the word ''knight'' makes us think first of all of the great figures, of Friedrich Barbarossa and Richard the Lion Heart or of Maximilian, the ''last'' imperial knight. Knighthood and nobility are inseparable in our understanding of the term. Nevertheless, we must now emphasize the paradoxical character of noble knighthood: paradoxical because the basic meaning of the word ''knight'' runs completely counter to the new content: a word denoting service becomes the essence of the life of the nobility.

This shift in meaning becomes clear when comparison is made with the old terms for ''hero.'' The words ''helt,'' ''degen,'' ''recke,'' and ''wîgant'' were used in precourtly literature and throughout the classical period without any class restrictions whatsoever in complete disregard of their very different origins.[2] A king and a great lord were called "wîgant" and "recke," "degen" and "helt" in exactly the same way as their men, particularly in combat, were called "wîgande" and "helde." The poets have a fondness for adding intensifying adjectives; they speak of "snellen helden" (bold heroes), "guoten degen" (good warriors), "küenen recken" (brave warriors), "tiuren wîganden" (fine fighters), but these epithets have only a decorative, not a distinctive significance and they can be encountered just as much in the lower as in the upper classes of fighters. The word "knecht" is the one exception. Whereas in English the word "knight" became a designation of nobility, the German "Knecht" never succeeded in freeing itself completely from the opposition to "Herr" (lord). It is true that the mass of fighting warriors goes by the name "knechte," without there being the least suspicion of denigration,[3] but it is impossible for a king to be designated "Knecht" without further explanation.[4] This changes when an emphatic adjective is added: in the forms *guoter kneht, vrumer kneht, edeler kneht* (good, faithful, noble servant) the word has the same value as the old words for hero and covers precisely the same areas of meaning. In the *Rolandslied* it is said of the emperor: "Karl ist selbe ein gut knecht" (Charlemagne is himself a good servant) (2259, s.706), and in the same way, of ordinary soldiers: "si sint gute knechte" (they are good servants) (1023 et passim).[5] The knight remains clearly distinguished from the group. The author of the *Rolandslied* neglected no opportunity to shower his heroes with heroic expressions, but he never calls one of them "ritter." The reason is obvious: it was impossible to think of kings and princes in terms of a word which basically denoted a man in the service of a lord. Intensifying adjectives were of no help either in getting over this obstacle.[6] It was not until the second half of the twelfth century that the word burst these bonds; it became socially acceptable and at the same time acquired a poetic overtone. In a short time it soared far above all the other words for hero.[7]

How the new usage developed from hesitant beginnings and only gradually established itself may be clearly read from the literary works. Onc single precursor may be found in the first half of the twelfth century in the *Millstätter Genesis*. There it is said of Joseph: "si verchoften in sâr einem riter putifar" (they thereupon sold him to a knight Potiphar) (77,7). Potiphar was a great lord: "der was (ein) gewaltich man, daz her was im undirtan" (he was a powerful man, the army was subject to him) (77,8). The title-writer of the miniatures is more accurate when he speaks of "einem fursten putifar" (a prince Potiphar) (77,5), for in the Vulgate, Potiphar is *princeps exercitus* (chief of the army) (Genesis 39 1), *princeps militum* (chief of the soldiers) (Genesis 40 3), *magister militum* (master of the soldiers) (Genesis 37 36), and *eunuchus Pharaonis* (a eunuch of

Pharaoh) (Genesis 37 36; 39 1).[8] Probably his military office was the bridge to the concept of knighthood, but this first noble knight remains extraordinary even in this formulation. The next piece of evidence is in the *Kaiserchronik*. In the story of Lucretia it is said of the prince Conlatinus: "ain furste was bi den zîten ze Triere, der gewan michel liebe ze Tarquînîô dem kunige. iz ergienc in baiden ubele. er was ain rîter vil gemait, Trieraere tâten im sô groziu lait, daz der helt vil guot ainen fursten dâ ze Triere ersluoch, der hiez Conlatînus" (there was in those days a prince in Trier who had great love for King Tarquin. Things went badly for both. He was an excellent knight. He hated the men of Trier so much that the good hero there in Trier killed a prince called Conlatinus) (4305–4315). This passage, whose confused syntax throws doubt on the correctness of the text, was read in various ways even in the Middle Ages. Four manuscripts of the later redaction replace *rîter* (4309) by *herre*, and three of the older redaction replace the second *furste* (4312) by *ritter*.[9] The different use of *helt* and *ritter* is significant. Conlatinus is "der helt" (4311) and beside that he is "ain riter vil gemait" (4309), that is to say, he is also an excellent soldier. The military side of the knighthood concept was the one least tied to rank, for on the battlefield all soldiers could be called "knights," irrespective of their rank and standing. But this princely knight remains an exception. There is no example of it in either the *Vorauer Alexander*[10] or in the *Rolandslied*. On one occasion Roland is urged on by his warriors: "voget der Karlinge, durch soteniu gimme, aller riter ere, ne spar si nicht mere!" (Lord of Charlemagne's men, by such a jewel, the honor of all knights, do not spare them any more) (5977–5980). He is the "comfort and glory of all warriors,"[11] as Oliver is later "the honor of all Christians" (aller cristen ere) (6340). In *König Rother*, the old Herlint says of the disguised king: "Iz ne mochte uffe der erdin, nie schonir ritar werden. Dan dietherich der degin" (There could not be any finer knight on earth than the warrior Dietrich) (2047–2049). Later King Constantine hears of Rother's trickery: "Geinir ritar erlich. Der danante dietherich. Daz was der koninc rother" (He was not a true knight, the man called Dietrich. He was King Rother). Rother had presented himself to the king as *armer man* (a poor man) (916) and had offered his service: "min dienest biedeich dich an" (I offer you my service) (928). In the king's service the alleged Dietrich can be called "knight"—until it emerges that the *ritar* is in fact a *koninc*, that the knight is a king. As king, Rother is never again alluded to as "knight." There is a similar situation in *Salman und Morolf*. There the king's brother Morolf is called *der ritter lobesam* (the famed knight) (160,2; 163,3; 180,2; 194,2; 198,2; 297,2; 712,3), *der stolze ritter balt* (the proud bold knight) (275,1), and *der ritter wol gemeit* (the excellent knight) (359,6). As the king's brother, Morolf is, of course, *furste* (prince) (305,3) but he is at the same time *sin dienstman* (his retainer) (101,5), and Salman himself calls him *mîn getrûwer dienstman* (my loyal retainer) (351,5; s. 208,5 and 356,2). Tristant is also one of this group of noble lords who are called knights in as much as they accept service under another lord. In the old Eilhart fragments he expresses the hope as a stranger in the land "daz man mich liepliche ane haz. behaldit ungehazzit. uñ mich ze ritter vazzit. uñ gift mir ros uñ perit" (that they accept me in kindly fashion without hate or dislike and give me a charger and palfrey) (M4^v 31–34). Here we still have the old terminology: "ze ritter vazzen" means to equip someone with weapons and thus make him into a knight.[12] A passage in *Herzog Ernst* A recalls the Conlatinus evidence in the *Kaiserchronik*. There it is said of Ernst: "der helit vil wale kunde aller slagte frumicheit ind was ein rittêre gemeit" (the hero was completely capable of every kind of correct behavior and was an excellent knight) (I, 9–11).[13] As in the case of Conlatinus, there is added to the usual epithet *der helt* the additional and careful expression *ein ritter gemeit* which designates primarily the military efficiency of the hero. Otherwise it is the old terminology which is dominant in *Herzog Ernst* A. Ernst is *der helit* (the hero) (I,9.29), *der helit gût* (the good hero) (II,20. 23; IV,9), *der degin her* (the noble warrior) (II,22), *der Tûrlîche degen* (the invaluable warrior) (IV,55), *der wîgant* (the champion) (II,17), and he and Wetzel are *die helede* (the heroes) (V,27), *di helede vil gôt* (the very good heroes) (V,35), *di degene düre* (the invaluable warriors) (V,37), *di wîgande* (the champions) (V,50), etc. Even in the B version of the thirteenth century the old terms for hero far outnumber those for the new noble concept of knighthood.[14] The Strassburg version of the Alexander romance is on the same level as the older *Ernst* poem. A comparison with the original version from Vorau demonstrates the changes in word-usage in a generation. In the Vorau version the Persian commander-in-chief Mennes is described as follows: "Mennes was ein herzoge genant, den Darios hete dar gesant, der was ein helt vrumeclîch" (Mennes was called a duke [or army leader] whom Darius had sent there. He was a competent leader) (1239–1241). For this the Strassburg redactor substitutes: "Mennes der wîgant, den Darius hete gesant . . . der hete manlîchen mût und was ouh ein rîter gût" (Mennes the champion, whom Darius had sent . . . he had a manly spirit and was also a fine knight) (1711 f.; 1715f.). From the *helt vrumelich* there has emerged a *rîter gût*.[15] Even about 1170 that was still exceptional.[16] Noble knights become more frequent only very gradually. In the old *Tundalus* fragments the hero is "Ein ridder wol virmezzin; Er was edele uñ wole bekant" (A well trained knight; he was noble and well known) (90f.). Similarly in the slightly later *Tnugdalus* version: "ein man, edel unt wol gitan . . . er was ein reiter gemaeit. Bediv chun unt balt" (a man noble and handsome . . . he was an excellent knight, both brave and bold'') (43,22f. and 27f.). In Veldeke's *Servatius* there is mention of a nun, Ute of Nivelles: "si was ouch selve wale geboren van vader ende van muder" (she was herself also well born on her father's and her mother's side) (5874f.) Ute "hadde einen bruder, einen riddere, einen ovelen man" (Ute had a brother, a knight, an evil man) (5876f.), who was thus the son of distinguished parents. Veldeke's *Eneit* stands on the threshold of the classical courtly terminology. It in Turnus is: "ein ritter gemeit unde ein stolzer jungelink" (an excellent knight and a proud youth) (117,4f.). And Aeneas laments over Pallas, a king's son, "edel ritter Pallas, wie ubel diu stunde was, daz dû worde erslagen" (Noble knight Pallas, how evil was the hour in which you were slain) (217, 33–35). That is all there is,[17] and it can be seen how far Veldeke still is from the word usage of later poets. He never calls his hero Aeneas a knight; the most he does is to use the word once in a comparative sense when he is talking about Aeneas's breeches: "sô nie ritter nehein scôner geleite an sîn bein" (never did any knight put anything more beautiful on his legs) (159,25f.). Hartmann von Aue is the first to break through to the new image of knighthood. In his *Erek*, kings' sons and princes are called knights entirely as a matter of course: we find "der ritter Îdêrs," (778), "der ritter Brîen" (1640), "der ritter Keîin," (5014), "der ritter Mâbonagrin" (9636), "der edel ritter Gâwein" (4785), and particularly "der ritter Erec" (3634, 4230, 5007, 5023, 5288, 6135, 8590), who is also called "der herre Erec" (4629[18], 7037, 8880) and "der künec Erec" (6763, 7233, 7911, 8520, 8896, 9405). The word *ritter*, which, on a lower level, merges into the concepts *dienestman* and *kneht* (retainer and servant) now becomes practically the equivalent of *herre* and *künec* in the province of the nobility. Great lords address one another, among themselves, as *ritter*[18] and the best reputation anyone can gain in this world is to be called "der beste ritter" (6844). The degree to which this first upward sweep of noble knighthood was the work of one poet, namely Hartmann von Aue, can be seen from the fact that afterwards modifications were made of it.[19] It was so in Hartmann's own later works,[20] and after him not only in poets who stood on the fringes of classical courtly epic, such as Herbort von Fritzlar,[21] the *Athis und Prophilias*,[22] and Konrad Fleck,[23] but even in Wolfram[24] and Gottfried.[25] The delight in knighthood we find in *Erek* appears later in its most vital form in Wirnt's *Wigalois* and, contrary to expectations, in the *Nibelungenlied*, whereas the *Nibelungenklage* avoids the noble concept of knighthood more than any other poem of the classical courtly period.[26] But these are nuances of minor significance. After Hartmann's *Erek* the title "ritter" has passed firmly into the possession of the aristocratic world. It has thrown off all ties with a particular social class and even an emperor can bear it: "er was ein edel ritter guot" (he was a noble and good knight) (228) is said of Emperor Otto in *Herzog Ernst* B.

From now on the knight concept is ambivalent and shifting. The new noble knight is to be found both next to and above the old service knights. From this parallel situation was derived the "perfectly unified knightly class" found in courtly poetry.[27] But the romantic idea that an emperor would have recognized a simple soldier as his social equal, or a lowly vassal, simply cannot be accepted at this stage. We have noted that there was a clear distinction throughout the whole classical period between knights and lords and that the core element in the concept of knighthood right up to the beginning of our period remained the service-connection to a lord's court. The fact that the lords themselves were now called knights demands an explanation. One thing should be made clear from the start: these noble knights, who appear from the time of the *Millstätter Genesis*, at first as isolated cases and then with increasing frequency, are not social climbers, former *ministeriales* perhaps, who have pushed their way up into the nobility. The kings and princes who are now called knights were princes and kings at an earlier period too. This means that we do not see the formation and consolidation of a new nobility in the literary sources. What we see from the philological point of view is not the rise of an institution but that of a word. What we are dealing with is not primarily a sociological problem or one of rank but a problem of the history of a word, with the question of how the old service word "knight" could rise to become a title of the highest distinction.

First we should look at France. It was from there that the word "chevalier" came, with courtly culture and the courtly romances. Almost everything that distinguishes the noble concept of knighthood in Germany was anticipated in it. According to its etymology, the term "chevalier" indicates a person who is sprung from the same lower level of society as the German "ritter," but it is obvious that the word did not establish itself in the vernacular until the word *caballarius* had ceased to mean "stablehand" but rather "the man who owns a horse" and who goes into battle mounted.[28] In any case the word "chevalier" had a more elevated meaning from the very beginning in the double sense of "l'aptitude au combat et la naissance noble"[29] (fitness for battle and noble birth). In the older *chansons de geste* it is still inferior as a term for a hero to *ber*; in the works of Chrétien de Troyes it has become the central concept of the courtly world.[30] The parallels with the German concept of knighthood become particularly apparent when, on the one hand, the *chevaliers* are counted among the *menue gent* (inferior classes), just like the *serjanz*, whereas, on the other hand, even a prince can be celebrated as *bons chevaliers* (good knight).[31] A new investigation of the meaning and use of the word in the texts of the twelfth and thirteenth centuries would be very desirable,[32] particularly in view of the new discussion of the connection between chivalry and nobility in France.[33] It can be said with certainty that Hartmann's breakthrough to the concept of noble knighthood was inspired by the *chevalerie* concept of his French sources and that the German concept of the knight during the classical period is inconceivable without the impulse from France. But it would be an oversimplification of the historical situation to regard the diffusion of the concept of knighthood as nothing more than a reflection of French conditions.[34] Influence from France had a significant effect on the development but it did not bring it about. The *Millstätter Genesis*, the *Kaiserchronik, König Rother*, and the old *Herzog Ernst*, which offer evidence of the first hesitant beginnings of the noble concept of knighthood, were independent of French sources. In France, as in Germany, the vernacular evidence is preceded by Latin testimony of the application of the old word for soldier, *miles*, to princes and upper nobility.[35] The rise of noble knighthood was a European phenomenon which only gradually becomes apparent in the vernacular literatures of the individual countries.

From the very beginning there was a poetic element in the noble concept of knighthood, to the degree that there is poetry in every metaphorical use of a word. Whenever the title "knight" broke out of its old limitations, it at once lost its character as a bald piece of objective description and became a metaphor. We encounter this tendency in many forms—as ornament, as a polite formula, as a verbal gesture. Its ornamental character can be determined from the numerous *epitheta ornantia* which are used more and more frequently in connection with it.[36] In Lamprecht's *Alexander* there are still six uses of *ritter* without a qualifying term as against two with one: *frumich rîter* (excellent knight) (156) and *rîter junch* (young knight) (925); in the *Kaiserchronik* it is seven to three: *edeler rîter* (noble knight) (1140), *guote rîter* (good knight) (4572) and *rîter vil gemait* (most excellent knight) (4309). In the *Nibelungenlied* the situation is reversed: in eighty-eight cases *ritter* is accompanied by an epithet as against thirty-five where it is not. The word becomes a formula of politeness in expressions of devotion by noble lords.[37] For example in the words of Iwein: "her Gâwein, lieber herre mîn, was mac ich sprechen mêre wan daz ich iuch êre als iuwer rîtr und iuwer kneht?" (Lord Gawain, my dear lord, what more can I say than that I honor you as your knight and your servant?) (*Iwein*, 7528–7531). Similarly in Stricker's *Daniel*: "der greve aber dô sprach . . . 'nû ist daz ouch mîn reht, daz ich iuwer ritter und iuwer kneht iemer darumbe sî.' " (But the count said: "Now it is my right too that I may be always your knight and your servant on this account.") (2316,21–23). When Laudine's first husband is lauded as "der aller tiureste man, der rîters namen ie gewan, von manheit und von milte" (the most precious of all men who ever bore the title "knight", in manhood and in generosity) (*Iwein*, 1455–1457), a metaphor is created by means of the connection with a concept of virtue

which frees the term "knight" from any social connections. Such formulations occur with considerable frequency. It is said of Siegfried in
the *Nibelungenlied*: "er ist an allen tugenden ein riter küen'unde guot"
(he is a bold and good knight in every characteristic) (230,4). In *Wigalois*:
"mir geviel nie rîter baz dan ir an rehter manheit" (no knight ever pleased
me more than you in his manhood") (3618f.) and in an obvious reminiscence of Hartmann: "ez ist ein der tiurste man der rîters namen ie
gewan an tugent und an manheit" (He is one of the most precious men
who ever bore the title "knight" in virtue and in manhood) (3921–3923).
Reinmar von Zweter permits the title "knight" to be used of noblemen
only in this metaphorical sense; he says that a free gentleman can indeed
be called "ein ritter sîner tât, der milte ein kneht" (a knight in his deeds,
a servant of his generosity) but not a knight without any qualification.

The derivatives of the word *ritter*, the adjective *ritterlich* (knightly,
chivalrous) and the adverb *ritterliche* (in knightly fashion, chivalrously)
allow us to recognize how the metaphorical usage led to the moralization
of the word and finally to making the whole world chivalrous.[38] At first
the military aspect is preponderant:[39] "daz swert ist ain riterlich gewant"
(the sword is a knightly apurtenance) (*Roland*, 5577);[40] "da wart riterlichen wol gestochin" (they thrust like knights there indeed) (ibid., 8280).
There is a great deal more evidence in later poetry too: the shield "was
genuoc ritterlîch" (knightly enough) (*Erek*, 2303); "mit manegem rîterlîchen slage" (with many a knightly blow) (*Iwein*, 7344); "rehte ritterlîche tât" (a right knightly deed) (Halberstadt, XXX, 84); "diu swert
si riterlîche erzogen" (they drew their swords in knightly fashion")
(*Eneit*; 315,10); "si dahten sich gelîche mit den schilten riterlîche" (they
thought themselves equals, chivalrous with their shields) (*Lanzelet*,
5283f); "mit zoumen wart gewendet vil riterliche dan" (then there was
much knightly use of the reins) (*Nibelungenlied* 185,3); "strîten rîterlîche"
(they fight chivalrously) (*Willehalm*, 44,4), etc.[41] It is much more important that these derivatives, unlike the basic word, were never subjected,
from the very beginning, to restrictions of social rank. Even kings fight
in knightly armor and achieve chivalrous deeds. As early as the *Rolandslied* it is said of King Estorgant: "da vacht der chunc riche vil hart
riterliche" (there the powerful king fought in true knightly fashion)
(4897f.) of the heathen commander Stalmariz "riterlichen stach er sin
spiz durch Beringeres schiltes rant" (in knightly fashion he thrust his
spear through the edge of Beringer's shield) (4996f.); and of the supreme
king Paligan: "sin gesune ware egeslich, sin gebarde were riterlich: sin
march gienc in sprungen . . ." (his appearance was terrifying, his ges-
tures knightly, his charger advanced in bounds) (8005–07).[42] Now that
princes fight chivalrously, it is also possible to speak of their "ritterlîchen
siten" (chivalrous manners), of their "ritterlîchen muot" (chivalrous

spirit), their "ritterlîchen prîs" (knightly fame).[43] From there it is a mere step to the connection with actual concepts of virtue: "Erec trûwete im (i.e., God) vil sêre umbe sîn ritterlîche êre" (Erec complained bitterly to God about his knightly honor) (*Erek*, 2498f.); pris uñ rum. Vñ ritterliche ere" (fame and glory. and knightly honor) (Herbort, 16527f.); "ein rehter adamas rîterlîcher tugende" (a true diamond of knightly virtues) (*Iwein*, 3257f.); "mit ritterlicher hubischeit" (with chivalrous courtliness) (Herbort, 12573); "mit rîterlîchen triwen" (with knightly loyalty) (*Parzival*, 631,20); "mit ritterlicher werdekeit" (with knightly dignity) (Gottfried, 5087). This extension of meaning is not to be explained merely as the result of an upward valuation of the term "knight." From the very beginning rather there is something in the word *ritterlich* which conveys distinction and superiority and which is lacking at first in the basic word. There is in particular a strongly visual element. *Ritterlich* and *ritterlîche* designate what strikes the eye as especially grand, the gleam of weapons for example,[44] but even outside the purely military sphere everything shining, splendid and glorious in appearance, in dress, and in physical development. As early as *Rother*, it is said of the king's messengers: "si trogen riterlich gewant" (they wore knightly clothes) (203), by which is meant their splendid clothing, not their armor.[45] The same words are used later to describe the dress of the ladies-in-waiting: "Die trogin ritarlich gewant. Von groceme overmote" (they wore knightly clothes because of their great pride) (1824f.) During the classical period *ritterlich* is a very common epithet for elegant clothing.[46] But the people who were them are called knightly too, and the word then indicates physical beauty. Thus it is said of Alexander: "sîn bûch ne was ime nit ze lanc noh ze breit: vil wol daz deme jungelinge steit. beide ubir vûze und ubir bein rîterlîch er ze tale schein" (His torso was neither too long nor too broad; it suited the young man perfectly. In his feet and legs he looked knightly right down to the ground) (*Strassburger Alexander*, 171–174). And about the Crane-people: "an ir lîbe nieman vant zer werlt deheiner slahte kranc, wan daz in die helse wâren lanc, ritterlîch übr al den lîp" (nobody in the world could find the least fault with their bodies; except that their necks were long, they were entirely knightly in their person) (*Herzog Ernst* B, 2872–2875). Parts of the body too, especially the legs, were praised as knightly: "sîn brust wol ûferhaben was, und iedoch enmitten smal, dar zuo was er über al wol geslihtet als ein zein. Er hâte ritterlîchiu bein unde wolstânde waden" (His chest was well developed but his waist was small and in general he was as well formed as an arrow. He had knightly legs and handsome calves) (*Flore*, 6850–6855); "obe den hunt iemen mac erloufen, rîterlîchiu bein die trage" (if anyone can catch up with the dog, he should have a knight's legs) (*Titurel*, 134,1f.) Like ladies' clothing, the beauty of the female body is also called knightly. As early as the

Strassburger Alexander there are "funf hundrit juncfrowen wol gewassen unde smal und rîterlîch ubir al, scône under den ougen" (five hundred young ladies, of good figure and slim, knightly in all respects, beautiful to the eye) (6046–6049). At a later period too, Hartmann von Aue similarly set up the model concept of knightly femininity:[47] "Hartman, gên wir schouwen ritterlîche vrouwen" (Hartmann, let us go and look at knightly ladies) (*MSF*, 216,31f.); "diu rîtterlîche magt" (the knightly maid) (Iwein, 387; similarly 1153); "ein ritterlîches wîp" (a knightly woman) (*Erek*, 3324, 1707; *Iwein* 6135). But he did not have many successors in this. The *ritterlîche wîp* is found once in Lanzelet, the *ritterlîche maget* once in *Kudrun*. That is all up to the middle of the thirteenth century. The significance of *ritterlich*, however, goes far beyond beautiful appearance. It can be applied to all actions and situations of a courtly person. Guests are "ritterlîche enpfangen" (received in knightly fashion) (*Wigalois*, 9325); they "gesellen sich ritterlîche" (consort in knightly fashion) with one another (*Erek*, 1945f.); they will be seated in knightly fashion ("ritterlîche setzen") (*Willehalm*, 263,24), cared for in knightly fashion ("ritterlîche pflegen" (*Wigalois*, 1166), and even bathed in knightly fashion ("ritterlîche baden") (ibid. 694); at court knightly companionship ("ritterlîche gesellekeit") (*Parzival*, 308, 29) and knightly happiness ("ritterlîchiu saelekeit") (*Lanzelet*, 2618) prevail. When Erek goes to church, that is a knightly journey ("ritterlîche vart") (*Erek*, 2489); and when rich gifts are distributed, it is knightly giving ("ritterlîche gâbe") (Thomasin 14596) which is mentioned. Courtly life is a knightly life ("ritterlîchez leben") (Gottfried, 5067). And social conscience is also knightly: then the virtuous Erec thought in truly knightly fashion of his father's-in-law poverty ("dô gedâhte der tugentrîche Erec vil ritterlîche an sînes swehers armuot . . ." (*Erek*, 1806–08). On the other hand, anyone who takes away a poor man's goods, has an unknightly spirit ("nimt sîn guot, der treit unrîterlîchen muot") (Thomasin, 7767f.). To think and act in knightly fashion becomes the standard by which courtly-aristocratic conduct is judged.[48]

It is the military side of aristocratic knighthood which can be perceived earliest and most clearly. The first applications of the title "knight" to noble lords refer entirely to their effectiveness in war. But this military aspect alone cannot explain the word's rise in status; it must remain a mystery why the old warrior terminology, which was much more poetic and in addition free of any class ties, was superseded by the knightly vocabulary.[49] Another aspect of social life at court was perhaps more important for the development of the aristocratic concept of knighthood, one at any rate whose influence on that development is hard to overlook, namely the concept of *Minne* (love). At the center of this idea of love, which was in its beginnings entirely aristocratic, we find the idea of service. The noble lord surrenders his rights as lord and enters the service of a lady. He serves for the reward of love and it is a distinction for him to be called "servant." The service-word *ritter* was a virtually automatic choice when a term was sought to describe this noble servant. It is courtly love-service which makes it possible to understand why the term "knight" was not only tolerated in aristocratic circles but even acquired a tone of distinction. It is true that aristocratic love-chivalry is remarkably late in appearing in the epic. Neither Veldeke nor, amazingly, Hartmann has a single instance. The evidence starts only with Herbort von Fritzlar, assuming that his *Liet von Troye* was written about 1190. In that word Prince Diomedes askes for a sleeve from his beloved Briseida and lets it fly from his lance during the battle, "so that people can tell from it that I am a lady's knight" ("Daz man erkenne da bi. Daz ich ein frowē ritter si") (9512f.). Nevertheless the early *Minnesang* (love-poetry) proves that the concept of knighthood was accepted into *Minne* terminology before the last decade of the twelfth century. As early as the middle of the century the the word appears quite frequently in the oldest poets: four times in the work of Der von Kürenberg and four times in that of Dietmar von Aist. It is found mostly in the *Frauenstrophen* (lines spoken by a woman) and designates the man to whom the *vrouwe* (lady) grants or denies her love. The lyric offers no information about the social position of these knights but we may regard it as certain that the noble love poets had noble lovers in mind. Are we also entitled to say that these lords are called knights because they serve their lady (*vrouwe*)?[50] It is customary to draw conclusions about the social condition of the poets from the evidence about knights drawn from the *Minnesang* and even to see in this evidence confirmation of the view "that the overwhelming majority of German love-poets belonged to the class of *ministeriales*."[51] However that may be, it is clear that when Emperor Heinrich has his lady say "I have devoted myself to a good knight ("ich hân den lîp gewendet an einen ritter guot") (4,26f.), in this passage at least it is not a *ministerialis* who is meant by the term "ritter" but obviously a great lord who is called "ritter" only in the applied sense. The old heroic terminology is eliminated much earlier in the *Minnesang* before Walther von der Vogelweide than it is in the epic and replaced by the knight-concept.[52] By 1200 the idea that a lord serves his lady as a knight is a commonplace of courtly literature. Gahmuret says to his brother, King Galoes; "You were a knight and a thief, you knew how to serve and deceive. If only I could steal love now! If only I had your skill and on the other hand true favor!" ("ir wâret ritter unde diep, ir kundet dienen unde heln: wan kunde ouch ich nu minne steln! Ôwê wan het ich iwer kunst und anderhalp die wären gunst!" (*Parzival*, 8, 22–6). The metaphorical system of *Minne* in relation to the term "knight" is here quite clear: the king is called knight as long as he serves ladies for the reward of love. Similarly in the love-decision made by little Obilot: "He (i.e., Gawain) is made for love and I shall have him as my knight. His service may well look for reward here" ("er ist sô minneclîch getan, ich wil in zeime ritter hân. sîn dienst mac hie lônes gern") (*Parzival* 352, 23–5); or when Gawain promises Queen Antikone: "If God preserves my life, I can do no other than constantly put at the service of your womanly kindness a life of service and a knightly temper" ("sol mir got den lîp bewaren, sô muoz ich dienstlîchez varen unt rîterlîch gemüete iwer wîplîchen güete ze dienste immer kêren") (ibid., 431, 7–11).[53] After Herbort and Wolfram[54], the lady's knight (*vrouwen ritter*) is a figure frequently conjured up in the courtly epic: Just as a lady's knight should ("reht als ein vrouwen ritter sol") (Gottfried, 9905); Can that be a lady's knight, who flees from chivalry like that? ("sol daz vrouwen ritter sîn, der ritterschaft sô vliuhet?") (Türheim, *Tristan*, 546, 10f.); "In the summer you shall become my knight and I your lady. Thus I shall grant all your desire" ("Du solt den sumer schone Min riter, ich din vrôwe sin, So laiste ich al den willen din") (Ems, *Willehalm*, 5160–2); the queen of Pullêbin asked him to be her knight for a year ("di konigin von Pullêbin bat daz he ir ritter wêre ein jâr") (Holle, *Demant*, 4318f.); in the summer I rode (or behaved) like a knight, as a lady's knight should ("den sumer fuor ich ritterlîch, reht als ein vrouwen ritter sol") (Lichtenstein, *Frd.*, 158,6f.).[55] In the image of the lady's knight the two essential elements of the courtly concept of the knight come together—nobility and concept of service. Even though no final determination can be made as to whether the idea of love-service effected the transfer of the title "knight" to the nobility, it appears certain that the development and establishment of aristocratic knighthood were affected by the idea of *Minne*.

Side by side with the aristocratic soldier-knight and the courtly lady's knight there exists a third type of aristocratic knighthood which has from the very beginning attracted most interest, namely, the "created" knight. The ceremonial conferring of the title "knight" at a dubbing ceremony is of great importance for our area in as much as the word "ritter" appears to lose its metaphorical overtones. It becomes a technical term, a "class-indicator." As the knightly class became consolidated as a social entity, the men who were called upon to perform knight's service even though they were already bearing arms, demanded a visible indication of their promotion in the new class . . . Nobody was born a knight; neither an emperor's son nor a king's son, neither upper nor lower nobility could achieve the status of knight without the formal act of dedication . . . belting on the sword, dedication, accolade, in these forms of acceptance into the knightly class there is a reflection of everything which, historically, had brought the class into being—as a military, social, and Christian class."[56]

Because of this connection with the formation of the class of knights, we must examine the dubbing ceremony as an institution more closely, even though it has already been the subject of thorough investigation on several occasions.[57]

Schwertleite, like *ritter*, is a word of its age and it appears in German source-material from the middle of the twelfth century, rather rarely, incidentally, when one thinks of the significance of the concept for courtly culture.[58] Here are the appropriate citations up to the middle of the thirteenth century:[59]

swertleite	Rother 5061. Melk Erin. 520. Eneit 347, 30. Gotfr. 4594. 4825. 4964. 4976. Stricker Dan. 8105. Ems Willeh. 5276. 5336. 6113
swertleiten stn.	Flore 7521
swert leiten	Kaiserchr. 8390. 8412 (= Tr. Silvester 584). 11380. Höxt. Aegidius 120. Erek 9485. Herbort 1425. Flore 7517. Ems Gerh. 3371. 4907. 4921. 4946. Ems Willeh. 5152. 5171. 5175. 5220. 5259. 5308. 5538f. 5719. 5820. 7263. 8593. Türheim Renn. 12885. Pr. Schönbach III, 239,30
wâfen leiten	Titurel 72, 1. Hz. Ernst B 113

The dubbing ceremony is the act by means of which a young man becomes a knight. This association of concepts is quite common in thirteenth-century texts, so that it is all the more remarkable that in the works of the twelfth century, although all of them except the *Höxter Aegidius* are aware of the word *ritter*, no direct connection exists between the concepts *swertleite* and *ritter*. Herbort's *Trojanerkrieg*, whose dating in the twelfth century is by no means certain, is the first work to make a loose connection between the two: "Da hilt vō troyge ein ritter bi. Ein vil kindischer man. Zu nestor er geran. Er was geheizzē Cedar. Ez was kume ein iar. Daz er geleit hette swert" (A knight of Troy was present there, a very childish man. He ran to Nestor. He was called Cedar. It was barely a year since he had been knighted) (1420–5). It is not until we reach source material of the next century,[60] Gottfried's *Tristan* and Fleck's *Flore* for example, that we find the two concepts closely connected with each other.[61] This remarkable separation for half a century can be understood if we note whose knightly initiation is being reported in the texts. In Heinrich von Melk, it is "eines chuniges sun" (a king's son) (*Erin.*, 511) who comes "zû der swertlaite" (to the dubbing) (ibid., 520). In the *Kaiserschronik* it is the sons of the emperor Narcissus who grow up "unz si daz swert mahten laiten" (until they could gird on the sword) (11380).[62] In *König Rother* we are told of the *suercleite* (5061) of young King Pippin. The *Höxter Aegidius* does not give explicit information about the rank of its hero. But Aegidius is "ein herre . . . uon uollime edele geborn" (a lord . . . of true aristocratic birth) (74f.) and the context shows that he is not only a lord but a ruler: "sine man ime rieten. er solde swert leitin" (his men advised him that he should gird on the sword) (119f.). Heinrich von Veldeke attaches to his well known mention of the court celebration at Mainz in 1184, at which the two sons of Friedrich Barbarossa received the sword, a remark "ichn vernam von swertleiten nie wârlîche mâre . . ." (I never heard true information about knighting ceremonies) (347, 30 f.)[63] In Hartmann's *Erek*, Mabonagrin, nephew of the king of Brandigan, says: "dô enwolde mir mîn oeheim des niht langer beiten, ich enmüeste swert leiten" (then my uncle was unwilling that I should wait any longer before being initiated into knighthood) (9483–5).[64] It is a closed group of people to whose initiation into knighthood the poets of the twelfth century testify. Without exception they are the sons of emperors and kings and the children of princes. From the beginning the initiation ceremony was an institution of the highest nobility, whereas the concept of knighthood rose only gradually into the aristocratic sphere. This means that "knight" and "initiation ceremony" are concepts of quite different origin and that it was only later that they were brought into connection with each other.

This conclusion is confirmed when the whole source material up to the middle of the thirteenth century is examined and note taken of the passages which do not speak explicitly of the *swertleite* but describe the act of dedication to knighthood by such expressions as "swert geben" (give the sword), "swert nemen" (take the sword), "swert emphân" (receive the sword) and later "ritter werden" (become a knight), "ze ritter machen" (make into a knight), etc.[65] Everywhere it is princes and great lords who solemnly receive the sword.[66] There are only a few passages where there can be any doubt about the social standing of the young knight.[67] And only once is there an account of the initiation of a non-noble—and that in a list of over forty such initiations.[68] It is the son of Der gute Gerhard in the work of Rudolf von Ems, the son of a merchant and a merchant himself (3368). This one case cannot be used to prove that, in *Der gute Gerhard*, the lower orders finally appear in the sources and that it now becomes clear that there are the same institutions among them as among the high nobility. The initiation of this merchant is rather one of the first pieces of evidence for the fact that, in the big cities, the upper stratum of the bourgeoisie had already become so rich and powerful in the first half of the thirteenth century that it was taking on the life style of the old nobility.[69] Thus this passage also is proof of the aristocratic character of the initiation ceremony. Investigation of the historical sources has led to the same result. Wilhelm Erben, who "collected and sifted all information in documents and chronicles as well as graphical representations of the initiation ceremony and the accolade",[70] produces forty-six examples up to the middle of the thirteenth century of the "initiation of young princes,"[71] whereas there is not one single piece of definite testimony for the dedication to knighthood of a non-noble.[72] In spite of this unambiguous discovery, it is possible to read everywhere that about 1200, the *ministeriales* shared the initiation ceremony with the upper nobility:

"The initiation ceremony was a custom which extended to all soldiers who fought on horseback, from kings down to *ministeriales*."[73] Aristocratic institutions, such as the initiation ceremony and the tournament, were current among knightly retainers."[74] Consequently the knightly dignity of the *ministeriales* is of decisive importance for an understanding of the knightly class under the Hohenstaufen, because their participation in the initiation ceremony is regarded as proof of their rise to noble rank and for putting them on the same level as the old nobility: "The dignity of knighthood was the means of the rise of the *ministeriales* in a legal sense."[75] In view of the importance of this question for class structure about 1200, it might be expected that all the sources which give any testimony about the knighting of a retainer would be most carefully collected. So far as my knowledge of the literature extends, however, there has been, astonishingly enough, only one attempt made to do so, that of Gustav Köhler,[76] who writes: "In the year 1156, the Archbishop of Mainz . . . presented the knight's belt to his *ministerialis* Mingota and at the same time Count Rudolf von Arnstein did the same to his. These are the first accounts in Germany of *ministeriales* being made knights. But it would be a mistake to assume that this at once spread to the whole mass of the upper stratum of *ministeriales*."[77] There must be unconditional agreement with the last sentence. But the two pieces of evidence produced by Köhler are valueless, since in one of them the text has been misunderstood: the account is not concerned with the initiation of ministeriales but of the Count of Arnstein himself;[78] and the other passage is suspected of being a seventeenth-century forgery.[79] So long as there is no reliable evidence for the initiation of retainers, no far-reaching conclusions can be drawn from mere assumption. This does not constitute a denial that individual *ministeriales* were initiated as early as the first half of the thirteenth century. There are two examples of it in the German source material,[80] and I have no doubt that further evidence could be found by a careful review of the historical sources,[81] but it is highly probable that in every case we are dealing with exceptional cases which cannot be evaluated as evidence for a general participation of *ministeriales* in aristocratic initiation ceremonies. Thus the foundation of the widespread acceptance of the initiation ceremony as "the outward sign of entry into the knightly class"[82] collapses. The dedication to knighthood does not indicate "elevation to the knightly class"[83] for the *ministeriales*, for "obtaining the dignity of knighthood, which was and remained something purely personal, did not in fact make the *ministerialis* equal to the hereditary nobles, whether he was a knight or not, nor did it separate him legally from his brothers and cousins who remained the retainers of nobles because of the cost."[84] Nor did the initiation ceremony have any socially formative significance for the upper nobility, since a king's son remained a king's son under any circumstances. Being dubbed knight could not possibly signify for the son of a great family either a proof of distinguished birth or acceptance into a company of selected men; he belonged to the class of selected men because of his birth. For him becoming a knight meant no more than formal permission to bear arms.''[85]

The aristocratic initiation ceremony was a purely social event,[86] whose only connection with social conditions was the fact that the formal entry of the young man into society was an expression of aristocratic life-style. Only the upper nobility was rich enough to put on a great celebration on such an occasion. There was never any compulsion to hold such an initiation[87] and there were no rights which derived from the reception of the knightly dignity.[88] The central feature of the ceremony was the solemn buckling on of the sword. The young prince was declared to be a man capable of bearing arms. The initiation ceremony carries on the aristocratic tradition of induction into armed service which can be demonstrated from Carolingian times and which perhaps goes back to Germanic institutions. The connection has often been noted and equally often disputed.[89] It can be easily proved from German sources. One of the first pieces of evidence, the initiation ceremony of the young Alexander, clearly retains the character of the induction:

> der chunich ne wolte es niwiht beiten
> er hîz daz chint bereiten.
> waz mage ich iu sundere gesagen:
> er det im wâfen fur tragen,
> sô mans unter eines chuniges
>   gesinden
> aller bezzest chunde finden;
> unt widerchurs Alexander,
> man gewunne im aber ander.
> Unt alsô daz chint nâch dem site
> was wol gewâfen unt geriten,
> dô was er ein scôner jungelinc.
> si grûzten in als ein chunich
>   (Vor. Alex. 357–68)

(The king was unwilling to wait at all. He ordered the young man to be prepared. What else can I tell you: he had weapons brought before him, the best that could be found in a king's household. If Alexander rejected any of them, others were brought to him. Thus the young man was well armed and mounted and was a fine youth. They hailed him as a king.)

The Adaptor of the Strassburg version replaces *nâch dem site* (365) by the words *nâh rîterlîchen site* (430) and shows by his alteration that the old induction had been developed into the courtly knightly dedication because of the introduction of chivalric terminology into the wording of the initiation ceremony. Throughout the whole classical period, the technical term for induction, "ze man werden" (to become a man), can be shown to be a synonym for *swert leiten* (buckle on the sword) and *ritter werden* (become a knight). It is used by Wirnt von Gravenberg in connection with the initiation of Wigalois: "sus wart her Gwîgâlois ze man" (thus Wigalois became a man) (1658). When Vivianz speaks of his initiation, he says: " 'dô ich ze Termis wart ein man' " (when I became a man at Termis) (*Willehalm*, 66,7) and in his despair over the death of his nephew, Willehalm asks: " 'Waz wold ich swerts umb dich gegurt? . . . war umbe hiez ich dich ein man?' " (" 'Why did I gird on your sword? . . . Why did I call you a man?) (67, 10 and 16). In *Der gute Gerhard* the remark is made before the son's initiation: "wan er niht worden was ze man nâch rîterlîchem rehte" (since he had not been made a man according to chivalric rites) (3548f.). The account of Flore's initiation ends with the statement: "er ist nû vollechlîche ein man" (He is completely a man) (*Flore*, 7774). When the statement is made about Charlemagne: "er vaterhalp hâte drî bruoder in den jâren, daz ir zwêne ritter wâren" (he had three brothers on his father's side who were at the age when two of them were knights) (Stricker, *Karl*, 146–8), this a clear expression of the fact that the initiation is the act by which a youth becomes a man. This is confirmed by the numerous accounts of the deeds undertaken by young princes in connection with the initiation. Almost invariably the dedication to knighthood immediately precedes the first public appearance, the proclamation as king or the coronation, accepting a fief, the first independent campaign, and, especially frequently, marriage. In several passages it is expressly stated that initiation into knighthood is a condition for the public functioning of a prince.[90] There were no regulations whether, when, or how the entry of the young lord into society should be celebrated. There was only an old *site* (custom) which arose from the taste or delight in display of the time. Gradually a courtly protocol developed in connection with it, as the poetic descriptions after 1200 demonstrate. But it was precisely among the poets that the effort to produce an exemplary form of the procedure had a unifying effect and even in the poetic sources the margin for variation was sufficiently broad.[91]

Let us go back to what is the most important question so far as we are concerned, namely, the reason why people arrived at the idea of calling a young aristocrat "ritter" when he was initiated into knighthood. What made the title so attractive that a noble regarded a service title as a distinction? To what "service" did the young man regard himself as bound? We may be sure, even though there is no evidence for it, that the ceremonial entry into the life of a lord gave rise to admonitions to the young man to prove himself in the arms which had just been granted to him and to conduct himself as a just and generous lord. But such a code of behavior had always been, by its very nature, part of the aristocratic ethic and hardly constituted an invitation to call oneself "knight." The change did not come about until the moment when Christian-ecclesiastical ideas and concepts found their way into what had been originally an entirely pagan institution, the granting of arms. It was the introduction of Christian ideas which made the old induction into arms into the initiation of the high Middle Ages, into the "dedication to knighthood."[92] In the collections of liturgical formulae, in manuscripts of the tenth and particularly of the eleventh century, first in Germany and later also from France and England, there are texts for the *consecratio ensis* (dedication of the sword) and for the *benedictio novi militaris* (benediction of the new knight) as well as documents on the blessing in church of swords and their bearers.[93] In one widely distributed version, a blessing is asked on the sword of a new knight" so that it may be a defense and protection of churches, widows and orphans, for all servants of God against the rage of the heathen, and that it may bring fear and horror to its enemies."[94] "According to the sense of this passage, induction into arms has itself become an act of ecclesiastical dedication and the military profession put under ecclesiastical patronage."[95] Doubt has occasionally been thrown on the value of these liturgical texts as historical testimony with the argument that contemporary narrative sources make no mention of the blessing of swords.[96] This may be explained by the character of the historical accounts; for the most part the only important consideration for them is the fact of initiation which can be expressed in one of the common formulae: *miles factus* (having been made a knight), *gladio* or *cingulo accinctus* (girded with the sword or belt).[97] If I understand the matter correctly, there is no detailed account of an initiation ceremony in the historical sources of our period but only reports on individual instances of it.[98] The assumption of the factual unimportance of the liturgical formulae is contradicted sharply by the fact that, after the eleventh century, the initiation ceremony was, for preference, celebrated on the high Christian holidays, especially frequently at Whitsuntide.[99] Such an adaptation of the knighting ceremony to the calendar of the church year is comprehensible only if the church ceremony was already a part of the initiation at this epoch.[100] The liturgical texts are supplemented and illustrated from poetical, not historical sources.[101] In courtly poetry there is not one detailed description of an initiation in which the blessing of the sword does not appear. The fact that this evidence does not appear until after 1200 cannot be interpreted as showing that it was not until this time that the blessing of the sword was made part of the proceedings of dedication to knighthood. It should rather be explained by the fact that the older poetry presents the initiation without giving any details.[102] About 1200 the idea that the blessing of the sword obliges the knight to protect widows and orphans is common to all poets. Wolfram talks about it in *Willehalm*:

"ein ieslîch rîters êre gedenke, als in nu lêre, do er dez swert enphienc, ein segen, swer rîterschaft wil rehte pflegen, der sol witwen und weisen beschirmen von ir vreisen . . ." (Let each think of a knight's honor, the blessing when he took the sword which told him that whoever wishes to cultivate knighthood truly should protect widows and orphans from the cruel) (299, 13–18). Walther von der Vogelweide recalls the blessing of the sword in the elegy: "dar an gedenkent, ritter; ez ist iuwer dinc. ir tragent die liehten helme und manegen herten rinc, da zuo die vesten schilte und diu gewîhten swert" (Think of it knights; it is your concern. You wear bright helmets and many a hard ring [armor] as well as tough shields and dedicated swords) (125, 1–3). Bruder Wernher mentions this blessing in the moral poem in which he laments the failure to observe the sacraments: "wer helt nû staete riterschaft, sît man niht swert durch schirmen segent witewen unde weisen?" (Who now observes faithful knighthood, since men no longer bless their swords by the protection of widows and orphans?) (42,7f.).

Carl Erdmann's researches have shown that the penetration of Christian ideas into the old aristocratic induction into arms must be considered in connection with the great reform movement of the eleventh century, which began as a reorganization of monastic life and spread in every direction, not only among church institutions but among secular ones too. In the latter the first evidence of its effect was the idea of the peace of God and it reached its peak in the concept of the crusade which was to have such important consequences. The main conclusion to be drawn from Erdmann's book can be said to be that, side by side with monastic and papal reform, "in third place lay knighthood was reformed."[103] For the first time the lay nobility was drawn into the great plan of division of Christian duties in this world. The ancient duty of the lord to maintain peace and law was not joined with specifically Christian duties—to take up the cause of widows and orphans, indeed of all the poor and oppressed, to protect the churches and respect their servants, and to combat heretics with fire and sword.[104] But the highest fulfillment of secular nobility would be to enter directly into the service of Christ as a Christian knight and to fight for the liberation of the Holy Places and for the spread of the Christian beliefs on the *reise über sê* (voyage overseas). This ideal picture of aristocratic-Christian knighthood appeared first in the polemics of the investiture struggle and receives its special emphasis in the Crusading propaganda of Urban II and his epoch.[105]

The terminology of the Christian ideal of knighthood is of great significance for our subject. The coinages of the primitive church, *miles Christi* (soldier of Christ),[106] *militia Christi* (forces of Christ), which designated first the apostles and then the ascetics and monks and in every case the unarmed defender of the faith and which, in consequence, were for a thousand years in sharp contrast to the *militia saecularis* (secular forces), were filled with new meaning in the second half of the eleventh century. Pope Gregory VII was the first to apply them, quite deliberately, to secular soldiers who were prepared to use their weapons for the cause of Peter.[107] From the Christian point of view, this was a linguistic revolution; up to that time the term *militia Christi* had meant victory through faith but now a man who entered the service of God with the sword of this world could also be called *miles Christi*. In this word there was implicit a great promise: remission of sins and expectation of eternal salvation. The Crusades were the realization of this new *militia Christi*. Basically the name was not connected with any particular social class; it applied to anyone who set out in the service of the faith whether he was a king or a retainer. But for noble lords the word must have had special overtones. In the title *miles Christi* there was for him the invitation to incorporate the religious idea of service into the lay nobility and to practice in the secular life of a lord the Christian virtues of *humilitas* and *misericordia* (humility and mercy).[108] We may note that at the same time as the church was developing the religious image of the knight the words *miles, militia, militaris* appear for the first time in liturgical formulae of blessing;[109] of still greater significance is the fact that in the years before and after the First Crusade the terminology of the aristocratic initiation in the historical sources changes in this respect, that the new *militia* concept now appears side by side with the old expressions *ense accinctus* (girded with the sword), *cingulo decorare* (distinguish with a belt), etc.[110] We may thus assume with some degree of certainty that there is an inner connection here and say that after the end of the eleventh century, when a noble lord is called *miles* (knight), the Christian image of knighthood of the reform and crusading movement is, consciously or unconsciously, in the background.

In German poetry, the *gotes ritter* (God's knight) is to be found side by side with the *vrouwen ritter* (lady's knight) and thus proves the living tradition of the religious concept of knighthood. One of the earliest texts, the *Millstätter Genesis* speaks of *gotes riteren* (God's knights) (139,12) and means the Children of Israel in Egypt. Even though in religious literature the old spiritual concept of *militia* was long retained,[111] in secular literature the word had its new overtones: in his last battle against the pagans, Roland is called *gotes ritter* (Stricker, *Karl*, 7918); the baptized pagan king Gamelerot is called *gotes ritter* even when he sets out to win *werde wib und hôhen pris* (noble women and high renown) (Türheim, *Rennewart*, 29677–9). The connection between God's knighthood and God's service becomes comprehensible when it is said of Jofrit: "In Gottes namen iuber mer Fuor der Gottes ritter sa Und was in Gottes dienste da Bis daz im der lip erstarp" (God's knight went overseas in God's name and was there in God's service until his life's end) (Rudolf von Ems, *Willehalm*, 15520–3).[112] The best expression of this idea is to be found in Hartmann von Aue, in the words of Gregorius: " 'ritterschaft daz ist ein leben, der im die mâze kan gegeben, sô enmac nieman baz genesen, er mac gottes ritter gerner wesen danne ein betrogen klôsterman' " ("knighthood is a life such that anyone who can bring moderation to it could not possibly spend his days better. He can rather be God's knight than a false monk") (1531–5).[113] The title "knight" which the aristocratic lord received at this initiation constitutes a duty to serve God while in this world and is a distinction even for kings and princes, because the service to which the title engages them is to the Highest.[114] This bond between the concept of knighthood and religious and ethical duty is nowhere more clearly expressed than by the clerical writer of didactic poetry, Thomasin von Zirklaere: "gedenket, rîtr, an iuwern orden: zwiu sît ir ze rîter worden? durch slâfen, weizgot ir ensît . . . wil ein rîter phlegen wol des er von rehte phlegen sol, sô sol er tac unde naht arbeiten nâch sîner maht durch kirchen und durch arme liute" (Think, knights, of your order: how did you become knights? By sleeping you certainly did not . . . if a knight really wants to practice what by rights he should practice, then he should suffer day and night according to his power for the church and for the poor) (7769–71; 77801–05).[115] It is not a question here of whether the noble lords about 1200 actually practiced the religious duty associated with the title "knight." The only thing of importance for us is that the aristocratic title of knight is in its origin and nature a cultural concept, a program of education which is of great significance in the history of ideas. For the first time it is put to the nobility that the highest realization of aristocratic life lies not in ruling but in serving, that it is not a diminution but on the contrary an enhancement of the life of a lord if it is put into the service of a higher power. It is this idea of service which is present in the word "knight," and it was the new meaning of the spiritual *militia* concept which gave the impulse to it. In courtly poetry the idea of service to the lady is to be found side by side with the idea of religious service and has the same value. This double obligation to service is made into a unified goal in the work of that master of great syntheses, Wolfram von Eschenbach in Willehalm's speech before the second battle which has already been cited:

> ,ein ieslîch ritter sîner êre
> gedenke, als in nû lêre,
> dô er daz swert emphienc, ein segen:
> ›swer ritterschaft wil rehte phlegen,
> der sol witewen und weisen
> beschirmen von ir vreisen‹:
> daz wirt sîn endelôs gewin.
> er mac sîn herze doch kêren hin
> ûf dienest nâch der wîbe lôn,

> dâ man lernet solhen dôn,
> wie sper durch schilte krachen,
> wie diu wîp dar umme lachen,
> wie vriundîn vriunts unsenftekeit
> senftet. zwei lôn uns sint bereit,
> der himel und werder wîbe
> gruoz . . .'
>
> (299, 13–27)[116]

("Let every knight think of his honor, as a blessing teaches him [which was given] when he received the sword: 'Whoever desires to practice chivalry truly must protect widows and orphans from the cruel.' That will be to his eternal profit. But he can nevertheless turn his heart to service for a reward from women, where one learns the sound that spears make crashing through shields, how the women laugh about it and how the discomfiture of her *ami* pleases a lady. There are two rewards that await us, heaven and the recognition of noble women'').

"Every account we have of the taking of the sword refers exclusively to the upper classes."[117] It was only for aristocratic lords that the title "knight" was a dignity, not for mounted soldiers or service knights, who bore the title anyway because they were in service. We still have to determine how wide the circle of aristocratic knighthood was. There is one phenomenon which can give some information about this; it has often been noted in the course of research but still not adequately evaluated. It is the so-called "Mass induction." So far as Germany is concerned, there is evidence after the end of the twelfth century that in connection with the initiation of young princes a number of other young men were made into knights.[118] In the poetic sources the numbers given vary from five (Holle, *Crane*, 1018f.) to 600 (*Nibelungenlied*, 646, 1; Stricker, *Daniel*, 6797; *Kudrun*, 178,4).[119] Even though these figures are mostly to be ascribed to poetic imagination, it is nevertheless interesting that "masses of knights appear here participating in the aristocratic dignity of knighthood. The most important question is who the people are who take the sword at the same time as the sons of princes and, unfortunately, it is not possible to give a clear answer to this, since in most cases only vague references are made to them. They are called *knechte* (servants), *knappen* (squires), *gesellen* (fellows), *reitgesellen* (mounted fellows), *schiltgesellen* (fellows of the shield), *degen* (warriors), *swertdegen* (sword-warriors), *swertgenôze* (companions of the sword), *recken* (heroes) or *kint* (young men), all words which make no distinctions of class. It is only rarely that an individual figure emerges from the anonymous group of sword-warriors. The most important witness is Ulrich von Lichtenstein, who himself tells us that in the year 1222, as one of 250 squires, he was made knight on the occasion of the marriage of the daughter of Duke Leopold of Austria in Vienna.[120] Ulrich came of a family of *ministeriales* and his initiation, with that of the son of Der Gute Gerhard, is the first of which we have testimony in German sources. The Lichtensteins were an important and powerful family whose life style could no longer be distinguished from that of the old noble houses. There is evidence that Ulrich himself was *dapifer* (steward) and later marshall of Styria and that he played a not insignificant role in aristocratic politics.[121] The rest of our information about the sword-warriors fits into this picture.[122] When there is in fact any remark about their social status, it is invariably the case that they are nobles: *edeliu kindelîn* (noble young men) take the sword at the same time as Siegfried (28,2); *kint dú öch von hoher arte sint* (young men who are of high class) and who are also called *juncherren wert* (noble young lords) take the dedication to knighthood with Willehalm of Brabant (Ems, *Willehalm*, 5337f and 5777); also invited are "Von Hanegö des fürsten man Der da wolte laiten swert" (the liegeman of the prince of Hanego who wished to take the sword) (5718f.); the companions of the shield in *Wolfdietrich* A are also called "juncherren" (young lords) (136,4).[123] The historical sources point in the same direction. In the year 1192, the *Reichersberger Chronik* reports that *multi comites et nobiles quam plurimi* (many counts and a very large number of nobles) took the sword at the same time as Duke Konrad of Swabia and Duke Ludwig of Bavaria.[124] We can see from this that mass initiation too was a matter for the nobility and that in consequence only the noble received the dedication to knighthood. It was not the reverse, that dedication to knighthood made a man noble. In no case was there any change of social class connected with it and in the case of these mass inductions too we must reject any idea that the ceremonial girding-on of the sword "signified elevation to the knightly class." It was an honor and a distinction to be permitted, as a sword-warrior, to take part in the dedication to knighthood of a prince. The aristocratic title of knighthood endowed its bearer with higher social esteem. In the women's apartments at the court of the Irish king, nobody recognizes Kurvenal with a greeting because he is not dressed as a noble. Brangaene asks: " 'Wer ist der man? . . . weder ist er ritter oder kneht?' " (Who is the man? . . . Is he a knight or a servant?) (Gottfried, 10766/9). Tristan answers: " 'vrouwe, swa vür irn geseht, er ist ein ritter unde ein man' " ("Lady, however, he looks, he is a knight and a liegeman") (ibid., 10770f.), and the chorus of ladies notes his fitness for polite society with the words: " 'a, saelic müezer iemer sin!' " ("Ah, may he always be happy!") (ibid., 10775). In the courtly society in Vienna people are discussing the newly dedicated companions of the shield [squires] and a lady is delighted "daz her Uolrich ist ritter hie warden . . . ich meine den von Liehtenstein" (that Lord Ulrich has become a knight here . . . I mean the one of Lichtenstein)

(Lichtenstein, *Frauendienst*, 44,f. and 8). Whoever bore the title of aristocratic knight belonged to aristocratic society.

But that is only one side of the matter. The initiation into knighthood had an unmistakable material side. In the ostentatious form of the courtly period, dedication to knighthood was an enormously costly production. A great festival was associated with it on every occasion, which often went on for days, and there was also the lodging and feeding of guests and the provision of expensive guests and the organization of a tournament in connection with the ceremony.[125] We know from historical sources that this delight in expenditure was not just poetry; the renowned court festival at Mainz in 1184, at which the sons of Friedrich Barbarossa were initiated, is only the best known example of a whole series. The glory of such a festival could only be enhanced if the largest possible number of young aristocrats took the blessing at the same time as the prince's son. The equipping of the squires was normally a matter for the promoter and the more expensive and fine it proved to be, the greater the reputation of the person who paid for it became. The young men received weapons, clothes, horses, and even cash. Willehalm boasts in front of the dying Vivianz: " 'ich gap hundert knappen swert durh dich . . . ich gap zwei hundert kastelân hundert den gesellen dîn mit harnasch, und diu künegîn ieslichem drier slahte kleit ûz ir sunderkamern sneit' " ("for your sake I gave a hundred squires their swords . . . I gave two hundred chargers to a hundred of your companions, with accoutrements and the queen tailored for each clothing of three kinds from her special store) (*Willehalm*, 63, 8f. and 10–14). The expense which King Sigebant undertook at the initiation of his son Hagen could hardly be exceeded: "sîn vater hiez in gâhen, daz er naeme swert mit hundert sînen helden: tûsent marke wert gaeb er ie vier gesellen vür ros und vür gewaete" (His father bade him hurry to be initiated with a hundred of his heroes; he gave the value of a thousand marks to four companions for horses and clothing) (*Kudrun*, 171, 1–3).[126] Thus many a "companion of the shield" [squire] was able to put himself into clothing such as his fathers and forefathers had never worn.[127] A special effect was produced when all the squires wore the same clothing as that of the prince's son. Thus Tristan, at his dedication to knighthood is "sînen gesellen ebengelich, ebenziere und ebenrich" (exactly like his companions, as decorative and as rich) (Gottfried, 4989f.).[128] But the poet lays great stress on the fact that the equality is external and does not affect their noble rank: "ich meine aber an der waete, die mannes hant da naete, niht an der an gebornen wat" (But I do mean the clothing sewn by human hands, not the clothing he was born with) (ibid., 4991–3). Nowhere are the squires made equal to the sons of princes by the act of dedication to knighthood. There was an obstacle to this which even the common concept of nobility could not overcome. After the initiation ceremony, they were called the *massenie* (entourage) of the young prince-knight (*Willehalm*, 63,19; Gottfried, 5014), his *cumpanie* (company) (Gottfried, 5130).[129] In the majority of cases there is no mention of a lasting relationship, but on a few occasions we do hear that a connection remained. After William of Brabant had taken the sword with a hundred companions, it is said "Sus was im ze ingesinde erkant Hundert ritter ze aller zit" (Thus a hundred knights were assigned to him as his household for ever) (Rudolf von Ems, *Willehalm*, 5786f.), and these knights accompany him later on his travels (5896ff.).[130] With this terminology—*ingesinde* (household), *massenie* (entourage) etc and especially in the equipping and clothing of the squires—we are almost back to the old service-knights and the distinction between the old unceremonious *ze ritter vazzen* (to take as knight) and the new ceremonial *ritter machen* (make into knight) fades into a fine shade of meaning. Indeed, in individual cases it often cannot be determined whether a man is called knight because he is in the service of a lord or because, as the squire of a lord he has taken the sword. At the lower fringe of the nobility the concept of aristocratic knighthood loses its significance, and it is certainly no accident that it is precisely these levels of society in the later Middle Ages who bore the title knight with particular pride, because they still shared in the aristocratic sense of the word by way of the mass inductions and they developed it further into a social-standing concept peculiar to themselves. But the distinction between the sons of princes, who received the sword, and the squires, who were permitted to participate, never disappeared. The title "knight" never had a socially distinctive or unifying meaning in the aristocratic sphere.

APPENDIX

1. Knightly Attributes

	ritter alt	Parz. 446, 10. Türlin Krone 29027
alter	*ritter*	Sächs. Weltchr. 262, 43. Holle Demant. 4429. 8400
		alter ritter wis: Holle Demant. 4734
	ritter arc	Thomasin 987
	ritter arm	Türlin Krone 16093
armer	*ritter*	Eilhart M 1ᵛ 13. Parz. 100, 29. 785, 7. Willeh. 72, 4. 428, 5. Sächs. Weltchr. 156, 21
		armer ritter guot: Thomasin 3779
	ritter balt	Nl. 926, 2. Zweter 221, 2. Holle Demant. 5759
barer	*ritter*	Türlin Krone 4250
bester	*ritter*	Erek 6844. Gregorius 2007. Lanzelet 329. 7921. 8020. Parz. 815, 18. Willeh. 229, 1. 291, 7. Wigalois 1237. 4010. 4795. 5823. Stricker Karl 212. 6270. 7289. Strikker Dan. 142. 360. 3530. 6327. Türlin Krone 5562. 16957. 18038. Ems Willeh. 7145. 7847. 7880. 7942. 14014. Holle Crane 3214. 3694. 3840
bezzerer	*ritter*	Lanzelet 2260. 8206. Parz. 750, 29. 771, 3. Willeh. 78, 17. Wigalois 577. 5602. 7946. Prosa-Lanz. M 410, 24f.

Stricker Karl 9610. Stricker Dan. 257. Türheim Renn.
12340. 12397. 21835. 25935. 29987. Holle Demant.
9932. Holle Crane 3211

ritter biderbe   Orendel 2583 [*r. b. und hêr*]. 3044 [*r. b. und junc*].
3068 [dito]. 3251 [*r. b. und hêr*]. Erek 4350 [*r. b. und
guot*]. Lanzelet 2506 [*r. b. und vrum*]. Kudrun 1088,
1

biderber   *ritter*   Prosa-Lanz. M 412, 15. Christoph. 65. Lichtenst. Frd.
1650, 4. 1673, 4

ritter blanc   Parz. 407. 12

blinder   *ritter*   Tagzeitengedicht 54

blôzer   *ritter*   Türlin Krone 4685

ritter edele   Kürnberg 8, 20. Dietmar 32, 21. Salman 279, 4. 775, 4.
Nl. 356, 1. 461, 2. 469, 1. 611, 2. 632, 2. 635, 1. 640, 4.
957, 1. 1188, 4 [*r. e. und guot*]. 1217, 4. 1347, 3 [*r. e.
biderbe und guot*]. 1907, 2. 1983, 2. 2146, 1. 2198, 4.
Gotfr. 10511 [*r. e. und ûz erkorn*]. Kudrun 121, 1. 478,
1. 511, 3. 583, 1 586, 2. 652, 1. 654, 4 [*r. e. und guot*].
1079, 1. 1247, 1. 1290, 1. 1337, 1. 1379, 1. 1622, 1.
Lichtenst. Frd. 256, 3 [*r. e. guot*]

edeler   *ritter*   Kaiserchr. 1140. Eneit 217, 33. Erek 957. 2694. 4785.
4803. 4989. 8030. 8813. 9325. Iwein 4930. Herbort
6549 11914. Lanzelet 6927. Morant 1802 [*e. r. und
rîche*]. 1948 [dito]. Nl. 32, 2. 836, 1. 1297, 3. 1535, 2.
1885, 4. Wigalois 423. 572. 1527. 2084. 2127. 2182.
2430. 3726. 4585. 5115. 5457. 6542. 7191. 9260. 10486.
Thomasin 1678. 7457. 7466. Sächs. Weltchr. 183, 29.
Türlin Krone 9601. 9934. 16945. 17584. 19532. 21868.
27819. Durne 1756. 2013. 2240. 5522. Stricker Dan. 311.
380. 2290. 2950. 3532. Ems Gerh. 1339. 1559. 3504.
4811. 6014. Ems Willeh. 8940. 13446. Türheim Renn.
13729. 18108. 18428. 30926. Zweter 48, 4 [*armer e. r.*].
265, 1. Lichtenst. Frd. 19, 4. 964, 5. 1318, 6. 1360, 6.
1503, 7. 1604, 2
edeler ritter balt: Nl. 969, 1
edeler ritter guot: Erek 898. Iwein 7393. Nl. 292, 3.
648, 2. 1069, 3. 1148, 1. 1405, 4. 1729, 3. 2114, 1.
Hz. Ernst B 228. Thomasin 7385. 7395. Ems Gerh.
5175. Kudrun 512, 1. 664, 3. 1161, 1. 1464, 1. 1484,
1. Türheim Renn. 203. 3681. 5050. 19358. Lichtenst.
Frd. 223, 7. 261, 2. 284, 8. 608, 6
edeler ritter hêr: Kudrun 1322, 3
edeler ritter hôchgemuot: Ems Gerh. 3295. 5832
edeler ritter klâr: Durne 4742
edeler ritter kluoc: Durne 1536
edeler ritter küene: Nl. 2293, 3
edeler ritter mære: Türlin Krone 18994
edeler ritter reine gemuot: Durne 2995
edeler ritter tiure: Halberstadt XXIV, 226
edeler ritter unervorht: Iwein 6730. Türheim Renn.
22515 [*e. r. vil unervorht*]
edeler ritter unverzaget: Türheim Renn. 22612
edeler ritter ûz erkorn: Türheim Renn. 31451
edeler ritter wert: Parz. 624, 14. Ems Willeh. 1480.
5720. Lichtenst. Frd. 1418, 6
edeler ritter wol bekleit: Ems Gerh. 664
edeler ritter wol geborn: Stricker Dan. 3178. Ems Alex.
8935

eigener   *ritter*   Lichtenst. Frd. 65, 5

einveltiger	*ritter*	Orendel 1123
	ritter ellende	Willeh. 267, 24. Türlin Krone 16062
	ritter ellens ríche	Parz. 802, 30
	ritter ellenthaft	Rubin XX, 2, 1. Holle Demant. 6191
ellenthafter	*ritter*	Ems Gerh. 6314
		ellenthafter ritter guot: Ems Gerh. 1533. Ems Willeh. 8893
elterer	*ritter*	Lanzelet 2046
	ritter êrbære	Türlin Krone 5809. 27223
êrbærer	*ritter*	Zweter 252, 10
	ritter êrlich	Rother 745. 2173. 2989. 3337. Oswald M. 1155. 1383. Holle Demant. 624
êrsamer	*ritter*	Christoph. 62
	ritter fier	Türlin Krone 3422
	ritter fin	Holle Crane 1510
geellenter	*ritter*	Türheim Renn. 28719
	ritter geêret	Wigalois 10419
	ritter gehiure	Türheim Renn. 170 [*r. vil g.*]
	ritter gemeit	Wien. Genesis 5061. Millst. Genesis 101, 29. Vor. Joseph 819. Kaiserchr. 4309 [*r. vil g.*]. Hochzeit 265. 305. Elmendorf 189. Eilhart 6435. Strassbg. Alex. 2211. Eneit 117, 4. 145, 33. 341, 14. Tnugdalus 43, 27. Hz. Ernst A I, 11. 17S. Hz. Ernst B 626. 1216. 2645 [*r. vil g.*]. 2831. Salman 359, 6 [*r. wol g.*]. 551, 2 [dito]. Herbort 1073. 4022. 17760. Lanzelet 2324. 3446. Nl. 79, 2 [*r. vil g.*]. 131, 2 [dito]. 153, 2 [dito]. 485, 2 [dito]. 707, 4. 722, 4. 1527, 4. 1713, 1 [*r. vil g.*]. Klage 394. Parz. 30, 8 [*r. vil g.*]. Wigalois 9266. Athis C* 38. Stricker Karl 2206. Stricker Dan. 1125. 2847. Holle Demant. 246. 304. 476. 2764. [*r. al g.*]. 2779. 3662. 5085. 6216. 7366. 8791. 8850. 10465. 10752. 10769. 11220. 11408. Holle Crane 1284. 1348. 1642. 4058. 4074. Lichtenst. Frd. 691, 3 [*r. vil g.*]
gemuoter	*ritter*	Türheim Renn. 4351
gerehter	*ritter*	Türheim Renn. 19693
gernder	*ritter*	Parz. 130, 6. Holle Demant. 4079 [Hs.: *gerne*] *êren gernder ritter*: Lichtenst. XXXVIII, 1, 1. Lichtenst. Frd. 1465, 7 *minne gernder ritter*: Türheim Renn. 31922
getageter	*ritter*	Prosa-Lanz. M 412, 15 [s. Lesart]
getoufter	*ritter*	Willeh. 425, 10
getriuwer	*ritter*	Lichtenst. Frd. 3. Büchl. 230
getriuwerer	*ritter*	Türheim Renn. 28889
getühtiger	*ritter*	Lanzelet 9023
gewâfeneter	*ritter*	Elmendorf 720. Sächs. Weltchr. 197, 2. Türlin Krone 4506. Pr. Schönbach III, 166, 18 [*wol g. r.*]
	ritter gewære	Gotfr. 8586
gewisser	*ritter*	Türlin Krone 15815
gewundeter	*ritter*	Holle Demant. 8142
gezimierter	*ritter*	Lichtenst. Frd. 1420, 7
grüener	*ritter*	Lanzelet 2961. 2978. 2990. 3010. 3106
	ritter grâ	Parz. 448, 1 [*r. g. gevar*]. 455, 24
grâwer	*ritter*	Parz. 446, 23. 447, 13 *grâwer ritter wert*: Parz. 514, 11
	ritter guot	Kaiser Heinr. 4, 27. Dietmar 39, 4. Eilhart 5059. 5817. 8828. Strassbg. Alex. 1716. Oswald W. 502. Eneit 24, 3. 113, 25. 181, 12. 191, 13. 243, 21 [*r. vil g.*]. 251, 9. Erek 2129. 2423. 4442. 4738 [*r. vil g.*]. 5776 [*r. alsô g.*]. 6946. 7960. 8482. Gregorius 2013. Lanzelet 5454.

		7975 [r. alsô g.]. Nl. 206, 4. 624, 2. 768, 2. 1167, 3. 1472, 3. 1486, 2. 1632, 1. 1647, 3. 1669, 3. Parz. 89, 17. 123, 21. 769, 13. 822, 13. Willeh. 76, 6 [r. als g.]. 348, 17. 389, 22. 443, 21. Wigalois 587. 2106. 6248. 6599. 7933. 8724. 9024. 9896. Thomasin 346. 3649. 7380. 8695. 8721. Stricker Karl 315. 3075. 3825 [r. alsô g.]. 4861. Stricker Dan. 906. 2909. 6323 [r. sô g.]. Türlin Krone 10711. 12302. 15954. 20304. 21035. 26917. Kudrun 196, 1. 420, 1. 549, 3. 966, 4. 969, 2. 1334, 2. 1405, 2. 1416, 1. 1449, 2. 1495, 1. 1513, 4. 1538, 2. Ems Willeh. 10743. 14695. Türheim Renn. 3277. 24513. 29813. Holle Demant. 664. 878. 3894. 4418 [r. alsô g.]. 5436. 7928. Lichtenst. Frd. 184, 5. 202, 2. 205, 5. 221, 5. 235, 8. 246, 3. 248, 3. 250, 8. 252, 2. 301, 7. 365, 1. 614, 7. 642, 1. 648, 7. 661, 3. 726, 1. 798, 5. 920, 4. 989, 1. 1013, 5. 1014, 3. 1061, 3. 1065, 5. 1352, 2. 1426, 3. 1438, 3. 1470, 1. 1479, 2. 1495, 8. 1521, 8
guoter	ritter	Kaiserchr. 4572. Regensburg 16, 2. Orendel 188. Erek 745. 2357. 4156. 4337. Gregorius 1565. Iwein 42. 2453. 5345. 7292. Herbort 3186. 14334. Lanzelet 2009. 2627 [g. r. und vrum]. 3429. Nl. 16, 4. 253, 4. 506, 1. 1354, 3. 2303, 2. 2364, 2. Parz. 768, 17. Willeh. 108, 11. Wigalois 3418. 7942. 8428. Thomasin 3832f. Prosa-Lanz. A II, 1. Sächs. Weltchr. 114, 9. 116, 17. 146, 20. Stricker Karl 4293. 6536. 6647. 9731. Stricker Dan. 280. 317. 3082. 3569. 4741. 4746. 7586. Türlin Krone 4570. 22612. Kudrun 647, 2. 1091, 4 1117, 1. 1147, 4. 1195, 4. 1410, 3. 1429, 4. 1466, 4. Lichtenst. Frd. 297, 3. 1498, 7. Lichtenst. Frd. 2. Büchl. 341. Pr. Schönbach I, 143, 10 [frevel und g. r.]
		guoter ritter gemeit· Nl. 146, 4. 861, 4
		guoter ritter wert: Freidank 93, 7
heimelicher	ritter	Pr. Schönbach I, 332, 5
	ritter hêr	Salman 177, 3. Nl. 1573, 1
	ritter hêrlich	Rother 131. Orendel 298. Eneit 144, 5. 191, 24. Stricker Karl 480
	ritter hôchgeborn	Salman 513, 2. Türheim Renn. 21976. 30412. Holle Demant. 912. 1583. 2446. Holle Crane 4277
	ritter hôchgemuot	Nl. 1815, 1. Türheim Renn. 5745. 19453. Rubin XX, 1, 5. Holle Demant. 9994. Lichtenst. Frd. 322, 6. 700, 8. 806, 1. 905, 1. 1527, 8. 1550, 3. 1574, 6. Lichtenst. Frb. 595, 18. 611, 9
hôchgemuoter	ritter	Ems Willeh. 6178. Lichtenst. XLIV, 1, 6. Lichtenst. Frd. 77, 7. 543, 2. 1050, 7
hovelicher	ritter	Ems Gerh. 4860
	ritter hövisch	Herbort 880 [r. h. und guot]. Ems Willeh. 1072 [r. h. und wert]
hövischer	ritter	Kürnberg 7, 21. Morant 2602. Lanzelet 1257. Gotfr. 10764. Stricker Dan. 6557. Lichtenst. Frd. 1484, 7
	ritter junc	Vor. Alex. 925. Orendel 443. 3138. Parz. 227, 18 [r. j. und alt]. 512, 29. Obdt. Servat. 2988. Stricker Dan. 6834. Holle Demant. 481 [r. j. und gemeit]. 4182. 4188. Holle Crane 2591. 3891
junger	ritter	Eilhart 527. Morant 5371. 5410. Lanzelet 820. 1084. 1244. 1896. 2938. Walther 24, 4. Athis C* 31. Wigalois 1801. 1912. 2300. 2785. 2950. 3016. 3074. 3116. 3237. 4040. 4797. 4863. 8459. 9371. Willeh. 357, 8. Holle Demant. 4171. 6901. Lichtenst. Frd. 1178, 4. Pr. Schönbach I, 120, 30

		junger ritter balt: Holle Demant 3860. Holle Crane 1398. 3000. 3474
		junger ritter vrum: Holle Demant. 2817
		junger ritter wis: Holle Demant. 3009 [*j. r. und w.*]. 3947 [dito]. 9124. 9270
kindischer	*ritter*	Herbort 5420
	ritter klâr	Parz. 604, 9. Durne 229. 3517. Türheim Renn. 32361
klârer	*ritter*	Parz. 639, 23. 722, 12
	ritter klein	Holle Demant. 7513. 7561. 9612
	ritter kluoc	Parz. 72, 26. 210, 19. 231, 15. Willeh. 394, 6
	ritter küene	Nl. 119, 4 [*r. k. und gemeit*]. 149, 4 [dito]. 203, 4 [*r. k. und guot*]. 230, 4 [dito]. 391, 4 [*r. k. und balt*]. 553, 1. 991, 4 [*r. k. und gemeit*]. 1718, 4 [dito]. 1759, 4 [*r. k. und guot*]. 2219, 4 [dito]. 2336, 4. Stricker Karl 1209. Kudrun 1620, 1. Holle Demant. 796 [*r. k. und wis*]
küener	*ritter guot*	Nl. 902, 2
	ritter kurtois	Parz. 593, 12. 632, 16. 753, 29. 797, 14. Willeh. 411, 18. Durne 1320
lieber	*ritter*	Sächs. Weltchr. 130, 10. Lichtenst. Frd. 1267, 7
	ritter lieht gemâl	Parz. 723, 23
	ritter lobelich	Nl. 552, 1. Kudrun 1663, 4. Holle Demant. 1046. Lichtenst. Frd. 253, 3. 286, 1. 907, 5
	ritter lobesam	Salman 68, 3. 160, 2. 163, 3. 180, 2. 191, 3. 194, 2. 196, 2. 198, 2. 202, 3. 212, 1. 297, 2. 640, 2. 644, 2. 712, 3. Orendel 1173. Strassbg. Alex. 1762. Herbort 13892
	ritter lustsam	Rother 1484 [Hs. H]. 2434 [*r. alsô l.*]. 2673. 2966. 3066. 3212. Eneit 135, 40. 147, 17. Wigalois 5044
mähtiger	*ritter*	Thomasin 7911
	ritter manhaft	Erek 8476 [*r. sô m.*]. Stricker Karl 1248. 5786
manlicher	*ritter*	Willeh. 304, 4
	ritter manlich getân	Parz. 763, 24
	ritter mære	Türlin Krone 8900 [*r. alsô m.*]
	ritter milde	Herbort 4009
	ritter minnehaft	Lanzelet 1826
müeder	*ritter*	Parz. 83, 4
	ritter muotes rich	Lichtenst. Frd. 599, 6. 1579, 6
offenbærer	*ritter*	Pr. Schönbach I, 332, 3
pfaflicher	*ritter*	Walther 80, 21
rehter	*ritter*	Herbort 13949
	ritter reine	Türheim Trist. 517, 25. Türheim Renn. 32432
reiner	*ritter*	Lichtenst. Frd. 1430, 6
		reiner ritter junc: Türheim Renn. 8472 [*edel r. r. j.*]
	ritter riche	Holle Demant. 717. 1442. 2605. 3340. 4534. 5630. 5738. 8126. 9348. 11205. Holle Crane 246. 1432. 1928. 4098. 4498
	ritter ritterlich	Lichtenst. Frd. 1493, 7 [*r. r. gemuot*]. 1528, 3
	ritter rôt	Parz. 170, 3. 176, 20. 206, 16. 218, 4. 221, 6. 276, 21. 280, 9. 305, 11. 309, 16. 315, 11. 383, 24 [*r. allenthalben r.*]. 388, 8. 392, 20. Türlin Krone 14209
rôter	*ritter*	Lanzelet 3282. 3291. 3334. 3381. Parz. 145, 16. 170, 6. 202, 21. 276, 4. 278, 25. 307, 18. 389, 4. 389, 29. Wigalois 2592. 2671. 2755. 2936
sæliger	*ritter*	Türheim Renn. 5112
		sæliger ritter guot: Türheim Renn. 13648. 20713. 31409
		sæliger ritter unverzaget: Türheim Renn. 31033
		sæliger ritter vil stæte: Türheim Renn. 13552
	ritter schæne	Holle Crane 2578
schæner	*ritter*	Kürnberg 10, 21. Lanzelet 6275. Wigalois 261

		schœner ritter brûnvar: Herbort 3174
		schœner ritter starc: Türlin Krone 26388
schœnerer	*ritter*	Rother 2048. Holle Demant. 8140
schœnster	*ritter*	Walther 80, 36. Holle Crane 4434
	ritter snel	Nl. 503, 2. Parz. 174, 10. 354, 19. Willeh. 425, 14. Craun 941
sneller	*ritter*	Nl. 757, 2
		sneller ritter balt: Kudrun 355, 1
		sneller ritter gemeit: Nl. 1900, 4
		sneller ritter guot: Nl. 1566, 1. Kudrun 1390, 4
		sneller ritter lobesam: Nl. 379, 4
	ritter starc	Morant 2996 [*r. wol s.*]. Nl. 891, 2
starker	*ritter*	Parz. 174, 18
	ritter stolz	Eilhart 561 [*r. alsô s.*]. Eneit 184, 38. Gr. Rudolf δ 6. Athis A* 86. Neidhart 20, 32. (XLVI, 6). Kudrun 115, 2 [*r. s. und guot*]. Türheim Renn. 2010. 23486. Holle Crane 3892 [*r. s. gemeit*]. Lichtenst. Frd. 954, 4
stolzer	*ritter*	Salman 20, 4. 66, 4. 74, 4. 540, 5. Orendel 352. Strassbg. Alex. 1718. Lanzelet 2402. 2503. 3790. Walther 124, 25. Wigalois 8940. Athis A* 128f. Neidhart 27, 22. Kudrun 1696, 4
		stolzer ritter balt: Salman 275, 1
		stolzer ritter gemeit: Orendel 1025
		stolzer ritter guot: Nl. 949, 1. 1214, 2. 1531, 1
		stolzer ritter hêr: Salman 48, 3
		stolzer ritter hôchgemuot: Ems Gerh. 5946
		stolzer ritter junc: Orendel 321
		stolzer ritter klâr: Holle Crane 1418
		stolzer ritter lobesam: Salman 650, 6
		stolzer ritter ûz erkorn: Holle Demant. 251
		stolzer ritter ûz gelesen: Holle Demant. 10176
		stolzer ritter vrum: Holle Demant. 1404. 10696. Holle Crane 1443
		stolzer ritter wert: Ems Gerh. 3601. Ems Willch. 6620. Türheim Renn. 22496 [*s. r. vil. w.*]
		stolzer ritter wis: Holle Demant 1909 [*s. r. und w.*]
süezer	*ritter reine*	Türheim Trist. 552, 16. Türheim Renn. 10148 [*s. r. vil r.*]
	ritter swarz	Türlin Krone 19124
	ritter tiure	Türlin Krone 21256
tiurer	*ritter*	Holle Demant. 6464
tiurerer	*ritter*	Türheim Renn. 23613. 28891. 29178
tiurester	*ritter*	Lanzelet 2736. Wigalois 1676. Türheim Renn. 22058
	ritter tôt	Parz. 249, 16
tôter	*ritter*	Wigalois 5866. Türlin Krone 14019
	ritter tugende vol	Türlin Krone 26557
	ritter tugenthaft	Türlin Krone 21181
	ritter tugentlich	Hz. Ernst B 1905 [*r. vil t.*]
übeler	*ritter*	Holle Demant. 2509
	ritter unervorht	Willeh. 370, 24. Durne 424. Stricker Dan. 2965. Türheim Renn. 29851. 31048
	ritter ungehiure	Holle Demant. 4692
	ritter unkunt	Lanzelet 611 .Türlin Krone 11806
	ritter unverzaget	Wigalois 10801. Türheim Renn. 8407. 13529. Holle Demant. 6885
unverzageter	*ritter guot*	Willeh. 360, 21
	ritter ûz erkorn	Herbort 13105. Nl. 73, 2. 876, 3. 2149, 2. Parz. 632, 25. Wigalois 10795. Kudrun 1302, 1. 1488, 1

ûz erkorner	*ritter*	Herbort 4789f.
	ritter ûz erwelt	Herbort 3998. Lanzelet 3132. 3298. 8356. Wigalois 10678. Stricker Karl 7286. Ems Willeh. 5710. Türheim Renn. 28637
	ritter ûz gekorn	Holle Demant. 7922
	ritter ûz gelesen	Holle Demant. 10739
	ritter ûz gesondert	Ems Willeh. 704
	ritter vermezzen	Priest. Wernher 1412 [*r. vil v.*]. Tundalus 90 [*r. wol v.*]. Herbort 14350 [dito]. Lanzelet 681. Türheim Renn. 8146 [*r. vil. v.*]. Holle Demant. 6250. 8248 [*r. sô v.*]
	ritter verwâfenet	Orendel 306
	ritter viurîn	Parz. 812, 20
	ritter volkomen	Iwein 1459 [*r. alsô v.*]
volmüeter	*ritter*	Gotfr. 10844
vorderer	*ritter*	Pr. Schönbach I, 279, 24
	ritter vrech	Durne 5985. Türheim Renn. 29811
vremeder	*ritter*	Rother 2487. Lanzelet 1906. 2427. 2658. 2799. 2941. 3398. 4659. Parz. 368, 17. 373, 19. Türlin Krone 7008. Holle Demant. 1734. 1901. 1971. 2839. 10266. 10422. Holle Crane 2621 *vremeder ritter rôt*: Ems Willeh. 11077
	ritter vreuden rîch	Lichtenst. Frb. 596, 1
vreveler	*ritter*	Sächs. Weltchr. 137, 5
	ritter vrum	Holle Demant. 330. 580. 701. 1644. 2140. 2752. 5318. 5404. Holle Crane 410. 1354. 1817
vrumeger	*ritter*	Vor. Alex. 156
vrumer	*ritter*	Salman 216, 5. Arm. Heinr. 1340. Iwein 1828. Herbort 119. Lanzelet 1059. Wigalois 1758. 3873. 4157. 5601. Thomasin 14695. Stricker Dan. 5349. Türlin Krone 2239. 14724. 17759. 20270. 21547. 21647. Türheim Renn. 22387
	ritter wæhe	Stricker Dan. 653
werder	*ritter*	Parz. 163, 18. 237, 4. 309, 27. 330, 7. 396, 4. 619, 18. 623, 4. 647, 4. 648, 15. 666, 24. Willeh. 139, 20. 263, 27. 312, 4. Durne 2056. Kudrun 803, 4. Ems Gerh. 574. 3508. 3941. 5358. Ems Willeh. 668. 1216. 2120. 2234. 3045. 7162. 7214. 7750. 7931. 10017. 13224. Ems Alex. 2824. Türheim Trist. 512, 3. 517, 4. Türheim Renn. 3709. 6022. 12382. 19419. 30529. 30536. 32110. Holle Demant. 3944. 7270. Lichtenst. Frd. 157, 7. 1311, 5. Lichtenst. Frb. 650, 6 *werder ritter fier*: Türheim Renn. 23449 *werder ritter gemeit*: Ems Gerh. 5941 [*w. r. vil g.*]. Holle Demant. 2571 *werder ritter guot*: Oswald M. 2042. Parz. 378, 30. Ems Willeh. 661. 10798. 10937. 14535. Türheim Renn. 26064. Holle Demant. 986. 2667. 3834. 5640. 5984. 11402 *werder ritter hôchgeborn*: Holle Demant. 2454. 8163 *werder ritter hôchgemuot*: Ems Barl. 287, 9. Türheim Renn. 13856. Holle Demant. 6257 *werder ritter kluoc*: Türheim Renn. 26260 [*reiner w. r. k.*] *werder ritter reine*: Holle Crane 1691 *werder ritter rîche*: Holle Demant. 4948. 6518 *werder ritter unverzaget*: Ems Willeh. 11431. Ems Alex. 7079. Türheim Renn. 31406. Holle Demant. 1249. 2580

werder ritter ûz erkorn: Ems Gerh. 1740. Holle Crane
    2532
werder ritter vrum: Holle Demant. 3620. Holle Crane
    2650. 3769. 4501 [stolzer w. r. v.]

werlicher	ritter guot	Parz. 376, 3. Willeh. 397, 3
	ritter wert	Morant 293. 3616. 5362. Parz. 203, 27. 318, 13. 682, 30 [r. w. erkant]. 768, 22 [dito]. Willeh. 143, 16. 238, 18. Thomasin 7753. 8671. Singenberg 9, 25. Christoph. 1143 [r. w. erkant]. Ems Gerh. 6075. Ems Willeh. 691. 11254 [r. w. und unverzaget]. 13871. Ems Alex. 11670. 18719 [r. w. erkant]. Türheim Trist. 579, 39. Türheim Renn. 11860. 21801. 23935. 25297. 25533. 25632. Lichtenst. Frd. 622, 7. 635, 1
	ritter wise	Türheim Renn. 14642. Holle Crane 3971
wiser	ritter	Parz. 678, 6. Holle Demant. 4989
	ritter wite erkant	Ems Gerh. 3644. Ems Willeh. 5897. 7533
wizer	ritter	Lanzelet 3095. 3118. 3182. 3207. 3217
	ritter wol bekant	Herbort 3993. Parz. 48, 23. Lichtenst. Frd. 251, 2. 291, 8. 712, 8
	ritter wol bekleit	Lanzelet 8858. Lichtenst. Frd. 850, 2 [r. w. gekleit]
	ritter wol bereit	Herbort 1479. Ems Alex. 3422. 11747
	ritter wol geborn	Eneit 311, 1. Wigalois 11288. Ebernant 1300. Holle Demant. 275
	ritter wol gelêrt	Herbort 14939 [r. harte w. g.]
	ritter wol gemuot	Lanzelet 972. 3329. 7497. Türheim Renn. 14419 [r. baz g.]. Winterstetten XIII, 1, 2. XXVIII, 1, 8. Lichtenst. Frd. 341, 6. 1581, 8 [r. baz g.]
	ritter wol gesluht	Dietmar 40, 5
	ritter wol gestalt	Holle Demant. 1510
	ritter wol getân	Eneit 241, 4. 337, 7. Lanzelet 5371. 5485. 8573. Nl. 328, 2. Klage 502. Holle Demant. 3615. Holle Crane 1170. 3847
	ritter wol gevar	Parz. 120, 25 [r. nâch wunsche var]. 361, 23. 669, 17
	ritter wol gezogen	Lanzelet 1762
wunder	ritter	Parz. 522, 26. Türlin Krone 9612. 13320
wünneclicher	ritter alt	Parz. 794, 2
	ritter wunt	Parz. 138, 30. 517, 4. 521, 20. 522, 11. Willeh. 431, 27. 439, 8 [r. sêre w.]. Türlin Krone 9573. Türheim Renn. 23982. 30199
	ritter zage	Thomasin 985
	ritter zart	Holle Crane 3454
zierer	ritter guot	Nl. 809, 4

2. The Adjective "Knightly" (Ritterlich)

ambet	Lichtenst. Frd. 757, 1
aneblic	Erek 7847
anekomen	Tirol F 7, 1
antpfanc	Lichtenst. Frd. 663, 7. 823, 1
arebeit	Willeh. 287, 24. Lichtenst. Frd. 150, 3. 220, 7. 235, 5. 290, 7. 292, 6. 295, 8. 398, 5. 556, 3. 831, 7. 872, 3. 920, 7. 963, 8. 1098, 5. Lichtenst. Frd. 1. Büchl. 168
art	Ems Gerh. 4949. Ems Willeh. 7495. Ems Alex. 3424. 10811. 21230
bein	Titurel 134, 2. Flore 6854
bejac	Türlin Krone 20289
bruoderschaft	Parz. 470, 19
burc	Parz. 534, 24
buhurt	Ems Gerh. 6038
degen	Priest. Wernher 1549

dienest	Lichtenst. Frd. 466, 7
dinc	Herbort 14676. Ems Gerh. 3662. Ems Willeh. 6777. Ems Alex. 4692. 12689. Zweter 114, 11. Lichtenst. Frb. 643, 17. 648, 15
ê	Nl. 33, 3
eit	Durne 4873. 4890. Ems Willeh. 2441. 11699
ende	Willeh. 88, 11. 354, 15. Stricker Karl 4707. Ems Alex. 12114
êre	Erek 2499. Iwein 6953. Herbort 14366. 16528. Türlin Krone 3737. 16064. 16134. Ems Willeh. 5879. Türheim Clig. 57. Türheim Renn. 19300. 27857. 28901
gâbe	Thomasin 14596
galopeiz	Willeh. 32, 11. Türheim Renn. 27566 [*walopiere*]
gast	Halberstadt XII, 30
gebærde	Roland 8006. Rother 1366. Lanzelet 2016. Lichtenst. Frd. 816, 8
gebâren	Ems Alex. 21138f.
gedanc	Türlin Krone 26697
gedranc	Ems Willeh. 5799
gelâz	Willeh. 33, 13
gemach	Lichtenst. Frd. 482, 3. 912, 1
gemüete	Parz. 431, 9. 474, 29. Willeh. 342, 14
ger	Gregorius 1622. Wigalois 10199. Willeh. 23, 21. Stricker Dan. 3486. Ems Willeh. 6487. Lichtenst. Frd. 1431, 5
gereite	Franciskus 474. 498
geschehen	Türlin Krone 2955
gesellecheit	Parz. 308, 29
getât	Durne 4992. Ems Willeh. 7091. Türheim Renn. 27576
gewant	Roland 5577. Rother 203. 1824. Nl. 66, 1
gewin	Wigalois 574. 2512. 3087. 3368
geziuge	Kudrun 1103, 4
gezoc	Lichtenst. Frd. 749, 1. 1005, 8
güete	Ems Willeh. 1689
guft	Ems Willeh. 7216
hantgetât	Türlin Krone 10691
heil	Ems Willeh. 1282
helt	Stricker Karl 3073. 9268
her	Ems Gerh. 5828
hövescheit	Herbort 12573
ingesinde	Christoph. 116
juncvrouwe	Strassbg. Alex. 6048
kleit	Lichtenst. Frd. 770, 4
komen	Willeh. 197, 18
kraft	Parz. 746, 16. Kudrun 582, 3. Ems Gerh. 3570. Ems Willeh. 719. 1277. 5628. 6352. 7139. 7257. 7461. 7636. 8389. 8437. 13272. 13865. Ems Alex. 12249. 12348. 17861. 18717. Ems Weltchr. 28751. Türheim Renn. 20246. Lichtenst. Frd. 590, 4. Lichtenst. Frb. 599, 16
kriegen	Türheim Renn. 22802
kür	Türheim Renn. 8368
lant	Parz. 478, 28
leben	Parz. 823, 19. Wigalois 2341. Gotfr. 5067. Ems Willeh. 12210. Ems Alex. 1408. Türheim Trist. 589, 13. Lichtenst. XXVII, 6, 4. Lichtenst. Frd. 1178, 8
lêre	Ems Alex. 7060
liet	Lichtenst. Frd. 1424, 8
lip	Stricker Dan. 4679
list	Stricker Karl 5538
lôn	Ems Alex. 6990. 11708. 12517
lust	Holle Demant. 3517. Holle Crane 953
maget	Iwein 387. Kudrun 14, 1
maht	Ems Gerh. 5978
man	Gotfr. 11101. Stricker Dan. 1935
manheit	Wigalois 3429. Ems Alex. 12289. Holle Demant. 9177
mære	Parz. 504, 26

muot	Gregorius 2014. Iwein 3581. Gotfr. 1682. Thomasin 7768 [*unritterlich*]. 11361. Stricker Karl 3076. 4878. 4888. 7851. Ems Willeh. 972. 6772. Türheim Renn. 3278. Lichtenst. Frd. 415, 4. 593, 8. 851, 8. 880, 7 [*unritterl.*]. 1388, 3. 1425, 8. 1589, 7 [*unritterl.*]
name	Halberstadt X, 442. Gotfr. 4409. Ems Willeh. 5613. 9203. Türheim Trist. 577, 17. Türheim Renn. 2402. 3037. 3281
orden	Türheim Renn. 6044
pflege	Türlin Krone 4272
prîs	Parz. 108, 26. 133, 9. 195, 3. 255, 27. Willeh. 22, 17. 48, 7. Gotfr. 1029. 4427. 5025. Craun 19. Türlin Krone 8898. Kudrun 471, 3. Ems Willeh. 677. 814. 933. 1176. 5852. 7765. 11022. 11383. Ems Alex. 7629. 11736. 12939. 17922. 20306. 21216. Ems Weltchr. 20276. Türheim Trist. 516, 22. Türheim Renn. 2103. 5052. 12723. 14641. 14780. 23729. Lichtenst. Frd. 3. Büchl. 238
puneiz	Ems Alex. 2204. Lichtenst. Frd. 262, 8. 1060, 1
reht	Wigalois 2332. Gotfr. 11205. Ems Gerh. 3549. Ems Willeh. 3490
rîcheit	Ems Willeh. 10987
ritter-	Ems Willeh. 5990 [*ritters site*]. Ems Alex. 11992 [*ritters lôn*]. Lichtenst. Frd. 645, 4 [*ritters spil*]. 1528, 3
ritterschaft	Lichtenst. Frd. 295, 5. 338, 1
ruom	Herbort 16708. Wigalois 9174. 11019. 11174. Türheim Renn. 12878
sache	Ems Willeh. 6358
sælecheit	Lanzelet 2618
sarwât	Türlin Krone 17033
schal	Erek 1519. 2374. Wigalois 9328. Ems Willeh. 3065. 9552
schande	Türlin Krone 3889
schar	Herbort 14412. Flore 221. Stricker Karl 9284. Türlin Krone 18856. Ems Gerh. 3458. 5958. Ems Willeh. 3672. Ems Alex. 6952. Türheim Trist. 507, 4. Türheim Renn. 2659. 3354. 5004. 5715. 7160. 7694. 8064. 17302. 19452. 23220. 26314. 27384. Lichtenst. Frd. 822, 6
schehen	Türlin Krone 876
schilt	Erek 2303
schimpf	Ems Alex. 1863
schîn	Türlin Krone 26855
schœnheit	Gotfr. 13113. Ems Alex. 17632
sic	Türlin Krone 20319
sicherheit	Parz. 15, 12. 198, 25. Ems Willeh. 481. 1482. 11422
sin	Parz. 204, 19. Stricker Karl 9419. Ems Willeh. 7670. Ems Alex. 15335
site	Oswald M. 1496. 2721. Strassbg. Alex. 430. Iwein 2815. 3560. Nl. 1307, 3. Parz. 173, 13. Wigalois 8430. 9027. 9564. 11068. 11419. Gotfr. 701. 2111. Stricker Karl 11149. Kudrun 708, 2. Stricker Dan. 656. Ems Gerh. 3583. 4989. Ems Willeh. 3063. 3477. 5715. 6716. 11959. 14862. Ems Alex. 2215. 3693. 3749. 7185. 7193. 15247. 21203. Ems Weltchr. 33097. Türheim Renn. 6056. Holle Demant. 2316. Lichtenst. Frd. 209, 1. 268, 6. 532, 6. 635, 3. 645, 2. 767, 4. 769, 5. 873, 6. 962, 8. 1064, 8. 1527, 4
slac	Iwein 7344
slihte	Ems Willeh. 14962
solt	Flore 502
spil	Kaiserchr. 4350. Wigalois 9796. Ems Gerh. 4888. Durne 1176. Türlin Krone 18033. Stricker Dan. 674. Türheim Renn. 29594
stæte	Lichtenst. XXV, 67. Lichtenst. Frd. 1619, 7. Lichtenst. Frb. 595, 7
stætecheit	Lichtenst. Frd. 424, 2
strît	Erek 1751. Wigalois 7639. Thomasin 7444
swanc	Lichtenst. Frd. 300, 6
tagalt	Obdt. Servat. 981
tât	Halberstadt XXX, 84. Parz. 510, 11. 559, 2. 695, 5. 768, 11. Willeh. 22, 15. 37, 12. 102, 9. 268, 27. 329, 17. 349, 5. Türlin Krone 27424. Ems Barl. 217, 7. Ems Willeh. 7831. Türheim Renn. 8413. 23453. 23505. 27838. 31428. Lichtenst. Frd. 207, 3. 426, 2. 575, 5. 919, 3. 1445, 5. 1849, 3. Lichtenst. Frd. Br. I, 115, 21
tjoste	Lanzelet 4472. Willeh. 27, 11. Lichtenst. Frd. 1547, 6
tôt	Wigalois 7950. Willeh. 344, 25

triuwe	Parz. 631, 20. Stricker Karl 9195. Stricker Dan. 4191. Türlin Krone 15587
tugent	Iwein 3258. Ems Willeh. 2621
tûre	Otte 5083
turnieren	Tirol 29, 5. Zweter 106, 1
vart	Erek 2489. Parz. 497, 15. Türheim Renn. 10837. Lichtenst. Frd. 462, 5. 471, 2. 982, 3. 1058, 4
velle	Türlin Krone 8960. 18262
vreude	Wigalois 9778. Ems Willeh. 14749
vrouwe	Hartmann 216, 32
vuore	Parz. 51, 6
wâpenkleit	Lichtenst. Frd. 1521, 4
wârheit	Ems Willeh. 13408
wât	Salman 11, 4. 12, 4. Gregorius 1559
wec	Lichtenst. Frd. Br. I, 217, 18
werc	Parz. 787, 25. Herbort 13938. Stricker Dan. 1496. Lichtenst. Frd. 190, 4. 1550, 2
werdecheit	Parz. 24, 17. Gotfr. 4411. 5087. Ems Gerh. 3904. 5842. Ems Willeh. 42. 170. 1062. 12093. 14852. Ems Alex. 2520. 12050. 12492
were	Nl. 2106, 2. Wigalois 7811. 10327. 10727. 11044. Franciskus 501. Ems Willeh. 6723. Ems Alex. 2338. 2856. 4999. 11723. 12016. 12389. 18636. 21170. Ems Weltchr. 30718. Türheim Renn. 23047. 23584. 24197. 31246. Holle Demant. 897. 8959
wip	Erek 1707. 3324. Iwein 6135. Lanzelet 978
wirde	Ems Willeh. 5864
wirtschaft	Ems Gerh. 5970
wise	Stricker Karl 5574. 9890. Ems Willeh. 14162
wort	Türheim Renn. 29608
zierheit	Gotfr. 4616
zuht	Nl. 371, 3
zunft	Parz. 122, 17

VI. The Knightly Class

When we speak of chivalric poetry, we mean in the first instance that the knightly class was the main support of the new literature. The Middle Ages had two expressions to designate the class, *orden* or *reht*.[1] It was not until the fifteenth century that the German word "Stand" took on the sense familiar to us "the designation of elements of the Empire which have a right to a share in the government" and still later "a designation of social rank."[2] The first extant evidence for *Ritterstand* (knightly class) is in the *Zimmerische Chronik*.[3] Before this, the German words *orden, ambet, art, ê, leben, name, reht*, etc. (order, office, class, honor, life, title, right) correspond to the Latin concepts *gradus, status, ordo, conditio* (rank, status, order, condition), etc. According to this, we should seek the linguistic manifestation of the knightly class of the High Middle Ages in the expressions *ritters orden* (order of knights), *ritters leben* (knights' life), *ritters reht* (knights' right), etc. A search through the evidence[4] immediately reveals that scarcely one of these expressions goes back into the twelfth century. The first instance of *ritters ambet* is in Thomasin von Zirklaere, of *ritters art, ritters leben*, and *ritters orden* in Wolfram von Eschenbach's *Parzival*. *Ritters reht* does go back to the eighties of the twelfth century, to Hartmann's *Erek*. The oldest and by far the most frequent formation is "ritters name." The first instances are in *König Rother* and in the *Kaiserchronik*. These, the oldest instances, are also the most interesting, because here the title "knight" still has a concrete meaning. In the *Kaiserchronik* it is said of King Constantine: "der kunic rihte sînen hof . . . : umbe herzogen unt umbe grâven unt alle di under in wâren, umbe alle rîteres namen, wi ir leben solte sîn getân . . .'' (the king organized his court . . . how it should be with the lives of the dukes, the counts and all those under them, with all those with the title of knight . . .) (8100, 02–05). Here, however, *name* does not mean "rank," "dignity," or "social standing," but is a periphrasis for a person, like *wîbes name* for *wîp, mannes name* for *man*.[5] The knights mentioned here are the old service-knights, who are *undertân* (subject to) lords and counts. The first instances of *ritters namen hân* also apply

107

to this group. Duke Adelger sends a message to all his men "swelhe lêhenreht wolten haben oder ritteres namen" (who desired to have feudal rights or the title of knight) (*Kaiserchronik*, 6800f.). From the beginning there is something distinctive in *ritters namen hân*, in this case, the distinction of being part of the entourage of a highly placed lord, and it is certainly no accident that we seldom encounter this expression in the sphere of the service-knights and then only outside truly courtly poetry.[6] From the time of Hartmann's *Erek* it is there reserved for aristocratic knighthood and is there connected with the ceremonial initiation in the formulation *ritters namen gewinnen*.[7] Where this concrete connection is not present, *ritters namen hân* means simply "to be a member of aristocratic society." The hero of the courtly romances is, at various times, *der aller tiureste, der höfschste, der küeneste, der schoeneste, der tugende rîcheste, der werdeste man, der ritters namen ie gewan* (the most precious, the most courtly, the bravest, the one richest in good qualities, the most worthy, who ever had the title of knight).[8] The noble lord bears *ritters namen* as an ethical obligation; the frequent rhyme with *schamen* is an indication of this.[9] Before an assembled court, Lunete declares Iwein to be " 'vür einen triuwelôsen man . . . und mac sich der künec iemer schamen, hât er iuch mëre in rîters namen, sô liep im triuwe und êre ist' " ("a faithless man . . . and the king may be ashamed for ever if he regards you as a knight any more, so long as loyalty and honor are dear to him") (*Iwein*, 3183, 87–9). There is no question here of birth or descent. It is simply that, in aristocratic circles, only a person who practiced the courtly moral laws of *triuwe* (loyalty) and *êre* (honor) could bear the *ritters namen*. " 'Ich sol mich gein in so bewarn daz wol min ritterlicher name belibet ane lasters schame' " ("I should so conduct myself towards him that my knightly title remains without the shame of sin.") (Türheim, *Rennewart*, 3280–2); "ein rehter hêrre . . . sol ouch ritters namen sô tragen, daz in der lîp iht müge verjagen ûs gêrten sîten in leckerlîchez luoder" (A true lord . . . should also so bear the name of knight [as to prevent] his body from ever driving him from honorable behavior into sensual temptation) (Zweter, 68, 1, 10–12).[10] The moral association of the title "knight" is clearest when the *ritters namen* is taken in an abstract sense as an instance of becoming involved by the abnegation of the individual: Tristan expresses the hope " 'daz ich . . . also ritter möhte sin, daz ich mich ritterliches namen und er min niht dörfte schamen und ritterlichiu werdekeit an mir niht würde nider geleit' " ("that I may be a knight in such a way that I may never be ashamed of the knightly title nor it of me and that chivalric nobility may never be laid down [debased] in me.") (Gottfried, 4407–12).[11] The ceremonial initiation takes the aristocratic lord "In die hohsten wirdekait Die diu welt mit namen trait, Ich maine ritterlichen namen" (to the highest dignity that the world has a name for, I mean the title "knight") (Rudolf von Ems, *Willehalm*, 5611–13). In courtly poetry, *ritters namen* is less a designation of class than a central concept of aristocratic ethics.[12]

This is true to a still greater degree of the expressions *ritters ambet, ritters leben, ritters reht*,[13] which everywhere refer to the moral obligations of the title of knight: "swer wil rîters ambet phlegen, der muoze mêre arbeit legen an sîne vuor dan ezzen wol . . . der mac niht rîters ambet phlegen, der niht enwil wan samfte leben" (Whoever desires to carry out a knight's duty must take on more toil in his way of life than eating well . . . he who wants nothing but soft living cannot perform the duties of a knight) (Thomasin von Zirclaere, 7785–7 and 91f.);[14] "sô man i'n dennoch mêre bî des helmes êre unt durch ritter ordentlichez lebn: dem sint zwuo rîche urbor gegebn, rehtiu scham und werdiu triwe gebent prîs alt unde niwe" (I admonish him then all the more by the honor of his helmet and by the ordered life of knights; to him two rich possessions are given, true modesty and noble loyalty give honor old and new) (*Parzival*, 321, 25–30)[15]; "er bat genâden den gast, Daz er in enpfienge Und iht übergienge Ritters reht an sîner bete" (He asked his guest's pardon for receiving him and omitting any part of a knight's rights that he requested) (Heinrich von dem Türlin, *Krone*, 9756–9).[16] It is true that *ritters art* is concerned with descent but the group of persons embraced by the word is so heterogeneous that it could hardly be fitted into a unified knightly class.[17] The expression which is most appropriate from our point of view and the most pleasant is *ritters orden* but, if we are to judge from the limited number of instances extant, it had little power of diffusion during the classical period. The unwritten laws of knightly duels, particularly in tournaments, are *ritters orden*: " 'ir müezet stechen Nâch ritters orden mit mir' " (You must joust with me according to the rules of knighthood) (Heinrich von dem Türlin, *Krone*, 9837f.);[18] in the post-classical epic, the ceremony of initiation: "und ist ritter worden nach ritterlichem orden" (And he became a knight according to the rules of chivalry) (Ulrich von Türhein, *Rennewart*, 6043f.).[19] Only in a few passages has the word a wider significance and then again in the sense of ethical duty which is laid on its aristocratic bearer by the title "knight": "owê der jaemelichen (ge)schiht daz diu werlt niht freuden hât! ir hoehstez leben mit grimme stât: daz ist rîters orden!" (Alas, a wretched event, for there can be no worldly joy! The highest point of their life rests on horror: that is the knight's way!.) (*Wigalois*, 11676–9). Thomasin had called attention to the religious duties of knighthood: "gedenket, rîtr, an iuwern orden" (Think of your rules, knights) (7769). Something of this religious sense is also exerting an effect when Anfortas asks Parzival, who has been reconciled to God and called to the Grail kingship: " 'sît ir vor untriuwe bewart, sô loest mich durch des helmes art unt durch des schildes orden' '' ("If you are protected from lack of faith, then free me by the helmet's style and by the way of the shield [i.e. by the rules of knighthood]'') (*Parzival*, 787, 19–21).

"The *ordo militaris* or *ordo equestris* (military order or knightly order) appears on the stage in the tenth century, originally in France. Richer, at the end of the tenth century, is the first to use the name and he gives us to understand that it constitutes a self-contained class with rights of inheritance."[20] The concepts *ordo equestris* and *ordo militaris* have often been produced as star witnesses for the early existence of the knightly class. There do not appear to be very many examples from Germany[21]: at the end of the eleventh century, Bruno mentions *famuli ordinis militaris* (servants of the military order) in the *Liber de bello Saxonico*; in the first half of the twelfth century *multi de equestri ordine* (many men of the equestrian order) are named as witnesses in a document of King Lothar. Usually the concepts appear with characteristic differentiations: *potiores in ordine militari* (the more powerful in the military order) (Richer), *milites ordinis secundi et tertii* (knights of the second and third order) (Bruno), *plures de equestri ordine majores et minores* (many of the equestrian order, greater and less) (Document of 1133), *primi et secundi ordinis milites* (knights of the first and second order) (Cosmas Continuation); in the same category are the contrasts between *gregarii milites* and *primi milites* (common soldiers and first-rank knights (Wipo), etc. It can be seen from this that the term *ordo militaris* is merely a vague paraphrase for the totality of vassals and soldiers whose social inequality was acknowledged by such differentiating epithets as *majores et minores, primi et secundi*, etc. (major and minor, first and second). "These words do not all constitute technical expressions or legal concepts."[22] Primarily these concepts do not reflect the social reality of the Middle Ages but are witnesses to a literary tradition. Ever since the time of Cicero *ordo equestris* had been the name of Roman "knighthood,"[23] which can be shown to have lasted until the fourth century. At that time the Roman word *eques* seems to have fallen into almost total oblivion and it was not until the high Middle Ages that it was revived by such authors as were closely associated with classical culture.[24] It would be interesting to find out whether the reappearance of the *ordo equestris* after the time of Richer of St. Remy can be explained as a corresponding Renaissance phenomenon. In any case the medieval concept is unthinkable without its Roman prototype. From the second half of the twelfth century we have an important piece of evidence that the old institution of a Roman equestrian order was known at the time and that the new concept of Christian-aristocratic knighthood was regarded as the fulfillment and even surpassing of classical knighthood. In the *Gesta Friderici*

Otto of Freising gives an account of the Roman nationalist movement under Arnold of Brescia, who·reported to the emperor that his object was "to reconstitute the sacred senate of the holy consecrated city and its equestrian order, so that by the decisions of that body and by the weapons of that order the ancient glory may return to the Roman empire and to your person."[25] To this Barbarossa gave the revealing answer: "Do you wish to learn about the ancient fame of your Rome, about the dignity of the senatorial order, about the ordering of its tents, about the virtue and discipline of its knightly class, about its unspotted and untamed bravery when it entered battle? Then look at our state! Among us you will find all this . . . Do I not reign in great fame, surrounded by a great and brave body of knights?"[26] It would be worthwhile to investigate to what degree the formation of the image of the knight in the high Middle Ages was determined by the revival of Roman legal concepts and ideas in the twelfth century.[27] Side by side with the classical tradition there is the Christian one, and as little light has been thrown on the one as on the other. As early as the fifth century, a comparison with the *militaris ordo* is made in a sermon which has been ascribed to Eusebius of Emesa.[28] In the Carolingian period *ordo militaris* has the same meaning as *ordo saecularis* (secular order) and is opposed to *ordo ecclesiasticus*[29] to "make the basic distinction between the church and the world."[30] In the twelfth century the concept acquired a new Christian sense in the spiritual orders of knighthood.[31] The Templars, the Knights of St. John, and the Teutonic knights were the only companies of knights which actually existed at this time.[32] Unfortunately there is no reliable testimony about the early social structure of the orders.[33] But for the Teutonic knights it is certain that the *ministeriales* played a significant role from the very beginning.[34] "In the orders the equality of hereditary ruler and retainer was stressed even to the point of dogma."[35] That is of great significance for the formation of the concept of knighthood, for here we encounter for the first time—and furthermore once again in the Christian-religious concept— a form of the idea which unambiguously includes both the old nobility and the *ministeriales*. But this equality of the brothers of a knightly order does not, of course, indicate an equality of social status according to the hierarchy of aristocratic classes but rather an equal footing within the order, just as all monks belonged to the common "class" of monks irrespective of their different social backgrounds. Nevertheless there was undoubtedly a far-reaching effect from the idea of a chivalric order, and still more from that of community which embraced the totality of Christianity in arms in a new *militia Christi*, namely the crusaders, and when, about 1200, we find constituted communities of knights outside the actual crusading movement, we may guess that they are a reflection of the idea of order formulated by the church.[36] The logical connections within the terminology are certain[37] but the social and cultural consequences of the crusades have been little investigated, at least in Germany.[38]

In German texts, we often encounter lists of ranks which allow us to determine the place of the knight in the medieval social hierarchy. Everywhere they are separate from the upper nobility: "Der kunic . . . Siben grafen vier herzogē. Manic ritter milde" (The king . . . seven counts, four dukes. many a generous knight.) (Herbort von Fritzlar, 4006 and 4008f.); "künge und fürsten . . . barûne und arme rîter" (kings and princes . . . barons and poor knights) (*Parzival*, 785, 6f.); "der fürste, der grâve, dirre und der, barûn unt d'anderen rîter" (some princes, some counts, some barons and other knights) (*Willehalm*, 264, 12f.); "Kúnge, fúrsten ritter wert" (kings, princes, worthy knights) (Rudolf von Ems, *Willehalm*, 13871). Most of these lists are connected with the collection of an army or with a tournament and there the knights with the common soldiers form the armed retinue of the great lords: "herzogen . . . andere groze herren . . . ritter unde knechte . . . kuchengesinde unde knaben" (dukes . . . other great lords . . . knights and soldiers . . . kitchen staff and boys) (*Oswald* W, 310f., 314f.); "Kinc, kuneginne. Ir kint ir furstē ir man. V die sie anders gehortē an. Ritter frowē manic knecht" (King, queen, their children, their princes, their liegemen. And the others who belonged to them. Knights, ladies many a soldier) (Herbort von Fritzlar, 13308–11); "die fursten ind die hēren . . . vrouwen . . . ind ritter" (the princes and the glorious ladies . . . and knights) (Holle, *Crane*, 1732f. and 1735); "vürsten ritter knehte" (princes knights soldiers) (Rudolf von Ems, *Alexander*, 19566); "ritter, herren, knehte" (Knights, lords, soldiers) (Rudolf von Ems, *Willehalm*, 9083); "künige . . . herzogen . . . grâven . . . bischofe . . . ritter unde knehte" (kings, dukes, counts, bishops, knights and soldiers) (*Oswald* M, 9, 11, 13, 15, 17); "herzogen und ouch graven . . . ritter und ouch geburen" (dukes and also counts . . . knights and also peasants) (*Orendel*, 2356 and 2358); "des keiseres sone, vorsten unde herren, riddere, man, wif unde kindere" (the emperor's sons, princes and lords, men, women and children) (*Sächsische Weltchronik*, 254, 33–255, 1). In many passages the knights are set apart from free men: "de vrien . . . rittere ind kneichte" (the free . . . knights and soldiers) (*Morant*, 3946 and 3949); "vrîen, grâven . . . ritter unde knehte" (free men, counts . . . knights and soldiers) (*Oswald* M, 105 and 107). In the *Lucidarius* their station is between the *vrîen* and the *eigen liuten* (the free and the bondsmen); "in des kuningis (sc. Melchisedech's) zite wurdin die livte geteilit in driv. von seme komin die vrien von iauet chomen die rithere. von cham komen die eiginin livte" (In the king's time the people were divided into three parts. The free came from Shem, the knights from Japhet. From

Ham came the bondsmen.) (148–51). This is taken literally from the *Imago mundi* of Honorius Augustodunensis "huius tempore divisum est genus humanum in tria: in liberos, milites, servos."[39] This station between free and unfree corresponds to the legal position of the *ministeriales*. Thus it is stated in the *Vorauer Moses* about the biblical division of mankind: "Daz sin dev geslahte . . . einez daz ist edele . . . die andere frigen luote . . . di driten daz sint dinestman . . . darunder wurden chnehte" (These are the classes . . . one is noble . . . the second, free people . . . the third consists of servants . . . among them bondsmen) (15, 1–7).[40] When there was a question of an exact legal designation, the poets preferred the word *dienestman* (servant, retainer) to the broader concept *ritter*. There is a fairly large number of such lists of social classes in which the knights are not mentioned but the retainers are:[41] "grâfen unde herzogen . . . vrîhêren unde dînestman" (counts and dukes . . . freelords and retainers) (Eilhart, 2017 and 2021); "marcgraven ende herzogen . . . graven ende vrien . . . burgare ende dinestman ende dat gemeine volc" (margraves and dukes . . . counts and free men . . . burghers and retainers and the common people) (*Servatius*, 515, 517, 519f.); "künige, fürsten, grâven . . . dienstman oder frî" (kings, princes, counts . . . retainers or free) (Reinbot von Durne, 1115f); "fûrsten, grâven, herzogen, vrîen unde dienestman" (princes, counts, dukes, freemen and retainers) (*Lanzelet*, 8380f.); "vürsten . . . grâven vrîen dienestman" (princes . . . counts, freemen retainers) (Herbort, 2555 and 2557; Zweter, 133, 3; Hardegger, 12, 8,9,10,12; Ulrich von Lichtenstein, *Frauendienst*, 186,2f.); "grâven vrîen dienstman" (counts, free men, retainers) (Rudolf von Ems, *Der gute Gerhard*, 3417 and 3477; Ulrich von Lichtenstein, *Frauendienst*, 992,7); "furstēfrigen dinstman" (princes, free men, retainers) (Herbort, 1231; 4201; 6237); "fúrsten, herren, dienestman" (princes, lords, retainers) (Rudolf von Ems, *Willehalm*, 5882); "herren, fürsten, dienestman" (lords, princes, retainers) (Rudolf von Ems, *Der gute Gerhard*, 5536), etc. Wherever the medieval "pyramid of power" is discussed, the conditions of increasing dependence from king down to the last *ministerialis*, the concept "knight" is no more than a substitute, a representative, for the more exact designation "retainer." Side by side with these lists there are others of quite different character in which the knights have a definite place and where the "retainers" are never named in their stead. These are the lists which include peasants and priests, bourgeoisie and merchants: "ritâre und gebûre, knehte unde koufman" (knights and peasants, soldiers and merchants) (*Eneit*, 48, 6f.); "koufman und gebûren, ritter unde hêren" (merchants and peasants, knights and lords) (ibid., 320,24f.); "Ritter vnd knechte. Bebure vnd koufman" (Knights and soldiers, peasants and merchants) (Herbort, 9846f.); "Vrauwen ind vrien . . . Ritter ind burgere . . . Garganten ind

knechte . . . Garzune ind geburen . . . Lodder ind spelman'' (Ladies and
free men . . . knights and bourgeois . . . freebooters and soldiers . . . pages
and peasants . . . knaves and itinerant minstrels (*Morant*, 5445; 5447,
5449; 5451; 5453); ''barune, pfaffen unde ritterschaft'' (barons, clergy,
and knights) (Gottfried, 15634f.); ''ritter, burger und knappen'' (knights,
burghers and squires) (Ulrich von Türheim, *Rennewart*, 10480); ''laein
vnt phaffen . . . reiter vnt gibouren'' (laymen und priests . . . knights
and peasants) (Tnugdalus, 51, 65 and 68); ''De alden mit den iungen.
Man ind vrauwen . . . Paffen ritter burgere (The old with the young.
Men and women . . . Priests knights burghers) (*Morant*, 5136f. and
5139); ''die phaffen . . . die gebour . . . die choufliut . . . frowen unt
rîter'' (Heinrich von Melk, *Erinnerung*, 423–5 and 427); in a sermon in
the *Speculum ecclesiae* the following are addressed in turn: ''ritere . . .
chŏflute . . . bulute'' (knights . . . merchants . . . peasants) (170, 14;
20; 28); in the *Kaiserchronik*, the various basics of the hierarchy are
combined with one another: ''der kunic rihte sînen hof . . . umbe herzogen unt umbe grâven unt alle di under in wâren, umbe alle rîteres
namen . . . umbe bûliute und umbe choufman'' (The king ruled his
court . . . the dukes, the counts, and all who were under them, all those
with the title ''knight'' . . . the peasants and the merchants) (8100, 2–4
and 12). It was Freidank who found the classic formulation: ''got hât driu
leben geschaffen: gebure, ritter unde pfaffen'' (God created three lives:
peasants, knights, and priests) (27,1f.).[42]

''In the Middle Ages there were really narrow-minded individuals
who quite seriously believed that there were only three occupational
classes, knights, peasants, and priests.''[43] It is not so much the narrow-
mindedness of medieval authors which is to blame for this as the naiveté
with which these sources have been interpreted as descriptions of the
actual state of the class structure. Medieval social literature was very
rarely concerned with distinctions of ruling, social, or economic group-
ings. ''Never . . . is there any question in this literature of the exposition
of the inner structure of a unit organized by classes but of a listing of
various classes set up according to varying principles of organization.''[44]
In the Middle Ages, the word ''class'' meant basically ''a position in a
large whole which was at one and the same time recognized and approved
[as part of the whole] or at least envisaged and accepted as given and
determined.''[45] And since this larger whole was always interpreted by
clerical authors as the Christian cosmos, ''the only classes which counted
as *status*, that is, classes in the full sense of the term were the great
member-communities of the natural and supernatural order of existence,
clerics and laity, secular clerics and the monastic orders, men and women,
married and single, the just and the sinners, the elect and the damned.''[46]
Understandably, a historian cannot do much with a class-concept of this

sort, which still persists in such expressions as "state of marriage" and "state of innocence." "The theoretical literature of the Middle Ages . . . needs first and foremost a connection with the historical reality from which it derives."[47] This is true also for the division of men into peasants, knights, and priests. The figure three is itself an abstraction, and the evidence from German sources has shown that there was no fixed or generally binding scheme but that the concepts were rather varied and interchanged. This division must be seen against the background of a long literary tradition which goes back to Plato and Aristotle and which remained vital throughout the Middle Ages.[48] In a poem of Bishop Adalbero on Robert the Pious it is stated: "Triplex ergo Dei domus est, quae creditur una. Nunc orant, alii pugnant, aliique laborant" (The house of God is threefold, although it is believed to be one. Some pray, others fight, and others work.)[49] In the *Gesta episcoporum Cameracensium* of the eleventh century mankind is divided into *oratores, agricultores, pugnatores* (prayers, tillers, fighters).[50] In many passages this topos is worked in with divisions of ruling classes,[51] but basically the idea of teaching class, farming class, and fighting class as pillars of the state is independent of the complicated hierarchical divisions of the Middle Ages. This is clearly expressed by Frauenlob, who is outside the limits of our period:

> In driu geteilet wâren
> von êrst die liute, als ich las.
> bûman, riltaer unt pfaffen,
> ieslich nâch sîner mâze was
> gelîch an adel und an art
> dem andern ie . . .
> (ed. Ettmüller, 244, 1–6)[52]

(As I have read, people were divided into three from the beginning, peasants, knights, and priests, and each, according to his measure was the equal of the other in nobility and function . . .). It is clear from this that when the knights are juxtaposed with peasants and priests they do not represent the nobility, which is above the others, and that indeed there is no legal classification implied here. "Knight" is simply a designation for all those who serve the human community with the sword.

"The medieval social framework was organized as a hierarchy of rule and birth. It had very little in common with what is today called "occupational classification."[53] In the old lordship state of the early Middle Ages there was "an unending and confusing diversity of formations and combinations, of conditions of lordship and dependence."[54] The social structure was determined by "the basic distinction on social life: overlordship and service."[55] It would, perhaps, be better not to speak of class organization at all in regard to this period, because the degrees of blood-money payment in customary law and the Carolingian distinctions between free and unfree were in any case something quite different from the class-structure of the later Middle Ages.[56] If ''the nature of the concept of class'' is to be seen in the fact ''that in a political lordship-grouping . . . the *meliores et majores terrae* (the superior and greater men of the land) 'represent' the whole, the 'Land' or the 'empire' before the ruler''[57] in a corporate organization, then we must not look for such a concept in Germany until after the end of the thirteenth century. The ''class-organization which developed from the feudal and aristocratic hierarchical structures and conditions of lordship''[58] demonstrates the far-reaching change in the medieval constitution, in the course of which the ''comitatus-state'' turned into a ''institutional geographic state'' (Theodor Mayer) and the medieval state became the modern one. The gradual ''fixing and condensation . . . in Western institutions and in Western society''[59] found its obvious expression in the class-structure of the late Middle Ages. The structuring of classes moved from the top downwards, not the other way round. ''The princes were the driving force of the classification movement.''[60] The consolidation of the class of imperial princes was the first step on the way to a state of social classes.[61] The development of a landed aristocratic organization of princes led to the incorporation of the old nobility which, in the territories, consolidated into a ''ruling class'' and cooperated from then on as the upper class in the territorial rule of the princes. Furthermore, the state-structure based on principalities also drew in the knights and the cities and made them into classes. The recognized classes of the late Middle Ages ''arose with the constitution of landed states'' and to this extent can ''be regarded as a creation of the landed rulers.''[62] ''So far as Germany is concerned . . . it is a fair assumption that, by the middle of the thirteenth century, the knights were definitely regarded as a separate class and that this fact was generally accepted, although there is no imperial law extant with the kind of rules which Frederick II put into his constitution for Sicily.''[63] The recognition of knights as a separate class coincides factually with the gradual reorganization of the various service dependencies into territorial landed classes.[64] No definite date can be assigned to this process; it was already well in train by the mid-thirteenth century. At the end of the century there is in most territories good evidence for the presence of knights attached to the land,[65] and, ''from the fourteenth century on,'' the only ''distinction made in the sources is between lords and knights.''[66]

The concept of nobility also underwent a shifting and consolidation at the same time as the formation of the new class system. The question of what ''nobility actually means legally, socially, economically, and politically''[67] is nowadays a central feature of historical research, since "the aristocratic organization of the medieval imperial constitution"[68] has been discovered to be the determining essential feature of the older state. It is true that "we are still a long way from being able to write a 'History of Aristocracy,' "[69] but there are some important preliminary studies, particularly on the late Carolingian period during which the bases of the later developments can be traced.[70] In the course of this it has been shown to be worthwhile to start from individual noble families and their history rather than from the institution of nobility which appears only dimly in the sources. In this way it becomes possible "to grasp the process of historical and social change in the framework of the nobility itself."[71] Thus the "multiple stratification and differentiation of the nobility" is clearly apparent.[72] "It is impossible to imagine how much graduation there was within the nobility."[73] As a result of this the conventional concept of nobility becomes very questionable indeed, since it invokes the fiction of unity where no unity existed, whether legal, social or economic. For this reason Heinrich Dannenbauer wanted to avoid altogether "the dubious and ambiguous word 'nobility' (adel) and for preference talk instead of 'lords and lordship' (Herren, Herrenstand)."[74] The numerous attempts to determine the nature of medieval nobility from the etymology of the word have not met with much success, since the desired meaning "superior race" could be arrived at only with considerable effort.[75] Gustav Neckel's arguments that an "unnoble aþal was the original form have never really been shaken.[76] It is indeed possible to trace a line from the meaning "property by descent, inherited property" to the medieval lordship over land as the most important feature of nobility, to the so-called "allodialism."[77] The meanings "paternal, what comes from the past, family, inherited nature, purity"[78] undoubtedly play an important role in the concept of nobility. But as long as the word covers "Ludwig the German right down to the smallest property-owner"[79] it is useless as a designation of the "old dynastic aristocracy."[80] We have to resign ourselves to the view that "the word nobility had originally no sense of class differentiation."[81] Otto von Dungern has demonstrated that "a small unified group of dynastic families held all power in their hands in Germany from the ninth to the end of the twelfth century."[82] If the smaller vassals and also the *ministeriales* are put side by side with this group of powerful lords and the whole lot are called "noble," then the one insurmountable social barrier which existed in the old lordship state is being overlooked.[83] Even the distinction between upper and lower nobility is misleading for the twelfth and thirteenth centuries,[84] for these concepts suggest a legal distinction which did not exist.[85] It is true that the old dynastic families can be called an aristocracy of birth[86] if by this it is meant that these dynastic families intermarried among themselves as a rule and that it was practically impossible to break into their circle, but in doing so there is a grave danger that the concept of class will be deprived of its meaning in law. What separated the prince from the minor "nobles" was "not a difference of legal standing but a political one based on power"; and there were also important economic and social differences.[87] Among the most important conclusions of recent research into the question of nobility is the observation that "from the tenth century on there must have been a far-reaching change in the structure of the nobility and in its sense of its own existence."[88] The clearest expression of this fact is the way the nobility from the eleventh century on began to call themselves after their principal place of residence and later the wearing of their own coats of arms. "By means of such distinguishing marks the noble families begin to set themselves off clearly one from another and to shape themselves to an ever increasing degree into families and particularly into great houses."[89] Hand in hand with this went the increase in the political power of the great dynastic nobility and the extension of their domains. "From the tenth century on the process of putting all state affairs on a basis of lordship advances rapidly."[90] From this there arose gradually a new grouping, which again went from top to bottom. As the class hierarchy of the latter Middle Ages established itself, the word *Adel* (nobility) also acquired for the first time a precise class meaning; it became the actual social designation for the lords and knights who were below the princes.[91]

The testimony of the German language is also interesting in this connection, for it shows that the new class concept of nobility was not completely accepted by the middle of the thirteenth century. Up to now the principal concern of studies of the subject has been the moral aspect of the concept of nobility in Middle High German, with ideas of nobility of principle and of soul.[92] In doing so, too sharp a distinction has some-times been made. Nobility of birth and nobility of principle are not opposites. They have a close internal bond. "The aristocratic world ever since Homer has lived for the conviction that a man of noble descent is born to 'virtue,' and that for precisely that reason this virtue is taken by them to be a sublime and strict demand."[93] A marked feature of the use of the word during the classical period is its extraordinary rarity when measured against the overwhelming significance of the aristocratic world in courtly poetry and also against the occurrences of the adjective *edele*; even the word *edelkeit* (nobility), derived from it, is far more common than *adel*. According to the dictionaries, the word is not found in Wolfram or Gottfried, nor in *Minnesangsfrühling* or Neidhart.[94] There is only one text of the period in which it is well represented, Thomasin's *Wälscher Gast*. There I have counted twenty-three instances. The word *adel* is never found in rank-lists of the type *vürsten, herren, dienestman* (princes, lords, retainers). It can be seen from this that the abstract concept of nobility was still of no significance in the courtly period. At this time, nobility was not an institution and therefore not a class in the legal sense, but always a personal quality of the individual which he acquired from his parents and forefathers.[95] Consequently an individual is called *edele*, because he himself is distinguished and because he comes from a distinguished family, not because the term means that he "is of the nobility." Nobility as a personal quality is often expressed in combination with a possessive pronoun.[96] A princess "mochte von ir adele. gezeme eime koninge" (could seem like a king in her nobility) (*König Rother*, 77f.); when aristocratic girls have to carry out lowly tasks, "mohten si ir adeles niht geniezen" (they could not have the advantage of their nobility) (*Kudrun*, 1007, 4).[97] Duke Ernst is suspected of intending to revolt against the emperor: "er wil sich genôzen in adel und an rîchheit" (he intends to be your equal in nobility and in riches) (*Herzog Ernst B*, 684f.). Morolt will fight only with an opponent "der von adele sî sô vrî, daz er mîn genôze sî" (who is so free as a result of his noble birth that he is my equal) (Eilhart, 413f.). It is said of Kaedin, a duke's son: "sîn adel von vürsten ist sô grôz daz er niht hôher möhte sîn" (his nobility [derived] from princes is so great that it could not be higher) (Ulrich von Türheim, *Tristan*, 537,4f.). The relative nature of the concept of nobility is here apparent: nobility is not the bond which ties all aristocratic families together but each family has its own nobility. "There are houses which are more noble than others."[98] It is the king who has the highest nobility. Nobility is conferred by God.[99] It is one of the *bona corporis* (goods of the body), of the qualities which are inherited, not won, which were recognized only with reluctance by medieval moral teaching. Thomas von Zirclaere names "diu sehs dinc, adel, maht, gelust, name, rîchtuom, hêrschaft" (the six things, nobility, power, joy, reputation, riches, lordship) (5745f; see also 5929f., 6114, 6723f.) and he is never tired of warning the lords not to relax in their nobility: "ein ieglîch biderbe herre sol . . . sich ouch niht hart verlân an sîn adel" (4209 and 4217). In courtly poetry the term "adel" is everywhere reserved for the people who are called *herren* and who have a *hêrschaft* (domain). Scarcely a trace remains of the old "unnoble nobility."[100] It was only later, after the idea had developed that knights, too, belonged to the nobility,[101] that it made sense to distinguish between upper and lower nobility.[102] It is only then that the *ritterlîche adel* to which a late gloss on the *Sachsenspiegel* gives testimony becomes a historical fact.[103]

We are close to the end. The investigation of the works written in German has led us to conceptions of knighthood which are basically different in nature. The word designates in the first place actual knights who are so called because they serve a lord and secondly noble lords who are called knights because they have solemnly taken the sword.[104] This is the explanation of the obscurity of the medieval image of the knight. At one time knighthood is celebrated as the highest form of noble life, in another context it is rejected with scorn. What the high and the low knights have in common is their appearance as a military phenomenon, that they are heavily armored cavalry and their common life at court no doubt acted as a unifying influence. Nevertheless the difference between lordship and service which determined the structure of society remained intact.[105] It has also proved to be the case that the concept of knighthood, at least until the middle of the thirteenth century, is not the most suitable instrument to fix the position of the individual in the medieval hierarchy of rule beyond the basic classification already mentioned. In the aristocratic sphere the title "knight" has no meaning in relation to differentiating classes;[106] and in the sphere of service the concept of knighthood refers only to the dependence on a lord, not to the personal quality of the person serving, who can be a king's son or a peasant.[107] To this extent our investigation produces negative results, but this does not, we hope, mean that the effort devoted to it was pointless. What was attempted was the critical examination of a doctrine which was in danger of becoming rigid dogma.[108] The aristocratic knighthood of which courtly poetry tells cannot be explained by shifting it into the social hierarchy. It is an educational and cultural idea of far-reaching significance and is a phenomenon of intellectual history rather than social history.[109] The reality of the nobility around 1200 obviously looked quite different. We hear of political murders, and the feuds of the great men were conducted with treachery, extortion, robbery, and arson.[110] In opposition to this crude reality the poets set up the chivalric ideal of virtue, the dream of the noble man who incorporates humility into his nobility and therefore strives to satisfy at one and the same time the duties of the world and claims of God. No source tells us that this image changed the aristocratic world of the time. The "decline of poetry" in the thirteenth century has frequently been interpreted "as the result of the moral decline of knighthood."[111] In fact, however, the development was exactly the reverse. It was not until the end of the classical courtly period that the knightly class became a social reality, and it was only in the late Middle Ages that the great lords tried to live according to the old rules of chivalry, half seriously, half in jest.[112] We may recall a remark of Otto von Dungern who designated the period "from about 1250 to 1450" as "the period of the finest flowering of chivalry in Germany."[113]

APPENDIX

The Knight's World[114]

ritters ambet	Thomasin 7785. 7791. Türlin Mant. 285
ritters art	Parz 123, 11. 520, 17. 544, 17. Willeh. 131, 1. Sachsensp. Lnr. 2 § 1. Sachsensp. Ldr. I 20 § 1. § 8. I 27 § 2. II 21 § 1. Türlin Krone 17600. 21527. 24732. Ems Alex. 21230 [*ritters ritterlîchiu art*]. Holle Demant. 6160
ritters âventiure	Durne 626
ritters banekîe	Türlin Krone 1171. 25876
ritters becher	Walther 20, 15
ritters behendecheit	Türlin Krone 2941. 7467
ritters bejac	Türlin Krone 29249
ritters bereitschaft	Gotfr. 4930
ritters bluot	Türheim Renn. 19419
ritters dienest	Türheim Renn. 31455. Holle Crane 1704. 3317. Lichtenst. Frd. 1389, 6. Lichtenst. Frb. 611, 15
ritters ellen	Parz. 37, 24. 60, 23. 196, 22. Türlin Krone 18668. 26895. 28007. Ems Willeh. 1288. Lichtenst. Frd. 1014, 7
ritters êre	Iwein 4718. Parz. 11, 26. 126, 13. 149, 16. Wigalois 518. 1306. Winterstetten XIII, 3, 5. Türlin Krone 860. 22597. Ems Willeh. 7589. Türheim Trist. 512, 3. Türheim Renn. 16006
ritters figiure	Gotfr. 6647
ritters gebære	Türlin Krone 7448
ritters gebeine	Titurel 133, 4
ritters gelt	Lichtenst. Frd. 254, 6
ritters gemach	Iwein 4360
ritters genôz	Herbort 9856. Holle Demant. 7279
ritters ger	Wigalois 11644. Stricker Karl 11554. Ems Alex. 2504. Lichtenst. Frd. 554, 2
ritters getât	Türlin Krone 27024
ritters gewise	Morant 2157
ritters gezouwe	Rother 301
ritters habe	Ems Willeh. 6563
ritters hant	Eilhart 6158. Parz. 69, 20. 203, 19. 220, 13. 372, 11. 440, 5. 519, 3. 749, 12. Ems Willeh. 6170. 12562. Holle Demant. 2931. 5505. 8555. 9309. Holle Crane 2348. 2585
ritters harnasch	Eilhart 1466
ritters herze	Parz. 130, 6 [*ritters herzen nôt*]. Holle Demant. 8251
ritters hôchgemüete	Ems Willeh. 14678
ritters kint	Stricker Ehre 340
ritters klagen	Lichtenst. Frd. 1034, 2
ritters kleit	Parz. 156, 27. Wigalois 1632
ritters knie	Lichtenst. Frd. 1578, 4
ritters kraft	Türlin Krone 20176. Ems Willeh. 990. 8761. 15239. Ems Alex. 7182. 10738. 12430
ritters kumber	Willeh. 3, 17
ritters künde	Neidhart 27, 28
ritters kunst	Stricker Karl 6633. Türlin Krone 26549. Lichtenst. Frd. 1422, 7
ritters leben	Zw. Büchlein 67. Parz. 117, 25. 321, 27 [*ritters ordenlîchez leben*]. Wigalois 9154. 9360. Ems Alex. 1399. [*r. l. unde strît*]. Lichtenst. XLIV, 6, 5. Lichtenst. Frd. 1242, 7. Lichtenst. Frb. 644, 25
ritters lêre	Zweter 106, 7
ritters liden	Türheim Renn. 25933
ritters lîp	Türheim Renn. 27486. 30536. 31922. Holle Demant. 2696 [?]. 3072. Lichtenst. XXXIV, 5, 6. XLIV, 1, 6. Lichtenst. Frd. 77, 7. 462, 4. 891, 4. 956, 6. 994, 4. 1034, 6. 1050, 7. 1307, 5. 1311, 3. 1311, 5. 1465, 7. 1650, 4. Lichtenst. Frb. 650, 6
ritters list	Ems Alex. 7495

ritters lôn	Ems Alex. 7354. 11992
ritters lop	Gotfr. 11097. Ems Alex. 7098. Lichtenst. Frd. 751, 7
ritters mâl	Parz. 179, 14. 315, 10. Winsbecke 21, 9. Türlin Krone 29881
ritters manheit	Ems Alex. 12231
ritters munt	Türheim Renn. 34986. Lichtenst. Frd. 1220, 6
ritters muot	Erek 899. 6947. Iwein 6. 2855. Parz. 362, 26. Türlin Krone 252. Ems Willeh. 6428. 7575. Türheim Renn. 13730. Zweter 48, 11. Lichtenst. Frd. 184, 6. 202, 1
ritters name	Kaiserchr. 6801. 8104. Rother 1331. Erek 4201, 5468. Gregorius 1665. Iwein 1456. 3038. 3188. Zw. Büchlein 70. Herbort 13042. Lanzelet 2222. 2643. 4652. Nl. 31, 4. Parz. 123, 9. Wigalois 996. 1940. 3922. 9851. Sächs. Weltchr. 196, 42. Otte 2393. Stricker Karl 4876. Stricker Dan. 146. 1166. Stricker Ehre D 495. Türlin Krone 8682. 8700. 8733. 11766. 13155. Ems Gerh. 3609. 4939. 4948. Ems Willeh. 5260. 5591. 5658. 5829. 8216. 14366. Ems Alex. 44. 2474. 7345. 17860. Türheim Renn. 11655. Zweter 68, 10. Holle Demant. 6155. Lichtenst. Frd. 1034, 7. 1518, 5. Pr. Schönbach I, 110, 14
ritters orden	Parz. 69, 4. 126, 7. Wigalois 11679. Türlin Krone 827. 9838. Ems Willeh. 5210. 7361. 7803
ritters ouge	Türheim Renn. 25700. Lichtenst. Frd. 1675, 2
ritters prîs	Herbort 14069. Parz. 98 21. 136, 11. 178, 30. 182, 10. 323, 23. 396, 15. 558, 20. 654, 10. Athis D 86. Türlin Krone 7491. 8969. 16242. 24093. 25842. 28082. Ems Willeh. 1407. 6314. 7413. 7490. 7742. 8807. 10940. 10967. Ems Alex. 4970. 6862. 6996. 10253. 12150. 12454. Ems Weltchr. 35367. Türheim Renn. 3070. 10845. 15771. Lichtenst. Frd. 152, 6. 1411, 7. Lichtenst. Frd. 1. Büchl. 84. 355
ritters rât	Parz. 66, 21. Ems Gerh. 3646
ritters reht	Erek 5412. 6647. Lanzelet 6472. Parz. 78, 10. Gotfr. 6518. 6684. Thomasin 7765. Stricker Karl 9733. Türlin Krone 3095. 3881. 5507. 9759. 16100 [*r. r. und triuwe*] 16568. 22676. Kudrun 180, 3. Ems Willeh. 7871
ritters ritterschaft	Türheim Trist. 586, 21
ritters schade	Lichtenst. Frd. 254, 7
ritters scham	Lichtenst. Frd. 1430, 6. 1439, 4
ritters schar	Sächs. Weltchr. 197, 8
ritters schimpf	Ems Alex. 3513
ritters schîn	Wigalois 9357. Türlin Krone 18207
ritters sicherheit	Türlin Krone 16570. 16702
ritters sin	Parz. 26, 2. Türheim Renn. 32998
ritters site	Parz. 179, 14. Türlin Krone 2099. 3932. 16632. 18030. 20195. Ems Willeh. 5763. 5990. 11068. Ems Alex. 7498. 7902. 11764. Türheim Renn. 23422. Lichtenst. Frd. 155, 8. 202, 5. 317, 7. 340, 2. 355, 4. 514, 2. 520, 2. 615, 8. 678, 4. 851, 2. 916, 2. 1352, 3. 1419, 6. 1425, 4. 1529, 8. 1587, 6. 1592, 4
ritters spil	Türlin Krone 29159. Ems Willeh. 6624. 6703. 7702. Lichtenst. Frd. 42, 4. 645, 4. 1355, 3
ritters spîse	Erek 386
ritters tât	Parz. 68, 27. 280, 29. 366, 15. 558, 4. 673, 4. Wigalois 11641. Türlin Krone 4998. 8901. 18327. 22655. 23994. 29053. Ems Alex. 4992. Türheim Renn. 25933. Lichtenst. Frd. 191, 6. 1408, 4. 1580, 4. 1588, 4
ritters tjost	Holle Demant. 3234
ritters tôt	Ems Willeh. 1216
ritters triuwe	Iwein 3173. Durne 3041. Türlin Krone 12344. 14478
ritters trût	Parz. 130, 1
ritters tugent	Lichtenst. Frd. 1033, 4
ritters urliuge	Türlin Krone 26926
ritters urteil	Parz. 98, 2
ritters vallen	Lichtenst. Frd. 865, 8
ritters vart	Türlin Krone 24733
ritters vreude	Ems Gerh. 4942
ritters vuore	Parz. 152, 12. 258, 22. 364, 1 Kudrun 48, 2
ritters wandel	Lichtenst. Frd. 1446, 4. 1580, 8

ritters wer	Wigalois 7800. 10153. Ems Willeh. 6733. 10744. Ems Alex. 4631. 11638. 12380. 12570
ritters werc	Lichtenst. Frd. 196, 6. 288, 7. 627, 2
ritters werdecheit	Ems Willeh. 6489. 11472
ritters wirde	Türlin Krone 27021
ritters wise	Türlin Krone 8992
ritters witze	Ems Willeh. 1113. Ems Weltchr. 30719
ritters zer	Ems Willeh. 6812
ritters zuht	Holle Demant. 3220. Lichtenst. Frd. 293, 4. 1439, 5. 1497, 7
ritters zuoversiht	Ems Willeh. 8391

VII. On the State of Research into Knighthood

hile medieval studies in France have long devoted a great deal of attention to the relationship between knighthood and nobility, recent investigation of knighthood in Germany did not begin until 1959, when Arno Borst published his essay "Das Rittertum im Hochmittelalter," itself intended as a program for study.[1] Borst defined knighthood as "a combination of lordship and service" (p. 216) and sought its historical roots in the actual life of the lower nobility as it had developed in various ways in France and Germany from the late Carolingian period. The particular merit of the essay lies in the fact that here, for the first time, the question of the relationship between idea and reality was made the central point and it is for this reason especially that it is a great pity that Borst has not up to now realized his plan for "a comprehensive history of medieval chivalry" (p. 213 n.). Many of his ideas and points of view are still exciting and topical today.

In its attempt at universality Johanna Maria van Winter's little book, *Rittertum, Ideal und Wirklichkeit* is related to Borst's essay. It was published in Dutch in 1965 and a German translation appeared in 1969.[2] It is intended for a wider circle of readers and in its effort to make a difficult subject simple, it sometimes goes so far that it is hard to discern the great technical knowledge of the author behind her formulations. In her investigations into the *ministeriales* in Dutch Guilderland,[3] J. M. van Winter has observed that between 1220 and 1230 the terms *nobiles* (sometimes *liberi*), which had up till then been usual in the lists of witnesses to documents, were replaced by *milites* and *famuli*, a new pair of terms. (Nobles, sometimes "free men," were replaced by "knights" and "servants.") It should not be concluded from this change in terminology that the class distinctions between nobles and *ministeriales* disappeared at that time—the legal distinction between the two groups lasted until the sixteenth century in the Netherlands according to the author's conclusions—but rather "the recognition that it was more important from the social point of view to have the status of a knight or squire than a noble or ministerialis" is here reflected (p. 21). Thus, she says, being a knight was not a class quality but rather meant "participation in a social status" (ibid.). In the course of this the author distinguishes between legally defined "orders" and socially determined "classes" and interprets knighthood "not as an order but as a social class"[4] (p. 22). This social class of knights grew out of "*ministeriales* and non-noble freemen in the twelfth century" (p. 87), and it was, in this form, at first sharply separated from the nobility. The author described the social status of the older form of knighthood in the following way: "the only thing that was demanded of a knight and his family was that he possessed enough to provide himself with a horse and armor and to be able to assume the life style of a knight. This latter meant in essence that he did not till his own soil . . ." (p. 84). At the same time she stresses the importance of service and particularly military service: "The distinguishing feature of the knight was his service" (p. 24). In the course of further development there was a far-reaching reshaping of knighthood and especially because it was "associated" later with nobility: "After the nobility began to join the knights at the beginning of the thirteenth century, this knightly order consisted of members of three different classes, which remained separate even within it, the *ministeriales*, the non-noble freemen, and the nobles" (p. 85). Particularly worthy of notice in this connection is the question "How did the nobility come to the stage of associating itself with knight-hood?" (p. 22). According to the author the answer to this is to be found in the ideal social concepts of knighthood. More than two thirds of her book are devoted to an exposition of the ideals of knighthood. The author has worked out the central role of the service-idea in the knightly ideology and distinguishes between three aspects of the idea of knightly service: 1. "service for the lord," which she explains as coming from the loyalty concept of feudal law and from the demands of clerical writers upon the making of war ("renunciation of booty and plundering" [p. 36]); 2. "service for the church and for Christianity," which is most clearly expressed in the formulae for the blessing of swords and standards and in crusading propaganda; and 3. "service to the lady" in the Latin treatise of Andreas Capellanus and in courtly poetry. This threefold idea of knight-hood, which was the object "of constant striving" after the end of the eleventh century was directed at "the actual fighting men of the time" and the result of this was that "they gradually developed a feeling of solidarity and thought of themselves as belonging to a kind of corporation, namely knighthood" (p. 77). By the thirteenth century, she says, the concept of knighthood had gained so much significance because of the value-concepts that were connected with it that it had become interesting and acceptable even to the nobility. As early as the twelfth century efforts were being made "to make the service ideals of knighthood into duties for the nobility" (ibid.), and finally "the nobility gave in to the pressure of conscience made by these ideals" (p. 87) and attached itself to knighthood. Thus there came about a "fusion on the social level (p. 78) between nobility and *ministeriales*, in which the author sees the characteristic features of later knighthood. In any case it was the movement of the nobility into the body of knights which brought about "the decline of the ideals of knighthood", for the old ideal had been completely determined by the ideal of service, and the noble lords had "no interest" in "maintaining the appearance of an ideal of service" (ibid.).

So far as I am concerned, the most important conclusions of J. M. van Winter's book are to be found in her conclusion that knighthood in the Middle Ages was much more a social phenomenon than a legal one and that it should therefore be examined from the point of view of social history rather than from the point of view of class law. In the second place, I find it a very important insight that knighthood is best understood when one makes sure of grasping its ideals. Some other points are in need of further clarification. It may be questioned whether it is a fortunate turn of phrase to designate knighthood as a social "class." In bourgeois class theory, the concept of class has a very specific place, so that its use in relation to the Middle Ages can only lead to misunderstandings.[5] A more important question is how the social ideal of older knighthood is to be determined historically. J. M. van Winter describes the knights of the earlier period as petty landowners (p. 84) and characterizes them elsewhere as "the armed retinue of a prince or nobleman" (p. 87). In France there is clearly good evidence for a class of *milites* in the eleventh century to which this description is to some degree applicable.[6] In Germany the conditions appear to have been somewhat different. The author does not go into these differences and indeed she does not pay enough attention in general to the significant topographical distinctions in her statements about "knighthood" in the high Middle Ages. According to her presentation "true knighthood" (p. 84) in the twelfth century consisted of members of two classes, the *ministeriales* and the "non-noble" freemen, which merged into a single community in the sense of knighthood, chiefly because of the triple ideal of service. According to this a central feature for the understanding of medieval chivalry is to be ascribed to the idea that the knightly service-ideal was originally the exclusive property of the non-noble body of knights and only later, in a second phase of development, was it taken over by the nobility. In these arguments of the author there are echoes of ideas which can be found, for example, as early as the work of Sidney Painter[7] or Arnold Hauser[8] and which are most decisively presented by the Romance scholar Erich Köhler.[9] His works anticipate the work of the Dutch scholar in terminology too, although she does not appear to be acquainted with his work, in so far as he ascribed the development of the courtly ideal of knighthood to a "lower group of knights." All these investigations work principally with the argument that the knightly idea of service must be interpreted from the point of view of a service stratum of society, because otherwise it would be incomprehensible. In my view, this line of argument does not go far enough whether it refers to the religious or the courtly concept of knighthood. Anybody who called himself *servus Christi, miles Christianus*, or *gotes ritter* and bound himself to service for the faith was not thereby designated as a servant in his social position. Kings and emperors bore these names and did not thereby infringe their nobility. There was thus a noble concept of service in the courtly sphere; it appears most clearly in the love-songs of princely poets but it is also present in other forms of courtly poetry.[10] If, like the author, one starts out from the idea that the idea of service to the lady applied originally only to such knights, for whom service and dependence were a social fact of life, it is virtually impossible to escape the assumption that the idea lost its real meaning when the nobility appropriated the chivalric ideology for itself: "For nobles did not feel themselves to be in a true service relationship to those above them and had also no interest in maintaining the appearance of a service ideal" (p. 78). Such pronouncements, however, can be reconciled only with the greatest difficulty with the known facts of literary history: as early as 1170–80 (i.e. half a century before the point at which the nobility is supposed to have associated itself with knighthood), there was at the German courts a flourishing courtly poetry with its specific ideal of knighthood. This poetry was not primarily in the hands of knights of the older type, that is to say, *ministeriales* and non-noble freemen, but was initiated by princely patrons and was intended for the noble society at major courts. The courtly ideal of chivalry, with its central concept of service obviously corresponded to the wishes and ideals of the princely patrons and the noble audience. It cannot be proved from literary history that "little more than an artificial flowering" was left of the "artistic beauty" and the "moral attraction" of the ideal of service in courtly literature (p. 87).

Hans Georg Reuter has expressed himself even more decidedly than J. M. van Winter against the traditional "knightly class theory"[11] and has subjected the whole of research into knighthood to thoroughgoing criticism, the historical research as well as that in German literature. He is convinced that practically everything written about knights in the last hundred years is wrong and that the reason is that everyone has taken as his starting point a concept of the knight which did not develop until the eighteenth century and which is reflected most clearly in the great work

of Jean Baptiste de la Curne de Sainte-Palaye. He says that the core of
this incorrect conception of the knight was the idea that there was a
unified knightly class in the Middle Ages within which the whole of the
nobility and *ministeriales* were merged. Reuter set himself the task of
checking whether the class explanation of the concept of knighthood
could be confirmed in the medieval sources and he came to a negative
conclusion; the medieval terms *miles* and *ritter* possess, according to his
conclusions, a mass of various meanings and cannot be interpreted in the
sense of the actual existence of knights as a social class. This result was
not, however, as surprising or as new in 1971 as the author believed.
The understandable desire to set off his own position from other efforts
which were similarly oriented unfortunately led the author to condemn
all the research, root and branch, without any differentiation, and even
to go so far as to be unwilling to allow that knighthood existed as a
historical phenomenon at all.

    The value of the work thus lies less in the general points of view
of the critical approach than in the presentation and analysis of the source
material. Here for the first time the historical sources in Latin and the
poetic sources in German for a limited area are investigated and compared
with one another with regard to the meaning and use of the words *miles*
and *ritter*. The Latin examples of *miles* and *militia* from the historical
writings of the eleventh to the thirteenth centuries in particular offer a
welcome addition to our knowledge. The author has organized his material
in such a way that the whole spectrum of meaning of the words *miles*
and *ritter* becomes clear. I would like to call particular attention to that
section of the *miles* chapter on "*miles* as a designation for the retainer"
(pp. 61ff.) and the discussion of the terminology of the initiation (pp.
70ff.). The author's conclusions that neither the military nor the service
meaning of *miles* permit any conclusions about class (p. 55 and p. 57)
are illuminating. The second conclusion, that "according to the sources
there can be no question of limiting the use to a particular social stratum"
(p. 64) must be examined by historians. In general, the chapter on the
German concept *ritter* is less fruitful because no new material is examined.
In respect of my investigations, Reuter has thrown doubt on the possibility
that the word "ritter" can designate a simple soldier and he declares that
the meaning "retainer" is not proved. Nevertheless numerous instances
can be produced from Middle High German texts for both the first and
the second meaning and the idea that the German word "ritter" is different
from the Latin word "miles" in both these respects does not get us any
further. The observation that the vernacular word hardly ever designates
a retainer whereas there are many instances of the use of the Latin word
miles in this sense is more interesting. The explanation that Reuter gives
for this, "that poetry is almost exclusively concerned with military and

courtly life and that legal relationships are hardly mentioned" (p. 111) is not very convincing. Otherwise his interest was everywhere directed towards showing that both the Latin and the German word had "various meanings . . . which cannot be explained in their totality in any unified fashion" (p. 107). From this the author draws the conclusion that no value could be attributed to the terminology of knighthood for the understanding of medieval social conditions. In the face of such an attitude, not much can be expected even from a comparison of German chivalric vocabulary with Latin, which in itself could be very informative. "The source-material which has been investigated does not permit any statement to be made other than that comparable conditions are sometimes designated by the words *miles* and *ritter*" (p. 167). The author appears to have an insufficient awareness of the possible uses of historical semantics for finding out information. His belief that he was compelled to deny any value as historical testimony to the poetical texts in any form ("historical actuality cannot be determined from poetry", p. 40) also put obstacles in the way of his work. The introductory chapter, "Poetry as the Reflection of Reality" (pp. 27ff.) merely shows that the author was not capable of dealing with the question.

During the last few years it has become more and more clearly recognized that the problem of knighthood is not, in the last instance, one of terminology. The historians are primarily concerned with the semantic history of *miles* and *militia* and up to now they have concentrated their attention on the eleventh century in particular, since it was then that the medieval use of the words appears to have developed. I may, perhaps, be permitted to discuss briefly some of the more recent studies on the subject because their results are of importance for all research into knighthood.

We should first mention the study on the origins of knighthood made by Georges Duby,[12] which is exemplary in its objective clarity and methodological circumspection. In its objectives it belongs in the larger context of French research into aristocracy, inspired chiefly by the theories of Marc Bloch, which is today on the way to working out the bases for a new understanding of the aristocracy of the high Middle Ages in France.[13] I cannot go into these problems but I would like to call attention to the fundamental significance of Duby's arguments. Duby's central point is the question of how it came about that the concepts "nobility" and "knighthood" in the thirteenth century were regarded as more or less identical. His starting point was a series of observations on the semantic history of *miles* ("it appeared methodologically sound to use a study of vocabulary as a starting point", p. 740) and he relied chiefly on documentary material. According to his findings the word *miles* occurs in the sense *vassus* or *fidelis* (vassal, faithful servant, retainer) for the first time in the southern French Mâconnais in 971;[14] for about a century the word remained fairly uncommon in the documents of the region then there followed a sudden extension of its use, both qualitative and quantitative and by the end of the eleventh century *miles* was applied without any social limitations to the greatest lords ("les plus hauts seigneurs de la région", p. 742). After this a regular distinction was made in the lists of witnesses between *milites* and *rustici* (knights and peasants). According to Duby, this means that after the end of the eleventh century the word *miles* designates "une qualité familiale et héréditaire" (a quality of family and descent) in the sense of the aristocracy of the high Middle Ages (p. 743). According to Duby's observations, the same development took place, with variations in time, in other districts of France; in Provence there is testimony to its application to the upper nobility as early as 1035; in the Ile de France the châtelains bore the title *miles* after 1060, in Northern France this stage of development was not reached until the last third of the twelfth century and still later in Lorraine; in the Netherlands and Germany a distinction was still being made between *nobiles* and *milites* in the thirteenth century. Duby emphasizes that many individual investigations are still needed into the regional use of the word before the detailed picture of the development can be drawn. It is already quite certain, however, that the rise in social standing of the word *miles* ("le succès du mot *miles*", p. 748) was one of the most important conditions in determining the specific sense of the knight-concept in the high Middle Ages.

Duby put three important questions in connection with his observations on the use of the word: 1. Why was the word *miles* preferred to *vassus, fidelis*, etc., to designate a "social superiority" (p. 757)? 2. Why were the ideas of value which were associated with the word *miles* capable of forming the basis of an aristocratic class-consciousness? 3. Why was the development which led to the equating of knighthood and nobility confined to France and why did the two concepts remain separated for so long in Germany? Duby answered the first question by referring to the military meaning of the word *miles*. There is no need for me to go any further into this. The second question goes to the heart of the problems of knighthood. According to Duby's observations, several factors were at work in the creation of the aristocratic ideal of knighthood. In the eleventh century, he says, the old idea that all mankind was divided into two *ordines* (classes), the *militia spiritualis* and the *militia saecularis* (spiritual warriors and secular warriors) was superseded by a threefold pattern, *oratores, agricultores, pugnatores* (men who pray, men who till, men who fight) (Gérard de Cambrai) in which the fighting men are distinguished from the working population of the country and thus positioned close to the nobility. At this same time a concept of spiritual knighthood was being developed which was applicable to both *principes* and *milites* in its requirement that the poor should be protected and the church defended and which also contributed to bringing closer together the concepts of *nobilitas* and *militia* (nobility and soldiery). In France in the eleventh century there also developed the supreme legal authority of the *châtelains* ("le ban"), to which the whole population of the country was subject—except the *milites*. As a result of this the social barriers between *milites* and *rustici* (knights and peasants) ("cette barrière sociale, désormais fondamentale", p. 758) were strengthened still more. The conditions for the peace of God, finally, operated to produce the same effect, since in their use of the term *militia* they made no distinction between noble lords and cavalrymen and consequently gave the impression that the two groups together formed a unit as regards knighthood. Duby attributed a great deal of significance to this last point.[15] It was there that he found the answer to his third question: the development he described had taken place only in France because the peace-of-God movement was confined to France and the specific supreme authority of the châtelains had developed only there. In Germany, however, the old distinction between princes and knights ("l'antique distinction qui séparait les chevaliers des princes", p. 761) remained intact and it was for this reason that the ideas of nobility and knighthood did not merge completely here.

Duby's essay demonstrates in exemplary fashion how historical and philological observations can supplement each other. The old service-concept *miles*, to which had been attached in the tenth century the additional ideas of subordination and dependence, "la soumission et le service" (p. 751), had become synonymous a century later with the highest social concept *nobilitas*. The fact that it was the military aspect of the word *miles* which brought about the improvement in the word's status is very illuminating. Of still greater significance, however, was the upgrading of the term because of the clerical *militia Dei* (warriors of God) concept which was widely diffused in the peace-of-God movement and in crusading propaganda. In the religious sphere, the idea of service which was present in the old expression *militia Christi* continued to possess a distinguishing significance. According to Duby, the transfer of the demand for religious service to the secular nobility was the moment of the birth of the knighthood of the high Middle Ages: "In France between 1030 and 1095, knighthood came to be regarded more and more clearly as one of the paths of the *militia Dei* ("la chevalerie apparut de plus en plus clairement en France, entre 1030 et 1095, comme l'une des voies de la *militia Dei*", pp. 759f.). In my opinion this is an idea of fundamental importance: knighthood was primarily an ideological phenomenon and even its visible realization in society can be understood only in the context of the development of the ideals of chivalry.

There are still unanswered questions in relation to the conditions in Germany. It must remain the task of the historians to investigate whether the development in France and in Germany really followed such different courses as would appear to be the case according to Duby's presentation. It is difficult to form a decision on this point because the *militia* terminology in Germany has not yet been clarified for the later period. It is to be assumed that regional differences are as significant here as they were in France. Even now it is permissible to suppose that the statement that the transfer of the *miles* concept to the upper nobility did not take place in Germany until the thirteenth century may, in this general form, be in need of limitation, even of correction.[16] Duby may, however, be right in his conclusion that in Germany the concepts of nobility and knighthood did not merge with one another in the same way as they did in France. This observation could also be of importance for German *ritter* terminology, since the situation which, according to Duby, characterizes the conditions in France had already been reached in German poetry by the end of the twelfth century. The first instance is in Hartmann's *Erec*, in which the formulations "der ritter Erec" and "der künec Erec" (Erec the Knight and Erec the King) have practically the same meaning and are virtually interchangeable (see above, p. 76). It remains to be investigated whether Hartmann's work reflects the linguistic usage of his French source.[17] There can be no final word on this question until it has been made clear how the aristocratic chivalric terminology of courtly poetry is related to the *miles* terminology of contemporary historical sources.

In contrast to Duby, P. van Luyn evaluated only narrative sources in his essay on French *milites* in the eleventh century.[18] His careful analysis of the rich material on the word led him to the conclusion that three components were to be distinguished in the *miles* concept of the eleventh century, military, social, and ideological. In the military sphere the word *militia* stands for a profession (p. 226). According to van Luyn, the *milites* formed a "social group" in society, distinguished on the one side from the great lords ("les grands") and on the other from the rural population ("des manants"). Van Luyn characterizes their place in the structure of society by the term *middle nobility* ("ils forment la media nobilitas", p. 225). Within this group of *milites*, according to van Luyn, a distinction should be made between "allodial knights," who often appear in the sources as property owners, as "grands propriétaires" (pp. 35ff.) and domestic knights (*milites domestiques*) who are to be encountered at courts and in the vicinity of great lords and who were frequently regarded as part of their *familia* (household) (pp. 193ff.). The common features of the "groupe sociale" were nevertheless of more significance than the differences. Finally, according to van Luyn, the word was already being applied to the upper nobility in the eleventh century and this leads to the third component of meaning: the entry of the upper nobility into the *militia* ("cette entrée des grands dans la *militia*", p. 216) is to be explained by the fact that the word *miles* had by now become a value-concept; the secular idea of knighthood—of the brave warrior—and the spiritual ideal—of the chivalric fighter for the faith and the church—had so elevated the value of the term that even the upper nobility felt it to be a distinction. Thus, he says, from the old nobility and the "ordinary milites" (*milites ordinaires*, p. 226) there was formed the *ordo militum* (order of knights) the knighthood of the high Middle Ages, which, in the eleventh century is not to be regarded as a "classe sociale" (l'*ordo militum*, qui n'est point une classe sociale", ibid.), because it incorporated in itself various groups—*milites, barones* and *primates* (knights, barons and princes), but as a community which is distinguished by its common profession of arms and its common ideal of knighthood.

Van Luyn thus set up a position which is in many respects related to that of J. M. van Winter. Both agree in distinguishing an older *militia*, which they understand to be a "classe sociale" from the later phenomenon of knighthood which included the upper nobility. It is true that van Luyn put the social standing of the older *milites* at a higher level than did van Winter, since he speaks of them as "lesser nobility," (*media nobilitas*) whereas van Winter stresses rather their inferior character. But van Luyn too emphasizes that, irrespective of their economic position, it was part of the obligations of the *milites* in the eleventh century to follow their lord at his summons ("l'obligation de suivre le seigneur à son appel", p. 202). Both investigations agree further that the later concept of knighthood is not to be approached from the point of view of social law, but must be explained by the concepts of a chivalric ideal. Like van Winter, van Luyn too speaks of a late "entry" of the upper nobility into the *militia* and it is here that the same reservations must be expressed as were made earlier. What makes van Luyn's essay valuable and important is chiefly the intelligent and extraordinarily well-documented analysis of the French occurrences of the word *miles* and it constitutes a considerable piece of preparatory work for a highly desirable history of the terminology of the word *militia*.

I would like to point even more emphatically to van Luyn's arguments about the knightly initiation ceremony (pp. 217ff. and 237ff.) It is characteristic of the state of research in this sector, which is of such great importance for the understanding of aristocratic knighthood, that the historical material has never been completely assembled. Essentially one must still refer to the collections put together by Wilhelm Erben,[19] which were very valuable in their day but have since been shown to be defective. Van Luyn has now produced eleven pieces of evidence for the initiation ceremony from France for the period between 1070 and 1125, most of them previously unknown, which, according to his observations, indicate that in France, unlike Germany, the initiation ceremony was not a prerogative of the upper nobility but was practiced by "ordinary" knights from the beginning ("l'adoube est pratiqué à tous les niveaux de la *militia*", p. 217). According to van Luyn's evidence, four of his eleven instances refer to sons of "*milites* ordinaires." There is here a wide open field for future research. The chief concern must be to investigate the terminology of the initiation ceremony to see whether formulations such as *ad militiam promovere, militem facere, armis militaribus adornare*, etc. (to advance to knighthood, to make a knight, to gird with the arms of knighthood) really refer always to a ceremonial act of initiation such as that for which there is historical evidence, particularly for the sons of princely families. In the German material on these terms, I have been able to observe that "ritter machen," "ze ritter vazzen," and similar expressions which occur in connection with the initiation ceremony in many passages mean no more than "equip as a soldier," "become a soldier," "muster" (see above, p. 31). In this connection it should also be mentioned that in the Latin sources the abnegation of worldly life may be expressed by the terms *cingulum militiae deponere* or *respuere* (to lay down the belt of knighthood or reject it (van Luyn, p. 218). It is not very likely that any ceremonial putting-off of the sword-belt actually took place when a *vir saecularis* (secular man) entered a monastery but if we are to assume that *cingulum militiae* had a metaphorical meaning here, then we must raise the question whether the same could not be true in a positive sense for such terms as *ad cingulum militiae promovere*.

Johann Johrendt's dissertation on the terms *milites* and *militia* in the eleventh century[20] appeared at the same time as van Luyn's essay. In part it covers the same area of source material as his but goes considerably beyond it in the amount of material evaluated. The work renders an important service largely through the fact that the *militia* terminology, especially of the narrative sources, of the eleventh century is here made available in considerable quantity. In his introduction Johrendt explains that he "has deliberately not attempted . . . to trace a total picture of knighthood" (p. 2). This need not be a disadvantage, since in the field of knighthood problems a great deal more research into details is still needed before a total picture can be drawn. In his first chapter, the author investigates the military function of the *milites*, in the second their position in the feudal system; the third deals with the economic circumstances of the *milites*, the fourth with the problem of their social rank. The work ends with two shorter sections on the secular ideal of knighthood in the eleventh century and on the spiritual *militia Christi* concept. The author emphasizes "that the designation *miles* in the eleventh century" does not yet permit any "clear distinction in law" (p. 6) and he consequently refuses to talk of a knightly class in the eleventh century (p. 235). The "approach to the *miles*-concept in the eleventh century" lies for him in the military sphere. "What binds all milites and what is common to all of them whatever the social distances between them is their professional pursuit of war" (p. 237). Thus Johrendt confirms at first what earlier investigations had shown. He does, however, lay particular stress on the professional character of this *miles* soldiering and keeps repeating "the common practice of their profession" (p. 236) and the "common professional attitude" of the *milites*. (p. 138). He designates them as "professional soldiers" (p. 237) who together formed a "professional class" (p. 182) which, according to him, whose sociological range stretched from king down to mounted *armiger* (man-at-arms, armor-bearer), even down to groom (p. 237). In my view, a terminology such as this can easily lead to misunderstandings. In discussing the professional practice of mounted military action it is better to confine oneself to the mercenary soldiery which so strongly marked the character of the feudal armies of the twelfth century. Naturally, there is no intention to dispute the fact that noble lords too took up arms and perhaps even spent a large part of their time in fighting and feuding; but they spent just as much time riding out to hunt or sitting in judgment and nobody today would dream of saying that they were for that reason professional hunters or professional judges. When a king or his vassals are called professional soldiers, the word "profession" loses any precise sense.

Johrendt ties the military meaning of *miles* closely to the meaning "vassal," in as much as he defines the "professional soldiers" more exactly as "vassal professional soldiers" (p. 6), as "free noble professional soldiers" (p. 187), as "noble war-vassals" (p. 229), and "fief-warriors" (p. 236). Behind this there is the view that "*miles* designates in general a member of the upper or middle stratum sociologically" (p. 171). Johrendt also calls upon the concept of freedom for his characterization of the older *militia*—"the professional class of the *milites* is defined unambiguously in law by its free status" (p. 182)—although elsewhere, in reference to the circumstances in Germany, he was able to discover "a mixture with unfree elements" (p. 145). For him the determining factor in the character of the older *milites* was their socially superior position "as a political and social elite" (p. 7); according to his definition the *militia* of the eleventh century "is to be regarded both theoretically and practically as an open leadership" and social framework of landed proprietary origin (ibid.). With this concept Johrendt takes completely the opposite view to that of J. M. van Winter in particular whose emphasis was on dependence and liability for service. In his efforts to work out the sharpest possible distinction between the concepts, Johrendt has chosen formulations which are more unambiguous than is justified by the findings in the sources. When he writes in his summary that "primarily there was no reference to be drawn about social origin from the designation *miles*" (p. 230), that means that the social position of the *milites* in the eleventh century cannot be thought of as unified. On the other hand, Johrendt is certainly right in saying that the value concepts which became associated with the word *miles* from the eleventh century on did not originate in the "lesser" nobility. Johrendt quotes a statement by Karl Bosl as a "basic insight into the nature of knighthood": "the sense and form of knighthood first developed in the upper levels of society but it was only gradually that the retainer class rose up into the cultural and social world of the knighthood of the great families" (p. 231).[21]

In his chapter on the ideal of knighthood, Johrendt adduces poetical texts as well as historical sources, particularly the Latin *Ruodlieb* and the French *Chanson de Roland*. The author was of the opinion that German research into the problem of knighthood could not escape the accusation of "being only too willing to regard literature as history" (p. 1), but the way in which he himself evaluates literary evidence shows how uncertain he is in dealing with this kind of source material. He does indeed emphasize that the real picture was very different from the representation of aristocratic life given in poetry (p. 200). In spite of this he does not succeed in making clear the specific declarative value of the poetic texts. "In the eleventh century all men born to knighthood underwent a systematic education between the ages of seven and fourteen, in spiritual and secular matters" (p. 214). "Ostensibly the knight may well fight for his country, his life, his freedom, and his knightly honor and loyalty, but in the West his combats do not receive any Christian sanction until he fights against the heathen Turk." (p. 199). "The *milites* watched for the heroic deeds of their leader and expected them as a matter of course" (p. 204). Statements like this, which merely take literally what is to be found in the poets and which are scarcely to be distinguished from what is to be found in the old cultural histories of knighthood, are virtually useless as historical findings. The juxtaposition of adjectival epithets (*honestus, gloriosus, praecellens*, etc.) which were associated with the word *miles* in the eleventh century, deserve more attention, as do the passages cited for the aspirations to *virtus, gloria* and *honor*, which Jorendt collected from historical sources (pp. 189ff.). It is obvious that these are epithets from the traditional praise of rulers and princes which are here applied to the *milites*, and Johrendt is no doubt right when he points out that the values associated with them "find their origin basically in aristocratic concepts" (p. 192).

It is scarcely possible to agree with the author in the contention he makes in his summary that his procedure was "primarily in the history of ideas" (p. 234), for the philological problems posed by the *militia* terminology are completely ignored. Johrendt never addresses the question of the social elevation of the word, which is what makes the *miles* concept so interesting from the semantic point of view. Unfortunately, the author made only limited use of the possible comparative examination of the conditions in France and Germany. It is true that on several occasions he does present separately French and German evidence in a way to deserve our gratitude and occasionally he points out the differences, for example in the chapter on the social rank of the *milites* and also in the tables in the appendix, but his individual observations are never combined into a complete picture. It is not easy to be fair to Johrendt's work in a brief summary of research. I do not regard it as my obligation to point out its weaknesses. I prefer to stress the positive aspect, especially the author's immense zeal for collecting material, to which we owe the fact that here, and especially in the huge annotation section and the detailed tables at the end, quantities of material are put at the disposal of research which can still be exploited on many occasions in future.

For the Germanist who is concerned with the problems of knighthood today the works of Josef Fleckenstein are of special interest, firstly because the conditions in Germany in the twelfth and thirteenth centuries are central, and secondly because Fleckenstein devotes special attention to the relationships between the historical development and the cultural circumstances. In the last few years, Fleckenstein has produced a number of essays which look at the central problems of research into knighthood from various viewpoints and which can be regarded as preliminary studies for "a comprehensive investigation into the relationships between knighthood and the lesser nobility" which he has announced.[22] I would like here to call particular attention to two of his essays. In 1972 there appeared his investigation on "Friedrich Barbarossa and Knighthood,"[23] in which he evaluates the significance of the courts at Mainz held in 1184 and 1188. According to Fleckenstein, the splendid assembly of 1184 in particular, at which the two sons of Friedrich I were initiated into knighthood "was a demonstration of the connection between imperialism and knighthood" (p. 1026); here, he says, the history of knighthood in Germany reached one of its high points. In concrete terms, this meant that the imperial court "had adopted chivalric norms for itself" (p. 1029) as may be seen most clearly from the fact that the ceremony of initiation, according to the pronouncements of contemporary sources, was an expression of "acceptance into knighthood" (ibid.). At the imperial court the "common nature of knighthood" was made clear terminologically by the fact that contemporary writers lump together "the chivalric-courtly society at the royal court of the Hohenstaufen" (ibid.) under the terms *milites* and *militia* and thus show that "all the members of the court" from king down to the legally unfree *ministeriales* "counted as knights" (p. 1029). It is true, he says, that the knights had already begun "to develop a class-consciousness" (p. 1030) under the influence of the church, but it was not until the imperial court acted as a "collecting point" and "catalyst" (ibid.) that nobility and *ministeriales* formed a community under the title of knights. This community could be understood by its recognition of courtly values, in its refinement of the forms of everyday intercourse, in its interest in chivalric poetry, and especially in its obligation to the crusading concept and the idea of the *militia Christi*. Fleckenstein then looked into the question of how the connection of the imperial court with knighthood developed. According to his conclusions, the most important impulse came in 1157 from the court held in Besançon; it was there, according to him, that Friedrich I first came in touch with the chivalric culture of Burgundy. The Empress Beatrix, who was herself well trained in literature and was associated with French poets at an early stage, played an important role in the acquisition of French chivalry. In addition to the direct influence of Burgundy, "the main entry port of the spirit of chivalry" (p. 1040), he believes that the example of West German princes who were oriented to France acted as a stimulant. But only the fact "that the emperor took his place at the head of his knights" (p. 1041) and opened the way at his court for the entry of the new concepts and ideals did the chivalric courtly culture of the West "become obligatory for the whole chivalry of the Hohenstaufen" (ibid.). This, he says, is the significance of the courts held at Mainz.

In a second essay, Fleckenstein took up "the problem of the determination of the knightly class."[24] He believes that, in attempting to answer the question whether there was a knightly class at the time of the Hohenstaufen, research has in part started from a false premise, namely that the knightly class must "be shown to be an objective and unified power" (p. 225). He believes it to be perfectly possible, however, that "knighthood comprises many variant groups and nevertheless felt itself to be a community" (p. 254). More recent research in France by Duby, van Luyn, and others had led to the conclusion that "knighthood" in France "had developed into a socially elevated class" (p. 256). In this context, he believes, the concept *ordo militaris* is of special significance because it demonstrates the existence of a knightly class in Germany as well as in France. According to Fleckenstein, all the people then called *milites*—and in the twelfth century, according to Fleckenstein, that included princes and great lords as well as the *ministeriales*—"irrespective of their varying status at law," were lumped together under this term (p. 260) and furthermore "as an ordo, a class" (p. 261). It is true that, to a degree, the term *ordo militaris* remained "ambiguous" (p. 263) because in Germany it was still used in part in the "older sense, sharply distinguished from the nobility" (p. 262); but so far as Fleckenstein is concerned it is "decisive" for the question of a knightly class that in Germany in the twelfth century "aristocrats of all ranks are attested, as well as *ministeriales*, under the term *milites*" (p. 263). In the medieval sense of social terminology—and that is Fleckenstein's major point—"knighthood constituted a class as early as the high Middle Ages, namely the *ordo militaris* (ibid.). With reference to the definition of this class, Fleckenstein emphasizes that there were in the Middle Ages open classes too: there was, for example, "no doubt that the *ordo clericorum* was a class" but "it was not closed"; entry into it came about by means of a particular act, the consecration" (p. 264). In the same way, he says, the knightly class was not "a class by birth" but "a class by profession" (p. 265) at first and a man was taken into it by a particular act, the initiation. Only later was "the aristocratic principle of equal birth" (p. 266) applied to the knightly class and it then effected a reshaping of the class. In the first half of the thirteenth century the legal definition of the class was complete and was made a matter of "legal statute" in various European countries (p. 267). He admits that, so far as Germany is concerned, there is "surprisingly no corresponding law" (ibid.) but it must be presumed that here too, in the thirteenth century, "definition was to be regarded as a rule" (p. 268). Reality did not, indeed, always correspond exactly to this legal development; at all times and at that period to an increasing degree there was in Germany "upward movement of non-knightly groups" into knighthood (ibid.). The decisive factor, therefore, is not to be found in the formal definition of the class but in the "change in structure" of knighthood (p. 269), which is most clearly expressed in the new concept *genus militare* (military class). This concept no longer applied "to a broad chivalric community" which embraced the aristocracy and the *ministeriales*, as the *ordo militaris* had done, but meant simply "*ministeriales* and ordinary knights" (p. 270). In reference to the total development, therefore, he believes it necessary to speak of "a knightly class in a double sense" (p. 271), firstly of the "knightly class of the high Middle Ages," which was "at first a purely professional class," and secondly of the "knightly class of the late Middle Ages," which became "a class by birth" once "the principle of knightly birth" had become established and which comprised "only the lower stratum of the old knighthood" (p. 270). The upper nobility then withdrew from the knightly class but, "paradoxically" (p. 271) it adopted knightly ideals and developed them further in the succeeding period.

Fleckenstein has performed a very useful service in making a central point of one question: In what sense can we speak at all of a knightly class? His conclusion that knighthood in the twelfth and early thirteenth centuries should not be interpreted as matter of birth fortifies the reservations that have been raised in regard to the traditional picture of the legal and constitutional aspects.[25] It is also illuminating that he insists on the necessity of starting from medieval concepts of class and of class-consciousness when the class-character of knighthood is examined. In medieval class theory, the word "class" means "position in a larger whole,"[26] and in this general sense the knights undoubtedly formed a class. The question nevertheless remains as to what concrete significance this class-concept could have for understanding the actual social conditions. In the sense of the medieval *ordo* concept the "class" of knights is to be regarded not only as belonging to a hierarchy running from kings to dukes, counts and freemen on the one side, from clerics to monks, merchants, and peasants on the other, but it must also include hermits, beggars, children, virgins, huntsmen, furnacemen, bawds, painters, dung-spreaders, fools, whores, murderers, and innkeepers, who had their own "class."[27] Otto Brunner emphasizes that medieval class-theory needs first and foremost "a relationship to historical reality,[28] and that is true for knights also. Fleckenstein has interpreted this connection with reality in the sense that he defines the older knightly class as a professional class. It is generally recognized that in medieval social theory there was frequent intertwining and mixing of hierarchical concepts based on ruling classes and professional classes. What is less clearly apparent is what significance a structure of society according to professional classes really possessed. It must be left to historians and legal historians to determine whether the concept "professional class" is really suitable for comprehending the true social state of knighthood in the twelfth century. It might be advisable to talk of the "class" of the knights only in connection with the later period in which there is historical evidence for stratification according to birth and for the development of a hierarchy of ranks. Knighthood of the period around 1200 can be described entirely as a social phenomenon, as a community of aristocratic life style and courtly ideals, as Fleckenstein did in his essay on Barbarossa and knighthood in which, I think I am right in saying, the word *Ritterstand* (knightly class) does not appear.

According to Fleckenstein, the clearest evidence of class formation for knighthood is the term *ordo militaris* (military rank, military class). For this Fleckenstein leans heavily on the research of Duby and van Luyn which, according to his presentation, lead to the conclusion that in France knighthood became constituted "as a class" (p. 257) and he opposes the interpretation which I support, that the concepts *ordo militaris* and *ordo equestris* must be seen against the background of a long literary tradition and that their value for understanding social history is questionable (see above, pp. 110f.). I am still of the opinion that the division of mankind into two or three *ordines* (classes), such as we often encounter in the ninth century among authors of clerical status,[29] should not be interpreted as the reflection of social reality, but that we should first determine how such concepts developed and what intellectual demands were associated with them. So far as the concept *ordo militaris* in particular is concerned, J. M. van Winter has shown in a valuable little study[30] that the term is used in the work of Richer of St. Remi in the tenth century in several meanings and that it can designate all soldiers taken together as well as the retinue of a lord. ("l'ordo militaris comprend tantôt tous les combattants qui forment l'armée, tantôt le groupe des serviteurs préférés du seigneur", p. 124). According to Fleckenstein's observations, this older meaning of *ordo militaris*, which did not include the nobility, was still alive in Germany in the twelfth century (p. 263). Obviously the juxtaposition of various components of meaning was just as characteristic of the concept *ordo militaris* as it was for the whole *militia* terminology. How far semantic findings can be projected on to socio-historical findings must first be determined by semantic and history of concepts research. Until this is done, the mere presence of the term *ordo militaris* cannot be evaluated as proof of the existence of a knightly class in the twelfth century any more than a *miles* at this time can be regarded without any question as a "knight."

Fleckenstein has produced very interesting testimony to show that in Germany, too, princes and great lords were designated as *milites* (p. 260, n. 48 and p. 1029, n. 36). It is obvious that the social elevation of the word *miles*, which Duby was able to prove for France, took place in similar fashion in Germany, although after a characteristic postponement in time. But the passages of testimony in Fleckenstein also show that in the sphere of the upper nobility the *miles* concept was applied chiefly with an adjectival epithet: *miles probus et largus, electi milites, egregius miles*, etc. (a fair and generous knight, chosen knights, brave knight). I have found it possible to make similar observations in the German material on the word. The word *miles* alone without any ornamental epithet seems to occur chiefly in connection with the initiation ceremony when it is used in connection with lords of princely or upper nobility status. That would agree with the findings in the German-language sources. By the end of the twelfth century anyway the word *ritter* is applied without any restraints to emperors and kings. This was obviously essentially a poetic use of the word. According to Fleckenstein's observations, the clearest expression of the new concept of knighthood is to be found in the fact that at the court of the emperor Friedrich I nobility and *ministeriales* are included in the term *militia*, and from that, he says, it can be deduced that "the whole court was included in knighthood" (p. 1029), from emperor to retainer. Since Fleckenstein gives considerable weight to this point, the instances he gives to support this use of the word deserve special attention (p. 1028, n. 35). In the military sphere, the word *militia* had always had an overlapping meaning (it is here that the formula *exercitus militum* (army of soldiers) in the *Historia de expeditione Friderici* belongs); furthermore the religious *militia* concept is scarcely to be referred back to the composition of chivalric society at the imperial court. It is here that the formulae *militia Christi* and *milites crucis Christi* belong, taken from various contemporary sources and further the instance from Arnold's *Slavenchronik*; "ad expugnandos inimicos crucis Christi robur militiae sue convertit", (IV, 7) (He turned the flower of his soldiery to destroy the enemies of Christ's cross). Thus the only passage which remains as evidence for "all members of the court" (p. 1029) is that taken from the *Hennegau Chronicle* of Gislebert of Mons, in which the number of *milites* who took part in the court held at Mainz in 1184 is given as 70,000: "congregatis equidem de toto imperio ex hac parte Alpium ad curiam principibus archiepiscopis, abbatibus, ducibus, marcionibus et comitibus palatinis et aliis comitibus et viris nobilibus et ministerialibus fuerunt numero juxta veram estimationem milites in illa curia 70 milia, exceptis clericis et cuiuscumque conditionis hominibus" (From all the empire on this side of the Alps were brought together at court princes, archbishops, bishops, abbots, dukes, marquises, and counts palatine and other counts, and noble men and *ministeriales* to the number of 70,000, not counting clerics and men of common condition) (ed. Vanderkindere, p. 155, lines 28ff.). It cannot be determined from the wording whether the figure given includes the princes and great lords or refers only to the "knightly" retinue of the upper nobility. According to the information provided by Gislebert, the Duke of Bohemia came to Mainz with 2,000 *milites*, the Duke of Austria with 500, the Duke of Saxony with 700, the Count of the Rhenish Palatinate with more than 1,000, the Count of Thuringia with the same number etc (p. 156, lines 9ff.).

When the aristocratic society at the court of Friedrich I is characterized as "chivalric society" (p. 1030), all that is meant is that the "chivalric forms and norms" which were then received at the imperial court were valid for all who belonged to the court's society, even for the legally still unfree *ministeriales*. In this sense "knighthood did become the aristocratic way of life" (p. 1032). Such terminology should not, however, be allowed to lead to the misunderstanding that courtly society thereby became a knightly society, that non-noble knights were accepted as members of it. The concept of aristocratic knighthood which we apply without question to the classical period of courtly culture, mainly under the influence of poetic texts, is not conditional upon the rise of knights but the elevation of the *word* "knight." The chivalric culture of the Hohenstaufen period was a culture of the upper aristocracy and the great courts of princes. We call it "chivalric" because the ideals of aristocratic society took shape in the person of the courtly knight and because the concept of the knight became the embodiment of aristocratic perfection. In several passages Fleckenstein has not made a sufficiently clear distinction between several shades of meaning in the term "knight"; he speaks of "the rise of knighthood" (p. 1025) and he bases his conclusion that the court of Friedrich I did not have "the stamp of chivalry originally" on the fact that no *milites* are mentioned in connection with earlier court-occasions (p. 1035). It would, however, be quite false to interpret him by concluding that the "courtly-chivalric culture" of the courts at Mainz (p. 1034) was, in his opinion, brought about by non-noble knights.

Fleckenstein attributes to the court of the emperor Friedrich I a decisive part in the spread and establishing of the new courtly culture brought in from France and he presents an impressive picture of the splendor and pervasive power of the courts held in Mainz in 1184 and 1188. In this connection it may be further pointed out that, even a generation before Friedrich I, the Hohenstaufen family had emerged as pioneers of French cultural influence. It cannot be accidental that the first chivalric tournament, which took place in Würzburg in 1137, was organized by Dukes Friedrich and Konrad of Swabia, the father and uncle of Friedrich I (Otto von Freising, *Gesta Frederici*, I, 27), and further that one of the earliest reports we have of the new aristocratic custom of the "knightly" initiation ceremony in Germany refers to Friedrich himself (*ibid.*, I, 27). We gather from this that the acceptance of modern French social forms was guided to a very important extent by the active interest of individual West German princely houses and that the Hohenstaufen played an especially prominent role in this. Nevertheless it is perhaps a one-sided picture which emerges if light is concentrated exclusively on the "chivalric Hohenstaufen" who "stepped to the head of his knights" and in doing so made the new courtly ideals binding "on the entire Hohenstaufen body of knights" (p. 1041). If we look at the general picture, the rich principalities of the northwest, particularly Flanders and Brabant, had a much larger part in transmitting French courtly culture and in the view of contemporaries it was not the Duchy of Swabia or the court of the Hohenstaufen emperors but Flanders, Brabant, and Hennegau which were the homes of courtly-chivalric excellence: "swelh ritter zHenegou, zBrâbant und zHaspengou zorse ie aller beste gesaz . . . "

(whatever knight rode best at Hennegau, at Brabant and at Haspengau) (Hartmann von Aue, *Gregorius*, 1575–7).[31] Literary history has turned away more and more from the idea, of which Hans Naumann was the proponent, that courtly literature in Germany was basically inspired by the Hohenstaufen court. The literary interests of the Hohenstaufen kings cannot be denied, but in its significance as a center of modern vernacular poetry the imperial court was overshadowed by others, especially the court of the Count of Thuringia and the Babenberg ducal court at Vienna.

I can deal much more briefly with Germanistic research on knighthood during the last few years. I shall confine myself to a few works which have concentrated on the connections between the image of the knight in literature and the historical reality. It need hardly be said that this restriction is the result of confining my attention to the problems which are here being discussed and does not imply any value-judgments. We are indebted to the French Germanist Daniel Rocher for an interesting review of research on knighthood and chivalric literature.[32] Basing his opinions on the latest research into nobility in France and Germany, he raises the question of "the social reality of knighthood" (p. 165) and in a second part he clarifies the various "spiritual aspects of chivalry" (p. 345). The announced third part, in which chivalric poetry is to be examined from sociological points of view, has not yet appeared. It is only recently that it has been pointed out that the terminology of knighthood plays a role within the context of the reception of the French "roman courtois" in Germany too. René Pérennec puts forward the thesis in an essay on the *Erec* of Hartmann von Aue and its French predecessor.[33] that the stronger moralizing and idealizing stress on the word *ritter* in the German poet should be seen in the context of the different social structures in France and Germany. Not the least of the attractions of the French texts for the audience at the great courts in Germany was certainly their interest in the representation of a modern courtly society. It is highly probable that sometimes attention to the differing nature of social conditions in Germany forced the poets to make changes in respect of their sources. (This has been known for a long time, for example, in regard to the initiation ceremony.)[34] In another connection Daniel Rocher[35] and particularly Gert Kaiser[36] have proved how fruitful this idea can be. Ursula Peters has provided an interesting commentary on it, with special stress on questions of knighthood.[37]

I would like to examine in somewhat more detail Werner Schröder's essay on "the image of the *ritter* in early Middle High German poets, which is directly related to my researches on the concept of knighthood.[38] Schröder attributes to me the opinion that "all *ritter* for whom there is literary testimony" up to the end of the twelfth century "were dependent men, mercenaries and retainers" (p. 335) and in the face of this he undertakes to prove that the word *ritter* was used as early as the early

Middle High German period "for the most part as a designating epithet" (p. 350). In order to make clear the nature of his criticism, I shall quote the passage in which Schröder takes me to task for the lack of philological accuracy in my work: "The supporting passages seem to have been bundled together in a very great hurry without the author's taking account in every case of the value in context. On p. 113 we find that "one of the earliest texts, the *Millstätter Genesis*, . . . already speaks of *gotes riteren* (139,12)' and that this means 'the people of Israel in Egypt.' In fact the passage comes from Exodus and it is the flies, one of the plagues of Pharaoh, not the Israelites, who are compared with *gotes riteren*—a not unimportant point for the interpretation of the passage" (p. 334). A reader who is not very well acquainted with early Middle High German biblical epics might get the impression that I had quoted a completely wrong work and further completely misunderstood the crucial passage. The passage about *gotes ritere* does indeed come from the second book of Moses, not from the first. It is, however, quite clear from the bibliography that I quote the Millstätter version of Genesis and Exodus from Diemer's edition, in which the two texts are printed one after the other, so that it was perfectly clear to the expert from the page numbering ("139,12") that I was talking of a passage from the second book. The relationship between the Genesis and the Exodus in the Millstätter version need not concern us here. In his literary history, De Boor talks about a "double work": "Thus we find the double work in the Millstätter manuscript and consequently call it "Millstätter Genesis and Exodus."[39] According to this my statement was not so very wrong. The most important feature in the matter is that the passage about *gotes ritere* is transmitted only in the Millstätter manuscript, a fact which is easily overlooked if the passage is ascribed to the "Old German Exodus," as Schröder does (p. 337).

In the "Millstätter Genesis and Exodus" *gotes ritere* are discussed in connection with the plagues which the god of Moses brought down upon the Egyptians. In the Middle High German text the third and fourth plagues are run together into the flies about which it is said, according to the new edition of Edgar Papp, Schröder's student:

> gotes rîtere wären si wilde;
> si hêten uile grôzze scare,
> uone gote chômen si dare
>
> (they were God's wild knights;
> they had many great bands,
> they came there from God)   (1482–4)

The flies, writes Schröder "are obviously presented as God's warriors, as *milites Dei*" (p. 337), an interpretation which has some tradition in Germanic research ("lice are the wild cavalry of God"[40]). It is in fact characteristic of the Exodus' style to "personify small creatures as knights" (Ehrismann): toads are presented as *helede* (heroes) (Diemer 137,37) and grasshoppers as *wigande* (warriors) (148,26). In spite of this it is not insignificant for the philologist that in the Millstätter manuscript we do not find *gotes rîtere* but as Diemer has written, *gotes riteren waren si wilde* (139,12). Diemer explains the passage in his glossary: "gotes rîteren wâren die hundes vliegen wilde 139,12—strange, i.e. they were free from them" (Vol. 2, p. 276); it was in this sense that Lexer put the passage in his Middle High German Dictionary (Vol. 3, p. 885). I do not propose to go into detail about the value of the conjecture *gotes rîtere* which has been preferred by editors ever since Kossmann's edition (1886) and which leads to a totally different understanding of the passage. (It might be urged in defense of the transmitted reading that the Israelites in Exodus are called *gotes diet* (God's people) (119,26) and *die gotlieben herren* (lords dear to God) (160,5). It could be pointed out in addition that in the biblical account of the fourth plague also the idea is present that the children of Israel were spared from it (c.f. Exodus viii 21–2). And finally the argument could be advanced that at least until the middle of the thirteenth century there is no instance of the expression "wilde ritter.") Unlike Werner Schröder, I am not a specialist in early Middle High German clerical poetry. He has not told his readers that his interpretation of the passage rests on a conjecture and he has not listed the reasons which caused him to agree with a change in the wording of the manuscript here. But if his reason for accusing me of philological inaccuracy is that I kept to the transmitted wording, that throws its own light on the principles of his critical method.

On the other hand, there seem in fact to be no basic differences between his point of view and mine. His investigations lead to the conclusion "that the word must have been beyond the first stages of its elevation, since early Middle High German poets make use of it" (i.e. the word *ritter*) (p. 351). Thus he confirms in essentials what I had determined earlier, that the word *ritter* rose from a lower social sphere and that the first traces of its elevation can be observed in the early twelfth century. I had designated the "knight" Potiphar in the *Millstätter Genesis* (77,7) as the "first aristocratic knight" in German literature in the vernacular (see above, p. 73). Schröder has not found any older one either. He is of the opinion that this instance "gave me plenty of trouble" (p. 337) because I called it "amazing in its formulation." I will gladly explain why the formulation "si uerschöften in sâr einem riter putifar" (they sold him to a knight Potiphar) (77,7) is in fact remarkable. Among the many thousand instances of the word *ritter* in Middle High German literature (and I know the material pretty well completely up to the middle of the thirteenth century), there are very few in which the word *ritter* stands immediately before the proper name as it does here. Only in Hartmann's *Erec* is this usage more common (cf. above p. 76 ff.). Konrad Zwierzina had already called attention to the fact that Hartmann stood "virtually alone among the older epic writers" in his use of this formulation[41] and he even played with the idea that "Hans Ried was the first who could have dubbed 'Herr' Erec knight" (p. 337). Zwierzina was acquainted with the corresponding formulations in Veldeke's *Eneit* but the oldest instances—*riter Putifar* in the *Millstätter Genesis* and *rîter Daclym* in the *Vorauer Alexander* (1299)—were not known to him. With such formulations as "der ritter Idërs" (778), "der ritter Brîen" (1640), "der ritter Erec" (3634), etc., Hartmann was obviously following an older tradition which first becomes tangible to us in the *Millstätter Genesis* but which was unable to establish itself in courtly poetry.

The first instance of the use of the word *ritter* is in the *Wiener Genesis*. There the story is told that Joseph, who had risen to high honor in Egypt, rode to meet his father with a large escort: "Ioseph sa dar reit, mit ime manich rîter gemeit" (Joseph rode there and with him many a fine knight) (5060f.). I do not see how it could be disputed that the *rîter* here form the "escort" of a great lord. (see above, p. 47) It appears to me very significant that the oldest instance of the word *ritter* testifies to exactly this meaning of the word. It is obviously the basic meaning from which we should start out. If Schröder declares that I saw in the knights who accompanied Joseph "courtiers who were unfit for military service," then that is his formulation, not mine (p. 336). His statement that "in the eyes of the poet, it would have been unworthy of this "powerful lord" to ride out with is household and courtiers" (ibid.) overlooks the old meaning of the word "Gesinde." The aristocratic lords living there also counted as part of the court retinue of a great prince. For example, in *Wigalois* it is said of King Arthur: "wol tûsent rïter er hêt ze gesinde tägelîche; der ieglîcher was sô rîche an rossen und an gewande, an bürgen und an lande, daz im nihtes gebrast" (he had a good thousand knights in his household every day; each of them was so rich in horses and clothing, in castles and land, that he lacked for nothing) (210–15). The knights in the retinue of a great prince cannot be accommodated under a formula of social rank; there can be king's sons among them and simple soldiers. What they have in common is not birth but, as van Luyn writes, "the obligation to follow their lord at his summons" (p. 202).

Schröder contradicts my opinion that a comparison of the *Strassburger Alexander* with the Vorauer version could show how the use of the word *ritter* had changed in the course of a generation (see above, p. 75). According to his view, the changes are principally "of a stylistic nature," and the larger number of instances of the word are allegedly found mostly in "doggerel lines of the crudest makeshift character" (p.

343). It is only rarely that we have the opportunity to trace the terminology of knighthood in the twelfth century as exactly as in making a comparison of the two Alexander poems. I should therefore like to present the material in its full form here (both texts from Kinzel's edition):

Vorauer Alexander	Straßburger Alexander
145 *sin bûch ne was ime ze lanc noh ze breit:* *a wie wole dem jungelinge daz stêt.* *scône er ze tale wert scein* *peidiu uber fûz unt uber pein.* *unt uber allen sînen lîp* 150 *sô was er als êrlih.*	171 *sin bûch ne was ime nit ze lanc noh ze breit:* *vil wol daz deme jungelinge steit.* *beide ubir vûze und ubir bein* *rîterlîch er ze tale schein.* 175 *unde ubir allen sînen lîb* *was er rehte hêrlîch.*
155 *Nû vernemt, wie sich Alexander vur nam:* *swâ sô ein frumich rî t e r zû zim chom,* *dem bôt er lîp unt gût.*	181 *Nû hôret, wî er sih fure nam:* *swâ ein frumich rî t e r zô ime quam,* *den bôt er lib unde gût.*
213 *unt wie er zen rî t e r n solti gebâren* *umbe daz, daz sim willich wâren.*	243 *und wî er zô den rî t e r e n solde gebâren* *zô diu daz si ime willich wâren.*
365 *Unt alsô daz chint nâch dem site* *was wol gewâfen unt geriten,* *dô was er ein scôner jungelinc.* *si grûzten in als ein chunich.*	430 *Dô daz kint nâh rî t e r lî ch e n site* *wol gewêfent was und geriten,* *dô was er ein scône jungelinc.* *si grûzten in alse einen kuninc.*
411 *Ein rî t e r hiez Lisias,* *der stolz unt redehaft was.*	482 *Ein rî t e r hîz Lysias,* *der stolz und redehaft was . . .*
923 *dâ mahti man manegen degen scouwen* *al durch den helm verhouwen,* *unde manegen rî t e r junch* *al durch die halsperge verwunt . . .*	1285 *man mohte dâ degene scowen* *durh den helmen verhowen.* *man sah dâ manigen rî t e r junc* *durh den halsberch sô verwunt . . .*
1239 *Mennes was ein herzoge genant,* *den Darios hete dar gesant,* *der was ein helt vrumeclich.* *ein hundert rî t e r hâter umbe sich* *mit swerten vil gûten,* *die tâten si im ze hûte.*	1711 *Mennes der wîgant,* *den Darius hete gesant* *Alexandro ingagen,* *alsih daz bûch hôrte sagen,* *der hete manlîchen mût* *und was ouh ein rî t e r gût.* *dô er di mêre vernam,* *stolzer rî t e r er nam* *ze sih zehen hundrit* 1720 *ûz sineme here gesundrit,* *di sîn solden hûten* *mit ellenthaften mûten.*
1247 *Alexander want sîn vanen,* *er begunde sine helide manen.* *er sprenget ze Mennes wert* *unt liez iz niuht durch die scarphen swert.* *durch alle die sine er brach.*	1725 *umbe karter sînen vanen* *und begunde sîne helede manen.* *Bucifale er verhancte,* *Mennese er zô sprancte.* *durh sîne rî t e r e er dô brach.*
1276 *ein rî t e r der hiez Daclym,* *der was mit Alexander dâ* *unde stunt ime des tages vil nâ.* *der ander hiez Jubal,* *der sich vil ungerne in dem sturme hal.*	1761 *vil schîre ime ouh ze helfen quam* *Daclym ein rî t e r lobesam.* *der was mit Alexandro dare comen . . .* 1772 *dâ was ouh ein ander,* *ein rî t e r, der hîz Jubal,* *der sih ungerne verhal.* *swâ iz in di nôt ginc.* *der was ein edele jungelinc.*

Vorauer Alexander   Straßburger Alexander

Vorauer Alexander	Straßburger Alexander
1299 *alsus sprach sîn rîter Daclym . . .*	1803 *des wart Daclym innen* *unde rief mit hôer stimmen . . .*
1371 *Unt Alexander sînen vanen wider gewan,* *Mennes aber ime zû chom . . .*	1887 *Dô nam Alexander sînen vanen* *und reit rîterlîche danen.* *dâ er wisse sîne man.* *Mennes ime aber zû quam . . .*
1443 *grâven chômen ime ouch* *zwei hundert unde sibenzoch.* *herzogen zim chêrten* *(daz sich sîne rîter mêrethen),*[42] *die zalt man, sô ich sicher bin,* *zaht hundert unde trîn.*	1970 *herzogen ime ouh quâmen* *zwei hundrit unde sibinzich* *unde dar zô manic grâbe rîch,* *di zô ime kêrten* *und sîne reise mêrtin.* *di quâmen alle mit gwalt.* *di grâben wâren gezalt* *rehte an eilif hundrit.*
	2207 *Abdirus was ein michel stat . . .* 2211 *dâ wâren rîtere gemeit* *und wâren zaller zît gereit* *ze wîge und ze sturme.*
	4371 *iz* [sc. der Elefant] *treget wol âne zwîhel* *in strîte und in sturme* *berhfriden unde turme* *und rîter dar inne.*
	4949 *mine rîter al di wîle* *wolden swimmen in den wâch.* *dâr ginc uns der scade nâh.* *cocodrillen quâmen,* *mîner gesellen si nâmen* *sibene unde zwênzic,* *di verloren dâ den lîb.*
	5957 *man mohte dar an* [sc. an dem Wandbehang] *scowen* *rîter unde frowen* *obene unde nidene* *mit wunderlîchen bilide.*
	6045 *ouh mohte man dâ scowen* *funf hundrit juncfrowen* *wol gewassen und smal* *und rîterlich ubir al . . .*

These instances show that even in the second half of the twelfth century the word *ritter* was making only very slow upward progress. The usage in the *Strassburger Alexander*, which is dated about 1170, gives very little reason for thinking that twenty years later the concept of knighthood would have become the distinguishing term for the new aristocratic courtly culture. Schröder's view that the word *ritter* in early Middle High German literature was used mostly "in a designating or distinguishing sense" (p. 350) finds no more confirmation here than it does in other texts of the period. *Ritter* still occur here, as they had a hundred years earlier in the *Wiener Genesis*, for the most part in the vicinity of great lords, they

are usually anonymous, and they often appear in large numbers, as soldiers in the army and as a retinue at court. Of the eight instances of *ritter*
in the *Vorauer Alexander*, five fall into this category. The remaining
three are only apparent exceptions: the "knight" Lisias is one of the
escort of Queen Cleopatra ("der was mit der brûte dar comen" [he had
come with the bride] is the wording of the Strassburg version, line 484;
in the *Historia de preliis* he is called "quidam ex discumbentibus"—one
of those at table, cf. Kinzel, p. 62); (Schröder changes him into a "distinguished Macedonian" on page 342 and into a "loyal subject of King
Philip" on page 341); the two "knights" Daclym and Jubal are brave
warriors, one of them a member of Alexander's bodyguard, the other of
the retinue of the Persian duke Mennes. In the Vorauer version there are
still no aristocratic knights. The most that can be said is that the word
has a sense of distinction when associated with a distinguishing epithet
(*frumich rîter*, 156; *rîter junch*, 925—excellent knight, young knight).
By comparing the two versions, a development of the terminology of
knighthood may be observed in the following particulars:

1. In the Strassburg version there is a considerable increase in the
   number of designating epithets; as well as *vrumec ritter* and *ritter
   junc* we find *ritter guot, stolzer ritter, ritter lobesam* and *ritter
   gemeit* (excellent knight, young knight, good knight, proud
   knight, famous knight, bold knight). The formulation *ritter gemeit* goes back to the eleventh century, but the *Strassburger
   Alexander* seems to provide the earliest evidence for the remaining
   expressions, a clear indication of its modernity;

2. The courtly formula *ritter unde vrouwen* is to be found only in
   the Strassburg version and, what is far more important, it is only
   here that we find the adjective *ritterlich* (and the adverb *ritterlîche*), which broke through class barriers earlier than the basic
   word *ritter* (cf. above pp. 79 ff.). Incidentally the same seems
   to be true for the Latin terms: a nobleman could be called *vir
   militaris* before the word *miles* had penetrated into aristocratic
   circles.[43] The words *ritterlich* and *ritterlîche* are even applied to
   Alexander at this point, to his splendid appearance ("rîterlîche
   er ze tale schein", p. 173) and to his military prowess ("und reit
   rîterlîche danen", p. 1888). At the same time the noble custom
   of admission to arms was made into *rîterlîchen site* (p. 430) and
   in the *Strassburger Alexander* there are for the first time "ritterliche" *juncvrouwen* (knightly young ladies) (6048), a usage
   which did not attain its full flower until Hartmann von Aue (cf.
   above, p. 81);

3. The *Strassburger Alexander* provides an important example of
   the rise of the word "ritter" into the sphere of the upper nobility

when it says of the Persian duke Mennes: "der hete manlîchen mût und was ouh ein rîter gût" (1715–6) (he had manly spirit and was a good knight). It is true that the duke is not directly designated as a knight but that it is stated simply that he was a fine warrior. Nevertheless the fact that the Strassburg adaptor changed the *helt vrumelîch* of the Vorauer text into *rîter gût* is a sign that the Strassburg version stood on the threshold of a new period in which the word "ritter" became the embodiment of courtly perfection.

In conclusion I would like to address several points of more general interest which require further clarification.

On the value of poetic texts as sources. Even today one still meets denigrating remarks about the utility of poetic testimony for the under-standing of historical connections in the Middle Ages. Such judgments are understandable as a reaction against the misuse of vernacular literature which used to be made in cultural history; statements in poetry were regarded as historical reality in completely uncritical fashion and were put together to form a picture of courtly culture which may have corre-sponded to romantic daydreams but not to the reality of life in the twelfth and thirteenth centuries. Weinhold's book on German women,[44] Niedner's treatment of tournaments,[45] and Alwin Schultz's major presentation of courtly life at the time of the *Minnesänger*[46]—I am deliberately men-tioning only such works as, with all their faults, have never been superseded as collections of material—can be called notorious examples of this sort of thing. But we should not fail to mention that even then there were critical voices raised against this sort of exploitation of poetic texts: Julius Petersen (1909)[47] and Paul Kluckhohn (1910)[48] each in his own way demonstrated that valuable information could be obtained from works of poetry if the questions were asked with the necessary caution. Edward Schröder should also be mentioned in this connection who, in the breadth of his historical interests and of his knowledge was superior to the majority of his contemporaries and who, in numerous studies demonstrated the value, one might even say the necessity, of cooperation between historians and philologists. Unfortunately his example inspired few successors; the researches of his student Schwietering on the history of the spear and sword in the twelfth century (1912)[49] remained an ex-ception. Today research must take up where it then left off. The whole area of the reality of courtly culture must be looked into afresh.[50] In doing so it will be important that the statements in historical sources and those in poetic ones, which are much richer in detail, throw mutual light on one another.

There is no formula, no patent method for the historical evaluation
of texts of fiction, or, putting it another way, I do not think that one can
get at the problem by a theory. It is hard to say anything against the
sentence "Knights in poetry are in principle fictional characters."[51] But
if one is convinced that medieval poetry was a social art and that it should
be looked at by way of its social conditions and assumptions, then one
will not be satisfied with such a conclusion. In general, it is true that one
must proceed with the greatest precaution and with the greatest effort to
be critical if one is to succeed in giving poetry a firm basis in history.
Most of all one must constantly take account of the aim towards which
one's desire for information is concretely directed. For example, it would
not seem to me to be very sensible to look in the poetic texts of the
courtly period for an answer to the question as to whether there really
was a knightly class at the time. I know that some critics have interpreted
the intention of my researches into the concept of knighthood in this sense
and I cannot exclude the possibility that some of my formulations may
have encouraged this view. But the fact of the matter was that I had to
take issue with the view that the knightly class was easier to perceive in
courtly poetry than it was in the historical sources ("In Wolfram's *Parzival* we encounter a completely unified knightly class.")[52] It was my
intention at that time to show that this view was wrong, that it was not
possible to use the poets as evidence for interpreting knighthood during
the classical period as a class phenomenon. It was perfectly clear to me
that any decision about the historic reality of the knightly class was the
business of the historians.

There is least dispute about the value of poetic texts as sources when
it is a question of historical semantics. One of the most important insights
of modern historiography is that the historical picture of the Middle Ages
which was put together in the nineteenth century was distorted and fal-
sified to a large degree by the fact that views on the state and on society
belonging to their own time were transposed to the quite different conditions of the Middle Ages. Otto Brunner especially emphasized over and
over again the importance of a conceptualization of history oriented towards the sources.[53] But since the historical source material is available
almost exclusively in Latin, the necessity of taking cognizance of vernacular tradition, for the most part poetic texts, is self-evident. Research
into early legal language has confirmed how fruitful such comparative
investigations can be. Edward Schröder should again be mentioned in
this connection, with his investigation into "duke" and "prince"[54] and
other studies and then, on the historical side, Walter Schlesinger in particular[55] and among more recent scholars perhaps Ruth Schmidt-Wiegand[56] or Gerhard Köbler,[57] in whose work historical and philological
interests come together in fruitful fashion. How successful work in this

area can be has been shown recently by the colloquium on "The Word and Concept 'Peasant.' "[58] My investigations into the concept of knighthood should be seen in this context. It would be desirable if the whole terminology of society in courtly literature could be gradually reworked: the concepts *adel* (*edele, edelkeit*—noble, noblemen, nobility), *hêrre* (*hêrschaft*—lord, lordship), *dienest* (*dienen, dienestman*—service, serve, servant or retainer), *vrî* (*vrîheit*—free, freedom), *geselleschaft geselle, gesellekeit*—society, companion, companionship), *hof* (*hövesch, hövescheit*—court, courtly, courtliness) and also *lêhen* (fief), *ingesinde* (household), *eigen* (possession, unfree man) etc are obvious candidates.

There is still another area in which poetry proves to be a historical source of the first rank. I would like to clarify this by means of one example from the *Krone* of Heinrich von dem Türlin. There we are told very circumstantially at what enormous expense the great court festival was prepared which King Arthur decided to celebrate at Tintagel (490ff.). Valuable presents, later to be distributed to the guests, were brought in from all over the world. Kei the seneschal, the highest court official, himself traveled to Spain where the best warhorses were to be found. White mules were fetched from Syria, richly decorated arms from France, dyed fabrics from Flanders, satin and silk stuffs from Greece, embroidered tapestries from Egypt, expensive furs from Russia, goldwork from London, and various jewelry from Ireland. To the best of my knowledge there is no historical source of the period which gives us in comparable detail such information about the most important import connections of the contemporary luxury trade. Every individual point can be historically verified. Naturally this does not mean that the events really happened on some particular occasion. The accumulation of every conceivable trade-connection is certainly poetry. What is more important is the fact that the account reflects a consciousness of what was regarded as necessary for the attainment of courtly perfection. This is true in general of the representations of society in courtly poetry. It is realistic in detail, but the reality which is represented in it is not primarily the actuality of real life but the actuality of aristocratic society's image of itself, the society that made this poetry possible and supported it.[59] In this respect the fairy-stories of King Arthur and his heroes have even more value as information than the whole body of chronicle writers of history who may indeed be more "reliable" in general, but who remained totally obligated to traditional Christian values in their concepts of social order and in their evaluations. So, incidentally, did the didactic literature in German of the courtly period. From the poetry, on the other hand, we can see that the aristocratic culture at the great courts originated in a sense of eliteness, which kept at a distance everything *dörperlich, vilain* (rustic, low) and which was supported by the feeling that it was part of a society which alone could afford the new luxury of material culture and which alone was master of the new code of courtly social intercourse and behavior which is reflected, for example, in the protocol for the knightly initiation ceremony or in the rules for chivalric tournaments. It can further be seen from the poetry that this social consciousness is conditioned to courtly and purely secular value-concepts, especially by the concept of courtly love which, as the *origo cunctorum bonorum* (origin of all good things) as it is called by Andreas Capellanus (ed. Trojel, p. 183), was made the central feature of this courtly canon of values. The fairly-tale nature of the Arthurian kingdom and the apparently unreal nature of the ideal characters at court, of the courtly knights and courtly ladies are not proof that poetry had no relationship to the concrete circumstances of society. It seems rather to have been the case that aristocratic society even in real life developed a consciousness of itself primarily and most clearly in the exalted mood of festivals rather than in the routine of domestic life. Nowhere does courtly culture become so comprehensible to us as a historical phenomenon as in the great court-festivals of the period with their material splendor and their social etiquette. These festivals were also the poets' hour. It was there that they found their patrons, it was there that they found their audience to whose ideas and expectations the social image of their love songs and courtly romances had to be related. When the writers of romance told of the splendid court-festivals which King Arthur celebrated with the knights of the Round Table, it was necessary for the listeners to be able to make a clear connection with the social reality of their own festivals, both in the courtly detail of the narrative and in the summons to equal the courtly excellence of the Arthurian heroes. One of the most important and certainly also one of the most rewarding tasks for research would be a comparative investigation of courtly festivals according to poetic and historical sources.

Word and Matter. Questions of Terminology. The fact that the word "knight" has been applied to the most varied historical phenomena causes particular difficulties. Even if we ignore the Greek ἰππῆς (cavalry) and the Roman *equites* (the "knightly class" of classical antiquity) and the armored cavalry of the Huns (the "knights" of the *Völkerwanderung*), etc., and confine ourselves simply to the high Middle Ages, there still remains enough terminological confusion. Even in more recent works, the instances of *miles* and *militia* in the twelfth and thirteenth centuries are usually translated without hesitation by the term "knight." (In the same way French research talks of "chevaliers" of the eleventh century as perfectly natural.) When the question is discussed as to the date from which the Latin words acquired the meaning "knight" and "knighthood," there is normally no thought given to what concept is connected with the word "knight." It can be observed at every step that our word usage has been determined by Romantic ideas which have become associated, for the most part unconsciously, with the concept of knighthood. In order to avoid the danger of looking at the real nature of knighthood in poetic fashion, and this is not a problem peculiar to historians of literature, it is necessary to investigate the field of application and the meaning of medieval words which shared in the verbal formulation of the concept of knighthood, namely the Latin word *miles* and its family, the French *chevalier*, and the German *ritter*. In the present state of research the most urgent matter is a reworking of the Latin terminology of *miles*. Georges Duby emphasizes that it will not be possible to sketch a clearer picture of the development of knighthood until it is possible to obtain an overview of the various local manifestations of the use of the word *miles*. This is particularly true of Germany, where territorial distinctions are much more pronounced than in France. Statements based on only two or three instances are of no help whatsoever. As long as there is no basic assessment of the verbal material, there will continue to be uncertainty on fundamental points.

It is already perfectly clear that the words *miles, chevalier*, and *ritter* could never be taken in such a narrow sense in any area or at any time as to be so semantically restricted as, for example, *princeps* or *baron* or *dienestman* are (prince, baron, retainer). The broad spectrum of meanings and uses is typical of the vocabulary of knighthood. At various times it was the military, the social, the religious, the ideological, or the hierarchical meaning of the word which was most prominent. For the most part they ran parallel to one another and it is fair to assume that there was mutual influence and that they overlapped. So what was a knight? In the military sense, every heavily-armed cavalryman was so named, whether he was a prince or a mercenary. All those who were part of the retinue of kings or great lords were also knights. In this case service was the one element common to all; the higher the status of the lord, the more distinguished were the people who were part of his retinue. Thirdly the whole nobility came to be numbered among the knights and in this sense the word designated a community of similar life style and similar ideals. Finally the word came to stand in addition for the lowest stratum of the nobility, which began to set itself off from those below as a knightly class in the territories from the thirteenth century on. In dealing with the sources we must take account of these four meanings at least and there is in fifth place the religious meaning of the *miles Christianus*. As a result, the question of who "the" knights really were in the eleventh, twelfth, and thirteenth centuries is mistaken. It can lead only to crass misunderstandings if an attempt is made to reconcile the various nuances of meaning of the concept of knighthood by identifying soldier-knights with court-

knights, collecting them into a knightly class, seeing in them the ad-
dressees of *miles Christi* propaganda, and deriving the concept of aristocratic knighthood from their rise into the nobility. Such confused ideas
can still be met. One particularly persistent idea which is constantly
repeated is that the application of the concept of knighthood to the upper
nobility was made possible only by the social rise of the mounted soldiers.
In doing so people lose sight of the fact that we are primarily concerned
here with the rise of a word when in the thirteenth century kings are
designated as knights and that the rise of a group of persons cannot
explain this word-usage. It remains an important task of research into
knighthood, indeed in a certain sense its central problem, to find an
answer to the question of how it came about that words which were
obviously based in the area of service came to be distinguishing epithets
of aristocratic life and how one and the same word came to have such
different meanings. It is good to keep in mind that the problem is twofold,
to establish the facts of word-usage in the sources and to interpret the
components of meaning in relationship to one another.

The Chivalric Ideal of Service—an Ideal for those who Serve? Various
value concepts come together in the courtly chivalric ideal. The traditional
ethics of the ruler with their central concepts of fairness and generosity,
specifically Christian demands on the nobility (protection for widows and
orphans, mercy to the vanquished, etc.), general moral values which, for
an educated man, could be put in the context of the system of cardinal
virtues (wisdom, constancy, courage, etc.)[60] All of these together were
related to the new value-concept of courtly love which imparted its courtly
character to the whole structure in its real sense. This courtly ideal of
chivalry is in need of further clarification as a whole and in its individual
components. In the same way it is not possible even today to answer with
certainty the question why the personification of courtly perfection should
be expressed in the word "knight". In this regard it seems very probable
that the most important precondition for it is to be found in the religious
miles concept of the peace of God and the crusading movement. It was
in the *miles Dei* (knight of God) ideal of the time of Urban II that the
idea was formulated consequentially that it could redound to the credit
of a noble lord to be called "servant"; the servant of a lord who stood
higher than any earthly power.

It is obviously not easy to see in concrete terms towards whom the
religious idea of service was directed. In attempting this a distinction
must be made between the works in which the concept of the *miles Christi*
developed and actual crusading propaganda. It is clearly impossible to
reduce to a social formula the group of people envisaged by Odo of Cluny
(in the *Vita Geraldi*), Bonito of Sutri (in the *Liber de vita christiana*),

Bernard of Clairvaux (in the *Liber ad milites Templi de laude novae militiae*), Jacob of Vitry (in the *Sermones ad fratres ordinis militaris*) and other clerical writers when they speak of the religious obligations of the *militia secularis* (secular soldiery). In principle the religious *miles*-concept was independent of the application of the word in secular society. Its traditional context was the *militia* terminology which went back to the early church.[61] When people began to talk about the *milites Christi* in connection with secular persons in the tenth century, the religious idea took on the nature of an appeal to social duty; it was easiest to combine with the military meaning of the lay concept of knighthood, for it was directed at everyone whose business was with the sword and who were in a position to fight for the church.[62] Carl Erdmann speaks of the "lay knighthood"[63] which stood in need of reform (p. 66) but he understood the concept of knight in such "broad" terms (p. 52) that he included even secular princes. Furthermore it is natural to take note of the fact that tracts written in Latin could not reach a lay audience directly. It is quite otherwise with the crusading sermons which, at the time of the first crusade, were clearly aimed at the whole population. ("Whereas the papal legates for crusades, the cardinals, bishops, and prelates directed their attention primarily to the secular and spiritual princes and often carried out their duties at court festivals, the preachers within the dioceses directed their attention principally to the broad mass of the population, to towns-people and peasants."[64]). It is probable, however, that later, at least in so far as there was direct recruiting for participation in crusades, that there was concentration more and more on the nobility, on the *maxime potentiores et nobiles*, on the very powerful and the noble.[65]

The idea of service is also central in the courtly concept of knighthood. Here the centre of attention is on love as the highest quality or concretely on the courtly *domna* (lady), the perfect *vrouwe* in virtue and beauty. In literary histories very little attention has been paid for a long time to the question of what the great lords, the princely *Minnesänger* and the lords of the upper nobility in the courtly romances, could do in order to get themselves recognized as the "knights" in service of their ladies. Only the more recent works in literary sociology, particularly those of the Romance scholar Erich Köhler,[66] who was able to continue the work of Wechssler,[67] and in Germanistics the investigations of Gert Kaiser,[68] have made this the point a central feature of interest and given new answers. For them the courtly ideal of service is an ideal for those who serve. Social groups on the lower fringe of the nobility, the "lesser knighthood" in France and the *ministeriales* in Germany, produced this courtly ideal of chivalry with its idea of service and used it, according to this view, to justify their own attempts at upward social movement. To the degree to which these groups were able to integrate themselves with the nobility, their chivalric ideal of upward striving became the ideology of the whole feudal class. I cannot here evaluate these theses in detail,[69] but I would not like to pass them over in silence because they are of fundamental importance for our subject. So I shall here confine myself to giving a brief account of the difficulties which, in my opinion, stand in the way of a system for explanation of this kind.

1. The thesis that the courtly ideal of chivalry was in its beginnings an ideal of the lesser knighthood contains a strong hypothetical element inasmuch as it rests on the assumption that this ideal found its first literary expression in a service-poetry no longer extant which must have chronologically preceded the literature which has actually been preserved. When the tradition began, in southern France with the songs of Count Guillaume of Poitou, in northern France at the courts of the Counts of Champagne and of Flanders, poetry was already unmistakably under the aegis of the upper nobility. In Germany too, courtly literature was from the beginning marked by the taste of princely patrons.

2. If the character of the courtly knight was inspired by the courtly interests of a serving class, then it has to be explained why the upper nobility also admired this character. Köhler has argued that the great lords adjusted the service ideology of the lesser knights to their own interests later and transformed it into an instrument for establishing discipline.[70] If that is regarded as true, then the question arises as to whether there was any need for an intermediate stage of a knightly ideal at all and whether it is not more probable that the idea of courtly service was not used from the very beginning in the sense of the upper nobility.

3. We would have to expect that it could be demonstrated historically how the social ideal of non-noble classes penetrated the courtly culture of the upper nobility. It must be shown to be likely that the lesser knighthood or the *ministeriales*, in the course of their rise into the nobility, not only took on the life style and self-awareness of the old nobility but that the aristocratic culture of the great courts was affected to a fundamental degree by these upcoming groups. In fact, however, there is no historical evidence for this assumption and it is not enough to conclude from the character of the courtly ideal of service that it must originally have been designed for those who serve.

The idea that courtly culture in Germany was principally in the hands of the *ministeriales* is a great deal older than the new literary-sociological interpretations. It goes back to Aloys Schulte[71] and Paul Kluckhohn[72] and obviously still has a good deal of support in Germanistic research. Anyone concerned today with understanding courtly poetry from the point of view of social history must take issue with this "*ministeriales* theory." I have dealt elsewhere[73] with one aspect of it, the thesis that the majority of courtly poets in Germany were themselves *ministeriales*. Here I would like to give a brief sketch of my views on several other points.

What we call courtly culture was, in Germany, the culture of the princely courts at which modern French styles of society and social behavior were accepted. Historically we can grasp this culture in its material aspects, in the splendid palaces and castles of the Hohenstaufen period, in the modern splendor of the clothes and armor (which we know otherwise almost only from pictures) and in the import trade in luxury goods. The self-awareness of this courtly society is reflected in the new aristocratic customs and forms of social intercourse the principal historical evidence for which is connected with the great court festivals. Literature was also part of this courtly culture, a large proportion of which had no other object than to present the forms of aristocratic life at court. Poetry went further in endowing courtly existence with meaning, particularly in the shape of the courtly knight. We have to interpret the social ideal of this poetry with reference to the expectations of the courtly audience, for there is historical evidence for the fact that poetry was recited at the great princely courts. It was the same princes who had the new palaces built and who put on the great court festivals who were the patrons of poetry and who commissioned it. The *ministeriales* were undoubtedly part of the aristocratic society at these courts around 1200. It is possible to make an approximate picture of the composition of the courtly audience if a comparison is made over a specific period between the lists of witnesses in the documents of individual princes and princely houses.[74] A fairly homogeneous group appears in these lists: members of the families of counts, clerical lords, barons (*nobiles*), and *ministeriales*. At the beginning of the thirteenth century, the more important *ministerialis* families may have been legally still distinct from the old nobility but they were not so in their life style. In so far as they lived like lords, they were part of aristocratic society. The most powerful of them appear as patrons of court poets themselves in the thirteenth century, a fact for which there is testimony in the case of the imperial butler Konrad von Winterstetten.[75] Furthermore a series of aristocratic *Minnesänger* sprang from families of *ministerialis* origin: the seneschal von Singenberg, Burkart von Hohenfels, Hiltbolt von Schwangau, the butler of Limburg, Ulrich von Lichtenstein and several more. To the degree that old families of counts and barons died out in the thirteenth century and the percentage of ministeriales increased, their part in the culture at the courts grew larger. There can be no question of diminishing their role, but it would be the equivalent of turning the historical development inside out if anyone insisted that courtly culture bore the mark of the *ministeriales* from its very beginnings.

The socio-historical preconditions for the development of court culture in the twelfth century are to be sought chiefly in the development of territorial principalities, not in the rise of the *ministeriales*. After the territorial princes had become rich enough and powerful enough to afford to keep court, their interest in art and literature began. They attracted poets to their courts and made sure that the poets became acquainted with the French texts which they had to put into German. The formation of courtly poetry must be seen in the context of the historical reception of French aristocratic culture. This is pointed up by the fact that in the adaptation of western literature there was characteristic selection; at the German courts the main interest was in those genres which were particularly suitable for the presentation of courtly social ideals, the *chanson* and the *roman courtois*. Many of the great lords themselves sang of love in the Provençal style and of their readiness for chivalric service to the lady they are wooing. Thus the powerful Swiss count Rudolf von Fenis-Neuenburg affirms in one of this songs: "Iemer mêre wil ich dienen mit staete" (I am determined always to serve with constancy) (*Minnesangsfrühling*, 81, 14), and many of his social equals said much the same. Naturally no biographical significance should be attributed to such statements but it would also be completely wrong to assume that the Count of Neuenburg intended to make an appearance in the mask of a *ministerialis*. The princes who called for this poetry had certainly no interest in the social drives of upward-striving lower orders. If they were glorified as courtly knights or called themselves knights, then the word "knight" had for them a sound which was high in the way that the word *miles* in the expression *miles Christi* had been earlier. In this several factors probably came together. The concept of knighthood had in the meantime penetrated into the terminology of the courtly initiation ceremony (see above p. 84ff.), and there was scarcely any occasion at which the self-awareness of this aristocratic court society was so clearly expressed as in the great pomp of the celebrations of the initiation of young princes. In addition to this, the word "knight" had a definitely masculine sound. In a society in which wars and feuds were an everyday occurrence, it must have been a distinction, even for a noble lord, if his effectiveness as a soldier and his mastery of the use of knightly weapons was praised. In my opinion, however, the focal point of the aristocratic concept of knighthood was to be found in the programmatic character of the word in the ethical sense. In this the thought could be perceived that dominion and nobility were not founded only in precedence of birth but must be justified also by virtue, and that it did not diminish the nobility of a lord but rather enhanced it if he declared himself the servant and knight of a personified courtly perfection. Service and dominion, worlds which were far apart in the social reality of the time, came together in courtly *Minne* ideology. This was expressed in so many words by Andreas Capellanus when he has a man of the upper nobility (*nobilior*) say to a noblewoman (*nobilis*): "et ideo maxima, quam habebam, vos videndi ac serviendi voluntas non modica suscepit augmenta et maiora ulterius incrementa cognoscet, quia liquide mihi constat et est manifestum, quod vobis servire solum est cunctis in hac vita regnare, et sine ipso nihil posset ab aliquo in hoc seculo dignum laudibus adimpleri'' (and thus the very great desire I have to see you and serve you has received not a little increase and will experience even greater strengthening because it is quite clear to me and it is obvious that to serve you is the only way to reign over everything in this life and without it nothing could be done by anyone in this life which would be worthy of praise) (p. 125). This has been translated, somewhat vaguely by Hanns Martin Elster.[76] It is clear that this aristocratic idea of service existed only in literature, only in poetry. How it is evaluated depends to a great extent on the point of view adopted by the modern observer. If the stress is put on the (alleged) unreality of the poetic representation of the knight and if the social image of courtly poetry is thought to be characterized by avoiding the actual political and social problems of feudal society, then the suspicion arises that the unpleasant sides of reality, which were quite obviously dominant at the time—we need think only of the cruelty of the conduct of war and feuds, of the violence in the exercise of political power, of the suppression of large sections of the population by the feudal economic system, etc.—were being passed over in silence in poetry. Nevertheless the other side of the picture seems to me to be just as important: the courtly ideal of knighthood with its idea of service, in which there is always a recognition of social duties, was directed towards humane and peaceful values, in as much as love was regarded as the highest social value. The European ethic of aristocratic behavior has been living on this ideal of knighthood for hundreds of years.[77]

Bibliography of Primary & Secondary Works

Source Materials

A. Collections

ATB.	*Altdeutsche Textbibliothek*, Halle[2]
ATU.	*Altdeutsche Texte für den akademischen Unterricht*, Halle
BGNL.	*Bibliothek der gesamten deutschen National-Literatur*, Quedlinburg-Leipzig
BLVS.	*Bibliothek des litterarischen Vereins in Stuttgart*, Leipzig[3]
DDM.	*Dichtungen des deutschen Mittelalters*, Leipzig
Diemer	*Deutsche Gedichte des 11. und 12. Jahrhunderts*, ed. Joseph Diemer, Wien 1849
DTM.	*Deutsche Texte des Mittelalters*, Berlin
EH.	*Editiones Heidelbergenses*, Heidelberg
GA.	*Germanistische Abhandlungen*, Breslau
GB.	*Germanische Bibliothek*, Heidelberg
Hahn	*Gedichte des XII. und XIII. Jahrhunderts*, ed. Karl A. Hahn, BGNL. 20, 1840
Kraus DG.	*Deutsche Gedichte des 12. Jahrhunderts*, ed. Carl Kraus, Halle 1894
Kraus LD.	*Deutsche Liederdichter des 13. Jahrhunderts*, ed. Carl von Kraus, 2. Bdd., Tübingen 1952/58
Kraus ÜB.	*Mittelhochdeutsches Übungsbuch*, ed. Carl von Kraus, 2. ed., GB. III 2, 1926[4]
Leitzmann	*Kleinere mittelhochdeutsche Lehrgedichte*, ed. Albert Leitzmann, Erstes Heft, 2. ed., ATB. 9, 1928
Massmann	*Deutsche Gedichte des 12. Jahrhunderts und der nächstverwandten Zeit*, ed. Hans F. Massmann, Erster Teil, BGNL. 3, 1; 1837
Meyer-Benfey	*Mittelhochdeutsche Übungsstücke*, ed. Heinrich Meyer-Benfey, Halle 1909
MGH. DC.	*Monumenta Germaniae historica, Scriptores qui vernacula lingua usi sunt (Deutsche Chroniken)*, Hannover
MSF.	*Des Minnesangs Frühling*, nach Karl Lachmann, Moriz Haupt und Friedrich Vogt neu bearb. von Carl von Kraus, Leipzig 1944
QF.	*Quellen und Forschungen zur Sprach- und Culturgeschichte der germanischen Völker*, Strassburg
RBHP.	*Rheinische Beiträge und Hilfsbücher zur germanischen Philologie und Volkskunde*, Bonn[5]
Waag	*Kleinere Deutsche Gedichte des XI. und XII. Jahrhunderts*, ed. Albert Waag, Halle 1890

B. Primary Works

Albertus: *St. Ulrichs Leben* von Albertus, ed. Joh. Andr. Schmeller, München 1844.
Anno: *Das Anno-Lied*, ed. Walther Bulst, EH. 2, 1946.
Arm. Hartm.: Der Arme Hartman, *Vom Glouben*, Massmann 1–42.
Arm. Heinr.: Hartmann von Aue, *Der arme Heinrich*, ed. Hermann Paul, 11. ed. v. Ludwig Wolff, ATB. 3, Tübingen 1958.
Athis: *Athis und Prophilias*, Kraus ÜB. No. 3.
Ava Johannes: Frau Ava, *Johannes*, ed. Paul Piper, *Die Gedichte der Ava*, ZfdPh. 19, 1887, 129–96; 275–321; Text 129–40.
Ava Jesu: Frau Ava, *Leben Jesu*, ibd. 140–96.
Brandan: *Sanct Brandan*. ed. Carl Schröder, Erlangen 1871.
Br. Wernher: Bruder Wernher, ed. Anton E. Schönbach, *Beitr. zur Erklärung altdeutscher Dichtwerke* 3/4, Sitzungsberichte der phil.-hist. Kl. der Kaiserl. Akad. d. Wiss. 148, Wien 1904, No. 7; 150, 1905, No. 1.
Christoph.: *Sanct Christopherus*, ed. Anton E. Schönbach, ZfdA. 26, 1882, 20–84.
Colm. Chrescentia: *Colmarer Chrescentia*, ed. Ernst Martin, *Colmarer Bruchstücke aus dem 12. Jh.*, ZfdA. 40, 1896, 305–31; Text 312–19.
Craun: *Moriz von Craûn*, ed. Ulrich Pretzel, ATB. 45, Tübingen 1956.
Dietmar: Dietmar von Eist, MSF. No. 7.
Durne: Reinbot von Durne, *Der hl. Georg*, ed. Carl von Kraus, GB. III 1, 1907.
Ebernant: Ebernant von Erfurt, *Heinrich und Kunigunde*, ed. Reinhold Bechstein, BGNL. 39, 1860.
Eilhart: Eilhart von Oberg, *Tristrant*, ed. Franz Lichtenstein, QF. 19, 1877[1].
Elmendorf: Wernher von Elmendorf, ed. Heinrich Hoffmann, ZfdA. 4, 1844, 284–317.
Ems Alex.: Rudolf von Ems, *Alexander*, ed. Victor Junk, 2 Bdd., BLVS. 272/74, 1928/29.
Ems Barl.: Rudolf von Ems, *Barlaam und Josaphat*, ed. Franz Pfeiffer, DDM. 3, 1843.
Ems Gerh.: Rudolf von Ems, *Der gute Gerhard*, ed. Moriz Haupt, Leipzig 1840.
Ems Weltchr.: Rudolf von Ems, *Weltchronik*, ed. Gustav Ehrismann, DTM. 20, 1915.
Ems Willeh.: Rudolf von Ems, *Willehalm von Orlens*, ed. Victor Junk, DTM. 2, 1905.
Eneit: Heinrich von Veldeke, *Eneit*, ed. Ludwig Ettmüller, DDM. 8, 1852.
Erek: Hartmann von Aue, *Erek*, ed. Albert Leitzmann, ATB. 39, 1939.
Erst. Büchl.: Hartmann von Aue, *Klage* (sog. *Erstes Büchlein*), ed. Moriz Haupt, *Der arme Heinrich und die Büchlein*, 2. ed. v. Ernst Martin, Leipzig 1881; Text 65–123.
Ezzo: *Ezzos Gesang*, Waag No. 1.
Flore: Konrad Fleck, *Flore und Blanscheflur*, ed. Emil Sommer, BGNL. 12, 1846.
Franciskus: Lamprecht von Regensburg, *St. Francisken Leben*, ed. Karl Weinhold, Paderborn 1880.
Freidank: *Fridankes Bescheidenheit*, ed. Heinrich E. Bezzenberger, Halle 1872.
Gandersheim: Eberhard von Gandersheim, *Reimchronik*, ed. Ludwig Weiland, MGH. DC. 2, 1877, 385–429.
Gotfr.: Gotfrid von Strassburg, *Tristan und Isolt*, ed. Friedrich Ranke, Berlin 1930.
Gregorius: Hartmann von Aue, *Gregorius*, ed. Hermann Paul, 8. ed. v. Albert Leitzmann, ATB. 2, 1948.
Gr. Rudolf: *Graf Rudolf*, Kraus ÜB.[1] No. 4.
Halberstadt: Albrecht von Halberstadt, ed. Karl Bartsch, BGNL. 38, 1861.
Hardegger: *Minnesinger*, ed. Friedrich H. v. d. Hagen, Bd. II, Leipzig 1838, No. 95; *Deutsche Liederdichter des 12. bis 14. Jhs.*, ed. Karl Bartsch, 4. ed. v. Wolfgang Golther, 2. Neudr. Berlin 1910, No. 45.
Hartmann: Hartmann von Aue, *Lieder*, MSF. No. 21.
Heimesfurt Urst.: Konrad von Heimesfurt, *Urstende*, Hahn 103–28,
Heiml. Bote: *Der heimliche Bote*, Meyer-Benfey No. 7.
Herbort: Herbort von Fritzlar, *Liet von Troye*, ed. G. Karl Frommann, BGNL. 5, 1837.
Himmel und Hölle: *Denkmäler deutscher Poesie und Prosa aus dem VIII.-XII. Jh.*, ed. Karl Müllenhoff u. Wilhelm Scherer, 3. ed. v. Elias Steinmeyer, 2 Bdd., Berlin 1892, No. 30.
Himml. Jerusalem: *Himmlisches Jerusalem*, Waag No. 7.
Hochzeit: *Die Hochzeit*, Waag No. 9.
Holle Crane: Berthold von Holle, *Crane*, ed. Karl Bartsch, Nürnberg 1858, 17–188.
Holle Darif.: Berthold von Holle, *Darifant*, ibd. 189–200.
Holle Demant.: Berthold von Holle, *Demantin*, ed. Karl Bartsch, BLVS. 123, Tübingen 1875.

Höxt. Aegidius: *Höxter Aegidius,* ed. Jacob Grimm, *Kleinere Schriften,* Bd. VI, Berlin 1882, 364–70.
Hz. Ernst A: *Herzog Ernst,* ed. Karl Bartsch, Wien 1869, 1–12[7].
Hz. Ernst B: Ibd. 13–186.
Iwein: Hartmann von Aue, *Iwein,* ed. Georg F. Benecke u. Karl Lachmann, 3. ed. Berlin 1868.
Jg. Judith: *Jüngere Judith,* Diemer No. 5.
Kaiserchr.: *Die Kaiserchronik,* ed. Edward Schröder, MGH. DC. 1, 1; 1892.
Kaiser Heinr.: Kaiser Heinrich, MSF. No. 8.
Klage: *Die Klage,* ed. Anton Edzardi, Hannover 1875.
Kudrun: *Kudrun,* ed. B. Symons, 3. ed. v. Bruno Boesch, ATB. 5, Tübingen 1954.
Kürnberg: Der von Kürnberg, MSF. No. 2.
Lanzelet: Ulrich von Zatzikhoven, *Lanzelet,* ed. Karl A. Hahn, Frankfurt a. M. 1845.
Lichtenst.: Ulrich von Lichtenstein, *Lieder,* Kraus LD. No. 58.
Lichtenst. Frb.: Ulrich von Lichtenstein, *Frauenbuch,* ed. Karl Lachmann, Berlin 1841, 594–660.
Lichtenst. Frd.: Ulrich von Lichtenstein, *Frauendienst,* ed. Reinhold Bechstein, 2 Bdd., Dt. Dichtungen des Mittelalters 6/7, Leipzig 1888[6].
Litanei: Kraus ÜB. No. 2.
Lob Salomons: Waag No. 3.
Lucidarius: *Lucidarius,* ed. Felix Heidlauf, DTM. 28, 1915.
Makkabäer: Kraus DG. No. 6.
Maze: *Die Maze,* Meyer-Benfey No. 6.
Meinloh: Meinloh von Sevelingen, MSF. No. 3.
Melk Erin.: Heinrich von Melk, *Erinnerung an den Tod,* ed. Richard Kienast, EH. 1, 1946, 30–57.
Melk Prl.: Heinrich von Melk, *Priesterleben,* ibd. 9–29.
Mfrk. Reimbibel: *Mittelfränkische Reimbibel,* Kraus ÜB. No. 1.
Millst. Genesis: *Millstätter Genesis und Exodus,* ed. Joseph Diemer, 2 Bdd., Wien 1862.
Millst. Sündenkl.: *Millstätter Sündenklage,* ed. Max Roediger, ZfdA. 20, 1876, 255–323.
Morant: *Morant und Galie,* ed. Erich Kalisch, RBHP. 2, Bonn-Leipzig 1921.
Neidhart: Neidhart von Reuental, ed. Edmund Wiessner, ATB. 44, Tübingen 1955.
Nl.: *Nibelungenlied,* nach der Ausg. von Karl Bartsch ed. Helmut de Boor, Dt. Klassiker des Mittelalters 3, 12. ed. Leipzig 1949.
Obdt. Servat.: *Oberdeutscher Servatius,* ed. Friedrich Wilhelm, *Sanct Servatius,* München 1910, 149–269.
Orendel: *Orendel,* ed. Hans Steinger, ATB. 36, 1935.
Oswald M.: *Münchener Oswald,* ed. Georg Baesecke, GA. 28, 1907.
Oswald W.: *Wiener Oswald,* ed. Georg Baesecke, GB. III 2, 1912.
Otte: Otte, *Eraclius,* ed. Harald Graef, QF. 50, 1883.
Parz.: Wolfram von Eschenbach, *Parzival,* ed. Karl Lachmann, 5. Ausg. Berlin 1891, 11–388.
Pass. Zacher: *Passionsgeschichte,* ed. Julius Zacher, *Bruchstücke aus der Sammlung des Frh. von Hardenberg,* 4. Reihe, ZfdPh. 15, 1883, 257–96; Text 277–80.
Pr. Jeitteles: *Altdeutsche Predigten aus dem Benedictinerstifte St. Paul in Kärnten,* ed. Adalbert Jeitteles, Innsbruck 1878.
Pr. Leyser: *Deutsche Predigten des XIII. und XIV. Jhs.,* ed. Hermann Leyser, BGNL. 11, 2; 1838[9].
Pr. Mone: *Altteutsche Predigten,* ed. Franz J. Mone, Anz. f. Kunde der teutschen Vorzeit 8, 1839, No. 9, 404–33; 509–30.
Pr. Schönbach: *Altdeutsche Predigten,* ed. Anton E. Schönbach, 3 Bdd., Graz 1886/88/91.
Pr. Wackernagel: *Altdeutsche Predigten und Gebete aus Handschriften,* ed. Wilhelm Wackernagel, Basel 1876[10].
Pr.br. Dieffenbach: *Mitteldeutsche Predigtbruchstücke,* ed. Lorenz Dieffenbach, Germ. 19, 1874, 305–14.
Pr.br. Grieshaber: *Predigt-Bruchstücke aus dem 12. Jh.,* ed. Karl F. Grieshaber, Germ. 1, 1856, 441–54.
Pr.br. Jeitteles: *Predigt auf Johannes den Täufer,* ed. Adalbert Jeitteles, Germ. 35, 1890, 170–81.
Pr.br. I Schönbach: *Predigtbruchstücke I,* ed. Anton E. Schönbach, ZfdA. 19, 1876, 181–208.
Pr.br. II Schönbach: *Predigtbruchstücke II,* ed. Anton E. Schönbach, ZfdA. 20, 1876, 217–50.

Pr.br. Zingerle: *Bruchstücke altdeutscher Predigten,* ed. Oswald Zingerle, ZfdA. 23, 1879, 399–408.
Priest. Wernher: Priester Wernher, *Maria,* ed. Carl Wesle, ATB. 26, 1927[11].
Prosa-Lanz.: *Lancelot,* ed. Reinhold Kluge, Bd. I, DTM. 42, 1948[12].
Regensburg: Burggraf von Regensburg, MSF. No. 4.
Rheinauer Paulus: Kraus DG. No. 2.
Rhein. Marienlob: *Rheinisches Marienlob,* ed. Adolf Bach, BLVS. 281, 1934.
Reinhart Fuchs: Heinrich der Glîchezâre, *Reinhart Fuchs,* ed. Georg Baesecke, 2. ed. v. Ingeborg Schröbler, ATB. 7, 1952.
Rittersitte: *Rittersitte,* ed. Hermann Menhardt, ZfdA. 68, 1931, 153–63.
Roland: *Das Rolandslied* des Pfaffen Konrad, ed. Carl Wesle, Neudr. ATU. 3, 1955.
Rother: *König Rother,* ed. Theodor Frings u. Joachim Kuhnt, Neudr. ATU. 2, 1954.
Rubin: Kraus LD. No. 47.
Sachsensp. Ldr.: *Sachsenspiegel, Landrecht,* ed. Karl A. Eckhardt, Germanenrechte 14, Göttingen 1955.
Sachsensp. Lnr.: *Sachsenspiegel, Lehnrecht,* ed. Karl A. Eckhardt, Germanenrechte 15, Göttingen 1956.
Sächs. Weltchr.: *Sächsische Weltchronik,* ed. Ludwig Weiland, MGH. DC. 2, 1877, 1–384.
Salman: *Salman und Morolf,* ed. Friedrich Vogt, Neudr. ATU. 1, 1954.
Servatius: Heinrich von Veldeke, *Servatius,* ed. Theodor Frings u. Gabriele Schieb, *Die epischen Werke des Henric van Veldeken* I, Halle 1956.
Singenberg: Ulrich von Singenberg, ed. Karl Bartsch, *Die Schweizer Minnesänger,* Bibl. älterer Schriftwerke der dt. Schweiz 6, Frauenfeld 1886, No. 2.
Specul. eccl.: *Speculum ecclesiae altdeutsch,* ed. Johann Kelle, München 1858[13].
Strassbg. Alex.: *Strassburger Alexander,* ed. Karl Kinzel, Germanistische Handbibl. 6, Halle 1885, 27–385.
Stricker Dan.: Stricker, *Daniel von dem blühenden Tal,* ed. Gustav Ehrismann, GA. 9, 1894.
Stricker Ehre: Stricker, *Frauenehre,* ed. Franz Pfeiffer, ZfdA. 7, 1849, 478–521[14].
Stricker Karl: Stricker, *Karl der Große,* ed. Karl Bartsch, BGNL. 35, 1857.
Summa Theol.: *Summa Theologiae,* Waag No. 2.
Tagzeitengedicht: *Bruchstücke eines Tagzeitengedichts,* ed. Hermann Degering, *Neue Funde aus dem 12. Jahrhundert,* Beitr. 41, 1916, 513–53; Text 526–28.
Tannhäuser: Tannhäuser, ed. Johannes Siebert, Halle 1934.
Thomasin: Thomasin von Zirklaria, *Der wälsche Gast,* ed. Heinrich Rückert, BGNL. 30, 1852.
Tirol: *Tirol und Fridebrant,* Leitzmann 1–10[15].
Titurel: Wolfram von Eschenbach, *Titurel,* ed. Karl Lachmann (s. o. Parz.), 389–420.
Tnugdalus: Hahn 41–66.
Tr. Aegidius: *Trierer Aegidius,* ed. Max Roediger, ZfdA. 21, 1877, 331–412.
Tr. Silvester: *Trierer Silvester,* ed. Carl Kraus, MGH. DC. 1, 2; 1895, 1–61.
Tundalus: Kraus DG. No. 11.
Türheim Clig.: Ulrich von Türheim, *Cliges,* ed. Albert Bachmann, ZfdA. 32, 1888, 123–28.
Türheim Renn.: Ulrich von Türheim, *Rennewart,* ed. Alfred Hübner, DTM. 39, 1938.
Türheim Trist.: Ulrich von Türheim, *Tristan-Fortsetzung,* ed. Hans F. Massmann, *Tristan und Isolt,* DDM. 2, 1843, 493–590.
Türlin Krone: Heinrich von dem Türlin, *Diu Crône,* ed. Gottlob H. F. Scholl, BLVS. 27, Stuttgart 1852.
Türlin Mant.: Heinrich von dem Türlin, *Der Mantel,* ed. Otto Warnatsch, GA. 2, 1833.
Urkunden: *Corpus der altdeutschen Originalurkunden bis zum Jahr 1300,* ed. Friedrich Wilhelm, Bd. I, Lahr 1932[16].
Vor. Alex.: *Vorauer Alexander,* ed. Karl Kinzel (s. o. Strassbg. Alex.), 26–172.
Vor. Joseph: *Vorauer Joseph,* ed. Joseph Diemer, *Beitr. zur älteren deutschen Sprache und Literatur* 20/21, Sitzungsber. der phil.-hist. Kl. der kaiserl. Akad. d. Wiss. 47, Wien 1864, 636–87; 48, 1865, 339–423.
Vor. Moses: *Vorauer Moses,* Diemer No. 1.
Walther: Walther von der Vogelweide, ed. Karl Lachmann, 11. ed. v. Carl von Kraus, Berlin 1950.
Walther-Epos: *Das mhd. Walther-Epos,* ed. W. Eckerth, 2. ed. Halle 1909[17].
Wien. Exodus: *Wiener Exodus,* ed. Ernst Kossmann, QF. 57, 1886.

Wien. Genesis: *Wiener Genesis*, ed. Viktor Dollmayr, ATB. 31, 1932.
Wigalois: Wirnt von Gravenberg, *Wigalois*, ed. J. M. N. Kapteyn, RBHP. 9, 1926.
Wild. Mann Veron.: Wilder Mann, *Veronika*, ed. Karl Köhn, Schr. zur germ. Philologie 6, Berlin 1891, 1–22.
Willeh. Wolfram von Eschenbach, *Willehalm*, ed. Karl Lachmann (s. o. Parz.), 421–640.
Winsbecke: Leitzmann 19–39.
Winterstetten: Ulrich von Winterstetten, Kraus LD. No. 59.
Wolfdietr. A: *Wolfdietrich A*, ed. Hermann Schneider, ATB. 28, 1931.
Zw. Büchlein: Pseudo-Hartmann, *Zweites Büchlein*, ed. Moriz Haupt (s. o. Erst. Büchl.), 124–48.
Zweter: Reinmar von Zweter, ed. Gustav Roethe, Leipzig 1887.

Secondary Literature

Abbreviations

AKG	Archiv für Kulturgeschichte
DVjs.	Deutsche Vierteljahrsschrift für Literaturwissenschaft und Geistesgeschichte
FmSt.	Frühmittelalterliche Studien
Hist. Jb.	Historisches Jahrbuch der Görres-Gesellschaft
HZ	Historische Zeitschrift
MIÖG	Mitteilungen des Instituts für Österreichische Geschichtsforschung
VSWG	Vierteljahrschrift für Sozial- und Wirtschaftsgeschichte
ZfbLG	Zeitschrift für bayerische Landesgeschichte
ZfdA	Zeitschrift für deutsches Altertum
ZGO	Zeitschrift für Geschichte des Oberrheins
ZRG GA	Zeitschrift der Savigny-Stiftung für Rechtsgeschichte. Germanistische Abteilung
ZRG KA	Zeitschrift der Savigny-Stiftung für Rechtsgeschichte. Kanonistische Abteilung

ACKERMAN, ROBERT F.: The Knighting Ceremonies in the Middle English Romances. In: Speculum 15. 1944. S. 285–313.
Adel und Bauern im deutschen Staat des Mittelalters. Hrsg. von THEODOR MAYER. Leipzig 1943. (Europa und das Reich.)
AHRENS, JAKOB: Die Ministerialität in Köln und am Niederrhein. Leipzig 1908. (= Leipziger historische Abhandlungen. 9.)
ALBERTS, W. JAPPE: Zur Entstehung der Stände in den weltlichen Territorien am Niederrhein. In: Aus Geschichte und Landeskunde. Forschungen und Darstellungen. Franz Steinbach zum 65. Geburtstag gewidmet von seinen Freunden und Schülern. Hrsg. von MAX BRAUBACH. FRANZ PETRI, LEO WEISGERBER. Bonn 1960. S. 333–349.
ANDRES, HANS: Das Rittertum des deutschen Hoch- und Spätmittelalters. In: Das deutsche Volk. Sein Wesen – seine Stände. Bd. 9. Die deutsche Soldatenkunde. Hrsg. von BERNHARD SCHWERTFEGER und ERICH O. VOLKMANN. Textband. Leipzig 1937. S. 26–49.
ANTON, HANS H.: Fürstenspiegel und Herrscherethos in der Karolingerzeit. Bonn 1968. (= Bonner Historische Forschungen. 32.)
ATKINS, HENRY G.: The Chivalry in Germany. In: Chivalry [s. dort]. S. 81–107.
AUBIN, HERMANN: Die Verwaltungsorganisation des Fürstbistums Paderborn im Mittelalter. Berlin, Leipzig 1911. (= Abhandlungen zur Mittleren und Neueren Geschichte. 26.)
AUE, KURT VON: Das Rittertum und die Ritterorden. Merseburg 1825.
AUER, JOHANNES: *Militia Christi*. Zur Geschichte eines christlichen Grundbildes. In: Geist und Leben. Zeitschrift für Aszese und Mystik 32. 1959. S. 340–351.
BADER, KARL S.: Herrschaft und Staat im deutschen Mittelalter. In: Hist. Jb. 62–69. 1942–1949. S. 618–646.
BALTZER, MARTIN: Zur Geschichte des deutschen Kriegswesens in der Zeit von den letzten Karolingern bis auf Kaiser Friedrich II. Leipzig 1877.
BARBER, RICHARD: The Knight and Chivalry. London 1970.
BASCAPÈ, GIACOMO C.: Gli ordini cavallereschi in Italia. Storia e diritto. Mailand 1971.

BAST, JOSEF: Die Ministerialität der Erzstifts Trier. Diss. Bonn 1918.

BATTY, JOHN: The Spirit and Influence of Chivalry. London 1890.

BEELER, JOHN: Warfare in Feudal Europe. 730–1200. Ithaca, N. Y. 1971.

BEINHAUER, MONIKA: Ritterliche Tapferkeitsbegriffe in den altfranzösischen Chansons de geste des 12. Jahrhunderts. Ein Beitrag zur Untersuchung ritterlicher Tugendbezeichnungen. Diss. Köln 1958.

Beiträge zum Berufsbewußtsein des mittelalterlichen Menschen. Hrsg. von PAUL WILPERT. Berlin 1964. (= Miscellanea Mediaevalia. 3.)

BELOW, GEORG VON: Ministerialität. In: Handwörterbuch der Staatswissenschaften. 3. Aufl. Jena 1910. Bd. 6. S. 710–714.

BENZ, ERNST: Über den Adel in der deutschen Mystik. In: DVjs. 14. 1936. S. 505–536.

BERGES, WILHELM: Die Fürstenspiegel des hohen und späten Mittelalters. Leipzig 1938. (= Schriften des Reichsinstituts für ältere deutsche Geschichtskunde [Monumenta Germaniae historica]. 2.) Neudruck 1952.

BEZZOLA, RETO R.: Les origines et la formation de la littérature courtoise en occident (500–1200). Bd. 1–3 [in 5 Bänden]. Paris 1944–1963. (= Bibliothèque de l'Ecole des hautes études. Sciences historiques et philologiques. 286. 313. 319. 320.)

BLOCH, MARC: Un problème d'histoire comparée: La ministérialité en France et en Allemagne. In: Revue historique de droit français et étranger. Sér. 4. Bd. 7. 1928, S. 46–91.

– La société féodale. Bd. 1–2. Paris 1939–1940. (= L'évolution de l'humanité. 34 – 34 bis.) Neudruck 1949.

BONENFANT, PAUL, et GEORGES DESPY: La noblesse en Brabant aux XIIᵉ et XIIIᵉ siècles. Quelques sondages. In: Le moyen âge 64. 1958. S. 27–66.

BORCH, LEOPOLD VON: Beiträge zur Rechts-Geschichte des Mittelalters mit besonderer Rücksicht auf die Ritter und Dienstmannen fürstlicher und gräflicher Herkunft. Innsbruck 1881.

BORN, LESTER K.: The Perfect Prince: A Study in Thirteenth and Fourteenth-Century Ideals. In: Speculum 3. 1928. S. 470–504.

BORST, ARNO: Das Rittertum im Hochmittelalter. Idee und Wirklichkeit. In: Saeculum 10. 1959. S. 213–231.

BOSL, KARL: Die Reichsministerialität als Element der mittelalterlichen deutschen Staatsverfassung im Zeitalter der Salier und Staufer. In: Adel und Bauern im deutschen Staat des Mittelalters [s. dort]. S. 74–108. Wieder in: K. B.: Frühformen ... S. 327–356.

– Die Reichsministerialität der Salier und Staufer. Ein Beitrag zur Geschichte des hochmittelalterlichen deutschen Volkes, Staates und Reiches. Bd. 1–2. Stuttgart 1950–1951. (= Schriften der Monumenta Germaniae historica. 10, 1–2.)

– Vorstufen der deutschen Königsdienstmannschaft. Begriffsgeschichtlich-prosopographische Studien zur frühmittelalterlichen Sozial- und Verfassungsgeschichte. In: VSWG 39. 1952. S. 193–214. 289–315. Wieder in: K. B.: Frühformen ... S. 228–276.

– Staat, Gesellschaft, Wirtschaft im deutschen Mittelalter. In: BRUNO GEBHARDT: Handbuch der deutschen Geschichte. 8. Aufl. Hrsg. von HERBERT GRUNDMANN. Bd. 1. Stuttgart 1954. S. 584–684. Selbständig [nach der 9. Aufl. 1970]: München 1973. (= dtv. Wissenschaftliche Reihe. 4207.)

– Das *ius ministerialium*. Dienstrecht und Lehnrecht im deutschen Mittelalter. In: Studien zum mittelalterlichen Lehenswesen [s. dort]. S. 51–94. Wieder in: K. B.: Frühformen ... S. 277–326.

– Freiheit und Unfreiheit. Zur Entwicklung der Unterschichten in Deutschland und Frankreich während des Mittelalters. In: VSWG 44. 1957. S. 193–219. Wieder in: K. B.: Frühformen ... S. 180–203.

– Über soziale Mobilität in der mittelalterlichen ‚Gesellschaft'. Dienst, Freiheit, Freizügigkeit als Motive sozialen Aufstiegs. In: VSWG 47. 1960. S. 306–332. Wieder in: K. B.: Frühformen ... S. 156–179.

– Herrscher und Beherrschte im deutschen Reich des 10.–12. Jahrhunderts. München 1963. (= Bayerische Akademie der Wissenschaften. Phil.-hist. Klasse. Sitzungsberichte. Jg. 1963. Heft 2.) Wieder in: K. B.: Frühformen ... S. 135–155.

– Frühformen der Gesellschaft im mittelalterlichen Europa. Ausgewählte Beiträge zu einer Strukturanalyse der mittelalterlichen Welt. München, Wien 1964.

– Castes, ordres et classes en Allemagne (d'après un choix d'exemples allemands). In: Problèmes de stratification sociale [s. dort]. S. 13–23. Erweitert unter dem Titel: Kasten, Stände, Klassen im mittelalterlichen Deutschland. Zur Problematik soziologischer Begriffe und ihrer Anwendung auf die mittelalterliche Gesellschaft. In: ZfbLG 32. 1969. S. 477–494.

– Macht und Arbeit als bestimmende Kräfte in der mittelalterlichen Gesellschaft. In: Fest-schrift Ludwig Petry. Bd. 1. Wiesbaden 1968. (= Geschichtliche Landeskunde. 5,1.) S. 46–64.
– Die Gesellschaft in der Geschichte des Mittelalters. 2. Aufl. Göttingen 1969. (= Kleine Vandenhoeck-Reihe. 231.)
– Die Grundlagen der modernen Gesellschaft im Mittelalter. Eine deutsche Gesellschafts-geschichte des Mittelalters. Bd. 1–2. Stuttgart 1972. (= Monographien zur Geschichte des Mittelalters. 4, 1–2.)

BOSL, KARL: Die horizontale Mobilität der europäischen Gesellschaft im Mittelalter und ihre Kommunikationsmittel. In: ZfbLG 35. 1972. S. 40–53.
– Die Unfreiheit im Übergang von der archaischen zur Aufbruchsepoche der mittelalterlichen Gesellschaft. München 1973. (= Bayerische Akademie der Wissenschaften. Phil.-hist. Klasse. Sitzungsberichte. Jg. 1973. Heft 1.)
– Die familia als Grundstruktur der mittelalterlichen Gesellschaft. In: ZfbLG 38. 1975. S. 403–424.

BOUTRUCHE, ROBERT: Seigneurie et féodalité. Bd. 1–2. Paris 1959–1970. (Collection historique.)

BRADLER, GÜNTHER: Studien zur Geschichte der Ministerialität im Allgäu und in Oberschwaben. Diss. Berlin F. U. Marburg 1973.

BRAUN, WERNER: Studien zum Ruodlieb. Ritterideal, Erzählstruktur und Darstellungsstil. Berlin 1962. (= Quellen und Forschungen zur Sprach- und Kulturgeschichte der germanischen Völker. N. F. 7.)

BRUNNER, HEINRICH: Der Reiterdienst und die Anfänge des Lehnwesens. In: H. B.: For-schungen zur Geschichte des deutschen und französischen Rechtes. Gesammelte Aufsätze. Stuttgart 1894. S. 39–74.
– Deutsche Rechtsgeschichte. 2. Aufl. Bd. 1. Leipzig 1906. Bd. 2. Neu bearbeitet von Claudius Frh. von Schwerin. München, Leipzig 1928. (= Systematisches Handbuch der Deutschen Rechtswissenschaft. Abt. 2. Teil 1. Bd. 1–2.)

BRUNNER, OTTO: Adeliges Landleben und europäischer Geist. Leben und Werk Wolf Helmhards von Hohberg. 1612–1688. Salzburg 1949.
– Die Freiheitsrechte in der altständischen Gesellschaft. In: Aus Verfassungs- und Landes-geschichte. Festschrift zum 70. Geburtstag von Theodor Mayer. Dargebracht von seinen Freunden und Schülern. Bd. 1. Konstanz 1954. S. 293–303. Wieder in: O. B.: Neue Wege . . . 2. Aufl. S. 187–198.
– Neue Wege der Sozialgeschichte. Vorträge und Aufsätze. Göttingen 1956. 2. Aufl. unter dem Titel: Neue Wege der Verfassungs- und Sozialgeschichte. 1968.
– ‚Feudalismus‘. Ein Beitrag zur Begriffsgeschichte. Wiesbaden 1959. (= Akademie der Wissenschaften und der Literatur in Mainz. Abhandlungen der geistes- und sozial-wissenschaftlichen Klasse. Jg. 1958, Nr. 10.) Wieder in: O. B.: Neue Wege . . . 2. Aufl. S. 128–159.
– Inneres Gefüge des Abendlandes. In: Historia Mundi. Ein Handbuch der Weltgeschichte in zehn Bänden. Hrsg. von FRITZ VALJAVEC. Bd. 6. Bern 1958. S. 319–385.
– Land und Herrschaft. Grundfragen der territorialen Verfassungsgeschichte Österreichs im Mittelalter. 5. Aufl. Wien 1965.
– Feudalismus, feudal. In: Geschichtliche Grundbegriffe [s. dort]. Bd. 2. S. 337–350.

BUMKE, JOACHIM: Parzivals ‚Schwertleite‘. In: Taylor Starck Festschrift 1964. Edited by WERNER BETZ, EVELYN S. COLEMAN, KENNETH NORTHCOTT. Den Haag 1964. S. 235–245.
– Ministerialität und Ritterdichtung. Umrisse der Forschung. München 1976. (Edition Beck.)

BÜSCHING, JOHANN G.: Ritterzeit und Ritterwesen. Vorlesungen. Bd. 1–2. Leipzig 1823.

CARO, GEORG: Beiträge zur älteren deutschen Wirtschafts- und Verfassungsgeschichte. Ge-sammelte Aufsätze. Leipzig 1905.

Chivalry. A Series of Studies to Illustrate Its Historical Significance and Civilizing Influence. Edited by EDGAR PRESTAGE. London 1928.

CLAVADETSCHER, OTTO P.: Nobilis, edel, fry. In: Historische Forschungen für Walter Schlesin-ger. Hrsg. von HELMUT BEUMANN. Köln, Wien 1974. S. 242–251.

COHEN, GUSTAVE: Histoire de la chevalerie en France au moyen âge. Paris 1949.

CONRAD, HERMANN: Geschichte der deutschen Wehrverfassung. Bd. 1. München 1939.
– Gottesfrieden und Heeresverfassung in der Zeit der Kreuzzüge. Ein Beitrag zur Geschichte des Heeresstrafrechts im Mittelalter. In: ZRG GA 61. 1941. S. 71–126.
– Deutsche Rechtsgeschichte. Ein Lehrbuch. Bd. 1. Frühzeit und Mittelalter. 2. Aufl. Karlsruhe 1962.

CONZE, WERNER, und CHRISTIAN MEIER: Adel, Aristokratie. In: Geschichtliche Grundbegriffe [s. dort]. Bd. 1. S. 1–48.

COPPIETERS, MAURITS: De ridders. Brüssel 1946. (= Ken uw volk. 11.)
– Ridderschap. Een cultuurhistorische verkenning. Antwerpen, Brüssel, Gent, Leuven 1948. (= Katholieke vlaamse hogeschooluitbreiding. Jg. 42. Nr. 2. Verhandeling 397.)

CORNISH, F. WARRE: Chivalry. 2. Aufl. London 1911.

COWDREY, H. E. J.: Cluny and the First Crusade. In: Revue Bénédictine 83. 1973. S. 285–311.

CURNE DE SAINTE-PALAYE, JEAN B. DE LA: Mémoires sur l'ancienne chevalerie considerée comme un établissement politique et militaire. 2. Aufl. Bd. 1–2. Paris 1826. Deutsch unter dem Titel: Das Ritterwesen des Mittelalters nach seiner politischen und militärischen Verfassung. Übersetzt von JOHANN L. KLÜBER. Bd. 1–3. Nürnberg 1786–1791.

DANNENBAUER, HEINRICH: Grundlagen der mittelalterlichen Welt. Skizzen und Studien. Stuttgart 1958.
– Adel, Burg und Herrschaft bei den Germanen. Grundlagen der deutschen Verfassungsentwicklung. In: Hist. Jb. 61. 1941. S. 1–50. Wieder in: Herrschaft und Staat im Mittelalter [s. dort]. S. 66–134. Wieder in: H. D.: Grundlagen ... S. 121–178.
– Königsfreie und Ministerialien. In: H. D.: Grundlagen ... S. 329–353.

DELBRÜCK, HANS: Geschichte der Kriegskunst im Rahmen der politischen Geschichte. Bd. 3. Das Mittelalter. 2. Aufl. Berlin 1923.

DESPY, GEORGES: Sur la noblesse dans les principautés belges au moyen âge. A propos de travaux récents. In: Revue belge de philologie et d'histoire 41. 1963. S. 471–486.

DOPSCH, HEINZ: Ministerialität und Herrenstand in der Steiermark und in Salzburg. In: Zeitschrift des Historischen Vereins für Steiermark 62. 1971. S. 3–31.

DROEGE, GEORG: Landrecht und Lehnrecht im hohen Mittelalter. Bonn 1969.

DUBY, GEORGES: La société aux XIe et XIIe siècles dans la région mâconnaise. Paris 1953. (= Bibliothèque générale de l'Ecole pratique des hautes études. Section 6.)
– La noblesse dans la France médiévale. Une enquête à poursuivre. In: Revue historique 226. 1961. S. 1–22. Wieder in: G. D.: Hommes et structures ... S. 145–166.
– Les origines de la chevalerie. In: Ordinamenti militari in occidente nell'alto medioevo. 30 marzo – 5 aprile 1967. Bd. 2. Spoleto 1968. (= Settimane di studio del Centro italiano di studi sull'alto medioevo. 15.) S. 739–761. Wieder in: G. D.: Hommes et structures ... S. 325–341.
– Situation de la noblesse en France au début du XIIIe siècle. In: Tijdschrift voor geschiedenis 82. 1969. S. 309–315. Wieder in: G. D.: Hommes et structures ... S. 343–352.
– Les féodaux. In: Histoire de la France. Publié sous la direction de GEORGES DUBY. Bd. 1. Paris 1970. S. 253–285.
– Lignage, noblesse et chevalerie au XIIe siècle dans la région mâconnaise. Une révision. In: Annales. Economies, sociétés, civilisations 27. 1972. S. 803–823. Wieder in: G. D.: Hommes et structures ... S. 395–422.
– Hommes et structures du moyen âge. Recueil d'articles. Paris, Den Haag 1973. (= Le savoir historique. 1.)

DUNGERN, OTTO FRH. VON: Der Herrenstand im Mittelalter. Eine sozialpolitische und rechtsgeschichtliche Untersuchung. Bd. 1. Papiermühle 1908.
– Adelsherrschaft im Mittelalter. München 1927. Neudruck Darmstadt 1967. (= Libelli. 198.)

EBEL, WILHELM: Über den Leihegedanken in der deutschen Rechtsgeschichte. In: Studien zum mittelalterlichen Lehenswesen [s. dort]. S. 11–36.

ELIAS, NORBERT: Die höfische Gesellschaft. Untersuchungen zur Soziologie des Königtums und der höfischen Aristokratie. Neuwied 1969. (= Soziologische Texte. 54.)

EMONDS, HILARIUS: Geistlicher Kriegsdienst. Der Topos der *militia spiritualis* in der antiken Philosophie. In: Heilige Überlieferung. Ausschnitte aus der Geschichte des Mönchtums und des heiligen Kultes. Eine Festgabe zum silbernen Abtsjubiläum des hochwürdigen Herrn Abtes von Maria Laach Ildefons Herwegen. Münster 1938. S. 21–50. Wieder im Anhang des Neudrucks von A. v. HARNACK: *Militia Christi* [s. dort]. S. 131–162.

ERBEN, WILHELM: Schwertleite und Ritterschlag. Beiträge zu einer Rechtsgeschichte der Waffen. In: Zeitschrift für historische Waffenkunde [abgekürzt: ZfhWk.] 8. 1918–1920. S. 105–167.

ERDMANN, CARL: Die Entstehung des Kreuzzugsgedankens. Stuttgart 1935. (= Forschungen zur Kirchen- und Geistesgeschichte. 6.) Neudruck Darmstadt 1955.

ETTMÜLLER, LUDWIG: Einiges über den Ritterstand und über die bei der Ertheilung dieser Würde einst üblichen Gebräuche. In: Mittheilungen der antiquarischen Gesellschaft in Zürich 11. 1856–1857. S. 91–100.

L'Europe aux IXe – XIe siècles. Aux origines des états nationaux. Actes du colloque international sur les origines des états européens aux IXe – XIe siècles, tenu à Varsovie et Poznań du 7 au 13 septembre 1965. Publiés sous la direction de TADEUSZ MANTEUFFEL et ALEKSANDER GIEYSZTOR. Warschau 1968. (Institut d'histoire de l'Académie polonaise des sciences.)

FAJKMAJER, KARL: Die Ministerialien des Hochstiftes Brixen. In: Zeitschrift des Ferdinandeums für Tirol und Vorarlberg [abgekürzt: ZdFTV]. Folge 3. Heft 52. 1908. S. 95–191.

FALKE, JACOB: Die ritterliche Gesellschaft im Zeitalter des Frauencultus. Berlin [1862.]

FASOLI, GINA: Lineamenti de una storia della cavalleria. In: Studi di storia medievale e moderna in onore di Ettore Rota, a cura di P. VACCARI e P. F. PALUMBO. Rom 1958. S. 81–93.

FECHTER, JOHANNES: Cluny, Adel und Volk. Studien über das Verhältnis des Klosters zu den Ständen (910–1156). Diss. Tübingen 1966.

FEHR, HANS: Das Recht in der Dichtung. Bern 1931. (= H. F.: Kunst und Recht. Bd. 2.)

– Vom Fürstenstand in der deutschen Dichtung des Mittelalters. In: Aus Verfassungs- und Landesgeschichte. Festschrift zum 70. Geburtstag von Theodor Mayer. Dargebracht von seinen Freunden und Schülern. Bd. 1. Konstanz 1954. S. 151–160.

FELDBAUER, PETER: Rangprobleme und Konnubium österreichischer Landherrenfamilien. Zur sozialen Mobilität einer spätmittelalterlichen Führungsgruppe. In: ZfbLG 35. 1972. S. 571 bis 590.

– Herrschaftsstruktur und Ständebildung. Beiträge zur Typologie der österreichischen Länder aus ihren mittelalterlichen Grundlagen. Bd. 1. Herren und Ritter. Mit einer Einleitung in das Gesamtwerk von Michael Mitterauer. München 1973. (Sozial- und Wirtschaftshistorische Studien.)

FICKER, JULIUS: Vom Reichsfürstenstande. Forschungen zur Geschichte der Reichsverfassung, zunächst im XII. und XIII. Jahrhunderte. Bd. 1. Innsbruck 1861. Bd. 2. Hrsg. von PAUL PUNTSCHART. Teil 1–3. Innsbruck bzw. Graz, Leipzig 1911–1923.

– Vom Heerschilde. Ein Beitrag zur deutschen Reichs- und Rechtsgeschichte. Innsbruck 1862.

FLECKENSTEIN, JOSEF: Bürgertum und Rittertum in der Geschichte des mittelalterlichen Freiburg. In: Freiburg im Mittelalter. Vorträge zum Stadtjubiläum 1970. Hrsg. von WOLFGANG MÜLLER. Bühl 1970. (= Veröffentlichungen des Alemannischen Instituts. 29.) S. 77–95.

– Friedrich Barbarossa und das Rittertum. Zur Bedeutung der großen Mainzer Hoftage von 1184 und 1188. In: Festschrift für Hermann Heimpel zum 70. Geburtstage am 19. Sept. 1971. Hrsg. von den Mitarbeitern des Max-Planck-Instituts für Geschichte. Bd. 2. Göttingen 1972. (= Veröffentlichungen des Max-Planck-Instituts für Geschichte. 36, 2.) S. 1023–1041.

– Zum Problem der Abschließung des Ritterstandes. In: Historische Forschungen für Walter Schlesinger. Hrsg. von HELMUT BEUMANN. Köln, Wien 1974. S. 252–271.

– Zur Frage der Abgrenzung von Bauer und Ritter. In: Wort und Begriff ,Bauer'. Zusammenfassender Bericht über die Kolloquien der Kommission für die Altertumskunde Mittel- und Nordeuropas. Hrsg. von REINHARD WENSKUS, HERBERT JANKUHN und KLAUS GRINDA. Göttingen 1975. (= Abhandlungen der Akademie der Wissenschaften in Göttingen. Phil.-hist. Klasse. Folge 3. Nr. 89.) S. 246–253.

FLOHRSCHÜTZ, GÜNTHER: Die Freisinger Dienstmannen im 10. und 11. Jahrhundert. In: Beiträge zur altbayerischen Kirchengeschiche 25. 1967. 9–79.

FOSSIER, ROBERT: Histoire sociale de l'occident médiéval. Paris 1970. (Collection ,U'. Série Histoire médiévale.)

– Chevalerie et noblesse au Ponthieu aux XIe et XIIe siècles. In: Etudes de civilisation médiévale (IXe–XIIe siècles). Mélanges offerts à Edmond-René Labande à l'occasion de son départ à la retraite et du XXe anniversaire du C. E. S. C. M. par ses amis, ses collègues, ses élèves. Poitiers [1975]. S. 293–306.

FRAUENHOLZ, EUGEN VON: Entwicklungsgeschichte des deutschen Heerwesens. Bd. 1. München 1935.

FRENSDORFF, FERDINAND: Das Recht der Dienstmannen des Erzbischofs von Köln. In: Mittheilungen aus dem Stadtarchiv von Köln [abgekürzt: MStK.] Bd. 1. Heft 2. 1883. S. 1–69.

FRESSEL, RICHARD: Das Ministerialenrecht der Grafen von Tecklenburg. Ein Beitrag zur Verfassungs- und Ständegeschichte des Mittelalters. Diss. Münster 1907.

FROMM, HANS: Nachtrag zu: PAUL KLUCKHOHN: Der Minnesang als Standesdichtung. In: Der deutsche Minnesang [s. dort]. S. 81–84.

FUNCK-BRENTANO, FRANTZ: Féodalité et chevalerie. Paris 1946.

FÜRTH, AUGUST FRH. VON: Die Ministerialen. Köln 1836.

GANAHL, KARL H.: Studien zur Verfassungsgeschichte der Klosterherrschaft St. Gallen von den Anfängen bis ins hohe Mittelalter. Innsbruck 1931. (= Forschungen zur Geschichte Vorarlbergs und Liechtensteins. 6.)
GANSHOF, FRANÇOIS L.: Etude sur les *ministeriales* en Flandre et en Lotharingie. Brüssel 1926.
— Qu'est-ce que la chevalerie? In: Revue générale belge 25. Nov. 1947. S. 77–86.
— A propos de la cavalerie dans les armées de Charlemagne. In: Académie des inscriptions et des belles lettres. Comptes rendus des séances 1952–1953. S. 531–537.
— Qu'est-ce que la féodalité? 3. Aufl. Brüssel 1957. Deutsch unter dem Titel: Was ist das Lehnswesen? Übersetzt von Ruth und Dieter Groh. 3. Aufl. Darmstadt 1970.
GANZENMÜLLER, WILHELM: Die flandrische Ministerialität bis zum ersten Drittel des 12. Jahrhunderts. Diss. Tübingen 1907.
GAUTIER, LÉON: La chevalerie. Nouvelle édition. Paris [1890.]
GENICOT, LÉOPOLD: Sur les origines de la noblesse dans le Namurois. In: Tijdschrift voor Rechtsgeschiedenis 20. 1952. S. 143–156.
— La noblesse au XIIᵉ siècle dans la région de Gembloux. In: VSWG 44. 1957. S. 97–104.
— L'économie rurale Namuroise au bas moyen âge. Bd. 2. Les hommes – la noblesse. Louvain 1960. (= Université de Louvain. Recueil de travaux d'histoire et de philologie. Série 3. Fasc. 20.)
— La noblesse au moyen âge dans l'ancienne ‚Francie‘. In: Annales. Economies, sociétés, civilisations 17. 1962. S. 1–22.
— La noblesse au moyen âge dans l'ancienne ‚Francie‘: Continuité, rapture ou évolution? In: Comparative Studies in Society and History 5. 1962–1963. S. 52–59.
— Noblesse, ministérialité et chevalerie en Gueldre et Zutphen. In: Le moyen âge 71. 1965. S. 109–116.
— Naissance, fonction et richesse dans l'ordonnance de la société médiévale. Le cas de la noblesse du nord-ouest du continent. In: Problèmes de stratification sociale [s. dort]. S. 83–92.
GERRITSEN, W. P.: Het beeld van feodaliteit en ridderschap in middeleeuwse litteratuur. In: Bijdragen en mededelingen betreffende de geschiedenis der Nederlanden 89. 1974. S. 241 bis 261.
GLADISS, DIETRICH VON: Beiträge zur Geschichte der staufischen Reichsministerialität. Berlin 1934. (= Historische Studien. 249.)
GLEICHEN-RUSSWURM, ALEXANDER VON: Der Ritterspiegel. Geschichte der vornehmen Welt im romanischen Mittelalter. Stuttgart 1923.
GOUGENHEIM, GEORGES: De *chevalier* à *cavalier*. In: Mélanges de philologie romane et de littérature médiévale offerts à Ernest Hoepffner par ses élèves et ses amis. Paris 1949. (= Publications de la Faculté des lettres de l'Université de Strasbourg. Fasc. 113.) S. 117–126.
GRAUS, FRANTIŠEK: Littérature et mentalité médiévales: le roi et le peuple. In: Historica 16. 1969. S. 5–79.
GREEN, DENNIS H.: The Carolingian Lord. Semantic Studies on Four Old High German Words: *balder, frô, truhtin, hêrro*. Cambridge 1965.
Grundbegriffe, Geschichtliche. Historisches Lexikon zur politisch-sozialen Sprache in Deutschland. Hrsg. von OTTO BRUNNER, WERNER CONZE und REINHART KOSELLECK. [Bisher:] Bd. 1–2. Stuttgart 1972–1975.
GRUNDMANN, HERBERT: Rotten und Brabanzonen. Söldnerheere im 12. Jahrhundert. In: Deutsches Archiv für Geschichte des Mittelalters 5. 1942. S. 419–492.
— Übersetzungsprobleme im Spätmittelalter. In: Zeitschrift für deutsche Philologie. 70. 1947–1948. S. 113–145.
GUDENATZ, RICHARD: Schwäbische und fränkische Freiherren und Ministerialien am Hofe der deutschen Könige 1198–1272. Diss. Bonn 1909.
GUILHIERMOZ, PAUL: Essai sur l'origine de la noblesse en France au moyen âge. Paris 1902.
GUTTENBERG, ERICH FRH. VON: Titel und Standesbezeichnungen des oberfränkischen Adels seit dem 11. Jahrhundert. In: Familiengeschichtliche Blätter 24. 1926. Sp. 97–103. 133–140
HAAN, M. J. M. DE: Van ridders abite. In: Leuvense Bijdragen 60. 1971. S. 115–135.
HAENDLE, OTTO: Die Dienstmannen Heinrichs des Löwen. Ein Beitrag zur Frage der Ministerialität. Stuttgart 1930. (= Arbeiten zur deutschen Rechts- und Verfassungsgeschichte. 8.)
HAGSPIEL, GEREON H.: Die Führerpersönlichkeit im Kreuzzug. Zürich 1963. (= Geist und Werk der Zeiten. 10.)

Handbuch der deutschen Wirtschafts- und Sozialgeschichte. Hrsg. von HERMANN AUBIN und WOLFGANG ZORN. Bd. 1. Stuttgart 1971.

Handwörterbuch zur deutschen Rechtsgeschichte. Hrsg. von ADALBERT ERLER und EKKEHARD KAUFMANN. [Bisher:] Bd. 1. Berlin 1971. Bd. 2. Lfg. 9–13 [Buchstabe K]. 1972–1975.

HANNING, ROBERT W.: The Social Significance of Twelfth Century Chivalric Romance. In: Medievalia et Humanistica N. S. 3. 1972. S. 3–29.

HARNACK, ADOLF VON: Militia Christi. Die christliche Religion und der Soldatenstand in den ersten drei Jahrhunderten. Tübingen 1905. Neudruck Darmstadt 1963.

HARTUNG, GÜNTER: Über Struktur und Stil höfischer Dichtung. In: Wissenschaftliche Zeitschrift der Ernst-Moritz-Arndt-Universität Greifswald. Gesellschafts- und sprachwissenschaftliche Reihe 15. 1966. S. 515–521.

HARVEY, RUTH: Moriz von Craûn and the Chivalric World. Oxford 1961.

HARVEY, SALLY: The Knight and the Knight's Fee in England. In: Past and Present 49. 1970. S. 3–43.

HAUSER, ARNOLD: Sozialgeschichte der Kunst und Literatur. Bd. 1–2. München 1953. Sonderausgabe in einem Band. 1967.

HEARNSHAW, FOSSEY J. C.: Chivalry and Its Place in History. In: Chivalry [s. dort]. S. 1–35.

HECK, PHILIPP: Der Ursprung der sächsischen Dienstmannschaft. In: VSWG 5. 1907. S. 116–172.

– Übersetzungsprobleme im frühen Mittelalter. Tübingen 1931.

HEIDSIEK, WILHELM: Die ritterliche Gesellschaft in den Dichtungen des Chrestien de Troyes. Greifswald 1883.

HEINEMANN, WOLFGANG: Zur Ständedidaxe in der deutschen Literatur des 13.–15. Jahrhunderts. In: Beiträge zur Geschichte der deutschen Sprache und Literatur (Halle) 88. 1966. S. 1–90; 89. 1967. S. 290–403; 92. 1970. S. 388–437.

HELBIG, HERBERT: Fideles Dei et regis. Zur Bedeutungsentwicklung von Glaube und Treue im hohen Mittelalter. In: AKG 33. 1951. S. 275–306.

– Der wettinische Ständestaat. Untersuchungen zur Geschichte des Ständewesens und der landständischen Verfassung in Mitteldeutschland bis 1485. Münster, Köln 1955. (= Mitteldeutsche Forschungen. 4.)

HELLMANN, MANFRED: Bemerkungen zur sozialgeschichtlichen Erforschung des Deutschen Ordens. In: Hist. Jb. 80. 1961. S. 126–142.

HELLWEG, MARTIN: Die ritterliche Welt in der französischen Geschichtsschreibung des vierten Kreuzzugs. In: Romanische Forschungen 52. 1938. S. 1–40.

HENNE AM RHYN, OTTO: Geschichte des Ritterthums. Leipzig [1893.] (= Illustrierte Bibliothek der Kunst- und Kulturgeschichte. 3.)

Herrschaft und Staat im Mittelalter. Hrsg. von HELLMUT KÄMPF. Darmstadt 1956. (= Wege der Forschung. 2.)

HINTZE, OTTO: Typologie der ständischen Verfassungen des Abendlandes. In: HZ 141. 1930. S. 229–248. Wieder in: O. H.: Feudalismus – Kapitalismus. Hrsg. und eingeleitet von GERHARD OESTREICH. Göttingen 1970. (= Kleine Vandenhoeck-Reihe. 313.) S. 48–67.

HIS, RUDOLF: Zur Rechtsgeschichte des thüringischen Adels. In: Zeitschrift des Vereins für thüringische Geschichte und Altertumskunde. N. F. 14. 1904. S. 1–35. Neudruck [selbständig] Darmstadt 1965. (= Libelli. 106.)

HOFFMANN, HARTMUT: Gottesfriede und Treuga Dei. Stuttgart 1964. (= Schriften der Monumenta Germaniae historica. 20.)

HOFFMANN, ULRICH: König und Reich im Urteil fränkischer und deutscher Historiker des 9.–11. Jahrhunderts. Diss. Freiburg i. Br. Bamberg 1968.

HOLLYMAN, KENNETH-JAMES: Le développement du vocabulaire féodal en France pendant le haut moyen âge. Etude sémantique. Genf, Paris 1957. (= Société de publications romanes et françaises. 58.)

HOMUTH, WILHELM: Vom Einfluß des Lehnswesens und Rittertums auf den französischen Sprachschatz. Bedeutungsgeschichtliche Untersuchungen. In: Romanische Forschungen 39. 1926. S. 201–266.

HORWATH, PETER: Concerning the Origin and Nature of the Tugendsystem of Medieval German Knighthood. In: Arts libéraux et philosophie au moyen âge. Actes du quatrième congrès international de philosophie médiévale. Université de Montréal. Montréal, Canada, 27 août – 2 septembre 1967. Montreal, Paris 1969. S. 1105–1111.

HUBY, MICHEL: L'adaptation des romans courtois en Allemagne au XIIᵉ et au XIIIᵉ siècle. Paris 1968. (Publications de la Faculté des lettres et sciences humaines de Paris-Nanterre.)

– Adaptation courtoise et société ou ‚la réalité dépasse la fiction'. In: Etudes germaniques 29. 1974. S. 289–301.

IMHOF, OTTO: Die Ministerialität in den Stiftern Straßburg, Speyer und Worms. Diss. Freiburg i. Br. 1912.

JACKSON, WILLIAM H.: *Prison et croisié.* Ein Beitrag zum Begriff *arme ritter.* In: ZfdA 101. 1972. S. 105–117.

JAKOBS, HERMANN: Der Adel in der Klosterreform von St. Blasien. Köln, Graz 1968. (= Kölner Historische Abhandlungen. 16.)

JAUERNICK, STEFANIE: Das theoretische Bild des Rittertums in der altfranzösischen Literatur. Diss. Göttingen 1961.

JOETZE, FRANZ: Die Ministerialität im Hochstifte Bamberg. In: Hist. Jb. 36. 1915. S. 516–597. 748–798.

JOHRENDT, JOHANN: *Milites* und *Militia* im 11. Jahrhundert. Untersuchung zur Frühgeschichte des Rittertums in Frankreich und Deutschland. Diss. Erlangen-Nürnberg 1971.

KAISER, GERT: Textauslegung und gesellschaftliche Selbstdeutung. Aspekte einer sozialgeschichtlichen Interpretation von Hartmanns Artusepen. Frankfurt/M. 1973. (Wissenschaftliche Paperbacks. Literaturwissenschaft.)

KAISERER, JAKOB: Geschichte des Ritterwesens im Mittelalter. Wien 1804.

KALLFELZ, HATTO: Das Standesethos des Adels im 10. und 11. Jahrhundert. Diss. Würzburg 1960.

KASTEN, INGRID: Studien zu Thematik und Form des mittelhochdeutschen Streitgedichts. Diss. Hamburg 1973.

KAUFMANN, GEORG: Wehrhaftmachung kein Ritterschlag. In: Philologus 31. 1872. S. 490–510.

KEUTGEN, FRIEDRICH: Die Entstehung der deutschen Ministerialität. In: VSWG 8. 1910. S. 1–16. 169–195. 481–547.

KIENAST, WALTHER: Rechtsnatur und Anwendung der Mannschaft (*homagium*) in Deutschland während des Mittelalters. In: Deutsche Landesreferate zum IV. Internationalen Kongreß für Rechtsvergleichung in Paris 1954. Hrsg. von ERNST WOLFF. Düsseldorf 1955. S. 26–48.

– Deutschland und Frankreich in der Kaiserzeit (900–1270). Weltkaiser und Einzelkönige. 2., völlig neu bearbeitete und stark erweiterte Aufl. Bd. 1–3. Stuttgart 1974–1975. (= Monographien zur Geschichte des Mittelalters. 9, 1–3.)

KLEBEL, ERNST: Territorialstaat und Lehen. In: Studien zum mittelalterlichen Lehenswesen [s. dort]. S. 195–228.

– Vom Herzogtum zum Territorium. In: Aus Verfassungs- und Landesgeschichte. Festschrift zum 70. Geburtstag von Theodor Mayer. Dargebracht von seinen Freunden und Schülern. Bd. 1. Konstanz 1954. S. 205–222.

KLEIN, HERBERT: Ritterlehen und Beutellehen in Salzburg. In: Mitteilungen der Gesellschaft für Salzburger Landeskunde [abgekürzt: MdGfSL] 80. 1940. S. 87–128.

KLEINSCHMIDT, ERICH: Herrscherdarstellung. Zur Disposition mittelalterlichen Aussageverhaltens, untersucht an Texten über Rudolf I. von Habsburg. Mit einem Editionsanhang. Bern, München 1974. (= Bibliotheca Germanica. 17.)

KLEWITZ, HANS-WALTER: Geschichte der Ministerialität im Elsaß bis zum Ende des Interregnums. Frankfurt/M. 1929. (Schriften des Wissenschaftlichen Instituts der Elsaß-Lothringer im Reich an der Universität Frankfurt.)

KLOCKE, FRIEDRICH VON: Untersuchungen zur Rechts- und Sozialgeschichte der Ministerialitäten in Westfalen. In: Westfälische Forschungen 2. 1939. S. 214–232.

KLUCKHOHN, PAUL: Die Ministerialität in Südostdeutschland vom 10. bis zum Ende des 13. Jahrhunderts. Weimar 1910. (= Quellen und Studien zur Verfassungsgeschichte des Deutschen Reiches in Mittelalter und Neuzeit. Bd. 4. Heft 1.)

– Ministerialität und Ritterdichtung. In: ZfdA 52. 1910. S. 135–168.

– Der Minnesang als Standesdichtung. In: AKG 11. 1914. S. 389–410. Wieder in: Der deutsche Minnesang [s. dort]. S. 58–81.

KÖBLER, GERHARD: Zur Lehre von den Ständen in fränkischer Zeit. In: ZRG GA 89. 1972. S. 161–174.

– Amtsbezeichnungen in den frühmittelalterlichen Übersetzungsgleichungen. In: Hist. Jb. 92. 1972. S. 334–357.

KÖHLER, ERICH: Zur Diskussion der Adelsfrage bei den Trobadors. In: Medium aevum vivum. Festschrift für Walther Bulst. Hrsg. von HANS R. JAUSS und DIETER SCHALLER. Heidelberg

1960. S. 161–178. Wieder in: E. K.: Trobadorlyrik und höfischer Roman. Aufsätze zur französischen und provenzalischen Literatur des Mittelalters. Berlin 1962. (= Neue Beiträge zur Literaturwissenschaft. 15.) S. 115–132.

— Observations historiques et sociologiques sur la poésie des troubadours. In: Cahiers de civilisation médiévale 7. 1964. S. 27–51. Deutsch unter dem Titel: Die Rolle des niederen Rittertums bei der Entstehung der Trobadorlyrik. In: E. K.: Esprit und arkadische Freiheit. Aufsätze aus der Welt der Romania. Frankfurt/M., Bonn 1966. S. 9–27.

— Vergleichende soziologische Betrachtungen zum romanischen und zum deutschen Minnesang. In: Der Berliner Germanistentag 1968. Vorträge und Berichte. Hrsg. von KARL H. BORCK und RUOOLF HENSS. Heidelberg 1970. S. 61–76.

— Ideal und Wirklichkeit in der höfischen Epik. Studien zur Form der frühen Artus- und Graldichtung. 2. Aufl. Tübingen 1970. (= Zeitschrift für romanische Philologie. Beiheft 97.)

KÖHLER, GUSTAV: Die Entwicklung des Kriegswesens und der Kriegführung in der Ritterzeit von Mitte des 11. Jahrhunderts bis zu den Hussitenkriegen. Bd. 1–3 [in 5 Bänden]. Breslau 1886–1889.

KOTZENBERG, WALTHER: Man, frouwe, juncfrouwe. Drei Kapitel aus der mittelhochdeutschen Wortgeschichte. Berlin 1907. (= Berliner Beiträge zur germanischen und romanischen Philologie. 33. Germanische Abteilung. 20.)

KRAUSS, HENNING: Ritter und Bürger – Feudalheer und Volksheer. Zum Problem der feigen Lombarden in der altfranzösischen und frankoitalienischen Epik. In: Zeitschrift für romanische Philologie 87. 1971. S. 209–222.

KROESCHELL, KARL: Deutsche Rechtsgeschichte. Bd. 1–2. Reinbek 1972–1973. (= rororo Studium. 8–9.)

KUHN, HANS: Altnordisch rekkr und Verwandte. In: Arkiv för nordisk filologi 58. 1944. S. 105–121.

KUHN, HUGO: Soziale Realität und dichterische Fiktion am Beispiel der höfischen Ritterdichtung Deutschlands. In: Soziologie und Leben. Die soziologische Dimension der Fachwissenschaften. Hrsg. von CARL BRINKMANN. Tübingen 1952. S. 195–219. Wieder in: H. K.: Dichtung und Welt im Mittelalter. 2. Aufl. Stuttgart 1969. S. 22–40. 250–251.

LE GOFF, JACQUES: Note sur société tripartie, idéologie monarchique et renouveau économique dans la chrétienté du IXe au XIIe siècle. In: L'Europe aux IXe–XIe siècles [s. dort]. S. 63–71.

LEMARIGNIER, JEAN-FRANÇOIS: Le gouvernement royal aux premiers temps capétiens (987 bis 1108). Paris 1965.

— Aux origines de l'état français. Royauté et entourage royal aux premiers temps capétiens (987–1108). In: L'Europe aux IXe–XIe siècles [s. dort]. S. 43–55.

— La France médiévale. Institutions et société. Paris 1970. (Collection ,U'. Série Histoire médiévale.)

LESSIAK, HANS: Die Entstehung der Ministerialität in Kärnten. In: Carinthia I 142. 1952. S. 226–248; 145. 1955. S. 275–303.

LEYSER, K.: The German Aristocracy from the Ninth to the Early Twelfth Century. A Historical and Cultural Sketch. In: Past and Present 41. 1968. S. 25–53.

LIEBERICH, HEINZ: Landherren und Landleute. Zur politischen Führungsschicht Bayerns im Spätmittelalter. München 1964. (= Schriftenreihe zur bayerischen Landesgeschichte. 63.)

LOESCH, HEINRICH VON: Das kürzere Kölner Dienstmannenrecht. In: ZRG GA 44. 1924. S. 298–307.

LÖHER, FRANZ VON: Über Ritterschaft und Adel im späteren Mittelalter. In: Sitzungsberichte der kgl. bayerischen Akademie der Wissenschaften. 1861. Bd. 1. S. 365–416.

LOT, FERDINAND: L'art militaire et les armées au moyen âge en Europe et dans le proche orient. Bd. 1–2. Paris 1946.

LÜBECK, KONRAD: Die Ministerialien der Reichsabtei Fulda. In: ZRG KA 35. 1948. S. 201–233.

LÜTGE, FRIEDRICH: Deutsche Sozial- und Wirtschaftsgeschichte. Ein Überblick. 3. Aufl. Berlin 1966.

LUYN, P. VAN: Les milites dans la France du XIe siècle. Examen des sources narratives. In: Le moyen âge 77. 1971. S. 5–51. 193–238.

MANGOLDT-GAUDLITZ, HANS G. W. VON: Die Reiterei in den germanischen und fränkischen Heeren bis zum Ausgang der deutschen Karolinger. Berlin 1922. (= Arbeiten zur deutschen Rechts- und Verfassungsgeschichte. 4.)

MANZ, LUISE: Der Ordo-Gedanke. Ein Beitrag zur Frage des mittelalterlichen Ständegedankens. Stuttgart, Berlin 1937. (= VSWG. Beiheft 33.)

MARANINI, LORENZA: *Cavalleria e cavalieri* nel mondo di Chrétien de Troyes. In: Mélanges de langue et de littérature du moyen âge et de la renaissance offerts à JEAN FRAPPIER par ses collègues, ses élèves et ses amis. Bd. 2. Genf 1970. (= Publications romanes et françaises. 112.) S. 737–755.

MARTIN, ALFRED VON: Kultursoziologie des Mittelalters. In: Handwörterbuch der Soziologie. Hrsg. von ALFRED VIERKANDT. Stuttgart 1931. S. 370–390.

MASSMANN, ERNST H.: Schwertleite und Ritterschlag, dargestellt auf Grund der mittelhochdeutschen literarischen Quellen. Diss. Hamburg 1932.

MAURER, FRIEDRICH: Über *Adel* und *edel* in altdeutscher Dichtung. In: Adel und Kirche. Gerd Tellenbach zum 65. Geburtstag dargebracht von Freunden und Schülern. Hrsg. von JOSEF FLECKENSTEIN und KARL SCHMID. Freiburg, Basel, Wien 1968. S. 1–5. Wieder in: F. M.: Dichtung und Sprache des Mittelalters. Gesammelte Aufsätze. 2. Aufl. Bern, München 1971. (= Bibliotheca Germanica. 10.) S. 463–468.

MAURER, HANS-MARTIN: Die Entstehung der hochmittelalterlichen Adelsburg in Südwestdeutschland. In: ZGO 117. 1969. S. 295–332.

MAYER, ERNST: Deutsche und französische Verfassungsgeschichte vom 9. bis zum 14. Jahrhundert. Bd. 1–2. Leipzig 1899.

MAYER, THEODOR: Die Ausbildung der Grundlagen des modernen deutschen Staates im hohen Mittelalter. In: HZ 159. 1939. S. 457–487. Wieder in: Herrschaft und Staat im Mittelalter [s. dort]. S. 284–331.

– Mittelalterliche Studien. Gesammelte Aufsätze. Lindau, Konstanz 1959.

MCDONALD, WILLIAM, with the Collaboration of ULRICH GOEBEL: German Medieval Literary Patronage from Charlemagne to Maximilian I. A Critical Commentary with Special Emphasis on Imperial Promotion of Literature. Amsterdam 1973. (= Amsterdamer Publikationen zur Sprache und Literatur. 10.)

MEISSBURGER, GERHARD: *De vita christiana*. Zum Bild des christlichen Ritters im Hochmittelalter. In: Der Deutschunterricht 14. 1962. Heft 6. S. 21–34.

MELLER, WALTER C.: A Knight's Life in the Days of Chivalry. London 1924.

MERZBACHER, FRIEDRICH: Die Bedeutung von Freiheit und Unfreiheit im weltlichen und kirchlichen Recht des deutschen Mittelalters. In: Hist. Jb. 90. 1971. S. 257–283.

MEYER, BRUNO: Das Lehen in Recht und Staat des Mittelalters. In: Zeitschrift für schweizerische Geschichte 26. 1946. S. 161–178.

Minnesang, Der deutsche. Aufsätze zu seiner Erforschung. Hrsg. von HANS FROMM. Darmstadt 1961. (= Wege der Forschung. 15.)

MITTEIS, HEINRICH: Lehnrecht und Staatsgewalt. Untersuchungen zur mittelalterlichen Verfassungsgeschichte. Weimar 1933. Neudruck Köln, Darmstadt 1958.

– Formen der Adelsherrschaft im Mittelalter. In: Festschrift für Fritz Schulz. Bd. 2. Weimar 1951. S. 226–258. Wieder in: H. M.: Die Rechtsidee … S. 636–668.

– Die Rechtsidee in der Geschichte. Gesammelte Abhandlungen und Vorträge. Weimar 1957.

– Recht und Dichtung. In: H. M.: Die Rechtsidee … S. 681–697.

– Der Staat des hohen Mittelalters. Grundlinien einer vergleichenden Verfassungsgeschichte des Lehnszeitalters. 8. Aufl. Weimar 1968.

MOHL, RUTH: The Three Estates in Medieval and Renaissance Literature. New York 1933. (Columbia University Studies in English and Comparative Literature.)

MOHR, WOLFGANG: Minnesang als Gesellschaftskunst. In: Der Deutschunterricht 6. 1954. Heft 5. S. 83–107. Wieder in: Der deutsche Minnesang [s. dort]. S. 197–228.

– *Arme riter*. In: ZfdA 97. 1968, S. 127–134.

– Mittelalterliche Feste und ihre Dichtung. In: Festschrift für Klaus Ziegler. Hrsg. von ECKEHARD CATHOLY und WINFRIED HELLMANN. Tübingen 1968. S. 37–60.

MOLITOR, ERICH: Der Stand der Ministerialen, vornehmlich aufgrund sächsischer, thüringischer und niederrheinischer Quellen. Breslau 1912. (= Untersuchungen zur deutschen Staats- und Rechtsgeschichte. 112.)

– Ständerechtsverhältnisse als Geschichtsquelle. In: HZ 170. 1950. S. 23–39.

MONZEL, NIKOLAUS: Geburtsstände und Leistungsgemeinschaften in der katholischen Soziallehre des Mittelalters und der Gegenwart. Bonn 1953. (= Bonner Akademische Reden. 10.)

MOORMAN, CHARLES: The First Knights. In: The Southern Quarterly Bd. 1. Heft 1. Okt. 1962. S. 13–26.

– A Knyght there was. The Evolution of the Knight in Literature. Lexington, Ky. 1967.

MOSBACHER, HELGA: Kammerhandwerk, Ministerialität und Bürgertum in Straßburg. In: ZGO 119. 1971. S. 33–173.

MOSER, HUGO: Dichtung und Wirklichkeit im Hochmittelalter. In: Wirkendes Wort 5. 1954 bis 1955. S. 79–91.

MÜLLER, EMIL: Die Ministerialität im Stift St. Gallen und in Landschaft und Stadt Zürich. Diss. Freiburg i. Br. 1911.

NAUMANN, HANS: Ritterliche Standeskultur in Deutschland. In: H. Naumann und Günther Müller: Höfische Kultur. Halle 1929. (= DVjs. Buchreihe 17.) S. 1–77.

– Der staufische Ritter. Leipzig 1936. (= Meyers kleine Handbücher. 3.)

– Germanische Grundlagen des Rittertums. In: Geistige Arbeit 4. 1937. Nr. 15. S. 1–2.

– Deutsche Kultur im Zeitalter des Rittertums. Potsdam 1938. (= Handbuch der Kulturgeschichte. Abt. 1.)

– Verhältnis des deutschen zum westlichen Rittertum. In: Von deutscher Art in Sprache und Dichtung. Bd. 2. Stuttgart, Berlin 1941. S. 169–188.

NECKEL, GUSTAV: Adel und Gefolgschaft. Ein Beitrag zur germanischen Altertumskunde. In: Beiträge zur Geschichte der deutschen Sprache und Literatur 41. 1916. S. 385–436. Wieder in: G. N.: Vom Germanentum. Ausgewählte Aufsätze und Vorträge. Leipzig 1944. S. 139–186.

NITZSCH, KARL W.: Ministerialität und Bürgerthum im 11. und 12. Jahrhundert. Ein Beitrag zur deutschen Städtegeschichte. Leipzig 1859. (= Vorarbeiten zur Geschichte der staufischen Periode. 1.)

NOTH, ALBRECHT: Heiliger Krieg und Heiliger Kampf in Islam und Christentum. Beiträge zur Vorgeschichte und Geschichte der Kreuzzüge. Bonn 1966. (= Bonner Historische Forschungen. 28.)

OMAN, CHARLES W. C.: A History of the Art of War in the Middle Ages. Bd. 1–2. 2. Aufl. New York 1924. Gekürzt unter dem Titel: The Art of War in the Middle Ages. A. D. 378–1515. Revised and Edited by JOHN H. BEELER. Ithaca, N. Y. 1953.

OSCHINSKY, HUGO: Der Ritter unterwegs und die Pflege der Gastfreundschaft im Alten Frankreich. Diss. Halle 1900.

OTTO, EBERHARD F.: Adel und Freiheit im deutschen Staat des frühen Mittelalters. Studien über *nobiles* und Ministerialen. Berlin 1937. (= Neue Deutsche Forschungen. Abteilung Mittelalterliche Geschichte. 2.)

– Von der Abschließung des Ritterstandes. In: HZ 162. 1940. S. 19–39.

PAINTER, SIDNEY: The Ideas of Chivalry. In: The Johns Hopkins Alumni Magazine 23. 1935. S. 218–232. Wieder in: S. P.: Feudalism and Liberty. Articles and Addresses. Edited by FRED A. CAZEL, JR. Baltimore, Md. 1961. S. 90–104.

– French Chivalry: Chivalric Ideas and Practices in Mediaeval France. Baltimore, Md. 1940. Neudruck Ithaca, N. Y. 1957.

PAULUS, NIKOLAUS: Die Wertung der weltlichen Berufe im Mittelalter. In: Hist. Jb. 32. 1911. S. 725–755.

PÉRENNEC, RENÉ: Adaptation et société: l'adaptation par Hartmann d'Aue du roman de Chrétien de Troyes ‚Erec et Enide‘. In: Etudes germaniques 28. 1973. S. 289–303.

PETERS, URSULA: Cour d'amour – Minnehof. Ein Beitrag zum Verhältnis der französischen und deutschen Minnedichtung und zu den Unterhaltungsformen ihres Publikums. In: ZfdA 101. 1972. S. 117–133.

– Niederes Rittertum oder hoher Adel? Zu Erich Köhlers historisch-soziologischer Deutung der altprovenzalischen u. mittelhochdeutschen Minnelyrik. In: Euphorion 67. 1973. S. 244—260.

– Artusroman und Fürstenhof. Darstellung und Kritik neuerer sozialgeschichtlicher Untersuchungen zu Hartmanns ‚Erec‘. In: Euphorion 69. 1975. S. 175–196.

PETERSEN, JULIUS: Das Rittertum in der Darstellung des Johannes Rothe. Straßburg 1909. (= Quellen und Forschungen zur Sprach- und Culturgeschichte der germanischen Völker. 106.)

PFEIFFER, G.: Studien zur Geschichte der fränkischen Reichsritterschaft. In: Jahrbuch für fränkische Landesforschung 22. 1962. S. 173–280.

PIETZNER, FRITZ: Schwertleite und Ritterschlag. Diss. Heidelberg 1934.

PLANITZ, HANS: Deutsche Rechtsgeschichte. Graz 1950.

PLASSMANN, JOSEPH O.: *Princeps* und *Populus*. Die Gefolgschaft im ottonischen Staatsaufbau nach den sächsischen Geschichtsschreibern des 10. Jahrhunderts. Göttingen 1954. (Schriften der Forschungshilfe.)

PLOTHO, WOLFGANG FRH. VON: Die Stände des deutschen Reiches im 12. Jahrhundert und ihre Fortentwicklung bis zum Schlusse des Mittelalters. Unter Berücksichtigung der Werke des Frhn. Otto von Dungern. In: Vierteljahrsschrift für Wappen-, Siegel- und Familienkunde 45. 1917. S. 1–59.

POTH, KARL: Die Ministerialität der Bischöfe von Münster. In: Zeitschrift für vaterländische Geschichte und Altertumskunde [abgekürzt: ZfvGA] 70. 1912. S. 1–108.

PÖTTER, WILHELM: Die Ministerialität der Erzbischöfe von Köln vom Ende des 11. bis zum Ausgang des 13. Jahrhunderts. Düsseldorf 1967. (= Studien zur Kölner Kirchengeschichte. 9.)

PRINZ, FRIEDRICH: Klerus und Krieg im früheren Mittelalter. Untersuchungen zur Rolle der Kirche beim Aufbau der Königsherrschaft. Stuttgart 1971. (= Monographien zur Geschichte des Mittelalters. 2.)

Problem, Das, der Freiheit in der deutschen und schweizerischen Geschichte. Hrsg. von THEODOR MAYER. Lindau, Konstanz [1955.] (= Vorträge und Forschungen. 2.)

Probleme des 12. Jahrhunderts. Reichenau-Vorträge 1965–1967. Konstanz, Stuttgart 1968. (= Vorträge und Forschungen. 12.)

Problèmes de stratification sociale. Actes du colloque international (1966). Publiés par ROLAND MOUSNIER. Paris 1968. (= Travaux du Centre de recherches sur la civilisation de l'Europe moderne. 5. = Publications de la Faculté des lettres et sciences humaines de Paris-Sorbonne. Série Recherches. 43.)

PRUTZ, HANS: Die geistlichen Ritterorden. Ihre Stellung zur kirchlichen, politischen, gesellschaftlichen und wirtschaftlichen Entwicklung des Mittelalters. Berlin 1908.

REIMANN, JOHANNA: Die Ministerialität des Hochstifts Würzburg in sozial-, rechts- und verfassungsgeschichtlicher Sicht. Diss. Berlin F. U. 1963. Wieder unter dem Titel: Zur Besitz- und Familiengeschichte der Ministerialien des Hochstifts Würzburg. In: Mainfränkisches Jahrbuch 15. 1963. S. 1–117.

REITZENSTEIN, ALEXANDER VON: Rittertum und Ritterschaft. München 1972. (= Bibliothek des Germanischen Nationalmuseums Nürnberg zur deutschen Kunst- und Kulturgeschichte. 32.)

REUTER, HANS G.: Die Lehre vom Ritterstand. Zum Ritterbegriff in Historiographie und Dichtung vom 11. bis zum 13. Jahrhundert. Köln, Wien 1971. (= Neue Wirtschaftsgeschichte. 4.)

RICHTER, DIETER: ,Ritterliche Dichtung'. Die Ritter und die Ahnengalerie des deutschen Bürgertums, In: Literatur im Feudalismus. Hrsg. von DIETER RICHTER. Stuttgart 1975. (= Literaturwissenschaft und Sozialwissenschaften. 5.) S. 9–39.

RIEMEN, ALFRED: Bedeutung und Gebrauch der Heldenwörter im mittelhochdeutschen Epos. Diss. [masch.] Köln 1954.

RITTER, JEAN-PIERRE: Ministérialité et chevalerie. Dignité humaine et liberté dans le droit médiéval. Thèse Lausanne 1955.

Rittertum. Schweizerische Dokumente. Hochadel im Aargau. Redaktion und Texte: HANS DÜRST. 2. Aufl. Aarau 1964. (= Dokumente zur aargauischen Kulturgeschichte. 2.)

Rittertum, Das, im Mittelalter. Hrsg. von ARNO BORST. Darmstadt 1976. (= Wege der Forschung. 349.)

ROCHER, DANIEL: ,Chevalerie' et littérature ,chevaleresque'. In: Etudes germaniques 21. 1966. S. 165–179; 23. 1968. S. 345–357.

– Henric van Veldeke und das Problem der ritterlichen Kultur. In: Heinric van Veldeken. Symposion Gent 23–24 oktober 1970. Verslag en lezingen uitgeven door Gilbert A. R. de Smet. Antwerpen, Utrecht 1971. S. 151–159.

ROSENAU, PETER U.: Wehrverfassung und Kriegsrecht in der mittelhochdeutschen Epik. Wolfram von Eschenbach, Hartmann von Aue, Gottfried von Straßburg, Der Nibelunge Not, Kudrunepos, Wolfdietrichbruchstück A, König Rother, Salman und Morolf. Diss. jur. [masch.] Bonn 1959.

ROTH VON SCHRECKENSTEIN, KARL H.: Geschichte der ehemaligen freien Reichsritterschaft in Schwaben, Franken und am Rheinstrome. Bd. 1–2. Tübingen 1859–1871.

– Das angebliche Ceremonial bei der Ritterweihe des Königs Wilhelm 1247. In: Forschungen zur deutschen Geschichte 22. 1882. S. 233–247.

– Die Ritterwürde und der Ritterstand. Historisch-politische Studien über deutsch-mittelalterliche Standesverhältnisse auf dem Lande und in der Stadt. Freiburg i. Br. 1886.

ROUSSET, PAUL: La description du monde chevaleresque chez Orderic Vital. In: Le moyen âge 75. 1969. S. 427–444.

RUST, ERNST: Die Erziehung des Ritters in der altfranzösischen Epik. Diss. Berlin 1888.

SANDBERGER, DIETRICH: Studien über das Rittertum in England vornehmlich während des 14. Jahrhunderts. Berlin 1937. (= Historische Studien. 310.)

– Die Aufnahme in den Ritterstand in England. In: AKG 27. 1937. S. 74–93.

SCHIECKEL, HARALD: Herrschaftsbereich und Ministerialität der Markgrafen von Meißen im
    12. und 13. Jahrhundert. Untersuchungen über Stand und Stammort der Zeugen mark-
    gräflicher Urkunden. Köln, Graz 1956. (= Mitteldeutsche Forschungen. 7.)
SCHLESINGER, WALTER: Die Entstehung der Landesherrschaft. Untersuchung vorwiegend nach
    mitteldeutschen Quellen. Bd. 1. Dresden 1941. (= Sächsische Forschungen zur Geschichte. 1.)
    Neudruck Darmstadt 1964.
— Herrschaft und Gefolgschaft in der germanisch-deutschen Verfassungsgeschichte. In: HZ 176.
    1953. S. 225–275. Wieder in: Herrschaft und Staat im Mittelalter [s. dort]. S. 135–190.
    Wieder in: W. S.: Beiträge ... Bd. 1. S. 9–52.
— Burg und Stadt. In: Aus Verfassungs- und Landesgeschichte. Festschrift zum 70. Geburtstag
    von Theodor Mayer. Dargebracht von seinen Freunden und Schülern. Bd. 1. Konstanz 1954.
    S. 97–150. Wieder in: W. S.: Beiträge ... Bd. 2. 92–147.
— Beiträge zur deutschen Verfassungsgeschichte des Mittelalters. Bd. 1–2. Göttingen 1963.
SCHMID, KARL: Zur Problematik von Familie, Sippe und Geschlecht, Haus und Dynastie beim
    mittelalterlichen Adel. Vorfragen zum Thema ‚Adel und Herrschaft im Mittelalter'. In:
    ZGO 105. 1957. S. 1–62.
— Über die Struktur des Adels im früheren Mittelalter. In: Jahrbuch für fränkische Landes-
    forschung 19. 1959. S. 1–23.
— Programmatisches zur Erforschung der mittelalterlichen Personen und Personengruppen. In:
    FmSt. 8. 1974. S. 116–130.
SCHMID, KARL, und JOACHIM WOLLASCH: Societas et Fraternitas. Begründung eines kommen-
    tierten Quellenwerkes zur Erforschung der Personen und Personengruppen des Mittelalters.
    In: FmSt. 9. 1975. S. 1–48.
SCHMIDT-WIEGAND, RUTH: Fränkische und franko-lateinische Bezeichnungen für soziale Schich-
    ten und Gruppen in der Lex Salica. Göttingen 1972. (= Nachrichten der Akademie der
    Wissenschaften in Göttingen. Phil.-hist. Klasse. Jg. 1972. Nr. 4.)
— Historische Onomasiologie und Mittelalterforschung. In: FmSt. 9. 1975. S. 49–78.
SCHMITTHENNER, PAUL: Das freie Söldnertum im abendländischen Imperium des Mittelalters.
    München 1934. (= Münchener Historische Abhandlungen. Reihe 2. Heft 4.)
— Lehnskriegswesen und Söldnertum im abendländischen Imperium des Mittelalters. In:
    HZ 150. 1934. S. 229–267.
SCHMITZ, HANS: Blutsadel und Geistesadel in der hochhöfischen Dichtung. Würzburg, Aumühle
    1941. (= Bonner Beiträge zur Deutschen Philologie. 11.)
SCHNÜRER, GUSTAV: Kirche und Kultur im Mittelalter. Bd. 1–3. Paderborn. Bd. 1: 3. Aufl. 1936;
    Bd. 2: 2. Aufl. 1929; Bd. 3: 1930.
SCHOWINGEN, KARL FRH. VON: Zum Ministerialenproblem: Eine Reichenauer Urkunde von
    1363. In: ZRG GA 61. 1941. S. 274–282.
SCHRADER, WERNER: Studien über das Wort höfisch in der mittelhochdeutschen Dichtung.
    Diss. Bonn. Würzburg 1935.
SCHRÖDER, EDWARD: Ritter oder Knecht? In: Anzeiger für deutsches Altertum 50. 1931.
    S. 213–214.
SCHRÖDER, RICHARD: Beiträge zur Kunde des deutschen Rechts aus deutschen Dichtern. In:
    ZfdA 13. 1866. S. 139–161.
SCHRÖDER, RICHARD, und EBERHARD FRH. VON KÜNSSBERG: Lehrbuch der deutschen Rechts-
    geschichte. 7. Aufl. Berlin, Leipzig 1932.
SCHRÖDER, WERNER: Zum ritter-Bild der frühmittelhochdeutschen Dichter. In: Germanisch-
    Romanische Monatsschrift 53. 1972. S. 333–351.
SCHULTE, ALOYS: Die Standesverhältnisse der Minnesänger. In: ZfdA 39. 1895. S. 185–251.
— Zur Geschichte des hohen Adels. In: MIÖG 34. 1913. S. 43–81.
— Der Adel und die deutsche Kirche im Mittelalter. Studien zur Sozial-, Rechts- und Kirchen-
    geschichte. 3. Aufl. Darmstadt 1958.
SCHULTZ, ALWIN: Das höfische Leben zur Zeit der Minnesinger. Bd. 1–2. 2. Aufl. Leipzig 1889.
SCHULZ, KNUT: Ministerialität und Bürgertum in Trier. Untersuchungen zur rechtlichen und
    sozialen Gliederung der Trierer Bürgerschaft vom ausgehenden 11. bis zum Ende des
    14. Jahrhunderts. Bonn 1968. (= Rheinisches Archiv. 66.)
— Die Ministerialität als Problem der Stadtgeschichte. Einige allgemeine Bemerkungen, er-
    läutert am Beispiel der Stadt Worms. In: Rheinische Vierteljahrsblätter 32. 1968. S. 184–219.
SCHUMACHER, KARL: Die Dienstmannschaft der rheinischen Stifter und Abteien und die
    Klosterreformen. In: Beiträge zur Geschichte des Niederrheins 25. 1912. S. 66–78.
SCHWER, WILHELM: Stand und Ständeordnung im Weltbild des Mittelalters. Die geistes- und
    gesellschaftsgeschichtlichen Grundlagen der berufsständischen Idee. 2. Aufl. Hrsg. von

NIKOLAUS MONZEL. Paderborn 1952. (= Görres-Gesellschaft. Veröffentlichungen der Sektion für Wirtschafts- und Sozialwissenschaften. 7.)

SEELIGER, GERHARD: Die soziale und politische Bedeutung der Grundherrschaft im früheren Mittelalter. Untersuchungen über Hofrecht, Immunität und Landleihen. Leipzig 1904. (= Abhandlungen der Kgl. Sächsischen Gesellschaft der Wissenschaften. Phil.-hist. Klasse. Jg. 22. Nr. 1.)

— Ständische Bildungen im deutschen Volk. Rektoratsrede. Leipzig 1905.

SEGELCKE, DOROTHEA: *Riten*. Studien zum Wortschatz des Reitens im Mittelhochdeutschen. Diss. Münster 1969.

SIEBEL, GÜNTER: Harnisch und Helm in den epischen Dichtungen des 12. Jahrhunderts bis zu Hartmanns ‚Erek'. Ein Beitrag zur Verwertbarkeit der Dichtung für die Realienforschung. Diss. Hamburg 1968.

SOENEN, MICHELINE: A propos de *ministeriales* brabançon propriétaires d'alleux aux XIIᵉ et XIIIᵉ siècles. In: Hommage au professeur Paul Bonenfant (1899–1965). Etudes d'histoire médiévale dédiées à sa mémoire par les anciens élèves de son séminaire à l'Université libre de Bruxelles. Brüssel 1965. S. 139–149.

SPANGENBERG, HANS: Vom Lehnstaat zum Ständestaat. Ein Beitrag zur Entstehung der landständischen Verfassungen. München, Berlin 1912. (= Historische Bibliothek. 29.)

SPROEMBERG, HEINRICH: Die feudale Kriegskunst. In: H. S.: Beiträge zur belgisch-niederlandischen Geschichte. Berlin 1959. (= Forschungen zur mittelalterl. Geschichte. 3.) S. 30–55.

Stadt und Ministerialität. Protokoll der IX. Arbeisttagung des Arbeitskreises für südwestdeutsche Stadtgeschichtsforschung. Freiburg i. Br. 13.–15. Nov. 1970. Hrsg. von ERICH MASCHKE und JÜRGEN SYDOW. Stuttgart 1973. (= Veröffentlichungen der Kommission für geschichtliche Landeskunde in Baden-Württemberg. Reihe B. Bd. 76.)

STAHLEDER, HELMUTH: Zum Ständebegriff im Mittelalter. In: ZfbLG 35. 1972. S. 523–570.

STEIN, ARTHUR: Der römische Ritterstand. Ein Beitrag zur Sozial- und Personengeschichte des römischen Reichs. München 1927. (= Münchener Beiträge zur Papyrusforschung und antiken Rechtsgeschichte. 10.)

STEINBACH, FRANZ: Geburtsstand, Berufsstand und Leistungsgemeinschaft. Studien zur Geschichte des Bürgertums. 2. In: Rheinische Vierteljahrsblätter 14. 1949. S. 35–96.

STENGEL, EDMUND E.: Über den Ursprung der Ministerialität. In: Papsttum und Kaisertum. Forschungen zur politischen Geschichte und Geisteskultur des Mittelalters. Paul Kehr zum 65. Geburtstag dargebracht. Hrsg. von ALBERT BRACKMANN. München 1926. S. 168–184. Wieder in: E. E. S.: Abhandlungen ... S. 69–86.

— Land- und lehnrechtliche Grundlagen des Reichsfürstenstandes. In: ZRG GA 66. 1948. S. 294–342. Wieder in: E. E. S.: Abhandlungen ... S. 133–173.

— Abhandlungen und Untersuchungen zur mittelalterlichen Geschichte. Köln, Graz 1960.

STEPHENSON, CARL: The Origin and Significance of Feudalism. In: The American Historical Review 46. 1941. S. 788–812.

STEPHENSON, CARL: Mediaeval Feudalism. Ithaca, N. Y. 1942. Neudruck 1956.

STÖRMER, WILHELM: König Artus als aristokratisches Leitbild während des späteren Mittelalters, gezeigt an Beispielen der Ministerialität und des Patriziats. In: ZfbLG 35. 1972. S. 946–971.

— Früher Adel. Studien zur politischen Führungsschicht im fränkisch-deutschen Reich vom 8. bis 11. Jahrhundert. Bd. 1–2. Stuttgart 1973. (= Monographien zur Geschichte des Mittelalters. 6, 1–2.)

Studien zum mittelalterlichen Lehenswesen. Lindau-Vorträge 1956. Lindau, Konstanz 1960. (= Vorträge und Forschungen. 5.)

Studien und Vorarbeiten zur Geschichte des großfränkischen und frühdeutschen Adels. Hrsg. von GERD TELLENBACH. Freiburg i. Br. 1957. (= Forschungen zur oberrheinischen Landesgeschichte. 4.)

STUKE, HORST: La signification du mot ‚Stand' dans les pays de langue allemande (Aperçu d'histoire des notions). In: Problèmes de stratification sociale [s. dort]. S. 37–49.

STUTZ, ULRICH: Schwertweihe. In: ZRG KA 9. 1919. S. 312–313.

— Zum Wesen und Ursprung des niederen Adels. In: Sitzungsberichte der Preußischen Akademie der Wissenschaften. Phil.-hist. Klasse. Bd. 32. Nr. 27. Berlin 1937. S. 213–257.

TELLENBACH, GERD: Vom karolingischen Reichsadel zum deutschen Reichsfürstenstand. In: Adel und Bauern im deutschen Staat des Mittelalters [s. dort]. S. 22–73. Wieder in: Herrschaft und Staat im Mittelalter [s. dort]. S. 191–242.

— Kritische Studien zur großfränkischen und alemannischen Adelsgeschichte. In: Zeitschrift für württembergische Landesgeschichte 15. 1956. S. 169–190.

- Zur Bedeutung der Personenforschung für die Erkenntnis des früheren Mittelalters. Freiburg i. Br. 1957. (= Freiburger Universitätsreden. N. F. 25.)
- Zur Erforschung des mittelalterlichen Adels (9.–12. Jahrhundert). In: Comité international des sciences historiques. XIIᵉ congrès international des sciences historiques. Vienne, 29 aout – 5 septembre 1965. Rapports. Bd. 1. Grands thèmes. Horn, Wien [1967]. S. 318–337.
- Irdischer Stand und Heilserwartung im Denken des Mittelalters. In: Festschrift für Hermann Heimpel zum 70. Geburtstag am 19. Sept. 1971. Hrsg. von den Mitarbeitern des Max-Planck-Instituts für Geschichte. Bd. 2. Göttingen 1972. (= Veröffentlichungen des Max-Planck-Instituts für Geschichte. 36, 2.) S. 1–16.

Territorialstaat, Der deutsche, im 14. Jahrhundert. Bd. 1–2. Hrsg. von HANS PATZE. Sigmaringen 1970–1971. (= Vorträge und Forschungen. 13–14.)

TREIS, KARL: Die Formalitäten des Ritterschlags in der altfranzösischen Epik. Leipzig 1887.

TRESTÍK, DUSAN, und BARBARA KRZEMIENSKA: Zur Problematik der Dienstleute im frühmittelalterlichen Böhmen. In: Siedlung und Verfassung Böhmens in der Frühzeit. Hrsg. von FRANTIŠEK GRAUS und HERBERT LUDAT. Wiesbaden 1967. S. 70–103.

Tugendsystem, Ritterliches. Hrsg. von GÜNTER EIFLER. Darmstadt 1970. (= Wege der Forschung. 56.)

Untersuchungen zur gesellschaftlichen Struktur der mittelalterlichen Städte in Europa. Reichenau-Vorträge 1963–1964. Konstanz, Stuttgart 1966. (= Vorträge und Forschungen. 11.)

VEDEL, VALDEMAR: Ridderromantiken i fransk og tysk middelalder. Kopenhagen, Kristiana 1906. Deutsch unter dem Titel: Ritterromantik. Mittelalterliche Kulturideale. 2. Übersetzt von Anna Grundtvig. Leipzig 1911. (= Aus Natur und Geisteswelt. 293.)

VERBRUGGEN, JAN F.: La tactique militaire des armées de chevaliers. In: Revue du nord 29. 1947. S. 161–180.

- Krijkskunst in West-Europa in de middeleeuwen (IXe tot begin XIVe eeuwe). Brüssel 1954 (= Verhandelingen van de kgl. vlaamse academie voor wetenschappen, letteren en schone kunsten van Belgie. Klasse der letteren. 20.)

WAAS, ADOLF: Herrschaft und Staat im deutschen Frühmittelalter. Berlin 1938. (= Historische Studien. 335.)

WACKERNAGEL, WILHELM: Ritter- und Dichterleben Basels im Mittelalter. In: W. W.: Kleinere Schriften. Bd. 1. Leipzig 1872. S. 258–301.

WAITZ, GEORG: Deutsche Verfassungsgeschichte. Bd. 1–8. Kiel 1844–1878. Bd. 1: 3. Aufl. 1880; Bd. 2: 3. Aufl. 1882; Bd. 3: 2. Aufl. 1883; Bd. 4: 2. Aufl. Berlin 1885; Bd. 5: 2. Aufl. Hrsg. von KARL ZEUMER. Berlin 1895; Bd. 6: 2. Aufl. Hrsg. von GERHARD SEELIGER. Berlin 1896; Bd. 7: Kiel 1876; Bd. 8: Kiel 1878.

WANG, ANDREAS: Der 'Miles Christianus' im 16. und 17. Jahrhundert und seine mittelalterliche Tradition. Ein Beitrag zum Verhältnis von sprachlicher und graphischer Bildlichkeit. Bern, Frankfurt/M. 1975. (= Mikrokosmos. 1.)

WEBER, KARL J.: Das Ritterwesen und die Templer, Johanniter und Mariner oder Deutsch-Ordens-Ritter insbesondere. Bd. 1–3. Stuttgart 1822-1824.

WECHSSLER, EDUARD: Frauendienst und Vassallität. In: Zeitschrift für französische Sprache und Literatur 24. 1902. S. 159-190.

WEDEL, HEINRICH VON: Deutschlands Ritterschaft. Ihre Entwicklung und ihre Blüte. 2. Aufl. Görlitz 1906.

WEIMANN, KARL: Die Ministerialität im späteren Mittelalter. Leipzig 1924.

WENTZLAFF-EGGEBERT, FRIEDRICH-WILHELM: Kreuzzugsdichtung des Mittelalters. Studien zu ihrer geschichtlichen und dichterischen Wirklichkeit. Berlin 1960.

WENZEL, HORST: Frauendienst und Gottesdienst. Studien zur Minne-Ideologie. Berlin 1974. (= Philologische Studien und Quellen. 74.)

WERNER, KARL F.: Untersuchungen zur Frühzeit des französischen Fürstentums (9. bis 10. Jahrhundert). In: Die Welt als Geschichte 18, 1958. S 256-289; 19. 1959. S. 146-193; 20. 1960. S. 87-119.

WESSELS, PAULUS B.: Der höfische Ritter, ein Wanderer zwischen zwei Welten. Nijmegen, Utrecht 1952.

WINTER, GEORG: Die Ministerialität in Brandenburg. Untersuchungen zur Geschichte der Ministerialität und zum Sachsenspiegel. München, Berlin 1922.

WINTER, JOHANNA M. VAN: Ministerialiteit en Riddershap in Gelre en Zutphen. Groningen 1962. (= Bijdragen van het Instituut voor Middeleeuwse Geschiedenis der Rijksuniversiteit te Utrecht. 31.)

—Riddershap. Ideaal en Werkelijkheid. Bossum 1965. (= Fibulareeks. 11.) Deutsch unter dem Titel: Rittertum. Ideal und Wirklichkeit. München 1969.

—'Uxorum de militari ordine sibi imparem'. In: Miscellanea mediaevalia in memoriam Jan Frederik Niermeyer. Groningen 1967. S. 113-124.

—De Middeleeuwse Ridderschap als 'classe sociale'. In: Tijdschrift voor Geschiedenis 84. 1971. S. 262-275.

—'Cingulum militiae'. Schwertleite en 'miles'-Terminologie als Spiegel van Veranderend Menselijk Gedrag. In: Tijdschrift voor Rechtsgeschiedenis 44. 1976. S. 1-92.

WINTERSWYL, LUDWIG A.: Der deutsche Ritterstand. Sinn und Gestalt. Potsdam 1937.

WITTICH, WERNER: Altfreiheit und Dienstbarkeit des Uradels in Niedersachsen. In: VSWG 4. 1906. S. 1-127.

ZALLINGER, OTTO VON: 'Ministeriales' und 'Milites'. Untersuchungen über die ritterlichen Unfreien zunächst in baierischen Rechtsquellen des 11. und 12. Jahrhunderts. Innsbruck 1878.

ZUTT, HERTA: 'Adel' und 'edel'. Diss. [masch.] Freiburg i. Br. 1956.

Notes

I. Introduction

1. Most recently Wolfgang Mohr, *Minnesang als Gesellschaftskunst*, Deutschunterricht 6, 1954, Heft 5, 83–107; repr. in: *Der deutsche Minnesang, Aufsätze zu seiner Erforschung*, Hans Fromm, ed., Wege der Forschung 15 (Darmstadt, 1961), 197–228.
2. Ehrismann, as interpreted by Eduard Neumann, *Der Streit um "das ritterliche Tugendsystem,"* in *Erbe der Vergangenheit*, Festgabe für Karl Helm (Tübingen, 1951), 137 55; quotation, p. 151.
3. Erich Köhler, *Ideal und Wirklichkeit in der höfischen Epik, Studien zur Form der frühen Artus- und Graldichtung* Beiheft 97 zur ZfrPh. (Tübingen, 1956), p. 68.
4. Hugo Moser, *Deutsche Sprachgeschichte der älteren Zeit*, in *Deutsche Philologie im Aufriss* I, Wolfgang Stammler, ed., 2 ed. (Berlin, 1957), Sp. 767ff.
5. See n. 3.
6. Friedrich-Wilhelm Wentzlaff-Eggebert, *Kreuzzugsdichtung des Mittelalters, Studien zu ihrer geschichtlichen und dichterischen Wirklichkeit* (Berlin, 1960).
7. See also Hugo Moser, Dichtung und Wirklichkeit im Hochmittelalter, *Wirk. Wort 5*, 1954/55, 79–91, where the word "Wirklichkeit" is understood primarily as the medieval grasp on reality rather than historical factual accuracy.
8. Hugo Kuhn, *Soziale Realität und dichterische Fiktion am Beispiel der höfischen Ritterdichtung Deutschlands*, in *Dichtung und Welt im Mittelalter* (Stuttgart, 1959), 22–40 (first published in *Soziologie und Leben*, Carl Brinkmann ed., (Tübingen, 1952), 195–219), quotation, p. 29.
9. Hans Naumann, *Deutsche Kultur im Zeitalter des Rittertums*, Handbuch der Kulturgeschichte, Part 1, Potsdam, 1938, pp. 11 and 13.
10. Ibid., p. 1.
11. Ibid., p. 2.
12. Ibid., p. 60.
13. Ludwig Tieck, *Minnelieder aus dem schwäbischen Zeitalter* (Wien, 1820), p. 14, "wörtlich nach dem Originale" of 1803. Similarly expressed by both

Schlegels in their lectures on literary history; see August W. Schlegel, *Vorlesungen über schöne Litteratur und Kunst*, Pt. III, Dt. Litt. denkmale 19 (Heilbronn, 1884), pp. 44ff.; Friedrich Schlegel, *Geschichte der europäischen Literatur* (1803/04), critical edition Ernst Behler, Vol. XI (Paderborn-München-Wien, 1958), pp. 180f.

14. *Mémoires sur l'ancienne chevalerie considerée comme un établissement politique et militaire*, 3 vols. (Paris, 1759–81); 2. ed., 2 vols., 1826; Johann L. Klüber trans., *Das Ritterwesen des Mittelalters*, 3 vols. (Nürnberg 1786–91).

15. I refer to: Jakob Kaiserer, *Geschichte des Ritterwesens im Mittelalter* (Wien, 1804); Karl J. Weber, *Das Ritterwesen und die Templer, Johanniter und Marianer oder Deutsch-Ordens-Ritter insbesondere*, 3 vols. (Stuttgart, 1822–24); Johann G. Büsching, *Ritterzeit und Ritterwesen, Vorlesungen*, 2 vols. (Leipzig, 1823); Kurt von Aue, *Das Rittertum und die Ritterorden* (Merseburg, 1825).

16. See Karl S. Bader, *Der deutsche Südwesten in seiner territorialstaatlichen Entwicklung* (Stuttgart, 1950), p. 165.

17. *Geschichte der ehemaligen freien Reichsritterschaft in Schwaben, Franken und am Rheinstrome*, 2 vols. (Tübingen, 1859/71); *Die Ritterwürde und der Ritterstand, historisch-politische Studien über deutsch-mittelalterliche Standesverhältnisse auf dem Lande und in der Stadt* (Freiburg, 1886).

18. The pamphlet by Ludwig A. Winterwyl, *Der deutsche Ritterstand, Sinn und Gestalt* (Potsdam, 1937), has no independent scholarly value.

19. August Frh. von Fürth, *Die Ministerialen* (Cöln am Rhein, 1836).

20. The last major contribution is by Karl Bosl, *Die Reichsministerialität der Salier und Staufer, Ein Beitrag zur Geschichte des hochmittelalterlichen deutschen Volkes, Staates und Reiches*, Schriften der MGh. 10, 2 vols., (Stuttgart, 1950/51); see also pp. 63ff., below.

21. Especially emphasized by Otto von Zallinger, *Ministeriales und Milites, Untersuchungen über die ritterlichen Unfreien zunächst in baierischen Rechtsquellen des 11. und 12. Jhs. (Innsbruck, 1878); more recent: Jean-Pierre Ritter, Ministérialité et Chevalerie, dignité humaine et liberté dans le droit médiéval*, Thèse de doctorat, Université de Lausanne, Fac. de droit (Lausanne, 1955); Paul Kluckhohn, *Die Ministerialität in Südostdeutschland vom 10. bis zum Ende des 13. Jhs.*, Qu. u. Stud. zur Verf, gesch. des Dt. Reiches IV, 1 (Weimar, 1910); this study is of particular value because of the inclusion of German sources. I was unable to consult the book by Johanna M. van Winter, *Ministerialiteit en Riddershap in Gelre en Zutphen*, Bijdragen van het Instituut voor Middeleeuwse Geschiedenis der Rijksuniversiteit te Utrecht 31 (Groningen, 1962).

22. Ludwig Ettmüller, *Einiges über den Ritterstand und über die bei der Ertheilung dieser Würde einst üblichen Gebräuche*, Mittheilungen der antiquarischen Gesellschaft in Zürich 11 (1856/57), 91–100; Karl Treis, *Die Formalitäten des Ritterschlags in der altfranzösischen Epik* (Leipzig, 1887); Wilhelm Erben, *Schwertleite und Ritterschlag, Beiträge zu einer Rechtsgeschichte der Waffen*, Zs. f. hist. Waffenkd. 8 (1918/20), 105–67; Ernst H. Massmann, *Schwertleite und Ritterschlag, dargestellt auf Grund der mhd.*

literarischen Quellen, Diss. (Hamburg, 1932); Fritz Pietzner, *Schwertleite und Ritterschlag*, Diss. (Heidelberg, 1934); Dietrich Sandberger, *Die Aufnahme in den Ritterstand in England*, AKG. 27 (1937), 74–93; Robert F. Ackerman, *The Knighting Ceremonies in the Middle English Romances*, Specul. 15 (1944), 285–313.

23. Julius Peterson, *Das Rittertum in der Darstellung des Johannes Rothe*, Qu. u. Forschgg. 106 (Strassburg, 1909).

24. Paul Kluckhohn, *Ministerialität und Ritterdichtung*, ZfdA. 52 (1910), 135–68; *Der Minnesang als Standesdichtung*, AKG. 11 (1914), 389–410; repr. in *Der deutsche Minnesang* (see above, n. 1), 58–81, with an important supplement by Hans Fromm, ibid., 81–84.

25. Among a great number of studies are: Jacob Falke, *Die ritterliche Gesellschaft im Zeitalter des Frauencultus*, Berlin (1862); Léon Gautier, *La Chevalerie*, Paris, 1884, nouv. éd. (1890); John Batty, *The Spirit and Influence of Chivalry* (London, 1890); Otto Henne am Rhyn, *Geschichte des Ritterthums*, Illustr. Bibl. der Kunst- u. Kulturgesch. 3, Leipzig (1893); F. Warre Cornish, *Chivalry* (London 1901; 2 ed. 1911); Heinrich von Wedel, *Deutschlands Ritterschaft, ihre Entwicklung und ihre Blüte* (Görlitz, 1904; 2. ed. 1906); Valdemar Vedel, *Ridderromantiken i fransk og tysk middelalder* (Kjøbenhavn-Kristiana, 1906); Ger. Trans. in: Aus Natur u. Geisteswelt 293 (Leipzig, 1911); Alexander von Gleichen-Russwurm, *Der Ritterspiegel, Geschichte der vornehmen Welt im romanischen Mittelalter* (Stuttgart, 1923); Walter C. Meller, *A Knight's Life in the Days of Chivalry* (London, 1924); *Chivalry, A Series of Studies to Illustrate Its Historical Significance and Civilizing Influence*, Edgar Prestage, ed., (London, 1928); Hans Naumann, *Ritterliche Standeskultur in Deutschland*, in: Naumann-Müller, *Höfische Kultur*, DVj., Buchreihe 17 (Halle, 1929); *Der staufische Ritter*, Meyers kl. Handbücher 3 (Leipzig 1936); *Verhältnis des deutschen zum westlichen Rittertum*, in: *Von dt. Art in Sprache u. Dtg.* II (Stuttgart-Berlin, 1941), 169–88; Sidney Painter, *French Chivalry: Chivalric Ideas and Practices in Mediaeval France* (Baltimore, Md., 1940; repr., Ithaca, N.Y., 1957); Frantz Funck-Brentano, *Féodalité et Chevalerie* (Paris, 1946); M. Coppieters, *De ridders*, Ken uw Volk 11 (Brüssel, 1946); *Ridderschap, Een cultuurhistorische Verkenning*, Katholieke Vlaamse Hogeschooluitbreiding, Jg. XLII, No. 2, Verhandeling 397 (Antwerpen-Brussel-Gent-Leuven, 1948); Gustave Cohen, *Histoire de la chevalerie en France au moyen âge* (Paris, 1949). See further the true cultural histories by Georg Grupp, Gustav Schnürer, Johannes Bühler, Justus Hashagen, etc. and the hopelessly antiquated but still irreplaceable work by Alwin Schultz, *Das höfische Leben zur Zeit der Minnesinger*, 2 vols., (Leipzig, 1879/80; 2nd ed., 1889).

26. Hans Naumann, *Dt. Kultur*, p. 4. Far be it from me to denigrate the achievements of recent research to which we owe a very much more profound understanding of the intellectual and artistic conception of knighthood. My criticism consists rather in questioning whether this ideal picture can be related without further ado to a reality which is assumed to be automatic.

27. I call attention to the most recent overall view of the German Middle Ages by Bruno Gebhardt, *Handbuch der dt. Geschichte*, ed, Herbert Grundmann,

8th ed., vol. I (Stuttgart, 1943; 4th repr., 1959). See especially para. 127, "Die Anfänge ritterlicher Kultur im 12. Jh." (pp. 337–39) in the contribution by Karl Jordan, *Investiturstreit und frühe Stauferzeit (1056–1197)* (pp. 242–340); see also the article in "Rittertum/Ritterstand" in *Sachwörterbuch zur dt. Geschichte*, Hallmuth Rössler and Günther Franz, eds. (München, 1958), 1064–66; for the Germanistic aspects see Helmut de Boor's introduction to the second volume of his *Geschichte der dt. Literatur*: Die höfische Literatur, (4th ed. München, 1960), pp. 1–20.

28. Aloys Schulte, *Die Standesverhältnisse der Minnesänger*, ZfdA. 39 (1895), 185–251, quotation p. 185. The other warnings evoked no response. Friedrich von Raumer wrote: "In any case, knighthood and chivalry was in many respects only a poetic fabrication, an idea which never became a real historical actuality in all its parts" (*Geschichte der Hohenstaufen und ihrer Zeit*, 3rd. ed., Vol. VI, Leipzig, 1858, p. 581); and in his superb study Franz von Löher called attention to the fact that "the common conception of the world of chivalry was nothing more than romantic (*Über Ritterschaft und Adel im späteren Mittelalter* [MSB. 1861, Vol. I, 365–416, quotation p. 366]). See also Léon Gautier's observation: "La chevalerie . . . est moins une institution qu'un idéal" (p. 2); F.J.C. Hearnshaw discusses similar attitudes in English research *Chivalry and Its Place in History*, in *Chivalry* (see above, n. 25), pp. 1–35, esp. p. 2.

29. I call special attention to the study by Sidney Painter (see above, n. 25), who concentrates on the question of the practical significance of chivalric ideals and gives his opinions on the subject with exemplary moderation. Little notice has been taken of the article by Eberhard F. Otto, *Von der Abschliessung des Ritterstandes*, HZ, 162 (1940), 19–39, who corrects the traditional picture in many respects, without, however, reaching totally clear conclusions himself. See also: Gina Fasoli, *Lineamenti di una storia della cavalleria*, in: *Studi di storia medievale e moderna in onore di Et. Rota* (Roma, 1958), pp. 81–93. I was unable to consult François-Louis Ganshof, *Qu'est-ce que la chevalerie?*, Revue générale belge 25 (Nov. 1947), 77–86.

30. Arno Borst, *Das Rittertum im Hochmittelalter, Idee und Wirklichkeit* (Saeculum 10, 1959), 213–31, quotation p. 213, n.

31. Ibid., p. 214. Arno Borst defines "knighthood as a connection between domain and service" (p. 216) and looks for its historical roots in the class of the small vassals, who gradually won for themselves a position of lords and then formulated a class morality. Of particular interest here is the different development in France and in Germany: "In France, chivalric literature, roughly speaking, reflects the reality of the nobility, while in Germany it reflects the ideal picture of men" (p. 228).

32. A few important essays have been collected in the volume *Herrschaft und Staat im Mittelalter*, ed. Hellmut Kämpf, Wege der Forschung 2 (Darmstadt, 1956). See also Walter Schlesinger, "Verfassungsgeschichte und Landesgeschichte," *Hess. Jb. f. Landesgesch.* 3 (1953), 1–34; Heinrich Dannenbauer, *Gruss und Dank*, in: *Aus Verfassungs- u. Landesgesch.*, Festschr. f. Th. Mayer, Vol. I (Konstanz, 1954), 5–7 ("Nothing is stable"); Theodor Mayer, *Ein Rückblick*, in: *Mittelalterliche Studien, Ges. Aufsätze* (Lindau-

Konstanz, 1959), pp. 463–503.
33. Otto Brunner, *Land und Herrschaft, Grundfragen der territorialen Verfassungsgeschichte im Mittelalter*, (4th ed., Wien-Wiesbaden, 1959), p. 163; *Neue Wege der Sozialgeschichte, Vortr. u. Aufsätze* (Göttingen, 1956); *"Feudalismus," Ein Beitrag zur Begriffsgeschichte*, Akad. d. Wiss. u. d. Lit. in Mainz, Abhlgg. d. geistes- u. sozialwiss Kl., Jg. 1958, No. 10 (Wiesbaden, 1959).
34. Philipp Heck, *Übersetzungsprobleme im frühen Mittelalter*, Tübingen 1931; see also Herbert Grundmann, "Übersetzungsprobleme im Spätmittelalter," *ZfdPh.* 70 (1947/48), 113–45; Walter Stach, "Wort und Bedeutung im mittelalterlichen Latein," *DA.* 9 (1952), 332–52.
35. Wilhelm Ebel, *Über den Leihegedanken in der deutschen Rechtsgeschichte*, in: *Studien zum mittelalterlichen Lehenswesen, Lindau-Vorträge 1956*, Vorträge u. Forschgg. 5 (Lindau-Konstanz 1960), pp. 11–36, quotation p. 16.
36. The method of translation has been used in an exemplary fashion by Walter Schlesinger, *Die Entstehung der Landesherrschaft, Untersuchung vorwiegend nach mitteldt. Quellen* I, Sächs. Forschgg. zur Gesch. 1 (Dresden, 1941); *Herrschaft und Gefolgschaft in der germ.-dt. Verfassungsgeschichte*, in: Wege der Forschung 2 (see above, n. 32), pp. 135–90 (originally in: *HZ.* 176, 1953, pp. 225–75); *Burg und Stadt*, in: Festschr. Th. Mayer I, 97–150. See also: Herbert Helbig, *Fideles Dei et regis, Zur Bedeutungsentwicklung von Glaube und Treue im hohen Mittelalter*, AKG. 33, 1951, 275–306; Karl Bosl, *Vorstufen der dt. Königsdienstmannschaft, Begriffsgeschichtlich-prosopographische Studien zur frühmittelalterlichen Sozial- und Verfassungsgeschichte* VSWG. 39, 1952, 193–214, 289–315; Joseph O. Plassmann, *Princeps und Populus, Die Gefolgschaft im ottonischen Staatsaufbau nach den sächsischen Geschichtsschreibern des 10. Jhs.*, Schr. der Forschungshilfe (Göttingen, 1954). That the use of this method is made more difficult "by the inconsistency of German legal terminology," is stressed by Karl S. Bader ("Herrschaft und Staat in dt. Mittelalter," *Hist. Jb.* 62–69, 1942–49, 618–46, quotation p. 643).
37. In any case, I have not discovered up to the thirteenth century any confirmation of chivalry in Latin contexts.
38. Numerous pieces of evidence have been collected and discussed by Alfred Riemen, *Bedeutung und Gebrauch der Heldenwörter im mhd. Epos*, Diss. (masch.), (Köln, 1954). The interest of this study is mainly directed towards the relationship of the concept of chivalry to the old hero-terminology, while the meaning of the word has never been in doubt: "In all epics knight is a class designation" (p. 8). I was unable to consult the typewritten dissertation by Wolfgang Bachofer, *Der Wortschatz der Vorauer Bücher Moses, Vorarbeiten zu einer Ausgabe* (Hamburg, 1961), which "investigates the fields of meaning 'Held-Ritter,' 'Knecht' and animal-names, taking account of all early Middle High German evidence" (Germanistik 3 (1962), 239–40: Selbstreferat).
39. Richard Schröder, "Beiträge zur Kunde des deutschen Rechts aus deutschen Dichtern," *ZfdA*, 13 (1866), 139–61, quotation p. 139.
40. See esp. Hans Fehr, *Das Recht in der Dichtung, Kunst und Recht* II (Bern,

1931); more recently, H einrich Mitteis, *Recht und Dichtung,* in: *Die Rechts-idee in der Geschichte, Ges. Abhandlungen u. Vortr.* (Weimar, 1957), pp. 681–97.

41. Paul Kluckhohn, pp. 6ff.; see also Julius Petersen, pp. 2f.

42. Paul Kluckhohn, p. 10.

43. This is, perhaps, the right place for me to justify my point of view in the face of criticism from Germanists. In several articles Werner Schröder has expressed his opposition to my interpretation of certain concepts in Wol-fram's *Willehalm* which have a religious stress. I had stated that when the poet talks of the "süezen wunden" of the martyr Vivianz (*Willehalm,* 62, 17), the adjective *süeze* has a different tone, a different meaning from that in the passages where it is merely a courtly cliché; and when he calls on God as he dies for his faith "uz süezem munde" (49, 15), I expressed the opinion that the "sweet" mouth of the hero expressed something more than and different from what is expressed by the "süeze minnichlîche munt" of some courtly lady. I saw in this an indication of Vivianz's holy death and particularly of the miracle of the fragrance which occurs at his death (69, 12ff.) and I understood the "süeze" of his body, which is said to have been enough to make the waters of the Dead Sea fresh (62, 11f.) as the "odor of sanctity." To this it is objected that one sweet mouth is the same as another and *süeze* must mean the same for both pagans and Christians. Schröder does not spare the coarse epithets in describing my interpretations as "irrelevant," "misleading," "arbitrary," "wrong," as "too facile," "not worthy of consideration," and "far-fetched" but he finally has to admit that Christ's "süeziu vart" (48, 15) must mean "holy earthly pil-grimage." It can be disputed whether this meaning is "very unusual in *Willehalm,*" Schröder himself regards it as "worth considering" in at least one other case. Nevertheless I can safely refute the implication that I had assumed "a common correspondence of *süeze* and holy. Something similar is true for the word *armuot.* Gyburg devotes herself to poverty ("ich wil armüete pflegen," [216, 2]); and when she measures her *lîbes armuot* not against pagan treasures but against "der sêle rîcheit" (216, 28f.), she is using a religious and Christian terminology even if all the evidence from the *Kaiserchronik* and other works state the contrary. It is undeniable that *armuot* means a state of non-possession and no long essay is needed to prove it. But it is equally certain that this non-possession can demonstrate a special value for a Christian for which ascetic literature offers abundant insights, and it can be seen from this literature that poverty is not only a question of standard of living but a matter of conscience. There is no longer any need for proof of the fact that there were aristocratic women in the thirteenth century who tried to live according to the apostolic ideal of poverty and in spite of this to carry out the obligations of their princely-secular position, that is, they undertook to realize this ideal within the secular world, not behind the walls of a nunnery. The figure of Gyburg reflects such an attitude, and a connection between Wolfram's poetry and the religious prob-lems of the laity of the period thus becomes apparent. The styling of the secular heroine in a spiritual sense attains its high point in Gyburg's appeal

as *heilic vrouwe* (403, 1). Schröder tries to weaken the significance of this passage by making it refer to her "holy death," about which nothing is said in the text. It is perfectly permissible for Schröder to see in Gyburg "perhaps the female figure in Wolfram with the most life" but the category "fullness of life" is scarcely the one most suitable to enable us to appreciate the essential nature of highly stylized courtly poetry. Our understanding of Wolfram will not be much advanced by simply denying the existence of religious problems in the work. In the present work I have again proceeded from the assumption that ten unambiguous pieces of evidence on knights do not prejudice the meaning of the eleventh and I am further convinced that lexicographical research into Middle High German is very little served when shades of meaning are explained away and everything forced into the same mold.

44. In an appendix to each section I have listed the evidence for some stereotyped uses of "ritter," which are supposed in part to illustrate the results of research or are otherwise characteristic of Middle High German usage. It is admittedly true that there can be differing opinions of the value of such lists. I do think, however, that if we were to possess such collections of formulaic expressions for the most important concepts, we would be able to arrive at more accurate conclusions not only about the linguistic interdependence of the poets but also about Middle High German stylistics as a whole. Within the framework of the time limits set (see the next note), the lists are intended to be complete. Because of the quantity of the literature under review, however, it is scarcely possible to prevent omissions and it is therefore to be expected that I have overlooked something here or there. I hope there are not too many such cases and that nothing important has escaped me. I would like to emphasize again that this study is concerned exclusively with German conditions. This limitation has to be accepted so long as there are no detailed studies of the vernacular sources in the various countries. On the relation of German knighthood to French, see Hans Naumann, in *Von dt. Art* II, 169ff.; Arno Borst, Saecul. 10, 213ff. Further literature concerning the conditions in France, see below, pp. 77.

45. So as to make it easier to understand which texts have been taken into account, I have accepted the concluding date of the second volume of Helmut de Boor's literary history and have included everything which is dealt with there, even when it goes slightly beyond the 1250 limit, and have left out everything not found there except that some *genres* which de Boor reserved for his third volume have been included: historical writing (*Gandersheimer Reimchronik, Sächsische Weltchronik*), learned prose-writings (Friedrich Wilhelm's *Denkmäler dt. Prosa des 11. u. 12. Jhs., Lucidarius*), and legal prose (*Sachsenspiegel, Mühlhauser Rechtsbuch, Urkunden*). Since Reinhold Kluge's edition of the *Prose-Lanzelet* is not yet complete, I have included only the two old fragments A and M. In the case of sermons, which in most cases cannot be accurately dated, I have used the *Speculum ecclesiae* and the collections mentioned by Gustav Ehrismann, *Geschichte der dt. Literatur b. z. Ausgang des Mittelalters*, 2 pts., Schlussband (München, 1935), pp. 413f., as well as the greater part of the fragments listed on p. 415. On the

other hand, I have not taken account of the small Middle High German narratives of the *Gesamtabenteuer*, since only a very small part of them could possibly date from the first half of the thirteenth century. Edward Schröder has called attention to the importance of the piece *Die beiden Knechte*, ed. Gustav Rosenhagen, DTM. 17, No. 178 for the knighthood question (see *Ritter oder Knecht?*, AfdA. 50, 1931, 213–14).

46. At this point I would like to express my heartfelt thanks to the historian Karl Ferdinand Werner for the long and for me extremely informative conversations we had on problems of knighthood and nobility.

II. The Word "Ritter"

1. In addition there is the form *riter* with a short open root syllable, see Moriz Haupt, note to *Erek* 8795; Carl von Kraus, note to Reinbot's *Hl. Georg* 93. We still need to investigate how this form, deduced from metric considerations, relates to the other two.

2. See Wilhelm Wilmanns, *Dt. Grammatik* II², 286, paragraph 223; Falk and Torp, *Norwegisch-dän. etymol. Wb.* II, 896.

3. See Bosworth-Toller, *Anglo-Saxon Dict.* (1882–98), 795 b; the Old High German *ritto* which is occasionally given in dictionaries is, however, not a proven form, but a conjectural one. See Verwijs-Verdam, *Middelnederlandsch Wb.* VI, 1030.

4. Ernst Martin, Rez. van Helten, Lit. bl. f. germ. u. rom. Philol. 9 (1888), Sp. 255.

5. Edmund Wiessner, *Höfisches Rittertum*, in: Friedrich Maurer and Friedrich Stroh, *Dt. Wortgesch.*, Pauls Grundriss 17, 2nd ed., Vol. I (Berlin, 1959), pp. 160f.

6. Seemingly without knowledge of Martin's statement ("not yet expressed anywhere") Edward Schröder repeated Martin's conjecture in 1897: Rez. Heyne, AfdA. 23 (1897), 158.

7. I restricted myself to the five volumes of glosses by Steinmeyer-Sievers and took only random samples of Karg-Gasterstädt and Frings (*Ahd. Wb.* I, Abkürzungsverzeichnis, p. 1) and of Herbert Thoma (*Reallexikon*² I, 579) supplements.

8. See Graff II, 722; there seem to be no examples in literary texts; in the glosses it occurs in only one St. Emmeramer Fragment (IV, 331, 20)—a modern copy of it is extant (see Steinmeyer-Sievers, ibid., n. 9). I was unable to consult Sanftl's Katalog of the St. Emmeramer Handschriften and was consequently unable to date the fragment.

9. The dating in this and following cases have all been taken from Steinmeyer-Sievers Handschriftenverzeichnis (IV, 371ff.; V, 50ff.).

10. In addition there is uncertain evidence, or evidence leading in a different direction: from the tenth century *Andleta, milis: chempho* (IV, 175, 6), *Tyrones, milites: du a* (read *diu a*) (IV, 320, 7); from the eleventh century *Miles gregarius: lithkneht* (II, 610, 47), *Cane milite: houe uuarte* (II, 512,

52f., 521, 51); from the twelfth century *Gregarius .i. miles: ainschiltiger, ainschilter* (IV, 215, 21f.); from the fourteenth century *Questū: reccho miles* (IV, 190, 36).

11. A brief list for the derivations will suffice: in the oldest manuscripts of the eighth/ninth centuries, *militia* is glossed by *dionost* (I, 458, 38f. 510, 8), *gisind* (I, 276, 51f. 284, 1) and *kampfheit* (I, 731, 57). The gloss *dionost* appears in later manuscripts also (II, 257, 60f.). In the ninth century *militiae cingulum* is translated by *uueralt-gegarauui* (II, 145, 45). From the tenth century on, we find *strît, wîg* for *militia* (I, 501, 35ff.) and *gistirni* for *militia caeli* (I, 369, 13ff. 454, 19. 454, 57ff. 605, 52ff. 683, 1ff. 744, 18ff.); in the eleventh century *heri* (II, 608, 10. 608, 58. 611, 78f.) and *degonod* (II, 663, 35. 712, 56); in the twelfth century *gedigene* (IV, 78, 51f. 151, 15f.) and *hereschaft* (III, 135, 7ff.). Since the tenth century *militare* has been translated by *strîtan* (I, 501, 15. 816, 32ff.) and *dionon* (II, 276, 22); in the ninth and tenth centuries *militares* by *knehta* (II, 342, 48f. 758, 18f.). In the tenth century *knehta* appears also for *militones* (II, 758, 21). *Heregesello* is used consistently for *commilitones* (I, 772, 16f. II, 569, 48. III, 135, 22ff. 183, 32f. 269, 69f. 315, 22f. 332, 62f. 348, 18f. 682, 23. IV, 136, 45.), and in the twelfth century *ginôz* (I, 772, 10).

12. In addition from the eighth/ninth centuries *Equites precursores quadrigarum: rohs foralouffono chanzuuagano* (I, 409, 53f.); from the ninth century *Uir. bige equitum . . . : reidimanno* (I, 618, 15ff.), from the tenth/eleventh centuries *Eques: derrisaman* (read *der reisaman*) (I, 339, 16); from the eleventh century *Eques: uuescunari* (II, 398, 72), *uueskinara* (II, 546, 32); from the eleventh/twelfth centuries *Eques: ridemun* (IV, 201, 24). Derivatives of *eques* are *equitatus*, which is always translated by *girit* (I, 327, 54ff. 335, 47. 552, 6. 553, 11. 692, 29ff. II, 663, 46. 713, 1), and *equester* for *rit(i)lich* in the eighth/ninth centuries (I, 279, 11), we find since the tenth century *reitman* (I, 704, 1ff. II, 369, 17) and *satelros* (I, 433, 46ff. 443, 6).

13. I don't know what Schade's authority is for his reference to the Low German *riddere* of the eleventh century (*Altdt. Wb.*[2] II, 719). It is not listed in Johann H. Gallée, *Vorstudien zu einem altndd. Wörterbuch* (Leiden 1903), and the evidence in Schiller-Lübben, *Mittelnddt. Wb.* III, 476 is all earlier.

14. See the collected evidence in the appendix to this chapter.

15. *Trübners Dt. Wb.* V, 419.

16. Even after the diphthongization of the long *i* there is no consistent distinction made between *ritter* and *reiter*, as the manuscripts of the fourteenth century show.

17. Evidence for rhymes: Karl Lachmann, Lesart zu *Iwein* 42; Georg A. Wolff, *diu halbe bir* (Erlangen, 1893), note to 59f.; Viktor Junk, *Zum Reimgebrauch Rudolfs von Ems*, Beitr. 27 (1902), pp. 446–503, esp. p. 466; Arno Schirokauer, *Studien zur mhd. Reimgrammatik*, Beitr. 47 (1923), Sonderabzug, pp. 51f. In my opinion the oldest evidence of rhyme for the form with a simple dental is to be found in Heinrich von Melk: *riter : gestriten* (Inf.) (Erin. 427f.), for the form with double-*t* in *Gregorius: ritter : bitter*

(1503f.). No conclusions can be deduced from this, since there is hardly any opportunity for rhyme for the form *rîter*.

18. Since I have not examined the manuscripts contained in the following list, I have to rely entirely on the statements of the editors so far as the composition and dating are concerned.

19. The dating and origin of the manuscript collections have recently been called in question again. Only the Strassburg manuscript remains unaffected, as before, "beendet 1187," is still valid. Hermann Menhardt suggests new solutions for the three others: *Die Vorauer Hs. kam durch Propst Konrad II. (1282–1300) aus dem Domstift Sazlburg nach Vorau*, Beitr. 78, Tüb., 1956, 116–59; *Zur Herkunft der Vorauer Hs.*, ibid., pp. 394–452; ibid., p. 80, Tüb., 1958, pp. 48–66; *Die Bilder der Millstätter "Genesis" und ihre Verwandten*; in: Festschrift f. Rud. Egger, *Beitr. zur älteren europäischen Kulturgeschichte*, Vol. III (Klagenfurt, 1954), pp. 248–371; *Der Millstätter Physiologus und seine Verwandten*, Kärntner Museumsschriften 14 (Klagenfurt, 1956); *Die Zweiheit Genesis—Physiologus und der Zeitansatz der Exodus*, ZfdA. 89 (1958/59), 257–71; *Regensburg ein Mittelpunkt der dt. Epik des 12. Jhs.*, ibid., pp 271–74. According to this all three manuscripts were written in Regensburg, the Wien manuscript about 1175, the Millstätt manuscript about 1180, and the Vorau manuscript about 1190. Reservations have, however, been voiced from various quarters against these findings: Pius Fank, *Kam die Vorauer Hs. durch Propst Konrad II. aus dem Domstift Salzburg nach Vorau?*, Beitr. 78 (Tüb., 1956), pp. 374–93; Ludwig Wolff, Rez. Menhardt, *Die Bilder . . .* , ibid., pp. 166–70; Friedrich P. Pickering, *Zu den Bildern der altdt. Genesis. Die Ikonographie der trinitas creator*, ZfdPh. 75 (1956), 23–34.

20. ". . . at the beginning of the second half of the twelfth century, possibly even before the second half" (Johann Kelle, *Speculum ecclesiae altdeutsch*, München, 1858, p. XII); "from the beginning of the second half of the twelfth century" (Gert Mellbourn, *Speculum eccl.*, Lunder germanist. Forschgg. 12, Lund-Kopenhagen, 1944, p. XV).

21. I am not concerned with either the form of inflexion or the derivation of the word; only the spelling of the word stem is in this case of importance.

22. Spelling and computation according to the Mellbourn edition.

23. Spelling and numbering of the manuscripts, unless otherwise stated, have been taken from the editions in the list of sources. For the dating I have followed the editors or the statements by Gustav Ehrismann and those in the Verfasserlexikon. Except for listing the manuscripts of the two sermons first, the order is arbitrary according to the chronology of the manuscripts.

24. No. 9 in Edward Schröder's Handschriftenverzeichnis.

25. Numbering, spelling, and line-count according to the edition of the *Tristrant*-Fragmente by Kurt Wagner.

26. Numbering according to the list of manuscripts in Otto Behaghel's edition; spelling taken from the reproduction of the Meran fragment by Joseph Zingerle, MSB. (1869), Vol. II, pp. 471ff. Verse numbering according to Ludwig Ettmüller's edition.

27. Spelling according to Friedrich Keinz, *Mitteilungen aus der Münchener*

Kgl. Bibliothek, Germ. 31 (1886), 74–90. Verse numbering according to Ettmüller. Gustav Ehrismann (II, 2, 1, p. 86) and the *Verfasserlexikon* (II, 357) designated this second manuscript the Münchner *Eneit*-Fragment; it is in reality the Münchner *Servatius*-Fragment.

28. The manuscript glosses which cannot be dated more precisely have for now not been taken into account. The form *ritter* does not all at appear in the manuscripts of the twelfth century; I found *rîter* or *riter* respectively eight times and *ríeter, ritbir* and *rithir* each once (see above, p. 10).

29. No. 13 in Edward Schröder's Handschriftenverzeichnis.

30. Numbering, spelling, and counting according to Friedrich Wilhelm, *Denkmäler dt. Prosa des 11. und 12. Jhs.*, no. 44; I compared the new reproduction by Marlies Dittrich, *Zur ältesten Überlieferung des dt. Lucidarius*, ZfdA. 77 (1940), 218–55.

31. Spelling according to Hermann Menhardt, ZfdA. 64 (1927), 211–35; verse numbering according to Bartsch-de Boor.

32. See Karl Lachmann, Lesart zu *Iwein* 42.

33. Even if the München manuscript of the *Specul. eccl.* or one in the manuscript glosses were earlier than the Wien Sammelhandschrift, the distance in time would be increased by only a few decades.

34. See the summary by Edmund Wiessner, in: *Dt. Wortgesch.* I, 157ff. Emil Öhmann, *Der romanische Einfluss auf das Deutsche bis zum Ausgang des Mittelalters*, ibid., I, 269–327, especially pp. 275ff.; Friedrich Kluge, *Dt. Sprachgeschichte* (Leipzig, 1920), pp. 274ff.; Emil Öhmann, *Die mhd. Lehnprägung nach altfranzösischem Vorbild*, Annal. Acad. Scient. Fennicae, Ser. B, Vol. 68, no. 3 (Helsinki, 1951).

35. Wherever there is no High German correspondence, the Flemish origin will either be proven through the articulation or through the fact that the words were unknown in southern Germany before then; this is applicable to *muote, baneken, vloite, blîde, trecken, gelücke*, etc.

36. There is no comparison possible with *truben*; it was at first common in the southern German poets as *draven, draben* and adopted the High German *t* only much later. See Edmund Wiessner, in: *Dt. Wortgesch.* I, 165. The relation between *hövesch* and *hübesch* is not clear; it is a fact that the southern German poets preferred the form *hövesch*, even though *hübesch* has to be considered as the translation into High German.

37. See Edmund Wiessner for the following statements.

38. The word *hövesch, hübesch* is an exception; it has been documented since the *Rolandslied*, Heinrich von Melk and the *Kaiserchronik*; see Werner Schrader, *Studien über das Wort "höfisch" in der mhd. Dichtung.* Diss., Bonn (Würzburg, 1935), pp. 4ff. The derivation, particularly of *hövesch*, from the Mnld. is by no means certain.

39. The fact that we find the oldest *ritter*-forms in manuscripts from Bavaria and Austria also argues the case against a borrowing from the extreme northwest. It was only in the second group of manuscripts that we found the form *ritter* in the mfrk. *Silvester*-Hs.; at the same time it occurred in the Vienna fragment of the *Kaiserchronik*, which again originates in Austria.

40. See Cleasby-Vigfusson, *Icelandic-English Dictionary* (1874), p. 497, s.v. *riddari*.
41. *Trübners Dt. Wb.* V, 419; Kluge-Mitzka, *Etymologisches Wb. der dt. Sprache* (17 ed. 1957), p. 602.
42. Friedrich Kluge, p. 274.
43. Quotation from John Earle/Charles Plummer, *Two of the Saxon Chronicles Parallel*, 2 vols. (Oxford, 1892/99; repr. 1952); I compared the older eds. by James Ingram (London, 1823) (examples of *die ritter* pp. 290. 302) and by Benjamin Thorpe, 2 vols. (London, 1861) (*examples* I, 353. 358) as well as the new ed. by Cecily Clark (Oxford, 1958) (*examples* pp. 9, 18). Any doubt about the reading of the manuscript is removed by the facsimile edition by Dorothy Whitelock, *Anglo-Saxon Chronicle* (*Bodleian Manuscript Laud Misc. 636*), Early English Manuscripts in Facsimile 4 (Copenhagen, 1954) (the evidence is on fo. 63a and 67b, pp. 125, 134). Description of the manuscript by Earle and Plummer II, pp. XXXIVf. See also Cecily Clark, *Studies in the Vocabulary of the Peterborough Chronicle, 1070–1154*, Engl. and Germanic Studies 5 (1952/53), 67–89, especially p. 84. The first part of the manuscript in which we find the evidence for knighthood was written after 1121.
44. *Trübners Dt. Wb.* V, 419; Kluge-Mitzka, *Etymol. Wb.*, p. 602. The allusion to the Middle English *riddēre* is found for the first time in the sixth edition of Kluge's *Wb.* (Strassburg, 1899); there is, however, again no source given.
45. The earliest evidence for *chevalier* occurs, to my knowledge, in the *Chanson de Roland*, a few decades after the *Wiener Genesis*; see Tobler-Lommatzsch, *Altfranzösisches Wb.* II, 358f. The French word cannot be credited entirely with the decisive impulse for the creation of the German word, since *ritter* originally had a wider meaning than *chevalier*. It was not until the second part of the twelfth century that the French term became of such significance for the formation of the German concept of knighthood. It may incidentally be pointed out that in German *ritter* may be found together with *rîter* as Old French *chevalier* together with *cavalier* (Kluge-Mitzka, p. 602; Edmund Wiessner, in: *Dt. Wortgesch* I, 160). There was, however, no Old French word *cavalier; cavalier* is rather the Old Provençal form which first came into French in the fifteenth century by way of Italy. But there was in Old French another word parallel to *chevalier* which designated a horseman only, namely *chevaucheor* (see Tobler-Lommatzsch II, 360). I am grateful to Professor Anna Hatcher for pointing this out.
46. From now on I shall no longer distinguish between *rîter* and *ritter*.
47. See appendix 1 to this section.
48. See appendix 2 to this section.
49. Edward Schröder, *Die Datierung des dt. Rolandsliedes*, ZfdA. 65 (1928), 289–96; quotation p. 295.
50. The *Vorauer Alexander* is the exception. *Wîgant* and *recke* do not occur here.
51. See appendix 3 to this section.

52. Not included are 1. evidence from glosses; 2. legends and epics of late transmission: Salman (38 times *ritter-*), Brandan (once), Orendel (20 times), Oswald M. (20 times), Oswald W. (3 times); 3. evidence from sermons because of the uncertainty in dating them. Because of the frequency in the occurrence of "Ritter" in the earlier sermons and because of the importance of the evidence on word-history I have compiled the following list: Specul. eccl. 47, 22. 48, 2 [*r.schaft*]. 170, 14. 18 [*r.schaft*]. Pr. Schönbach I, 65, 28. 77, 22 [*ritteren*]. 109, 29. 110, 13. 14. 20. 27. 120, 24. 30. 143, 10. 144, 3. 279, 24. 27. 331, 23 [*r.schaft*]. 26. 332, 1. 3. 5. 355, 9 [*r.schaft*]. 9f. [*r.schaft*]. 24. 27. II, 17, 10. 19, 26. 40, 23. 53, 1. 1. 95, 40. 108, 13. 169, 28. III, 166, 18. 239, 30. 31 [*r.schaft*]. 36. Pr. Leyser 129, 22 [*r.schaft*]. Pr. Wackernagel XII, 53. Pr. Mone 528. 529. Pr. Jeitteles 79, 16. Pass. Zacher 279, 4. 24. 24. 28. Pr.br. Grieshaber 450a, 26. 27. 30. Pr.br. Dieffenbach A IV, 2, 9. Pr.br. Jcitteles 172, 8. 26. 174, 18. Pr.br. Zingerle 407, 12. 33. 37. 408, 4. Pr.br. I Schönbach 188, 6. 10. 197, 26. Pr. br. II Schönbach 225, 24 [*r.schaft*]. 249, 6 [*r.schaft*] (2 times). 20. 22. I do not lay any particular stress on the chronological order of the listings but merely accept the customary starting points.

53. In the first column I list the actual number of instances, in the second and third the relative frequency of the word; i.e., the second column gives the number of instances per thousand lines, while the third gives the number of verses with one instance of *ritter* each. For each work there appears on the first line the number of instances for the word *ritter* and on the second line the numbers for the whole family of words. The list is arranged after the first number in the second column and also according to the relative frequency. Religious-didactic literature as well as short epics and fragments have not been considered, since the conversion to a thousand verses would be rather hypothetical.

54. I count 11,032 verses.

55. Of the counted instances of *ritter* only three are to be found in B (2570. 3078. 3620), and only two in C (60. 4563).

56. In the case of *Wolfdietr.* A, *Kudrun*, and the *Nibelungenlied* I count 1 Str. = 8 Verses.

57. Only the instances in the text of Bartsch-de Boor have been considered here.

58. I count 18,530 verses.

59. This topic has most recently been dealt with by Alfred Riemen, loc. cit. He produces on p. 126 a tabulated survey of the percentual relationship of the words to each other (*knappe* and *gast* have been considered there also) in twenty-three epics, beginning with Lamprecht's *Alexander* up to Konrad's *Trojanerkrieg*. Since the counting was done on the basis of excerpts from the individual works, a somewhat lopsided picture is received from the percentage figures. An example, the listing for Herbort von Fritzlar: *wîgant* 12.5%; *degen* 0%; I noted, however, *wîgant* only once and *degen* thirty times. See also the summary by Edmund Wiessner, in: *Dt. Wortgesch.* I, 181f. with references to special studies. My figures are possibly in a

few instances not quite exact: I collected the terminology for "hero" only additionally. The list is in approximate chronological order, works by the same author have, however, been kept together.

60. In addition once *lussamer kneht*.
61. In addition once *hêrlîcher kneht*.
62. In addition once *hêrlîcher kneht* and once *sneller kneht*.
63. In addition once *tiurer kneht* and once *tiurlîcher kneht*.
64. In addition three times *tiurer kneht* and once *vrumer kneht*.
65. In addition seven times *volcdegen* and once *dietdegen*.
66. According to Edward Schröder, ZfdA. 65, 295 *guoter kneht* appears twenty-five times.
67. In addition once *volcdegen*.
68. In addition once *kneht balt*.
69. In addition once *hêrister kneht*.
70. In addition once *dietdegen* and once *swertdegen*.
71. In addition once *sneller kneht*.
72. The omissions after v. 508 and v. 2037, which were filled in by Kinzel according to the Basel manuscript, have not been considered here.
73. In addition once *dietdegen* and once *swertdegen*.
74. In addition three times *tiurer kneht* and once *sneller kneht*.
75. In addition once *tiurer kneht*.
76. I counted the instances in only one of the two manuscripts, also wherever the fragments of the Prag and Sagan manuscripts overlap.
77. In addition three times *dietdegen*.
78. In addition once *brûtdegen*.
79. In addition once *swertdegen*.
80. Once *starker kneht*.
81. In addition once *edeler kneht*.
82. See Paul Schütze, *Das volkstümliche Element im Stil Ulrichs von Zatzikhoven*, Diss. Greifswald 1883, p. 23.
83. In addition once *dietdegen* and once *volcdegen*.
84. The number of instances is according to the *Wörterbuch* by Bartsch, without consideration of the share of the individual manuscripts.
85. In addition once *swertdegen*.
86. In addition once *edeler kneht* and once *rîcher kneht*.
87. See Ernst Cucuel, *Die Eingangsbücher des Parzival und das Gesamtwerk*, Diss. Heidelberg 1936, pp. 26f.
88. Ernst Cucuel, p. 27 does not list the instance 416,26.
89. In addition three times in B and two times in C.
90. In addition nine times in B and sixteen times in C.
91. In addition eight times in B, once in C; and in addition once *volcdegen*.
92. In addition three times in B and eleven times in C.
93. In addition eight times in B and twelve times in C.
94. The manuscripts AJa deviate.
95. In addition once *werder kneht*.
96. In addition once *dietdegen*.

97. In addition once *getriuwer kneht* and once *wîser kneht*.
98. In addition once *vrumer kneht*.
99. The supplement has not been considered.
100. In addition once *swertdegen*.
101. Once *stolzer kneht*.
102. In addition once *swertdegen*.
103. Once *tugentrîcher kneht*.
104. The supplement has not been considered.
105. In addition once *volcdegen*.
106. In addition once *dietdegen*.
107. In addition once *swertdegen*.
108. See Edmund Wiessner, in: *Dt. Wortgesch.* I, 182.
109. In addition once *swertdegen*.
110. In addition three times *swertdegen*.
111. In addition three times *edeler kneht*.
112. In addition once *swertdegen*.
113. Once *wünneclîcher kneht*.
114. The didactic poem and the epic fragments have been combined.
115. The *Hofzucht* has not been taken into account.

III. The Knight as Soldier

1. For the various theories of the Middle Ages about the origin of knighthood see Julius Petersen, pp. 68ff; for its beginning under Romulus esp. pp. 74f.
2. Hermann Conrad, *Dt. Rechtsgeschichte, Ein Lehrbuch*, I. *Frühzeit und Mittelalter* (Karlsruhe, 1954), p. 394.
3. *Trübners Dt. Wb.* V, 419; see also Grimm's *DWB.* VIII, 1053.
4. This is known also to Wernher von Elmendorf: "da waren gewafenete ritter inne" (720) and Herbort von Fritzlar: "Da warē drizzic inne. Rittere verborgē" (16159f.).
5. *Ritter* as an occupation force of a city occurs also in Veldeke: in Karthago every castle gate was under the protection of a count, "der die borch mâre mit drin hundert rittern solde weren" (*Eneit* 26, 26f.); also Sächs. Weltchr. 87, 2f. Albertus 807ff. 924f., etc.
6. In Hartmann's *Gregorius*: "nû vant man aller tegelîch ritterschaft vor der stat . . . zorse und ze vuoze" (1972f. 75); in *Wigalois*: "man vant dâ rîterlîche wer ze rosse und ouch ze vuoze" (11044f.).
7. Edward Schröder, *ZfdA.* 65, 294.
8. Statements about shield-bearers in literature differ widely; the explanation for this is that the later instances became mixed up with the early examples. Only in the thirteenth century did they become "attendants of knights, who usually had one and later on two in their retinue" (Paul Kluckhohn, p. 140).

9. See also Türlin's remark, "daz ritters kraft Wær ze vuoze ûf der erde Gerechent ze kleinem werde, Wie küene ein ritter wære" (*Krone*, 20176–79).

10. Rennewart receives the advice: "du solt die rîter stôzen, die gewâpendn und die blôzen, mit der stangen ûf die erden" (*Willehalm*, 417, 5–7).

11. In Herbort it is said of the Argonauts: "Sper phile vnd swert. Des die ritterschaft noch gert. Des hettē sie gefuget ir schar" (323–25); and later on of Hupus and Cupesus: "Man saget daz ir ritterschaft. Were harte nvtze. Mit maniger hande geschutze" (4002–04). During the martyrdom of St. Sebastian *riter* appear as archers (Pr. Schönbach I, 279, 27. Pr.br. I Schönbach 188, 10).

12. See the evidence in the appendix to this section.

13. Gustav Köhler, *Die Entwicklung des Kriegswesens und der Kriegführung in der Ritterzeit von Mitte des 11. Jhs. bis zu den Hussitenkriegen*, Vol. III, Sect. 2, Breslau 1889, pp. 19ff.; Ernst Mayer, *Dt. und französische Verfassungsgeschichte vom 9. bis zum 14. Jh.*, Vol. II, (Leipzig, 1899), pp. 185ff.; Hans Delbrück, *Geschichte der Kriegskunst im Rahmen der politischen Geschichte*, Vol. III (2nd ed. Berlin, 1923), pp. 321ff.; Eugen von Frauenholz, *Entwicklungsgeschichte des dt. Heerwesens*, Vol. I (München, 1935), pp. 177ff. I was unable to consult Peter U. Rosenau's unprinted legal dissertation, *Wehrverfassung und Kriegsrecht in der mhd. Epik. Wolfram v. Eschenbach, Hartmann v. Aue, Gottfried v. Strassburg, Der Nibelunge Not, Kudrunepos, Wolfdietrichbruchstück A, König Rother, Salman u. Morolf* (Bonn, 1959).

14. Eugen v. Frauenholz I, 119.

15. Alfred Riemen writes concerning this: "The line in which Iwein addresses the giant as 'rîter . . .' is totally out of place; . . . this is either an error by Hartman . . . , or the word is used by Iwein to designate a warrior in general" (p. 59). In Stricker's *Daniel, ein rise* (411), *ein ungefüeger knabe* (504), also is addressed by König Artus as "ritter guot" (906).

16. Instances: Rhein. Marienlob 861; Wild. Mann Veron. 427ff.; Heimesfurt Urst. 113, 14ff.; Pass. Zacher 279, 4ff.; Pr. Schönbach II, 52, 38ff.; Pr. Mone 528; Pr. Wackernagel XII, 53; Pr. Jeitteles 79, 16ff. Later instances in Schmeller, *Bayer. Wb.* II, 182 and in Julius Petersen, pp. 66f.

17. There is frequent testimony to the fact that it was impossible to determine the social standing of a man in knight's armor; thus the defeated Mabonagrin asks his conquerer, Erek, to tell him his name, for "hâtz ein unadels man getân, sô enwolde ich durch niemen leben" (Erek, 9349f.).

18. Arno Borst, Saecul. 10, 216; "The servant whom his lord had provided with a horse and equipped as a cavalry soldier had socially nothing in common with his lord who was equipped in the same way" (Otto von Dungern, *Der Herrenstand im Mittelalter, Eine sozialpolitische und rechtsgeschichtliche Untersuchung* I, Papiermühle, 1908, p. 347).

19. Priamus dispatches messengers: *daz im ritter quemē* (Herbort 1751); *nâch ritterschaft hât er gesant der edel keiser rîche* (Ebernant 2048f.); *vart wider heim in iuwer lant, besendet iuwer ritterschaft* (Gotfr. 6410f.), etc.

20. I.e. in Türlin's *Mantel* the knights receive armor and horses as presents:

Artús der êren stam der hiez den rittern alsam gewæfen geben unde kleit, ros bedecket . . . (188–91).

21. Christ's grave is guarded after a sermon *von den rittern. die die Juden gemietet heten* (Pr. Mone 529). I was not able to find any further examples for the expression *ritter mieten* in the literature up to 1250. Konrad von Heimesfurt says: *daz er* [sc. Jesus] *wurde behût. Gaben si phenninge. den reitern mit gedinge. Daz si in des grabes phlagen. vnt da bei gewaffent lagen* (Urst. 113, 14–18).

21a. For future reference see Karl F. Werner, *Die Entstehung des Fürstentums (8.–10. Jh.), Studien zur fränkischen Reichsstruktur, zum Fürstenbegriff und zur Geschichte des nichtköniglichen Herrschertums* (1963).

22. Hans Delbrück admittedly says: "The *Scharmeister* or *Rittmeister* who occasionally appears in the epics and obviously had the task of keeping the knights in order, is never found in actual history" (III, 293). Further Middle High German instances of *Rottmeister* in Gustav Köhler III 2, 204, n. 3.

23. It is perhaps no accident that the old authorities in research on knighthood had a viewpoint which is different from this: "Feudality has nothing in common with chivalry" (Léon Gautier, p. 20); "the dignity of knighthood gave just as few political privileges, as might be expected since it had no standing in feudal law" (Roth von Schreckenstein, *Ritterwürde*, p. 328).

24. Hermann Conrad I, 394.

25. Hans Delbrück III, 242.

26. Eugen von Frauenholz I, 66: "the knight could not have existed had it not been for the fief" (K.-J. Hollyman, *Le développement du vocabulaire féodal en France pendant le haut moyen âge, Etude sémantique*, Société de publications romanes et françaises 58, Genève-Paris, 1957, p. 129); "In Germany, as elsewhere, chivalry had its material basis in feudalism" (H. G. Atkins, *The Chivalry in Germany*, in: *Chivalry*, pp. 81–107, quotation p. 81); "The means a knight needed for his equipment and his campaigns were provided by his landed possessions" (Gustav Schnürer, *Kirche und Kultur im Mittelalter*, Vol. II, 2nd ed. Paderborn, 1929, p. 258).

27. "It is principally free holders of fiefs who are called *milites*" (Julius Ficker, *Vom Reichsfürstenstande, Forschungen zur Geschichte der Reichsverfassung zunächst im 12. und 13. Jahrhunderte*, Vol. II, Pt. 1, Paul Puntschart, ed., Innsbruck, 1911, p. 218). On the use and meaning of *miles* in the Middle Ages, see also: Georg Waitz, *Dt. Verfassungsgeschichte*, Vol. V (Kiel, 1874), pp. 436ff.; Julius Ficker, *Vom Heerschilde, Ein Beitrag zur dt. Reichs- und Rechtsgeschichte* (Innsbruck, 1862), pp. 179f.; Du Cange, *Glossarium med. et inf. latinitatis* IV, 396ff.; Roth von Schreckenstein, *Ritterwürde*, pp. 93ff.; Otto von Zallinger, pp. 4ff.; Paul Kluckhohn, pp. 49ff.; and esp. Paul Guilhiermoz, *Essai sur l'origine de la noblesse en France au moyen âge* (Paris, 1902), pp. 332ff.

28. Richard Schröder, *Lehrbuch der dt. Rechtsgeschichte*, 6th ed. by Eberhard Frh. von Künssberg (Berlin-Leipzig, 1922), p. 171. Instances for the

German word *ritterlêhen* are to be found only in the fifteenth century; Herbert Klein, MdGfSL. 80, 91 (see below, n. 48) shows that the word appears for the first time in sources from Salzburg in 1491; Lexer II, 467 only gives the reference to Haltaus's *Glossarium germanicum*. The term *feudum militare* occurs in Germany from the end of the eleventh century on. See François L. Ganshof, *Was ist das Lehnswesen?*, Ruth and Dieter Groh trans. (Darmstadt, 1961), pp. 118f.; the term *beneficia militaria* is classical Roman. See Alfons Dopsch, *Wirtschaftliche und soziale Grundlagen der europäischen Kulturentwicklung aus der Zeit von Caesar bis auf Karl d. Gr.*, Vol. II (2nd ed. Wien, 1924), p. 293.

29. "It is in the mounted Germanic retinue that we must look for the origins of Western knighthood" (Hans Naumann, *Dt. Kultur*, p. 11; see also Hans Naumann, *Germanische Grundlagen des Rittertums*, Geistige Arbeit 4, 1937, no. 15, 1–2; F. Warre Cornish, p. 29). It is on this point in particular, incidentally, that views are widely divided. Roth von Schreckenstein began his history of knighthood with "the chivalric character of the Indogermanic people" (*Ritterwürde*, p. 20). Otto Henne am Rhyn begins the development with the Greek ἱππῆς (p. 11). From the point of view of armament knights have been derived from the late classical armored cavalry-men, whom the Romans created according to the model of Asiatics: "The 'medieval' knight makes his appearance from the end of the third century on" (Ferdinand Lot, *La fin du monde antique et le début du moyen âge*, L'évolution de l'humanité 31, Paris, 1927, p. 19). The social type of the medieval knight is first found in the late Carolingian period: "The hour of knighthood's birth is . . . the late ninth century" (Arno Borst, Saecul. 10, 216). But if stress is laid on the ethics of chivalry, "then it may be said with complete accuracy that it was the call to the Crusade which created knighthood" (Adolf Waas, *Geschichte der Kreuzzüge in zwei Bänden*, Freiburg, 1956, Vol. II, p. 58). Julius Petersen complained long ago "The various and often contradictory use of the word 'Ritter' gives rise to misunderstandings and ambiguities" (p. 59).

30. "According to statements in documents, *miles* in the eleventh century still means a free vassal" (Karl Bosl, *Das ius ministerialium, Dienstrecht und Lehnrecht im dt. Mittelalter*, in: Vorträge u. Forschungen 5 [see above, p. 189, note 35], 51–94, quotation p. 54); see also Paul Kluckhohn, p. 21 and the literature given in note 27.

31. For example Hermann Conrad I, 396; Hans Planitz, *Dt. Rechtsgeschichte* (Graz, 1950), p. 108.

32. Julius Ficker, *Reichsfürstenstand* II 1, 218.

33. "The great vassals were completely equal to the owners of allodial domains but the smaller knights of free condition, whose possessions moved within narrower limits, were also regarded as nobles" (Richard Schröder, p. 470).

34. Ibid., p. 472.

35. Gustav Köhler, III 2, 71.

36. ". . . the fusion of free knights and unfree retainers in one class" (Hermann Conrad I, 396); ". . . the fusion of both classes into a unified

knightly class'' (Paul Kluckhohn, p. 116); ''. . . the merging of the *min-isteriales* with the unfree and free knights into a unified knightly class''
(Hans Planitz, p. 108), etc.

37.   Heinrich Brunner, *Der Reiterdienst und die Anfänge des Lehnwesens*, in:
H. B., *Forschungen zur Geschichte des dt. und französischen Rechtes,
Ges. Aufsätze*, (Stuttgart 1894), pp. 39–74 (originally in: ZRG. GA. 8,
1887, 1–38) quotation p. 62.

38.   Hermann Conrad, *Geschichte der dt. Wehrverfassung*, Vol. I, (München,
1939), p. 86.

39.   Heinrich Mitteis, *Lehnrecht und Staatsgewalt, Untersuchungen zur mittelalterlichen Verfassungsgeschichte*, (Weimar, 1933), p. 131.

40.   Ibid., p. 438.

41.   Heinrich Mitteis, Rez. Schlesinger, in: *Die Rechtsidee* . . . (see above,
p. 189, note 40), pp. 458–73 (originally in: HZ. 168, 1943, 145–61),
quotation p. 465. There is no real evidence in the texts of our period that
could testify to the spreading of Eike's feudal theory. The words *ritter*
and *lêhen* are occasionally loosely associated, as in Rudolf von Ems:
''die ritter lêhen silber golt, von gesteine rîchen solt enphiengen von dem
künege dâ'' (Gerh. 6411–13). Only once are the two terms so closely
associated that we are tempted to see in this an anticipation of the *Sachsenspiegel*. It is stated in the *Kaiserchronik* that Adelger, the Bavarian
duke, ordered his people to cut off their robes at the knee and in that way
share with him the humiliation inflicted on him by the Roman emperor:
''er sante ze Baiern in daz lant, er gebôt in allen bî der zeswen hant:
swelhe lêhenreht wolten haben oder ritteres namen, si êrten den herzogen
dâ mite, daz si daz gewant ab sniten'' (6798–6803). This case unfortunately evades an exact interpretation, since the decisive *oder* could be
intended either as an association or as a separation. Martin Baltzer is,
however, of the opinion (*Zur Geschichte des dt. Kriegswesens in der Zeit
von den letzten Karolingern bis auf Kaiser Friedrich II.*, Leipzig, 1877,
p. 17) that here ''the expressions *lêhenreht* and *ritters namen* have obviously been used as synonyms.'' Alfred Riemen writes: ''the poet sep-
arates by the use of the connecting word *oder* the enfiefment and the
knightly initiation'' (p. 9). I am personally inclined toward Riemen's
point of view. There is almost simultaneously with the *Kaiserchronik* a
quite similar Latin wording; in 1145 Konrad III forbids the Abbot of
Allerheiligen in Schaffhausen to grant any fiefs from the abbey's property
or to make any knights: ''quicquam . . . in beneficium dare aut milites
aliquos creare (quotation Wilhelm Erben, ZfhWk. 8, 127). This also has
been differently interpreted, see below, p. 234, note 81.

42.   I call special attention to *Studien zum mittelalterlichen Lehenswesen* (see
above, p. 189, note 35) with the important essays by Wilhelm Ebel, Karl
Bosl, Ernst Klebel and others. Some of the more recent monographs on
fiefdom are still dominated by the traditional idea obtained from legal
texts; Heinrich Brunner's famous ''Arab-Thesis,'' in particular, has widespread impact even today. Even though the assumption that the invasions
of the Arabs in the eighth century formed ''the initial impulse for a

systematic increase of the cavalry" (*Forschungen*, p. 73), has been refuted (see Hans G. W. von Mangoldt-Gaudlitz, *Die Reiterei in den germanischen und fränkischen Heeren bis zum Ausgang der dt. Karolinger*, Arbeiten zur dt. Rechts- u. Verfassungsgesch. 4, Berlin, 1922; François L. Ganshof, *A propos de la cavalerie dans les armées de Charlemagne*, Académie des inscriptions et des belles lettres, Comptes rendus des séances 1952/53, pp. 531–37) the basic idea of the old doctrine, that is, "that the need for cavalry . . . brought about the development of feudalism" (Heinrich Brunner, *Forschgg.*, p. 45) is still very much alive today, in spite of considerable criticism. See Alfons Dopsch, *Beneficialwesen und Feudalität*, MIÖG. 46, 1932, 1–36; H. A. Cronne, *The Origins of Feudalism*, Historical Revisions XCI, History 24, 1940, 251–59; Marc Bloch, *La société féodale*, 2 vols., L'évolution de l'humanité 34/34 bis (Paris, 1939/40, repr. 1949), esp. I, 235f.; Heinrich Mitteis, pp. 124ff.; Heinrich Mitteis, *Der Staat des hohen Mittelalters, Grundlinien einer vergleichenden Verfassungsgeschichte des Lehnszeitalters* (4th ed. Weimar 1953), pp. 55ff., including further literature; Friedrich Lütge, *Dt. Sozial- und Wirtschaftsgeschichte, Ein Überblick*, Enzyklopädie der Rechts- u. Staatswiss., Abt. Staatswiss. (Berlin-Göttingen-Heidelberg, 1952), pp. 51ff. Even the latest legal history teaches that feudalism was "originally a legal institution which predominantly served military purposes (Hermann Conrad, *Rechtsgesch.* I, 353); of similar opinion are: François L. Ganshof, *Qu'est-ce que la féodalité?* (3rd. ed. Bruxelles, 1957), esp. p. 30; Carl Stephenson, *Mediaeval Feudalism* (Ithaca, N.Y. 1942, repr. 1956), esp. p. 43; Bruno Meyer, *Das Lehen in Recht und Staat des Mittelalters*, Zeitschr. f. Schweizer. Gesch. 26 (1946), 161–78. The picture of early feudal conditions will look very much different once the results of the researches of Theodor Mayer and Heinrich Dannenbauer have been incorporated into the handbooks: the dogma of the general liability to military service of the free Germanic peoples is now questionable (see Heinrich Dannenbauer, *Die Freien im karolingischen Heer*, in: H.D., *Grundlagen der mittelalterlichen Welt, Skizzen und Studien*, Stuttgart 1958, pp. 240–56 [first published in Festschrift Th. Mayer (see above, p. 188, note 32) I, 49–64]; Walter Schlesinger in: Wege d. Forschg. 2, 143), and the so-called "King's free men" are recognized as the most important instrument of Carolingian military policy (see Theodor Mayer, *Königtum und Gemeinfreiheit im frühen Mittelalter*, in: *Mittelalterl. Studien* [see above, p. 188, note 32], pp. 139–63 [first published in: DA. 6, 1943, 329–62]; several articles by Heinrich Dannenbauer on this subject are collected in his volume *Skizzen und Studien*).

43.   Georg Waitz, Vol. IV (2nd ed. Berlin, 1885), p. 218; see Gerhard Seeliger, *Die soziale und politische Bedeutung der Grundherrschaft im früheren Mittelalter, Untersuchungen über Hofrecht, Immunität und Landleihen*, Abhandlgg. der phil.-hist. Kl. der Kgl. Sächs. Ges. d. Wiss. 22, no. 1 (Leipzig, 1904), esp. p. 34.

44.   See Friedrich Keutgen, *Die Entstehung der deutschen Ministerialität*,

VSWG. 8, 1910, 1–16, 169–95, 481–547, esp. p. 506.

45. Walther Kienast, *Rechtsnatur und Anwendung der Mannschaft (homagium) in Deutschland während des Mittelalters*, Dt. Landesreferate zum IV. Internat. Kongress für Rechtsvergleichung in Paris 1954, Ernst Wolff, ed. (Düsseldorf, 1955), pp. 26–48, quotation p. 44.

46. Karl Bosl in: Vortr. u. Forschgg. 5, 61; see Walther Kienast in: Landesref., p. 33.

47. Heinrich Mitteis, *Lehnrecht*, p. 231.

48. See Herbert Klein, *Ritterlehen und Beutellehen in Salzburg*, Mitteilungen der Gesellschaft für Salzburger Landeskunde 80 (1940), 87–128; Ernst Klebel, *Freies Eigen und Beutellehen in Ober- und Niederbayern*, Zeitschrift für bayerische Landesgeschichte 11, 1938, 45–85; Otto Brunner, pp. 355f.; Walther Kienast in: Landesref., p. 44; Karl Bosl in: Vortr. u. Forschgg. 5, 61.

49. Herbert Klein, MdGfSL. 80, 92.

50. Marc Bloch 1, 315. "The nobility is obviously older than the hierarchy of society which developed from feudalism and vassalage" (Heinrich Dannenbauer, *Adel, Burg und Herrschaft bei den Germanen, Grundlagen der dt. Verfassungsentwicklung*, in: Wege der Forschung 2, 66–134 [originally in: Hist. Jb. 61, 1941, 1–50; also in *Skizzen u. Studien*, pp. 121–78], quotation pp. 71f.). "The old law of nobility established itself again in the shape of a special feudal law" (Eberhard F. Otto, *Adel und Freiheit im dt. Staat des frühen Mittelalters, Studien über "nobiles" und Ministerialen*, Neue Dt. Forschgg., Abt. Mittelalterl. Gesch. 2, Berlin, 1937, p. 136).

51. Walther Kienast, *Lehnrecht und Staatsgewalt im Mittelalter, Studien zu dem Mitteis'schen Werk*, HZ. 158, 1938, 3–51, quotation p. 12. "The attempt to convert feudal law to state law did not succeed" in Germany (Theodor Mayer, *Die Ausbildung der Grundlagen des modernen dt. Staates im hohen Mittelalter*, HZ. 159, 1939, S. 457–87, quotation p. 486); see also Heinrich Mitteis, *Lehnrecht*, p. 444; Wilhelm Ebel in: Vortr. u. Forschgg. 5, 35; Adolf Waas, *Herrschaft und Staat im dt. Frühmittelalter*, Hist. Stud. 335, Berlin 1938, pp. 340f.; Georg Droege, *Lehnrecht und Landrecht am Niederrhein und das Problem der Territorialbildung im 12. u. 13. Jh.*, in: *Aus Geschichte u. Landeskunde, Forschgg. u. Darstellungen*, Franz Steinbach zum 65. Geb., Bonn 1960, pp. 278–307.

52. Heinrich Mitteis, Rez. Kienast, in: *Die Rechtsidee . . .* (see above, p. 186, note 40), pp. 184–92 (originally in: ZRG. GA. 52, 1932, 520–28), quotation p. 189. Otto von Dungern calls feudal law "a permanent rule of order which never applied to the German nobility but which instead established itself in the thirteenth century in the minds of the theoreticians as a well-ordered system" (p. 245). See Marc Bloch, II, 84.

53. See Otto Frh. von Dungern, *Adelsherrschaft im Mittelalter*, München 1927; Heinrich Mitteis, *Formen der Adelsherrschaft im Mittelalter*, in: *Die Rechtsidee*, pp. 636–68 (originally published in: Festschr. Fritz Schulz, Weimar 1951, pp. 226–58); Karl Bosl, *Der "aristokratische*

Charakter" *europäischer Staats- und Sozialentwicklung, Prolegomena*
zu einer allgemeinen Verfassungsgeschichte, Hist. Jb. 74, 1955, 631–42;
see also the chapter "Die europäische Adelsherrschaft" in Friedrich Heer,
Mittelalter (von 1100 bis 1350), Kindler's Kulturgeschichte (Zürich,
1961), pp. 28–44. Of special importance is the observation that feudal
law had a much lesser part to play in the territories than in the constitution
of the empire. See Ernst Klebel, *Territorialstaat und Lehen*, in Vortr. u.
Forschgg. 5, 195–228; Ernst Klebel, *Vom Herzogtum zum Territorium*,
in: Festschr. Th. Mayer I, 205–22; Otto Brunner, pp. 355f.; Heinrich
Mitteis, *Lehnrecht*, p. 237.

54.   See Heinrich Brunner, *Dt. Rechtsgeschichte*, Vol. II, 2nd ed., especially
by Claudius Frh. von Schwerin (München-Leipzig, 1928), pp. 353f.;
Walther Kienast in: Landesref., pp. 28f.

55.   Paul Guilhiermoz, p. 334.

56.   "Among the people who are designated as *milites*, the element of service,
however, is so intrusive that we might be tempted to translate them
frequently as 'servants or mounted mercenaries' " (Roth von Schreckenstein, *Ritterwürde*, pp. 96f.). The explanation that the word *miles* was
used for vassals is much less plausible, because the "fonctionnaires roy-
aux," who were called *milites* during the time of the Merovingians, had
entered into the king's vassalage at the time of the Carolingians (Paul
Guilhiermoz, pp. 336f.).

57.   See Hans Delbrück III, 255; Charles W.C. Oman, *A History of the Art*
of War in the Middle Ages (2nd ed. New York 1924), Vol. I, p. 105.

58.   Hans Delbrück III, 255.

59.   See Edmund E. Stengel, *Über den Ursprung der Ministerialität*, in: *Pap-*
sttum und Kaisertum, Forschungen zur politischen Geschichte und Geis-
teskultur des Mittelalters, Festschrift Paul Kehr, München 1926, pp.
168–84, esp. p. 171.

60.   Evidence by Paul Guilhiermoz, p. 140, n. 9 and pp. 165ff. We are
permitted an interesting glimpse of the *milites* by the report of Ekkehard
IV under Abbot Notker, in the second half of the tenth century (*Casus*
Sancti Galli c. 135): those were vassals of the monastery of St. Gallen,
and Ekkehard sharply distinguishes between them and the *comites aliique*
potentes. We can surmise their lowly social status from the treatment with
which they have to put up from the abbot—he required them to perform
regular court service and supervised the education of their children. Text
and interpretation by Karl H. Ganahl, *Studien zur Verfassungsgeschichte*
der Klosterherrschaft St. Gallen von den Anfängen bis ins hohe Mitte-
lalter, Forschgg. zur Geschichte Vorarlbergs und Liechtensteins 6 (Innsbruck, 1931), p. 160.

61.   See Marc Bloch I, 233ff.; Paul Guilhiermoz, pp. 242ff.

62.   Heinrich Brunner II, 359.

63.   See Walther Kienast in: Landesref., p. 42.

64.   Evidence by Georg Waitz V, 436; Otto von Zallinger, pp. 8f.; Ernst
Mayer II, 184ff. A rich treasure-trove for further evidence of unfree
milites are the individual investigations on the problem of *ministeriales*.

65. See Georg Waitz V, 436; Edmund E. Stengel in: Festschr. P. Kehr, p. 172.
66. Erich Molitor, *Der Stand der Ministerialen vornehmlich auf grund sächsischer, thüringischer und niederrheinischer Quellen*, Untersuchgg. zur dt. Staats- u. Rechtsgesch. 112 (Breslau, 1912), p. 48.
67. "The statement that in the tenth and eleventh centuries *milites* were *always* designated as free vassals only is an exaggeration" (Friedrich Keutgen, VSWG. 8, 493, n. 1); Karl Fajkmajer arrives at the same conclusion, *Die Ministerialen des Hochstiftes Brixen*, Zeitschr. des Ferdinandeums für Tirol u. Vorarlberg, 3. Folge, Heft 52, 1908, 95–191, esp. p. 136.
68. Dietrich Schäfer, *Die "agrarii milites" des Widukind*, Sitzungsber. der kgl. Preuss. Akad. d. Wiss., phil.-hist. Kl., Jg. 1905, no. 27 (Berlin, 1905), 569–77, quotation p. 572; with ref. to the *milites agrarii* see also Friedrich Keutgen, VSWG. 8, 8, n. 1; Edmund E. Stengel in: Festschr. P. Kehr, p. 173, n. 1; Hans Delbrück III, 111ff.; Marc Bloch I, 277f.
69. Otto von Dungern, *Herrenstand* I, 345; also Roth von Schreckenstein: "By the designation *miles* . . . nothing about the social status at birth of a particular man has been stated" (*Reichsritterschaft* I, 159).
70. Hermann Conrad, *Rechtsgesch.* I, 356.
71. Hans Fehr, *Dt. Rechtsgeschichte*, Lehrbücher und Grundrisse der Rechtswiss. 10 (4th ed. Berlin, 1948), p. 87.
72. Richard Schöder, p. 559.
73. Friedrich Keutgen's opinion is rather sceptical: "Nothing could have been further removed from the strict organization of the agrarian administrations during their heyday than to hand fiefs to dependent people solely for the creation of an army" (VSWG. 8, 540).
74. Eugen von Frauenholz I, 62. "The feudal state did not, in the end, prove to be a sound basis for the shaping of the military potential" (ibid., p. 63). "The army as it developed through the feudal system, was a rather imperfect means for conducting wars" (Gustav Köhler III 3, Breslau, 1889, p. 1).
75. "When the liegelord proceeded to present or grant to his people land without dismissing them . . . , then the relationship between lord and man has, in most respects, undergone a rapid and thorough change. The vassal then became . . . a feudal liegeman or *Junker*. He himself became a lord, even though not a very important one" (Hans Kuhn, *Die Grenzen der germanischen Gefolgschaft*, ZRG. GA. 73, 1956, 1–83, quotation pp. 4f.). "As a knight endowed with property as a pension ceased to live with his lord and stayed more or less distant from his person, it was inevitable that the services he owed should diminish" (Paul Guilhiermoz, p. 255).
76. Charles W. C. Oman's judgment is the most sharp: "Assembled with difficulty, insubordinate, unable to maneuver, ready to melt away from its standard the moment that its short period of service was over, a feudal force presented an assemblage of unsoldierlike qualities" (*The Art of War in the Middle Ages A.D. 378–1515*, rev. by John H. Beeler, Ithaca, N.Y., 1953, pp. 57f.).

206   THE CONCEPT OF KNIGHTHOOD IN THE MIDDLE AGES

77.   See Ferdinand Lot, *L'art militaire et les armées au moyen âge en Europe et dans le proche orient*, 2 vols. (Paris, 1946); the important work by J. F. Verbruggen, *Krijkskunst in West-Europa in de Middeleeuwen (IXe tot begin XIVe eeuwe)*, Verhandlingen van de Kgl. Vlaamse Acad. voor Wetenschappen, Letteren en Schone Kunsten van Belgie, Kl. der Letteren, Verhandlg. 20 (Brüssel, 1954), was not available to me; see the review by Ferdinand Stöller, MIÖG. 65 (1957), 132–36, and the detailed acknowledgement by Heinrich Sproemberg, *Die feudale Kriegskunst*, in: H.S., *Beiträge zur belgisch-niederländischen Geschichte*, Forschgg. zur mittelalterl. Gesch. 3, Berlin, 1959, 30–55. J. F. Verbruggen expressed the basic ideas of his work in a series of articles; see esp. *La tactique militaire des armées de chevaliers*, Revue du Nord 29 (1947), 161–80. "The old-fashioned opinion that the knight engages in individual hand-to-hand combat and that battles and military campaigns therefore show a total void of systematic leadership, is conclusively refuted" (Heinrich Sproemberg, Rez. Verbruggen, DA. 12, 1956, 619–20, quotation p. 620). The German sources are also of importance for questions concerning military tactics: Wolfram describes, for example, in *Willehalm* a consolidated cavalry-attack (389, 20ff.), the orderly withdrawal from individual encounters during the battle (413, 22ff.), the manœuvring with reserves (423, 1ff.), etc.
78.   Walther Kienast, HZ. 158, 44; see Heinrich Mitteis, *Lehnrecht*, p. 445.
79.   The earliest example in 982 is the conscription by Otto II, reproduced by Eugen von Frauenholz I, 181ff.; for an interpretation see Ernst Klebel in: Festschr. Th. Mayer I, 207ff.
80.   See Heinrich Mitteis, *Lehnrecht*, p. 428.
81.   Ibid., p. 603.
82.   See Paul Guilhiermoz, pp. 276ff.; Hans Delbrück III, 97ff.; Heinrich Mitteis, *Lehnrecht*, pp. 602ff.; Eugen von Frauenholz I, 91f.
83.   Heinrich Mitteis, *Lehnrecht*, p. 605.
84.   Ibid., p. 602.
85.   Hans Delbrück III, 259; see Edmund E. Stengel in: Festschr. P. Kehr, pp. 170f.
86.   "*Principes in expeditionem solemni indictione evocavit, sed . . . omnes pariter miliciam detrectabant. Ipse tamen . . . gregario tantum ac privato milite contentus, infesto exercitu ingressus est Ungariam*" (quoted from Paul Guilhiermoz, p. 250, note 16); *milites speciales* are documented by the Lauterberger Chronik in Philipp's von Schwaben army (see Martin Baltzer, p. 29, note 29).
87.   Text by Friedrich Keutgen, VSWG. 8, 485.
88.   In addition Hans Fehr writes: "It is questionable whether the poet regards the peasants as an integral part of the army or only as pioneers and sappers" (Hans Fehr, *Kunst u. Recht* II, 105). An unprejudiced reading of the text, however, does not allow for such doubts. The peasant is, in Neidhart von Reuental also, "a man quite able to bear arms" (Hans Fehr, ibid., p. 194).
89.   Hans Fehr, *Das Waffenrecht der Bauern im Mittelalter*, ZRG. GA. 35,

1914, 111–211, quotation p. 183. Legal history shows, however, that "the peasant lost the right to bear arms at the end of the eleventh century" (Hans Fehr, *Rechtsgesch.*, p. 86). But then, according to Friedrich Keutgen, "can the theory that sons of peasants had no access to knighthood from the time of the Hohenstaufen be maintained with any certainty" (VSWG. 8, 182, n. 1); see also Edmund E. Stengel, DA. 14, 402; Karl Bosl, VSWG. 39, 304.

90. See above, p. 25.

91. "*Et si evenerit, ut in qualibet ecclesia vel in sancto loco plures brunias habeat quam ad homines rectores eiusdam ecclesiae sufficiant, tunc principem idem rector ecclesiae interroget, quid de his fieri debeat*" (quotation from Eugen von Frauenholz I, 166; trans. ibid., p. 30).

92. "*Et hoc in arbitrio dominorum pendeat, quos ducant, a quibus stipendia accipiant, quibus halspergas concedant*" (quotation from Eugen v. Frauenholz I, 258).

93. Franz Joetze, *Die Ministerialität im Hochstifte Bamberg*, Hist. Jb. 36, 1915 516–97, 748–98, quotation p. 534; see also Paul Guilhiermoz, pp. 298ff. for evidence from German sources.

94. Examples in Paul Guilhiermoz, pp 245f. Roth von Schreckenstein, *Ritterwurde*, p. 147; Georg Waitz V, 436; Paul Kluckhohn, p. 29, note 1; Wilhelm Ganzenmüller, *Die flandrische Ministerialität bis zum ersten Drittel des 12. Jhs.* Diss. Tübingen, 1907, pp. 15f. There are obviously many more examples than could be surmised from this compilation. A new summary would indeed be welcome. Concerning the concept of *familia*, see Gerhard Seeliger in: Abhandlgg. 22, 137; Edmund E. Stengel in: Festschr. P. Kehr, p. 178, note 2.

95. On the subject of domestic rule as the core of overlord-power and on the structure of medieval domain in general, see Otto Brunner, pp. 240ff.; Otto Brunner, *Inneres Gefüge des Abendlandes*, in: *Historia Mundi*, Vol. VI (Bern 1958), 319–85, esp. pp. 331ff.; Otto Brunner, *Das "ganze Haus" und die alteuropäische "Ökonomik"*, in: *Neue Wege . . .* (see above, p. 189, n. 33), pp. 33–61; Walter Schlesinger in: Wege d. Forschg. 2, 135ff.; Karl Bosl, *Staat, Gesellschaft, Wirtschaft im dt. Mittelalter*, in: Gebhardt's *Handbuch* (see above, p. 187, note 27), pp. 584–684, esp. pp. 616ff.

96. Gerhard Seeliger in: Abhandlgg. 22, 191.

97. This process of change has been observed in relation to Brixen by Karl Fajkmajer (ZdFTV. 52, 125). The same biased point of view which makes the vassal-*milites* the same as aristocratic lords, often tries to see only *ministeriales* in the unfree *milites*, although Otto von Zallinger long ago called attention to the fact that at least in southern Germany "there was as early as the eleventh century a class of unfree knights which was to be distinguished from the *ministeriales* and which was subordinate to them" (p. 2). More details above, pp. 60.

98. See Georg Waitz, Bd. VIII, Kiel 1878, pp. 164ff.; Alwin Schultz II, 162ff.; Gustav Köhler III 2, 146ff.; Hans Delbrück III, 329ff.; Charles W.C. Oman, *A History* I, 375ff.; Eugen von Frauenholz I, 85f.; Ferdinand

Lot, *L'art militaire* II, 423ff.; also: Bryce D. Lyon, *The Feudal Antecedent of the Indenture System*, Specul. 29 (1954), 503–11; Bryce D. Lyon, *From Fief to Indenture, The Transition from Feudal to Non-Feudal Contract in Western Europe*, Harvard Historical Studies 68 (Cambridge, Mass. 1957).

99.   Hans Delbrück III, 330. Ibid., p. 274, an interesting passage from the *Gesta episcoporum Leodicensium*, according to which Bishop Wazo of Liège conducted his wars in the eleventh century predominantly with the help of mercenaries.

100. See Eugen von Frauenholz I, 89.

101. See Richard Schröder, p. 563.

102. See Paul Schmitthenner, *Das Freie Söldnertum im abendländischen Imperium des Mittelalters*, Münchener Hist. Abhandlgg., Reihe 2, Heft 4, München 1934, especially pp. 76ff.; Paul Schmitthenner, *Lehnskriegswesen und Söldnertum im abendländischen Imperium des Mittelalters*, HZ. 150, 1934, 229–67; Herbert Grundmann, *Rotten und Brabanzonen, Söldnerheere im 12. Jahrhundert*, DA. 5, 1942, 419–92; Herbert Grundmann, *Söldnerheere in der Stauferzeit*, Forschgg. u. Fortschr. 18 (1942), 303–05.

103. Herbert Grundmann, DA. 5, 482. "Conducting of wars no longer seemed feasible without mercenaries from the thirteenth century onward" (Gustav Köhler III 2, 164).

104. See Charles W.C. Oman: ". . . a force of mercenaries who were, for most military purposes, infinitely preferable to the feudal array" (*The Art. . .* , p. 66). In another passage Oman describes the mercenaries "inferior in morale to the feudal force" (p. 65); the editor adds to this: "This is a misconception. The mercenaries . . . proved more faithful, so long as their salaries were paid, than did the feudal baronage . . . There is nothing to indicate that they were inferior in courage or morale to any soldiers of the period" (n. 7). In reference to the battle of Bouvines, the *scientia et virtus bellandi* of the Brabanters are highly praised (see Martin Baltzer, p. 11, n. 42).

105. Roth von Schreckenstein, *Ritterwürde*, p. 93.

106. Paul Schmitthenner, HZ. 150, 233.

107. Paul Kluckhohn, p. 116.

108. Otto von Dungern, *Herrenstand*, p. 350.

109. Karl Bosl in: Vortr. u. Forschgg. 5, 55.

110. Eugen von Frauenholz I, 60.

111. Julius Petersen, p. 59.

112. Hans Planitz, p. 108; see Claudius Frh. von Schwerin, *Grundzüge der dt. Rechtsgeschichte* (München-Leipzig 1934), pp. 117f.; Wolfgang Frh. v. Plotho, *Die Stände des dt. Reiches im 12. Jh. und ihre Fortentwicklung bis zum Schlusse des Mittelalters unter Berücksichtigung der Werke des Frhn. Otto v. Dungern*, Vierteljahrsschr. f. Wappen-, Siegel- u. Familienkunde 45, 1917, 1–59, esp. p. 24.

113. Hans Delbrück III, 256.

114. "Rulers, aristocrats and nobles are anyway part of the warrior class"

(Eugen von Frauenholz I, 67); they "were all themselves professional soldiers" (Heinrich Sproemberg, *Beiträge*, p. 39). From this point of view the practice of all non-military lordship rights would be an incidental occupation of the princes: "The soldier carries out . . . all higher functions as a secondary occupation" (Hans Delbrück III, 258). Otto von Dungern's judgment is more to the point: "For all these dynasts, knighthood was neither a distinction nor a special calling but simply the result and obligation of their social position, into which they were born" (*Herrenstand*, p. 348).

115.   The old dispute as to whether service at court or service in war brought about the rise of the *ministeriales* may be regarded nowadays as settled, and recent research has accepted almost unanimously Edmund E. Stengel's formulation: "The impulse for the creation of a class was not a defined professional activity performed by groups of officials and soldiers classified according to profession . . . ; it was service in itself which provided the decisive force" (in: Festschr. P. Kehr, p. 175).

116.   It is seldom that we are provided with such an exact picture of the social rise of definite classes as in the report of Ekkehard IV on the situation of the *Meier* in St. Gallen in the tenth century: ". . . *Servantibus, majores locorum, de quibus scriptum est, quia servi, si non timent, tument, scuta et arma polita gestare incoeperant . . . , nos beneficia nostra curemus et venatui, ut viros decet indulgeamus!*" (Casus c. 48, quotation according to Karl Ganahl, p. 119, see also the interpretation there provided). Here the series of upward steps is perfectly clear: in the administrative service of the abbey the *Meier* move upwards; they are then made feuditories, and the income from the fiefs make it possible for them to arm themselves like lords.

117.   Otto von Dungern, *Herrenstand*, p. 350.

118.   Paul Schmitthenner, HZ. 150, 252.

119.   Ibid., p. 254.

120.   Otto von Dungern, *Herrenstand*, p. 342.

121.   This list shows the knights as an anonymous mass. It is obvious that the numbers given have no historical credibility; this is proved by the preference for round numbers. I am deliberately beginning with twenty knights and am producing only such instances as those in which the numerals stand either directly next to or close to the word *ritter*. The qualification of the figure given (c.g., *wol hundert ritter oder mêr*) is not considered, nor is the position or method of writing the numerals.

IV. The Knight as Retainer

1. Gustav Köhler III 2, 16.

2. Hermann Schneider, *Heldendichtung, Geistlichendichtung, Ritterdichtung; Geschichte der deutschen Literatur* I (2.ed., Heidelberg, 1943), p. 285.

3. Wolfgang Stammler writes on the *Wiener Genesis*: "The patriarchs are

helede and *riter*, they are landed peasants, like the knights of their time"
(*Die Anfänge weltlicher Dichtung in deutscher Sprache, Eine neue Ken-
nung*, ZfdPh. 70, 1948/49, 10–32, quotation from p. 25). In the *Wiener
Genesis*, however, I have found only the one instance of *ritter*, and here
it is not the patriarchs but their servants who are called *ritter*.

4. Walther Kotzenberg finds in Exodus (ed. Massmann, 6243) a "foreshad-
owing" of the "trivialization of the word *frouwe* which was not carried
through until much later" at the beginning of the twelfth century (*man,
frouwe, juncfrouwe, Drei Kapitel aus der mhd. Wortgeschichte*, Berliner
Beiträge zur germanischen und romanischen Philologie 33, Germ. Sect.
20, Berlin, 1907, p. 67). Later instances ibid., pp. 78, 81, 94ff. Wolfram
even gives the title *frouwen* to the *trippâniersen* and *soldiersen* in the
baggage train of an army (Parzival 341, 19). Kotzenberg does not go into
the question of the expression *ritter unde vrouwen*.

5. Parallel with these there are *ritter unde vrouwen* outside the lord's court
too. In the *Kaiserchronik* it is stated with reference to the martyrdom of
Peter and Paul: *daz lantfolc zôch allenthalben zuo, rîter unt frowen* (4208f.;
similarly 5764ff.). In Herbort too: *Daz lantvolc quam durch wūder dare.
Ritter uñ frauwē* (1172f.). And in Otte: *die herren von dem lande . . . sie
fuoren ze Rôme und kâmen dar, manec wunneclîchiu schar von rîtern und
von frouwen* (1826. 33–35).

6. See the instances given above. Knights as an escort when hunting Eilhart
6396f., Eneit 60, 36ff., Nibelungenlied 926, 2f., Sächsische Weltchronik
136, 32ff., Holle Crane 4033f.

7. Further instances: Salman 373, 1f., Erek 10018ff., Wigalois 680ff.,
1141ff., 3973ff., 8563f., 11448f., Parzival 183, 28; 227, 18; 624, 14; 802,
28ff., Klage 3208f. (B), Flore 2130ff., Ems Willehalm 3072ff., 3488ff.,
14549ff., Türheim Rennewart 16684f., Stricker Daniel 1133ff., Türlin
Krone 10911f., 14724f., Durne 1536ff., Kudrun 115, 2f; 1658, 1ff, Holle
Demant 7022ff., 8124ff.

8. In other passages the knights are served in their turn: *den rîtern an ir want
diende manec sarjant* (Parzival 637, 7f.); *die dienesthaften knehte nâch
dienestlîchem rehte dienten sie den rittern dâ* (Ems Alexander 6891–93),
etc.

9. See also: *. . . dem waren als wir vns enstan. hundert reiter vndertan*
(Heimesfurt Urst. 112, 49f.); *. . . der gebot wârn undertân ouch tûsent
rîter unversaget* (Wigalois 10800f.), etc.

10. See Durne 1461ff., Ems Weltchronik 33090ff., Holle Demant 1560ff.,
10088ff. These passages should in their turn be distinguished from those
in which the knights are given presents of clothes, horses, and money (see
above p. 200, n. 20). Emperor Charlemagne sends out an invitation to a
Whitsun feast: *"Her solen komen vp den dach. Tzwentzich dusent riddere
wert. Den sal ich orss cleider pert. Geuen riche ind schone"* (Morant
292–95). At Gahmuret's wedding there is *"araebesch golt geteilet . . . armen
rîtern al gemeine* (Parzival 100, 28f.). Gawan presents *harnasch al der
rîterschaft* (ibid., 666, 19). At the wedding of King William of England:
daz varnde volc mit vreude enphie manege rîche gâbe hie, die ritter lêhen

silber golt, von gesteine rîchen solt enphiengen von dem künege dâ die ellenthaften fürsten sâ (Ems Gerhard 6409–14). The distinction between presents and pay is sometimes not clear.

11. It is certainly no accident that in both cases the title "knight" is used of the king's sons only for the purposes of comparison: *als noch vil dicke ein rîter tuot* (Parzival 17, 12); *nie herre ez rittern baz gebôt* (Türheim Tristan 516, 38).

12. Further instances, mostly from more recent sources, in *Deutsches Rechtswörterbuch* V, 794f.

13. Instances of the use of the title "herre" for "representatives of the lower classes" in Walther Kotzenberg pp. 7f. *Herre* is purely a formula of courtesy in the expressions *hêr wirt* (Walther von der Vogelweide 31, 23), *hêr gast* (ibid., 31, 24), etc. See *Mittelhochdeutsches Wörterbuch* I, 664b ff. "The connection with the knightly class in the sense that it is stated that the only retainer who could bear the title 'Herr' was one who had been formally admitted into the knightly orders by an initiation ceremony is untenable" (Otto von Dungern, *Herrenstand*, p. 284); see also Paul Kluckhohn, pp. 116f.; Julius Petersen, pp. 131ff. Hans Kuhn has called attention to the fact that the word "herre" itself "was to be found far down" [the social order] (ZRG. GA. 73, 61).

14. Instances of the opposition of *miles* to *dominus* or *senior* in Paul Guilhiermoz, p. 343 and n. 61.

15. Hans Fehr writes about this *Spruch*: "The social class structure here is: 1. the lords, based on free birth, to which the knights and the servants . . . belong; 2. . . . . retainers; 3. . . . . bondsmen" (*Kunst und Recht* II, 164). Such an interpretation finds no support in the clear and unambiguous statements in the text. Ready-made theories on class are here being forced on to the transmitted material.

16. The word is remarkably uncommon in the legal texts from which one would expect the earliest clear information about the social rank of knights. It appears neither in the *Mainzer Landfrieden* of 1235 nor in the *Mühlhauser Reichsrechtsbuch*. It appears once in the feudal law of the *Sachsenspiegel* (2 #1, see above p. 36), in the Landrecht seven times (I 20 #1, #8, I 27 #2 [twice], II 21 #1, II 27 #2 and once *riddereperd* III 51 #2), mostly in the rules on laws of inheritance and marriage. It is laid down *wat iewelk man van ridderes art moge geven sime wive to morgengave* (I 20 #1), namely *enen knecht oder ene maget . . . unde tune unde timmer unde veltginge ve* (ibid.). If one compares what *alle de van ridderes art nicht ne sin* (I 20 #8) may give to their wives: *dat beste perd oder ve dat se hebbet* (ibid.), it can be seen that the gap between the groups cannot have been very great. This becomes even clearer when we compare the figures given in the *Schwabenspiegel* (ed. Wackernagel, chap. 19) on the size of the dowry. There *fursten und ander hohe vrie herren* give to the value of 100 marks, the *miteln herren vrien* to the value of ten marks, the *dienstman* to the value of five marks (pp. 21f.); then follow bondsmen knights (*ist ein eigen man ritter*), *koufman, gebure* and *eigenman* (p. 22). Eike von Repgow also knows of landed tenants who were of "knightly class": *de*

tinsman, swe he si, he erft sin gebuw oppe sinen erven oppe tinsgude, it ne si en man van ridders art, de it sime wive to morgengave hebbe gegeven (Ldr. II 21 #1). Veldeke's *Servatius* offers further evidence of tenants of knightly birth: *du was te Huys in der stat ein sente Servases eigen man* (5260f.); *he was van gerechter scolt sculdech cins van sinen houvede* (5270f.); it is then said of this man: *van sines vaderes siden was he van ridderscap geboren* (5276f.). The rules in the *Sachsenspiegel* on knights' horses are remarkable; no compensation is attached to them (Ldr. III 51 #2). Eike distinguishes them from *rideperden: dat rideperd, dar de rideman sime herren oppe denen scal, dat gilt men mit eneme punde* (III 51 #1).

17. A good picture of the functions of a "knight of the feudal period" is given by Paul Guilhiermoz: "They can be summed up by saying that they had to follow him (i.e., their lord) anywhere that he decided to take them and that they had to carry out any duties that he decided to entrust to them. Thus we find them close to his person, not only in war . . . and at the court of his sovereign but also on his travels and during all his movements, on the hunt, in prison, in all the important circumstances of his life" (pp. 251–53).

18. See Falk and Torp under the word *Red* (II, 885) and under *Ride* (II, 897).

19. Hans Kuhn, ZRG. GA. 73, 64; Karl Bosl, *Über soziale Mobilität in der mittelalterlichen "Gesellschaft"; Dienst, Freiheit, Freizügigkeit als Motive sozialen Aufstiegs*, VSWG. 47, 1960, 306–32, esp. p. 313.

20. Hans Kuhn, ZRG. GA. 73, 81; see also Hans Kuhn, *Altnordisch rekkr und Verwandte*, Arkiv 58, 1944, 105–21.

21. Even if one maintains the position that the horse was essential to the knight from the beginning, it still does not follow from this that the primary function of a "ritter" was military. From the Carolingian period on, there is considerable evidence for people who were required to provide horses or act as messengers (the best known are the *scararii* or *scaremanni* in the Trier region) and who play a significant part in the early history of the *ministeriales*. See Karl W. Nitzsch, *Ministerialität und Bürgerthum im 11. und 12. Jahrhundert. Ein Beitrag zur deutschen Städtegeschichte, Vorarbeiten zur Geschichte der staufischen Periode* I, Leipzig 1859, pp. 22ff.; Friedrich Keutgen, VSWG. 8, 515ff.; Edmund E. Stengel in Festschrift P. Kehr, pp. 175ff.; Erich Molitor pp. 20ff.; Josef Bast, *Die Ministerialität des Erzstifts Trier*, diss Bonn 1918, pp. 100ff.; Heinrich Dannenbauer, *Paraveredus—Pferd* in *Grundlagen* . . . (see above, p. 203, n. 42), 257–70 (originally in ZRG. GA. 71, 1954, 55–73). Their service is paraphrased as *equitando servire, equitare quocumque iubetur illi praecipitur* (instances in Karl W. Nitzsch, pp. 25, 26, 39). In a document from St Gallen of the second half of the ninth century, it is required of these people that "equitent ubicumque eis praeceptum fuerit" (quotation from Karl H. Ganahl, p. 146); "it is permissible to see in this a typical formulation and to deduce from it a new proof of the general spread of the institution" (ibid. p. 147). The Latin term is *scaram facere*; Caesarius of Heisterbach defines it thus: *scaram facere est domino abbati, quando ipsi iusserit, servire et nuncium*

eius seu litteras ad locum sibi determinatum deferre (quoted from Edmund E. Stengel, p. 177, note 1). The corresponding German word is *reide*; in Erfurt it was later part of the duties of the *ministeriales: reide, quod significat nuncios qui ad preceptum episcopi mittendi exiguntur* (quoted from Friedrich Keutgen, p. 531, n. 1). In the fourteenth century there was in Trier a *Rydehuva, quem nullus debet possidere nisi miles vel armiger, qui tenetur esse eques in servitio dum requisitus fuerit* (quoted from Erich Molitor p. 22, n. 1; see Josef Bast p. 104). These mounted servants conform exactly to the picture of the retainer in the Middle High German sources. I do not exclude the possibility that in using the word *rîter* (Reiter), the sources are primarily concerned with such people.

22. Paul Kluckhohn, p. 15.
23. See Paul Piper's glossary, 1887, p. 522.
24. See Edward H. Sehrt and Wolfram K. Legner, *Notker-Wortschatz*, 1955, p. 103.
25. Paul Kluckhohn does not make a clear distinction between the instances "in the older glosses," for which he refers to Graff (II, 745) and those "in glosses of the eleventh century or later" (p. 14). So far as I can see, *dienestman* does not occur in the major gloss-manuscripts of the ninth century. Most of the instances in the glosses are from manuscripts of the twelfth and thirteenth centuries. Before this time the word is attested in only two manuscripts of the tenth century (Vienna 2723 and 2732) and in one manuscript each from the tenth/eleventh century (London Arundel 514) and the eleventh century (Munich 18140) and the eleventh/twelfth century (Munich 14689).
26. In addition there is the gloss *pedissequus:dienestman* IV, 270, 20; V, 5, 30.
27. Also perhaps II, 124, 58, where one manuscript writes *dinoman* for *curiales* (Clm 14689), whereas all others have *dincman*.
28. Paul Kluckhohn draws this conclusion expressly from the instances in glosses (p. 15), but the *dienestman* glosses offer no support for this. Therefore Kluckhohn bases his case on the rendering of the words *militia, militare* by *dionost, dionon* (ibid., p. 14), from which the only conclusion that can be drawn is that the *militia* concept in the Middle Ages was not confined to military service but designated a service-relationship in general. See Paul Guilhiermoz, pp. 332f.
29. Solomon's servants are also indicated by the sentence: *von similîchir ginôzschaf vil michil was sîn hêrschaf* (181f.), a proof of the fact that lordship and relationship were interdependent concepts. See on this subject Walter Schlesinger in: Wege der Forschung 2, 135.
30. Walther Kotzenberg, p. 24. The oldest evidence, to my knowledge, for the inclusion of the term for retainer in the scale of lordship is in the *Vorauer Moses: einez daz ist edele, di hant daz hantgemahele. di andere frige lûte. di tragent sich mit gûte. di driten daz sint dinestman. also ich uirnomen han. darunder wurden chnehte. daz sint dev geslahte* (15, 2–7).
31. Unfortunately, these interesting instances have never been collected; some of them are in the *Deutsches Rechtswörterbuch* under *Dienstmann* (II,

906ff.) under the sub-heading "Latin forms"; others are to be found here and there in the literature on the *ministerialis* problem. According to Otto Imhof (*Die Ministerialität in den Stiftern Strassburg, Speier und Worms*, diss. Freiburg i. Br. 1912, p. 6) the German word apparently is to be found in a Strassburg document of 1070.

32. Philipp Heck, *Der Ursprung der sächsischen Dienstmannschaft*, VSWG. 5, 1907, 116–72, quotation from p. 125. But it should be pointed out that the Middle High German *ambetman, ambetliute* agree more closely with the technical meaning of *ministerialis, minister* than does *dienestman*. In Wolfram, for example, it always designates the bearers of offices at court (*Parzival* 667, 10; *Willehalm* 173, 15; 211, 19; 212, 6; 261, 19), while *dienestman* appears only in a general sense.

33. See Walther Kotzenberg, p. 45. In a non-genuine song of Reinmar we find: *ich was ie der dienest dîn* (176, 11). In Walther von der Vogelweide *dienstman* occurs once, in the *Spruch* 85, 17: *er sî dienstman oder frî* (85, 18); it is also found in one passage of Neidhart, the first instance in lyric of the transference of the retainer-concept to the love relationship: *sî endarf mîn niht ze dienestmanne jehen* (95, 16). It is not until the lyric of the thirteenth century that this usage becomes more frequent. See Kotzenberg pp. 46ff; Paul Kluckhohn, ZfdA. 52, 135ff. As a result of this state of affairs, the conclusion of Kluckhohn's investigation "that the dependent situation of the lover towards his mistress in German *minnesang* is often depicted through the image of the *ministerialis* relationship" must be reexamined (ibid., p. 147).

34. Many instances are given by Walther Kotzenberg, pp. 18ff. and Paul Kluckhohn, pp. 125ff. Additional evidence from early Middle High German sources: Ava Leben Jesu 635; Litanei 807; Tr. Aegidius 1557; Tr. Silvester 517. The word is relatively common in the *Rolandslied* (seven instances), the *Kaiserchronik* (seventeen instances), Heinrich von Melk (five instances) and in *Salman*, whose extant form is late (eleven instances), but in Eilhart I have found only three (1472, 2021, 8341), in *Morant und Galie* two (2148, 3009), in *Lanzelet* three (8381, 8628, 8926) in Hartmann altogether eight (*Erst. Büchlein* 1568, *Erek* 6278, 6332, 6361, 9762, *Gregorius* 201, *Armer Heinrich* 5, Iwein 7477), in *Parzival* five (see Senn-Lehmann p. 37), in *Willehalm* two (211, 18; 463, 18), in Gottfried four (see Valk, p. 14), in Herbort von Fritzlar, if I have counted correctly, eight (228, 1231, 2347, 2557, 2696, 3947, 4201, 6237), in *Wigalois* six (4829, 8615, 8713, 9308, 9676, 9856). In the post-classical epic it is more frequent only in Rudolf von Ems; he uses it nine times in *Der gute Gerhard*, ten in *Barlaam* and then always as a religious metaphor, in *Willehalm*, fourteen, in *Alexander*, six, and in the *Weltchronik* (apart from the continuation), twenty-seven. In Türheim's *Rennewart* I have counted eight instances (443, 3122, 3136, 3811, 12693, 13391, 19090, 31518), in Stricker's *Daniel* two, 5987, 6053)., in Türlin's *Krone* two (20426, 28138), two in Holle's *Demantin* (335, 8875), and one in Holle's *Crane* (4680).

35. Thus Walther Kotzenberg; "Courtly epic is, in its beginning, feudal . . . The poet of *Graf Rudolf* and Freiherr von Veldeke had never mentioned *di-*

enestman, the *ministeriales* Hartmann and Wolfram, Meister Gottfried and their successors use the word frequently . . .'' (p. 49; see also p. 32). The second part of this statement has already been contradicted by Paul Kluckhohn (p. 127). The first part is also wrong; Veldeke uses *dienestman* eight times in the *Servatius* (see the glossary in the Frings-Schieb edition). Incidentally, surely no one believes nowadays that Veldeke was a Freiherr.

36. Paul Kluckhohn, p. 127.

37. Paul Kluckhohn points to the numerous instances of *dienestman* in *Wolfdietrich* and concludes: "Thus the *Dienstmannen* play a major role in the so-called *Volksepos* earlier than they do in the courtly epics" (p. 127). In fact, *Wolfdietrich* A, with twelve instances of *dienestman*, is an interesting case. It is the only epic of our period in which the word *dienestman* is more common than *ritter* or one of the old *Heldenwörter*. In this, however, I see not a typical feature of the so-called *Volksepos*, rather something due to the lateness of the manuscripts. After the middle of the thirteenth century *dienestman* appears to become generally more frequent. See Walther Kotzenberg p. 50. In the *Münchener Oswald* it appears twenty times.

38. Walther Kotzenberg p. 23; Paul Kluckhohn, p. 126. In precourtly poetry the religious usage is predominant and not only in religious texts. In the *Kaiserchronik*, ten of seventeen instances are religious metaphors, in the *Rolandslied*, six out of seven. In the classical period this use is rare, e.g. Gottfried 6885, *Willehalm* 463, 18, but in post-classical epic, especially in Rudolf von Ems, it again becomes very common.

39. Paul Kluckhohn p. 126; AKG. 11, 398ff. It is noteworthy that the courtly metaphor is employed not only in regard to ladies but also to men, e.g. *Iwein* 7477; Gottfried 6549. The earliest instance of *dienestman* of a *vrouwe* that I know of is in Hartmann's *Erstes Büchlein* 1568.

40. See Walther Kotzenberg pp. 36ff.

41. Ibid., pp. 34ff.

42. First in the *Roland* 8906: *er were fri oder dinist man*. Similarly *Morant* 2148, 3009 and *Willehalm* 211, 18: *der dienestman und der vrîe*. I see no difference here, whereas Paul Kluckhohn (pp. 126f.) classifies the *Roland* example as "class designation" and writes of the three great epic authors that "none of the three ever uses [the word] as a class designation, even though he also cites the *Willehalm* passage.

43. Walther Kotzenberg p. 13; similarly on p. 11.

44. Ibid. p. 13, note 22; the instances cited there from the earlier period contain only parts of Kotzenberg's order of ranking.

45. Similarly in the description of the tournament at Friesach; *fürsten, grâven, frîen gar hân ich genant, swaz ir kom dar; nu nenn ich iu die dienestman* (192, 1–3), and after a long listing of retainers there follows: *nu nenne ich iu die ritter gar* (200, 1); finally they are all summarized under the formula *herren unde ritter* (201, 1).

46. Walther Kotzenberg p. 39.

47. See Otto von Zallinger pp. 41ff., Paul Kluckhohn pp. 130f.; *Deutsches Rechtswörterbuch* II, 913.

48. See August von Fürth pp. 24ff.; Georg Waitz V, 428ff.; Otto von Zallinger

pp. 12ff.; Paul Kluckhohn pp. 15ff.; Erich Molitor pp. 6ff.; Karl Bosl, VSWG. 39, 197ff.

49. Roth von Schreckenstein, *Ritterwürde* p. 157.
50. Karl Bosl, VSWG. 39, 289.
51. In Trier the *ministeriales* are called *milites* as early as 1135 (see Josef Bast p. 82), in Bamberg "from 1179 on" (Franz Joetze Hist. Jb 36, 533), in the foundations of the Upper Rhine apparently as early as the beginning of the eleventh century (see Otto Imhof pp. 13f.), in documents from Köln not until 1219 (see Jakob Ahrens, *Die Ministerialität in Köln und am Niederrhein*, Leipziger historische Abhandlungen 9, Leipzig, 1908, p. 90), and in St Gallen too, from the beginning of the thirteenth century on (see Emil Müller, *Die Ministerialität im Stift St. Gallen und in Landschaft und Stadt Zürich*, diss. Freiburg i. Br., 1911, pp. 68f.) I was unable to obtain François L. Ganshof, *Etude sur les "ministeriales" en Flandre et en Lotharingie*, Brussels, 1926.
52. See Julius Ficker, *Reichsfürstenstand* II 1, 223ff.: August von Fürth p. 68; Otto von Zallinger p. 19; Paul Kluckhohn p. 77, pp. 130f.; Karl Fajkmajer ZdFTV. 52, 125 and 133; Josef Bast p. 96; Franz Joetze, Hist. Jb. 36, 772f.; Karl Poth, *Die Ministerialität der Bischöfe von Münster*, Zeitschrift für vaterländische Geschichte und Altertumskunde 70 (1912), 1–108, esp. p. 72; Rudolf His, *Zur Rechtsgeschichte des thüringischen Adels*, Zeitschrift des Vereins für thüringische Geschichte und Altertumskunde N.F. 14 (1904), 1–35, esp. p. 9.
53. Paul Kluckhohn p. 129.
54. Ibid. p. 50.
55. Erich Molitor p. 37.
56. Ibid. p. 37.
57. Franz Joetze, Hist. Jb. 36, 520.
58. Gustav Köhler III 2, 64.
59. Josef Bast p. 51.
60. Edited by F. Frensdorff, *Das Recht der Dienstmannen des Erzbischofs von Köln*, Mittheilungen aus dem Stadtarchiv von Köln, I 2 (1883), 1–69; text pp. 4–10.
61. Ibid., p. 5.
62. Ibid., p. 9.
63. Ibid., pp. 9f.
64. In the list of witnesses from two documents from Strassburg from the beginning of the thirteenth century, the terms *ex ordine ministerialium* and *ex ordine militum* are used for the same group of people (see Otto Imhof p. 13). It has long been recognized in investigations into the terminology of the sources that the words *miles* and *ministerialis* stand for one and the same thing and hence are interchangeable (See Julius Ficker, *Reichsfürstenstand* II i, 218; Roth von Schreckenstein, *Ritterwürde* p. 335; Josef Bast pp. 51f.; Franz Joetze Hist. Jb. 36, 533f.; Emil Müller pp. 7f. Erich Molitor: "In fact the two expressions were also very frequently interchanged with one another" (p. 37). In spite of this, even later studies have clung to the special "ritter" interpretation of the "miles" titles. This

can be explained only by assuming that the doctrine of the Hohenstaufen knightly class was regarded as untouchable.

65. F. Frensdorff paraphrases the "miles fuerit" as follows: "the younger son, who has exercised himself in knightly arms . . ." (MStK. I 2, 19). This meaning emerges even more clearly in the shorter version of the old Köln service law, which is also from the second half of the twelfth century (ed., Heinrich von Loesch, *Das kürzere Kölner Dienstmannenrecht*, ZRG. GA. 44, 1924, 298–307, text pp. 298–307). In this version the sentence *Quicumque frater suus miles fuerit* . . . is replaced by *Cum ministerialis sancti Petri primo miles effectus fuerit* . . . (#1, p. 298). This short version was translated into German after the middle of the thirteenth century (ed., F. Frensdorff MStK. I 2, 39–45; dating ibid., pp. 45ff.; Heinrich von Loesch p. 300), and there the passage runs; *As sente Peters dienztman van eirste ritter wirt* . . . (#1, p. 39); *ritter werden* here means nothing more than reaching the age at which weapons could be worn.

66. See Richard Schröder pp. 472ff.; Georg von Below, *Ministerialität* in: *Handwörterbuch der Staatswissenschaften*, 3. ed. Jena, 1910, VI, 710–14. Erich Molitor speaks of "a unified class of *ministeriales*" (p. 49), Friedrich Keutgen of a "class limited by inheritance and law" (VSWG. 8, 486), F. Frensdorff of a "class limited by birth" (MStK. I 2, 20), etc.

67. Individual researches provide many instances of this. The term here produced *comes* from a document of 1257 cited in Erich Molitor, p. 95. Werner Wittich's theory (*Altfreiheit und Dienstbarkeit des Uradels in Niedersachsen*, VSWG. 4, 1906, 1–127), according to which the *ministerialis* class was substantially created by the entry of free elements, has been generally rejected. See Friedrich Keutgen, VSWG. 8, 9ff. Nowadays opinions are sharply divided on the extent and significance of such transitions, most recently the sharply critical remarks on the subject by Karl Bosl I, 27.

68. Karl Bosl in: Gebhardt's *Handbuch* I, 633.

69. Hermann Aubin, *Die Verwaltungsorganisation des Fürstbistums Paderborn im Mittelalter*, Abhandlungen zur Mittleren und Neueren Geschichte 26 (Berlin-Leipzig, 1911), p. 2.

70. See F. Frensdorff, MStK I 2, 23ff.: Richard Fressel, *Das Ministerialenrecht der Grafen von Tecklenburg, Ein Beitrag zur Verfassungs- und Ständegeschichte des Mittelalters*. Diss. (Münster, 1907), pp. 14ff.

71. In a document of 1291 from Bamberg we find: *Nullus clericus vel ministerialis cuiuscunque status, nominis et condicionis* (see Franz Joetze, Hist. Jb. 36, 540). As late as the fourteenth century there are in Magdeburg *ministeriales . . . duplicis generis* with varying legal classification (see Erich Molitor p. 39). Instances of *meliores, optimi, optimates* among the *ministeriales* in Georg Waitz V, 441f. See also Jakob Ahrens p. 37 ("The gap between the higher and lower *ministeriales*"); Otto Haendle, *Die Dienstmannen Heinrichs des Löwen, Ein Beitrag zur Frage der Ministerialität*, Arbeiten zur deutschen Rechts- und Verfassungsgeschichte 8, Stuttgart 1930, p. 76 ("Separation of the class into an upper and a lower stratum"); Karl Freiherr von Schowingen, *Zum Ministerialenproblem: Eine Reichen-*

auer Urkunde von 1363, ZRG. GA. 61, 1941, 274–82, esp. pp. 280f. ("double *ministerialis* condition"); Friedrich Keutgen, VSWG. 8, 171f.; Karl Bosl II, 606f.; Karl Schumacher, *Die Dienstmannschaft der rheinischen Stifter und Abteien und die Klosterreformen*, Beiträge zur Geschichte des Niederrheins 25, 1912, 66–78, esp. p. 67.

72. Friedrich von Klocke, *Untersuchungen zur Rechts- und Sozialgeschichte der Ministerialitäten in Westfalen*, Westfälische Forschungen 2, 1939, 214–32, quotation p. 216, n. 9. "Actually one and the same domain could very well have knightly and peasant *ministeriales* at the same time, naturally with different duties, different laws, and different social position" (ibid., p. 220, note 35).

73. Eberhard F. Otto, p. 231. The principal theses of Otto's book have been in part sharply rejected. See Ulrich Stutz, *Zum Wesen und Ursprung des niederen Adels*, Sitzungsberichte der Preussischen Akademie der Wissenschaften, Jahrgang 1937, phil.-hist. Kl., no. 27 Berlin 1937, 213–57. Nevertheless his criticism of the class-unity of the *ministeriales* has been taken up again in recent research. See Herbert Helbig, *Der wettinische Ständestaat, Untersuchungen zur Geschichte des Ständewesens und der landständischen Verfassung in Mitteldeutschland bis 1485*, Mitteldeutsch Forschungen 4, Münster-Köln, 1955, p. 280; Karl Bosl in: Vorträge und Forschungen 5, 82 emphasizes that "it is impossible to talk about *one* service law or *one* class of *ministeriales* . . . There are types differentiated socially, legally, and politically, there are classes of *ministeriales* which are fully developed, half developed, and underdeveloped but there is no ideal type."

74. To say that the *ministeriales* "were as a rule poor" (Arno Borst, Saecul. 10, 223) is appropriate only of the lower strata of retainers. Conclusions should not be drawn from the way in which Wolfram and Walther lived, since it is impossible to show that either of them belonged to the *ministeriales*.

75. Hans Naumann, *Deutsche Kultur* p. 1; most recently Jean-Pierre Ritter: "an enormous juridical and social revolution" (p. 112).

76. Karl Bosl II, 616.

77. The thesis of the free origin of the *ministeriales*, first proposed by Georg Caro (*Zur Geschichte der Grundherrschaft in der Nordostschweiz*, in: G.C., Beiträge zur älteren deutschen Wirtschafts- und Verfassungsgeschichte, Ges. Aufsätze, Leipzig, 1905, 78–100, esp. pp. 95ff.) and later defended by Eberhard F. Otto (pp. 216ff.) in an extreme form, has been rejected again and again. Nevertheless, it has not been without influence on research. The problem has taken a new turn through the work of Heinrich Dannenbauer, *Königsfreie und Ministerialen*, in: Grundlagen . . . (see above p. 204, n. 42), 329–53. On this subject see Karl Bosl in: Vorträge und Forschungen 5, 69ff.

78. On the medieval concept of freedom, see the collection *Das Problem der Freiheit in der deutschen und schweizerischen Geschichte*, ed., Theodor Mayer, Vorträge und Forschungen 2, Lindau-Konstanz (1955); further Karl

Bosl, *Freiheit und Unfreiheit, zur Entwicklung der Unterschichten in Deutschland und Frankreich während des Mittelalters*, VSWG. 44, 1957, 193–219, who speaks of "free bondage" (ibid., p. 210), the reverse of the expression "unfree nobility" (e.g., Eberhard F. Otto p. 11).

79. Karl Bosl I, 28; see Paul Kluckhohn p. 18; Hans-Walter Klewitz, *Geschichte der Ministerialität im Elsass bis zum Ende des Interegnums*, Schriften der wissenschaftlichen Institut der Elsass-Lothringer im Reich an der Universität Frankfurt, Frankfurt, 1929, p. 8.

80. Eberhard F. Otto, p. 221; see Georg Caro, Beiträge p. 98.

81. See Georg Waitz V, 331; Richard Schröder p. 474; Ernst Mayer II, 192f.; Paul Kluckhohn p. 48.

82. See Karl H. Ganahl: "The large amount of landed property owned by the church demanded on the one hand administration by an organized bureaucracy and on the other provided the economic basis for the formation of a military vassal establishment" (p. 152, similarly p. 175). Karl Fajkmajer points in the same direction: "The *ministeriales* within the households of great foundations seem to have been employed to by far the greatest extent in economic administration" (ZdFTV 52, 116, note 1). Fajkmajer points out that the split within the *ministeriales* is to be attributed to the fact "that a separation took place between episcopal mensal properties and the property of cathedral chapters; as a result the officials had to be separated too (ibid. p. 119). The importance of the *ministeriales* for local administration is stressed in all detailed research studies, especially by Friedrich Keutgen: "The *ministeriales* are to be explained by the fact that owners of domains needed a staff of officials whose position involved a high degree of independence and trust and this raised them far above the mass of dependents and petty officials" (VSWG. 8, 546).

83. Friedrich Keutgen emphasizes the connection between the condition of *ministerialis* and enfiefment: "My thesis on the contrary is that certain services were regularly connected with the receipt of a fief from the beginning; those entrusted with them had a claim to a fief and it is here that the *ministeriales* are distinguished from the lower office-holders" (VSWG. 8, 505; similarly pp. 508f.); see also Heinrich Mitteis, *Lehnrecht* pp. 446f.; Hans-Walter Klewitz p. 27; Erich Molitor p. 31. There is evidence for fiefs and ownership by *ministeriales* as early as the eleventh century. See Karl Fajkmajer, ZdFTV. 52, 112 ("at the time of their first appearance"); Jakob Ahrens, p. 57 ("almost from the beginning"); Josef Bast, pp. 75f.; Otto Imhof, pp. 59 and 67; Erich Molitor, pp. 166ff.; and also Jean-Pierre Ritter, pp. 57ff.

84. Karl Bosl I, 29; see Georg Caro; "Service to his lord, at court in the administration of his property, and in the field forms the basis of the social position of the retainer" (*Beiträge* p. 97) and Edmund F. Stengel in: Festschrift P. Kehr, pp. 174f. On "service, freedom, freedom of movement as motives in social advancement," see Karl Bosl, VSWG. 47, 306ff.

85. See Karl Bosl: "the special nature of service" (II, 615).

86. See Karl Bosl, VSWG. 39, 203f. "The new formation of the class of

ministeriales is, however, only a repetition of a procedure which had been going on in Germany and among the Germanic peoples for a thousand years, whenever the time was favorable" (Karl Bosl, VSWG. 47, 315).

87. See Otto von Zallinger pp. 41ff.

88. See Dietrich von Gladiss, *Beiträge zur Geschichte der staufischen Reichsministerialität*, Hist. Stud. 249 (Berlin, 1934), pp. 8f.

89. The imperial *ministeriales* in southwest Germany who could escape local rule later provided the germ of imperial knighthood. The peasant *ministeriales* and the retainers in the lower town offices took no part whatsoever in the formation of the class. See Friedrich Keutgen, VSWG. 8, 172; Otto von Dungern, *Herrenstand*, p. 216: "The *ministeriales*, who, until the end of the thirteenth century, never had property which could support a family living in aristocratic style, never became nobles."

90. The "noble" status of the knights of the late Middle Ages should not be thought of too highly. "Originally they did not live in castles but 'fortified houses' on 'gentlemen's seats . . . A knight or noble retainer who lived on a domain of some sixty yokes of arable land had an income scarcely higher than that of the upper strata of the peasantry" (Otto Brunner, *Zwei Studien zum Verhältnis von Bürgertum und Adel* in: Neue Wege . . . [see above p. 189, n. 33], 116–54, quotation p. 138. See also Otto Brunner, *Land und Herrschaft* p. 343; Herbert Klein, MdGfSL. 80, 118; Karl Bosl in: Gebhardt's *Handbuch* I, 617.

91. *Sachwörterbuch zur deutschen Geschichte*, s.v. *Rittertum, Ritterstand* p. 1065; see also Friedrich Heer, *Die Tragödie des heiligen Reiches* Stuttgart 1952, p. 271: "The courtly world of 1180 to 1220 is based essentially on the sociological dynamics of the new German nobility," in which the *ministeriales* are understood to be included.

92. Friedrich Keutgen, VSWG. 8, 515. Many differences between individual retainerships are to be explained by the different ranks of the domain-holders. See Julius Ficker, *Reichsfürstenstand* II 1, 226; Paul Kluckhohn, p. 42; Karl Bosl, VSWG. 39, 209.

93. Hermann Aubin calls attention to the small monastery of Böddeken, which paid money to its own steward to influence him to exercise his duties not more than three times a year: "it could not afford more frequent visits" (p. 51). There is evidence everywhere of disputes between lords spiritual and their *ministeriales*. In *Die Ministerialen der Abtei Fulda*, ZRG. 66, KA. 35 (1948), 201–33, Konrad Lübeck gives a vivid picture of the situation which admittedly remains one-sided in the sense that the conduct of the *ministeriales* is explained simply as the result of "insatiable greed" and "a powerful hunger for land" (p. 209). The conditions in Brixen are very interesting; here the Graf von Tirol played off the bishop against his *ministeriales*. "This clever policy made the most important contribution . . . to the development of the dominant position in the region of the Graf von Tirol" (Karl Fajkmajer, ZdFTV. 52, 162f.).

94. See Erich Molitor p. 33; Franz Joetze, Hist. Jb. 36, 755, etc.

95. Most recently this has been shown in the case of Meissen: Harald Schieckel, *Herrschaftsbereich und Ministerialität der Markgrafen von Meissen im 12.*

und 13 Jahrhundert, Untersuchungen über Stand und Stammort der Zeugen markgräflicher Urkunden, Mitteldeutsche Forschungen 7, Köln-Graz, 1956; see also Hermann Aubin, p. 1; Hans Walter Klewitz, p. 42; Erich Molitor p. 40; pp. 195f.; Karl H. Genahl, p. 182; Karl Bosl II, 620ff.

96. Josef Bast, p. 51.
97. Franz Joetze, Hist. Jb. 36, 760.
98. Paul Kluckhohn, p. 143.
99. Romanticism already regarded knights as "free and noble" (Johann G. Büsching II, 263), and not a great deal has changed. Recent research also calls "nobility and knightly class the same thing" (Hans Neumann, *Deutsche Kultur*, p. 2): "The medieval noble class was determined by knighthood. Nobility and knighthood gradually merged into one. Membership of the knightly class conferred nobility" (Hermann Conrad, *Rechtsgeschichte* I, 394). On the concept of aristocratic knighthood and the *ministeriales'* share in it, see the next section.
100. Roth von Schreckenstein, *Reichsritterschaft* I, 161.
101. This question is at the center of the sharp controversy between Otto von Dungern and Aloys Schulte. Otto von Dungern was of the opinion that "the lower nobility and *ministeriales* are to be equated as early as the period around the mid-twelfth century and later" (*Herrenstand* p. 354). Aloys Schulte on the other hand emphasized: "I believe that, about 1300, the class of retainers was regarded as noble but about 1200 the lower members of the masses of freemen still ranked higher than retainers, except for a few imperial *ministeriales*" (*Der Adel und die deutsche Kirche im Mittelalter, Studien zur Sozial-, Rechts-, und Kirchengeschichte*, 3. ed. Darmstadt, 1958, pp. 21f.); see Otto von Dungern, Rez. Schulte, MIÖG. 32, 1911, 506–16; Aloys Schulte, *Zur Geschichte des hohen Adels*, MIÖG. 34, 1913, 43–81. There is no doubt that Aloys Schulte was literally correct in this question of dating; Otto von Dungern later corrected his opinion: "Not until the thirteenth century does the change take place. Some powerful families of retainers . . . did succeed in moving upward into the circle of the successors of formerly dynastic families" (*Adelsherrschaft*, p. 59). Nowadays, since the question is no longer of decisive importance, it is rather the common ground in the work of Schulte and Dungern which is recognized and both are revered as pioneers of the new concept of the medieval aristocratic state.
102. On the lower Rhine "a distinction was made at least until the end of the thirteenth century . . . between *ministeriales* and free vassals" (Jakob Ahrens, p. 89); the same in Trier (see Josef Bast, p. 88). In southeast Germany this distinction was alive "even as late as the fourteenth century" (Paul Kluckhohn p. 121), in Switzerland to the end of the fourteenth century (see Emil Müller p. 72) and in Münster also to the end of the fourteenth century (see Karl Poth, ZfvGA. 70, 77). On the upper Rhine "the distinction between *nobiles* and *ministeriales* is demonstrable for the last time . . . in 1406" (Otto Imhof, p. 87). There is much evidence that this separation was not a mere legal fiction but had practical effects on the arranging of marriages, the sale of property etc. I was not able to obtain

the work of Karl Weimann, *Die Ministerialität im späteren Mittelalter* (Leipzig, 1924).

103. Karl Bosl I, 27; similarly II, 605.

104. "Even though life-style and ideals of conduct . . . brought the two classes of upper nobility and *ministeriales* closer together, they could not bridge the legal differences in property- and marriage-law and in social structure. It is therefore misleading to speak of a unified knightly class" (Erich Freiherr von Guttenberg, Rez. Winterswyl, DA. 3, 1939, 291–92, quote on p. 291).

105. The dependence of the knight is shown most clearly by the possessive pronoun or the possessive genitive. Paul Guilhiermoz calls attention to "the innumerable texts in which *miles* and *chevalier* occur with a possessive (*miles noster, miles alicuius*)" (p. 345); see also Hans Kuhn, Ark. 58, 105f. Emphatic possessives of the type *mîn herre Gâwein* and the instances of *sîne ritterschaft* = "seine ritterliche Tüchtigkeit" (his chivalric capability) are not counted. The position of the possessive pronoun before or after the word *ritter* is not indicated; no distinction is made between singular and plural.

106. Where the possessive pronoun refers to a lady, the figures are in italics.

107. Instances of the type *der Kriechen ritterschaft* are not included, nor are *gotes ritter-(schaft), des tiuvels ritter-(schaft)*; the spelling of *ritter, ritterschaft* has been normalized.

108. In formulaic juxtapositions of knights with other groups of persons, it is sometimes the connective element which dominates, sometimes the divisive, e.g., *ritter unde vrouwen* as against *ritter unde pfaffen*. In principle, only the stereotype, simple pairings are included, not juxtapositions of a more individualized nature, but an exact distinction is not easy to make. In instances of the type *die ritter und die vrouwen* no note is taken of the case. The spelling is normalized.

V. The Noble Knights

1. August von Fürth, p. 70.

2. Even in precourtly poetry the words for "hero" were largely synonymous. Continuing shades of meaning have been traced into the classical period by Alfred Riemen, *passim*.

3. For example, in the *Vorauer Alexander: si chômen mit funzich tüsint chnehten, die wole getorsten vehten* (1453f.); and in the *Annolied: Da vanter inne . . . Manigin helit güdin, Die dere burg huhdin. Wiliche Knechti dir werin . . .* (XX, 3. 5–7). But this is not a common usage in the classical period.

4. The emperor can be called *knecht* only in relation to God, e.g., Roland 3055, 7004. Later the word also designates an aristocratic lord who has not yet been initiated into the bearing of arms.

5. Edward Schröder writes that *guoter knecht* "disappears . . . at the begin-

ning of the thirteenth century (ZfdA. 65, 295f.). I do not know whether that is to be taken literally; the list above on pp. 19ff. shows that the expression is still to be found in Holle's *Crane*. See also Paul Kluckhohn, p. 139, n. 5.

6. From the beginning decorative epithets are attached to *ritter: ritter gemeit, ritter guot, edeler ritter, stolzer ritter* (see Appendix 1 to this section), without at first influencing the meaning of the word.

7. In the course of this the further development of an old ethical vocabulary was stunted. Derivatives of *degen* and *kneht* which are not uncommon in Old High German texts and glosses appear only rarely in Middle High German: *degenheit* (Himml. Jerusalem 454; Rother 762, 1307; Kaiserchronik 11740; Melk Prl. 157; Eilhart 1671; Graf Rudolf F 26; Eneit 201, 2; Athis F 111; Nibelungenlied 108, 1; Herzog Ernst B 7; Ems Weltchronik 30865); *degenschaft* (Lanzelet 2588); *degenlich* (Ava Jesu 506; Vorauer Moses 54, 29; Jg. Judith 174, 18; Graf Rudolf B^b 14; Erek 8542; Nibelungenlied 500, 2, 2077, 2 [C], 2084, 2 [C]; Christoph 1104; Ems, Weltchronik 20255, 30866); *degenlîche* (Roland 8511; Nibelungenlied 102, 2, 204, 4, 236, 3 [A], 2209, 2; Klage 1235; Lanzelet 6281; Herzog Ernst B 5146; Türlin Krone 4621); *knehtheit* (Roland 7793; Kaiserchronik 4605, 13852); *knehtlîche* (Jg. Judith 178, 23; Litanei S 28; Eneit 193, 7). The legacy was taken over by the derivatives of *ritter*.

8. In the Vienna and Vorau versions, Poiphar is never called anything but "herre.": *si uerchouften in sâre zu eineme herren hiez Putifâr* (Wiener Genesis 3675f.; Vorauer Joseph 115).

9. See the variants to lines 4328 and 4331 in Hans F. Massmann's ed.

10. Because of Kinzel's misleading punctuation, there is one passage where the impression might be given that knights were counted among the princes. Darius assembles his army. (I give parallel passages from the Vorauer and Strassburg versions.)

die fursten wil ich zellen
unt die menige, diu mit samit in chom,
alsô Dario wol gezam . . .
ze zwein unde drîzech wâren sie gezalt
die chunige, die zim chômen,
dô si sine nôth vernâmen.
grâven chômen ime ouch.
zwei hundert unde sibenzoch
herzogen zim chêrten,
daz sich sine rîter mêrethen.
die zalt man, sô ich sicher bin,
zaht hundert unde trîn.

(Vor. 1434–36. 40–48)

gagen Dario quâmen gevaren
zwêne und drizich kuninge,
daz wizzit âne lugene,
di sine nôt vernâmen.
herzogen ime ouh quâmen
zwei hundrit unde sibinzich
unde dar zô manic grâbe rich,
di zô ime kêrten
und sine reise mêrten.
di quâmen alle mit gwalt.
di grâben wâren gezalt
rehte an eilif hundrit.

(Str. 1966–77)

Kinzel's punctuation is obviously based on the number of dukes: only when he connects line 1144 of the Vorauer text to the next line is the number the same in both versions. He also took note of the fact that the dukes in line 1143 are remarkably isolated. The Strassburg text, however, makes it clear that only kings, dukes, and counts are counted; there is not a word about knights. Thus the passage must be read as follows:

> *grâven chômen ime ouch*
> *zwei hundert unde sibenzoch.*
> *herzogen zim chêrten*
> *—daz sich sîne rîter mêrethen—,*
> *die zalt man, sô ich sicher bin,*
> *zaht hundert unde trîn.*
>
> (Vor. 1143–48)

What line 1146 says, therefore, is this: the Persian army was strengthened by the soldiers whom the dukes brought to the king, by *die menige diu mit samit in chom* (1135). Lists of princes in which the counts appear before the dukes are occasionally to be found elsewhere: *künge, grâven, herzogen* (Parzival 5, 17); *der kunic . . . Siben grafen vier herzogen* (Herbort 4006/08). The person who reworked the Strassburg version changed the titles *grâven* and *herzogen* around and thus restored the normal order.

11. See Edward Schröder (''Zierde aller Reitersleute''), who regards this as ''the first glimmering of a new value for the word (ZdfA. 65, 295). The expression *aller ritter êre* is not uncommon in courtly literature: Erek 9674; Lanzelet 951; Parzival 209, 14; Türlin Krone 17002.

12. The main later tradition takes exception to this and writes: ''*daz man mich schôner unde baz haldit unde nicht en hazzet und mit zwênzig rittern vazzet, und gibit in ros unde pfert*'' (3592–95). The idea that anyone ''ze ritter vazzet'' a king's son was obviously strange to the remodelers. But otherwise the late tradition too uses the knight concept in the sense of the precourtly period. When Tristrant is disguised as a fool, he says: ''Ich bin ein ritter gût'' (8828) and this is the only passage where he is called ''ritter.'' A friend of Tristrant at Marks court is introduced as *der ritter ein* (7742) and is then called *der ritter* (7754, 7760, 7787, 7796); in the same way a second friend (7533); we are told nothing about their social standing. Delakors schevalier, who is called *ein ritter gut* (5059) is in any case a nobleman. Otherwise it is only the two men who are supposed to kill Brangaene who are called *ritter* (2873, 2876, 2886, 2902, 2909, 2959, 3001, 3022).

13. Here too the text is not completely above suspicion. In the Saganer A fragments the word *ritter* is missing at this point; there the lines run: *der helt wol kunde. aller slachte vrumekeit. er was zu aller zit gemeit* (75–77 S). But the B version reads: *ein ritter gemeit* (626); this argues for the genuineness of the Prague A text.

14. Ernst is there called *der helt* eleven times, *der degen* five times *der recke* twice, and *der wîgant* twenty-seven times but never simply *der ritter*. He is called (once each) *der ritter gemeit* (1216), *ein ritter gemeit* (626), *ein ritter vil tugentlîch* (1905). Altogether Ernst is called *ritter* three times, *helt* twenty-five times, *degen* nineteen times, *recke* twelve times and *wîgant* forty-four. No account is taken here of the two occasions where he and Wetzel are called *ritter* together (2645 and 2831).

15. There is another noble knight in the *Strassburger Alexander: ein rîter, der hîz Jubal . . . der was ein edele jungelinc* (1773, 76). This Jubal was a *rîter* as early as Lamprecht (1279, s. 1276): a Persian soldier who threatens Alexander in the battle. It was the person who reworked the Strassburg version who first raised him to the nobility.

16. At this same period *Graf Rudolf* remains completely unaffected by aristocratic knighthood. The word ritter occurs only once and refers to Rudolf's troops (δ 6). Rudolf himself is referred to as *greve* (often), as *vürste* (once), as *herre* (eight times), and he is designated by the old words for hero: *helt* (ten times), *degen* (twelve times), *recke* (once), and *wîgant* (once).

17. Nisus, who guards the castle gate, *was ein ritter gût, edile unde hêre* (181, 12f.); other than this we find out nothing about his origin. There is also *ritter Tarcûn ein harde hobesch Troiân unde ein ritter wol getân* (241, 2–4; see 242, 25), with no remark as to his social standing. It is said of the princess Camilla: *si gebârde als ein jungelink unde schûf selbe ir dink, als si ein ritter solde sîn* (147, 5–7) and *sî was gebalzieret als ein ritter lussam* (147, 16f.) but this refers not to her nobility but to her Amazon qualities.

18. Erek is addressed as *ritter* (4347, 9319, 9669), *edel ritter* (4803, 8813, 9325), *ritter guot* (4442), *ritter vil guot* (4738); Keiin as *ritter* (4747, 4770), *edel ritter* (4989); Guivreiz as *edel ritter* (8030), *ritter guot* (6946), *ritter biderbe unde guot* (4350). This form of address is mostly used only when it is not known who is inside the armor. But it does occur when Gawain says *edel ritter* in conversation with Keiin.

19. The proud expression *der ritter Erec* in particular never became established. It was in fact not a new term but one connected with older usage, for example, *riter putifar* in the *Millstätter Genesis*, *rîter Daclym* in the *Vorauer Alexander* (1299), *ritter Tarcûn* in the *Eneit*. The corresponding formula *der ritter Iwein* is no longer found in *Iwein*, and I have not been able to find a single instance in either *Wolfram* or *Gottfried*. The usage is rare in the late courtly epic too. In the *Nibelungenlied* there is one use of the form of address edel ritter Hagene (1535, 2).

20. *Iwein* is closest to *Erek*. In addressing individuals, the simple form *ritter* (six instances) is predominant over *edel ritter guot* (once). In the *Gregorius* the hero is called *ritter* both before and at his initiation (1499, 1503, 1647, 1649, 1654, 1665) but not after that. Later he practices with weapons for so long *daz er wesen kunde ritter swie man gerte, ze sper und ze swerte* (1986–88). Der arme Heinrich is never called *ritter*; only as a basis for comparison is it said of him that lacked no quality *die ein ritter . . . haben sol* (34f.) and that he endured abuse *als ein vrumer ritter sol* (1340).

21. Scarcely ten of the total of 113 instances of the use of *ritter* can be regarded as applying to aristocratic lords and in most cases they are designated as outstanding fighting men: Jason *wappente sich wol . . . Daz nie ritter gemeit. Zv strite baz was bereit* (1071, 73f.); *Troylus sich ane liez. Daz er ein gut ritter hiez . . . Er konde manigē gutē slac* (3185f. 89); of Prothesilaus *Man saget daz er do strite. So rechte ritterliche. Daz in deheime riche. Nie ritter baz gestreit* (4282–85). Jason is also called *der frume ritter* (119) and *ein ritter hubisz und gut* (880); *Hektor ein schone ritter brunfar*

(3174); Theseus *ein kindisch ritter . . . Vñ iedoch ein kvne degen* (5420f.) Achilles is addressed as *edel ritter* (11914), Diomedes as *ritter* (9920). On the subject of Diomedes *frowen ritter* (9513), see below.

22. There are no aristocratic knights in *Athis*. The word is used only as a collective (A* 86, 104, 129, 141; A** 14; C* 31, 38, 136, F3) and once as a general expression *an rittirs prise gehoit* (D 86f.).

23. Flore is made *ze ritter* by the Amiral (7504); otherwise only as a collective (162, 401, 1407, 2131, 6510, 7526, 7634, 7651) or as a general expression (7514).

24. Wolfram is rather reticent in calling his hero Parzival "ritter." (I have not counted the passages in which Parzival is regarded as or designated as a knight by others; every unknown man in armor is called "ritter" in the courtly epic). Parzival calls himself "ritter" in recalling his initiation: "*mich hiez ein künec ritter sîn*" (163, 22); he is called *ritter* in relation to Cunneware (see below); throughout the Gawan books he is anonymously *der rôte ritter*; he is *aller ritter bluome* (109, 11), *schûr der rîterschefte* (678, 22); *ezn wart nie rîter baz getân* (695, 9); he displays *ritters site und ritters mâl* (179, 14), he *treit diu rîters mâl* (315, 10); *er tet ouch ritters ellen schîn* (1966, 22); but nowhere does the poet call him simply "knight." On the other hand Gahmuret is called *unser rîter* (16, 19) in the easy-going narrative plural and *der ritter* (33, 11; 95, 28); in the same way Ither (154, 27), Gawan (574, 7 and 15). Kingrimursel is *ein rîter* (319, 21; 415, 29) the king of Gascony *ein rîter kluoc* (72, 26), King Schirniel and his brother *zwên ritter snel* (354, 19), Gramolflanz *ein rîter clâr* (604, 9), Beakurs *der clâre rîter* (722, 12). In the *Titurel* the word is used only as a collective (11, 1; 30, 4) and in a general sense (50, 4; 133, 4). In the prayer in the prolog, Wolfram calls his hero *ein ritter* (2, 27), but the designation does not occur later, except once as a basis for comparison: *ê wart nie rîter baz gezogen und âne valsch sô kurtoys* (153, 16f.). When Willehalm says to people to whom he is unknown: "*ich pin ein rîter, als ir seht* (113, 1), the designation "ritter" refers to his equipment. Graf Milon is *ein rîter* (413, 9); two heathen kings *wâren rîter als guot, gein strîte rehte flinse* (76, 6f.); it is said of Arofel: *undr al dem Terramêres her was ninder bezzer rîter dâ* (78, 16f.)

25. Tristan is called "ritter" at his initiation (5024) and later at the battle with Morolt: *sit do er uf daz ors gesaz . . . do was der ritter lobelich* (6694 and 6697). In the fight with the giant Urgan he is *der ritter* from Urgan's point of view (15978, 16070). At the Irish court Tristan is turned out *also wol, als ein volmüete ritter sol* (10843f.). In Tristan's eyes King Mark is *zem sper und zem schilte ein ritter edel und uz erkorn* (10510). As in Wolfram, (Parzival 123, 21) "ritter" is used only once in Gottfried as a term of address: Isolde uses it to Tristan the Dragon-slayer (9464).

26. At the initiation of Gunther's son it is said: *man machete rîter daz kint* (4363). Otherwise the word occurs only as a collective: (394, 502, 852, 2855, 3208[B] = 3209[C]; there are three other instances in B and two in C (2570, 3078, 3620 and 60, 4563). The old terms are kept for the great figures of the destruction of the Burgundians: *helt, degen, recke, wîgant*.

27. "In Wolfram's *Parcival* we encounter a completely unified knightly class" (Paul Kluckhohn p. 9).
28. See K.-J. Hollyman pp. 129ff. Wilhelm Homuth (*Vom Einfluss des Lehnwesens und Rittertums auf den französischen Sprachschatz, Bedeutungsgeschichtliche Untersuchungen*, Romanische Forschungen 39, 126, 201–66) explains "chevalier" as a "neologism created at the rise of medieval knighthood" (p. 215).
29. K.-J. Hollyman p. 134. "The knight stands before us finished, perfect, splendid in the oldest version of the *Chanson de Roland*" (Léon Gautier p. 28); see also Georges Gougenheim "*De "chevalier" à "cavalier"*" in: *Mélanges de philologie romane et de littérature médiévale offerts à Ernest Hoepffner*, Publications de la faculté des lettres de l'université de Strasbourg, fasc. 113 (Paris, 1949), 117–126.
30. See the chapters "Chevalerie et chevaliers dans les chansons de geste" and "La Chevalerie dans le roman courtois" in Gustav Cohen pp. 43ff. and 69ff. The material on knights in the *Chansons* laid the groundwork for Léon Gautier's great exposition.
31. See Martin Hellweg, *Die ritterliche Welt in der französischen Geschichtsschreibung des vierten Kreuzzugs*, Romanische Forschungen 52, 1938, 1–40, esp. pp. 10 and 36ff.
32. As well as in the works already mentioned in note 30 above, material on the subject may be found in: Hugo Oschinsky, *Der Ritter unterwegs und die Pflege der Gastfreundschaft im Alten Frankreich*. Diss. (Halle, 1900); Ernst Rust, *Die Erziehung des Ritters in der altfranzösischen Epik*. Diss. (Berlin, 1888); Wilhelm Heidsiek, *Die ritterliche Gesellschaft in den Dichtungen des Chrestien de Troyes* (Greifswald, 1883).
33. The old theory of Paul Guilhiermoz that there was no nobility in France which was determined on socio-legal grounds until after the formation of knighthood, and that the concepts *chevalerie, noblesse, liberté* and *vassalité* were thereafter identical (see in particular pp. 370ff and 462ff.) was essentially supported by Marc Bloch (II, 58ff.) and by Ferdinand Lot: "In the tenth century vassality, knighthood, and nobility merged. A single term designates them all: *chevalerie* (knighthood) (*L'art militaire* II, 421). In recent research, on the other hand, objections have been raised by various people. There is a judicious rejection by Robert Boutruche, *Seigneurie et féodalité*, Vol. I, Collection historique (Paris, 1959), p. 189. The equation *chevalerie = vassalité* is disputed by Georges Duby, *La société aux XIe et XIIe siècles dans la region mâconnaise*, Bibliothèque générale de l'école pratique des hautes études, sect. VI (Paris, 1953), pp. 233f. The identification of *chevalerie* and noblesse is opposed by P. Bonefant and G. Despy, *La noblesse en Brabant aux XIIe et XIIIe siècles, Quelques sondages*, Le Moyen Age 64, 1958, 27–66: "Nobility, in its origins, was independent of knighthood" (p. 36). Léopold Génicot's essays point in the same direction: *De la "noblesse" au "lignage," Le Cas des Boneffe*, Revue belge de philologie et d'histoire 31 (1953), 39–53; *Le destin d'une famille noble du Namurois, Les Novilles aux XIIe et XIIIe siècles*, Annales de la société archéologique de Namur 46 (1953), 157–232; *Sur les origines*

de la noblesse dans le Namurois, Tijdschrift voor Rechtsgeschiedenis 20 (1952), 143–56; *La noblesse au XIIe siècle dans la région de Gembloux*, VSWG. 44 (1957), 97–104.

34. Arno Borst, Saecul. 10, 223f. stresses the different social structure of knighthood in France and Germany.

35. Instances in Georg Waitz V, 436f.; Roth von Schreckenstein, *Ritterwûrde* p. 292, n. 4; Paul Guilhiermoz pp. 343f.; Otto von Dungern, *Herrenstand* p. 346.

36. See Appendix 1 to this section.

37. On this see Paul Kluckhohn, AKG. 11, 402ff.

38. The word *ritterschaft*, the oldest derivative of *ritter*, shows the same tendency, although less clearly. The first instance is in the *Wiener Exodus: iz* (i.e., das Heer) *ne fuorte schilt noh daz swert, noh die hutten noh gezelt, helm noh die brunne, neheimer riterschephte wunne, in rossen noh in molen, in gereiten vile tiuren, noh den scaft noh den bogen . . .* 1343–49; = Millstätter Genesis 137, 17–20). It is not clear here whether *ritterschaft* means "group of knights" or "weapon-practice, battle-game". There is testimony for both meanings in the *Rolandslied*: among the pagans there is *tanz unde riterscaft unt ander manige hochuart* (287f.); and it is said of them: *habent si grozer riterscaft, got gibet uns urmare craft* (5811f.). Otherwise in the early period the collective meaning "a number of knights" is predominant (Rother 246; Kaiserchronik 110, 480, 4565, 4876; Melk Erinnerung 354, etc.). From the time of Veldeke's *Eneit* this meaning gives way to the new one "combat with knightly weapons." In the *Eneit* we find for the first time the terms *ritterschaft tuon* (143, 22 *et passim*), *ritterschaft üeben* (254, 23), *ritterschefte pflegen* (237, 27) *sich ritterschefte underwinden* (254, 18f.), *sich an ritterschaft kêren* (147, 24f.). These terms are found frequently later and for the most part are formed on French models (*feire chevalerie*, etc.). The reference to descent in Veldeke's *Servatius* is an isolated instance: *van sines vaderes siden was he van ridderscap geboren* (5276f.). Hartmann then developed the notion further, particularly in the *Gregorius*, whereas in the Arthurian romances he stayed on the path laid down in the *Eneit*. Now *ritterschaft* becomes a general term for an aristocratic lifestyle: *ritterschaft daz ist ein leben, der im die mâze kan gegeben, sô enmac nieman baz genesen* (Gregorius 1531–33). From there the word becomes a personal attribute and can designate the aristocratic-warrior nature of a man: *durch sîne ritterschaft und durch sîner übermüete kraft ist mîn veter zuo gevarn . . .* (Lanzelet 1715–17). It is in this sense that Gottfried speaks of the *ritterschaft* of Blanscheflur; *al ir trost und al ir craft, ir tuon und al ir ritterschaft, ir ere und al ir werdekeit, daz allez was do hin geleit* (1761–64).

39. Up to about 1180 there are nine instances each of *ritterlich* and *ritterlîche* (see above pp. 000f.). Up to the middle of the thirteenth century there are almost 500 instances of *ritterlich* and more than 350 of *ritterlîche*.

40. Edward Schröder translates: "The sword also is part of the equipment of a cavalryman and can also be used in a cavalry fight" (ZfDA. 65, 294). In my opinion the context does not justify the assumption of any special reference to a cavalry battle.

41. Further instances of the adjective in Appendix 2 to this section.

42. Similarly later: *dô nam Alexander sinen vanen und reit rîterlîche danen* (Strassburger Alexander 1887f.); *Enêas ime daz vergalt harde rîterlîche wider* (Eneit 211, 40f.); *gên im kam ritterlîche der herzoge* (Herzog Ernst B 5570f.), etc.

43. See Appendix 2 to this section.

44. Herzog Ernst and Wetzel *wârn sô ritterlîch gevar* in their equipment (Herzog Ernst B 2802); it is said of Parzival: *sin zimierde ist rîche: dez harnasch stuont rîterlîche* (Parzival 164, 21f.); similarly 447, 3f.); in the description of a castle: *ein ritterlîcher aneblic ziertez hûs innen* (Erek 7847f.), etc.

45. The text itself does not expressly state this, but when the messengers arrive at the king's court, people are amazed at their rich clothes. (222ff.).

46. In the *Eneit* there appear *funfzich ritter wol getân, schône unde lobesam . . . wol gezieret mit gewande und vil ritterlîche, wand si wâren rîche* (337, 7f., 12–14); Baron Gandin *kam schone gecleit mit ritterlicher schonheit* (Gottfried 13113f.); of Tristan: *sin geschepfede und sin wat die . . . bildeten under in zwein einen ritterlichen man* (11098–101); Gregorius asks: *"gebet mir ritterlîche wât"* (1559) and by this he means fine clothing. Hartmann mentions *cleider die nâch rîterlîchen siten sint gestalt ode gesniten* (Iwein 2814–16). It is said of Queen Camilla: *ir gewant al daz si trûch daz stunt ir ritterlîche* (Eneit 146, 34f.); and of Iblis: *ir roc was gezieret, wol gefischieret rîterlîche an ir lîp* (Lanzelet 5801–03); see also Nibelungenlied 66, 1; 276, 4(A); Parzival 148, 18; Ems Gerhard 2890, 3570f.). In Ulrich von Lichtenstein knightly clothing is specifically distinguished from equipment: *ich wart entwâpent snelle dâ, dar nâch vil ritterlîch gekleit* (Frauendienst 1435, 6f.).

47. It is said of Belacane: *si hete wîplîchen sin, und was abr anders rîterlîch, der touwegen rôsen ungelîch* (Parzival 24, 8–10); and of Herzeloyde: *dâ vor was si ritterlîch; ach wênc, daz wirt verkêret gar, si wirt nâch jâmer nu gevar* (104, 20–22). Girls are brought to Josaphat, *gestalt sô ritterlîche wol, daz des niemen wundern sol, ob ir volge ein junger man* (Ems, Barlaam 298, 29–31).

48. This also appears in expressions such as *daz dûhte den künec . . . ritterlich unde guot* (Stricker, Daniel 886f.); *diz dûhte s'alle ritterlich* (ibid., 2990); *ob er daz tuot, dêst ritterlîch* (Lichtenstein, Frauendienst 55, 8; similarly 1061, 7); *waz ich taete dâ, daz waere ritterlîch* (ibid. 213, 5/7); *dêswâr, daz was unritterlich* (Ems. Alexander 8315; similarly 11299), etc.

49. It is not even certain that the technical meaning "heavily armed cavalryman," which in many respects is the connecting link between the old horsed fighting man and the aristocratic knight, had actually become accepted before the word was taken into the aristocratic sphere.

50. In at least one of the early anonymous poems the terms "ritter" and "Frauendienst" are associated: *"mir hât ein ritter"* sprach ein wîp *"gedienet nâch dem willen mîn . . ."* (6, 5f.)

51. Paul Kluckhohn, ZfdA. 52, 149.

52. According to Heffner-Petersen, *Word-Index*, the words *wîgant, recke* and *kneht* do not occur at all in *Minnesangs Frühling*. *Degen* is found once in Spervogel (31, 2) and once in Rugge (98, 19), *helt* twice in Spervogel (20,

25; 21, 3), twice in Rugge (98, 22; 99, 3, with both these examples and the *degen* example in his *Kreuzleich*), and once in Pseudo-Dietmar (37, 25). On the other hand there are twenty-two examples of *ritter* in *Minnesangs Frühling*.

53. Also in Wolfram: *swelch ritter pflac der sinne, daz er dienst bôt nâch minne* (Parzival 639, 25f.); *bi ieslîchr (sc. vrouwe) ein rîter der ir pflac unt der sich diens dar bewac* (ibid. 670, 15f.); see also Parzival 26, 10; 368, 17f.; 440, 4ff.; 458, 6f.; 632, 15ff.; 811, 24; Titurel 30, 4; Craun 263ff.; Türheim Rennewart 27486; 31454f.; Pseudo-Hartmann, Minnesangs Frühling 214, 34ff. and especially frequently in Ulrich von Lichtenstein: XXXIV, 5, 6f; XXXVIII, 1, 1f.; XLIV, 6 5f.; Frauendienst 19, 4f.; 77, 4f.; 150, 3f.; 152, 6f.; 419, 6f.; 424, 4f.; 836, 2ff.; 1052, 7f.; 1388, 2ff.; 1389, 5ff.; Frd. 2. Büchl. 381ff.

54. Ampflise orders Gahmuret: *"du solt ouch mîn ritter sîn im lande ze Wâleis"* (Parzival 77, 8f.); he answers her messenger *"vart wider, sagt ir dienest mîn; ich sül iedoch ir ritter sin"* (98, 3f.); *aldâ wart von Gahmurete geleistet Ampflîsens bete, daz er ir ritter waere* (78, 17–19). Parzival serves Cunneware as knight: 284, 7; 305, 16f. In *Willehalm* the queen has to allow it to be said to her that *Tybalt der Arâboys waere ir rîter manegen tac* (153, 18f.).

55. See also Craun 602f.; Gottfried 13127f.; Ems Willehalm 5155; 6312f.; 7490ff.; 8598f.; Ems Alexander 2917ff.; Türlin Krone 752ff.; Türheim Rennewart 31440f.; Holle Demant 7948f.; Lichtenstein XLIV, 7, 4; Frauendienst 45, 4f.; 148, 2f.; 197, 3f.; 390, 1f.; 559, 3f.; 1014, 7f.; 1639, 5ff.; Frd 1 Büchl. 63f.; 69f.; Frd. 2 Bücl. 37ff. In the light of this evidence, Paul Kluckhohn's conclusion needs to be corrected: "Other words, too, which designate the vassal, such as the word ''ritter,'' are never used by the German *Minnesänger* to express their relationship to their lady. Only Ulrich von Lichtenstein calls himself so on one occasion and then with the addition *eigen*: 'ir eigen ritter' (Frauendienst, 17, 17)" (ZfdA. 52, 145).

56. Ludwig A. Winterswyl p. 81 and p. 87.

57. As well as the special studies on knightly initiation and dubbing already mentioned (see above p. 000, note 22), see Léon Gautier pp. 245ff.; Paul Guilhiermoz pp. 393ff.; Hans Delbruck III, 274 ff.; Marc Bloch II, 46ff.

58. The most remarkable thing is that it is precisely the works with the most instances of the word *ritter*—Wolfram's *Parzival*, Wirnt's *Wigalois*, Türlin's *Krone*, Holle's *Demantin* and Lichtenstein's *Frauendienst*—which do not use the word *Schwertleite*.

59. The lists made by Ernst H. Massmann pp. 14f. and von Fritz Pietzner p. 26 are partly defective. For the period after 1250, Pietzner cites the word from only two sources, Konrad's *Partonopier* and *Der jüngere Titurel*. It is not until after the middle of the fourteenth century that dubbing supplants the initiation ceremony in Germany (see Pietzner pp. 112ff.).

60. The passage of preaching on St. Martin cannot be dated with certainty: *do wart er des betwungen, daz er mŭse swertleiten unde riter mŭse werden* (Pr. Schönbach III, 239, 29f.).

61. In describing the creation of knights, Eilhart (521ff.) and Veldeke (Eneit

174, 8ff.) did indeed use the term "ritter," but in these pssages the word *swertleite* does not appear.

62. The remaining instances from the *Kaiserchronik* are unclear. Emperor Konstantin ordered *uber elliu sîniu rîche, swer daz swert laite, er chôme ze helfe der christenhaite* (8411–13); and exactly the same is said of his mother's call to arms: *und alle di swert mahten laiten si chômen wider der christenhaite* (8390f.). Here the word does not have the meaning of a technical act of creation of knights but designates quite simply the capability of bearing arms or liability to military service.

63. Even if the Hohenstaufen part of the *Eneit* is not Veldeke's work, it must have been inserted at a very early date (see Theodor Frings and Gabriele Schieb, *Drei Veldekestudien*, Abhandlungen d. dt. Akad. d. Wiss. zu Berlin, phil.-hist. Kl., Jg. 1947, no. 6, Berlin 1949, pp. 75ff.).

64. It is said of St. Martin: *do notte in sin herre der chůnic Julianus. daz er riter muse werden. wand er riche und edel was* (Pr. br. Grieshaber 450a, 25f.).

65. Numerous instances of this and other formulations in Ernst H. Massmann pp. 36ff.

66. Instances in: Vorauer Alexander 358ff.; Kaiserchronik 13933/14183f.; 16449; Orendel 178; Eilhart 516ff.; Eneit 174, 22ff.; Erek 555f.; Gregorius 1646f.; Herbort 1719/4773; 14900; Morant 3612ff.; 5356ff.; Lanzelet 4699; Parzival 97, 25; Titurel 39, 1; Willehalm 66, 8f.; Wigalois 1627f.; Gottfried 5011ff.; 18704; Nibelungenlied 31, 4; Kalge 4362f.; Flore 7510ff.; Herzog Ernst B 118f.; Otte 4625f.; Durne 131ff.; Sächsische Weltchronik 139, 38f.; 232, 8f.; Stricker Daniel 8103ff.; Türlin Krone 424f.; Kudrun 19, 1ff.; 171, 1ff.; Ems Gerhardt 4946ff.; Ems Willehalm 5586ff ; Türheim Rennewart 2654ff.; 12884f.; Holle Crane 1122.

67. This is true for Cedar in Herbort 1424f. already mentioned. There is nothing about his origin but it is possible to draw some conclusions from his behavior; he fights with Greek kings and moves freely over the battlefield; furthermore a relation of his is mentioned on the Trojan side (1457); only nobles are represented like this. The noble origin of Hagen's father Aldrian causes less difficulty (his initiation is mentioned in the *Nibelungenlied,* 1755, 3). It is clear from the reference to the Walther saga that he is thought of as a prince. In Gottfried's *Tristan* the two sons of Tristan's foster-father Rual are presented with the sword (5728f.). Rual is, indeed, only *ein herre von dem lande* (467) but even under Riwalin he acts as director of the land (465f.), and later Tristan hands over to him and his sons his whole *urbor* (5796) as an *erbelehen* in Parmenie (5803), so that Rual now becomes the most powerful man in the territory. In the *Sächsische Weltchronik* there is an account of the initiation of the future emperor Valentinian: *Durch de sterke wart he to riddere gemaket unde wart des heres meister* (128, 19). Eike says nothing about his origin except that he was *van Ungeren geboren* (128, 16). But it is indicated by the observation: *Julianus de keiser hadde ene untridderet unde vordreven, wande he cristen was* (128, 20) that he had had a higher rank earlier. In Holle's *Demantin* the deputy ruler of a margrave is made into a knight (10568); we learn nothing about his social

position. Nevertheless, the margrave testifies for him: "*he was geweldig ober mîn rîche . . . zu zinse twang he al mîn lant*" (10571/77); he was in any case a great lord. Apart from this, in all these dubious cases, with the exception of that of the two sons of Rual, nothing is said about the form of the initiation and the accompanying circumstances. There are significant differences.

68. No account is taken here of the interesting passage in Gottfried's *Tristan* where Queen Isolt, *diu mortraete* (12723), dangles before the two men who are supposed to kill Brangaene the possibility that their reward may be "*daz ich iuch morgen an dem tage mit rilicher sache beide ritter mache*" (12738–40). Apart from the fact that this never happens and that Isolde's vague promise is never again mentioned, the social position of the two men is not definite; we know only that they were *zwene knehte* (12713), and the term *knecht* is flexible, since even around 1200 it could designate the young noble who had not yet been initiated to arms. King Oswald gives a similar promise to a *schifkneht: "unde ist mîn rabe komen her ûs Engellant, drîzic marc goldes gibe ich dir in dîn hant unde mache dich ze ritter"* (Oswald M. 1914–16). The often cited complaint in *Wigalois* (see Fritz Pietzner pp. 49f.) about the lords who *dem immer swert gegeben der daz rîterlîche leben niht behalten künne* (2340–42) does not allow us to decide whether the poet is there thinking of a formal initiation or not.

69. Gerhard belongs to the upper bourgeoisie in Köln, indeed he has a position of honor superior to that of all other burghers. Emperor Otto at an assembly recognizes at once that Gerhard is *vor in der êrste* (759). In his dress, appearance, and life style he is scarcely to be distinguished from a great aristocratic lord. He has close relations with the archbishop and plans to marry his son to a princess. It is important that this son is appointed as one of the *ministeriales* of the archbishop (3475ff.) and acquires *dienstmannes reht* (3370; 3483) before he is initiated. It is his father, however, not his liegelord, who starts the process of initiation: ". . . *wan ich ze dirre hochzît mînem sun wil geben swert*" (3402f.). Wolfgang Mohr has kindly pointed out to me that even in Gottfried's *Tristan* there is at least the possibility of a merchant's son's being initiated. Tristan, allegedly a merchant's son, serves at first as *jegere* (3482) and *hoveman* (3487) at the English court and receives rich rewards from Mark for his offerings at court ("*schoeniu cleider unde pfert, der gibe ich dir swie vil du wilt*" 3734f.). He is raised to the position of personal hunstman and *trut gesinde* (3743). There is no question at this point of Tristan's initiation. But when Rual comes to Cornwall and asks *einen getageten hoveman* (3906) about Tristan he receives the answer: "*ein knappe ist hier gesinde, der sol schiere nemen swert*" (3914f.). No statement is made as to whether the king has made a corresponding decision in the meanwhile or whether the words merely reflect the general expectation of the court. Only after Tristan's royal origin is made known does Rual take the initiative and invite Tristan: "*minen herren dinen oeheim den bite, daz er dir helfe heim und dich hie ritter mache*" (4391–93). Mark at once declares his readiness to do so (4402ff.). On the close-knit relationship between knighthood and upper bourgeoisie

in the thirteenth and fourteenth centuries, see Roth von Screckenstein, *Ritterwürde* pp. 396ff.; Otto Brunner, *Neue Wege* pp. 116ff.

70. Confirmed by Ulrich Stutz, *Schwertweihe*, ZRG. KA. 9 (1919), 312–13, quotation p. 313.

71. Wilhelm Erben, ZfhWk. 8, 108ff.

72. Wilhelm Erben writes: "It is certainly at least partly due to the lack of suitable sources that we are unable to produce more numerous instances of the initiation of young men of non-royal standing as early as the twelfth and early thirteenth centuries" (p. 121). The "more numerous" refers to two celebrated passages from the *Gesta Friderici* of Otto von Freising which are, in fact, worthless for the conditions in Germany. Otto's astonishment that in Italian states the *cingulum miliciae* was bestowed on craftsmen and people of low estate merely confirms that there was no such thing in Germany (II, 13: *inferioris conditionis iuvenes vel quoslibet contemptibilium etiam mechanicarum artium opifices*, Georg Waitz, ed., MGH., Script. rer. Ger., 2. ed. (Hannover, 1884), p. 93). And the story of the "ordinary soldier" (*strator*), whom the emperor wished to make into a knight in 1154 as a reward for an outstanding exploit near Tortona and who refused on the ground that his own social position was good enough for him is to be explained on the basis of Italian rather than German law (II, 23: *quem rex ad se vocatum militari cingulo ob tam praeclarum facinus honorandum decrevit . . . cum plebeium se diceret in eodemque ordine velle remanere, sufficere sibi conditionem suam* [ibid., p. 101]). The same is true of the procedures from the chancellery of Frederick II for the elevation of non-nobles to knighthood. See Roth von Schreckenstein, *Ritterwürde* pp. 197ff.; Wilhelm Erben, ZfhWk. 8, 121; Fritz Pietzner p. 50.

73. Roth von Schreckenstein, *Ritterwürde* p. 204. "The custom held good for everyone from the king down to the *ministeriales*" (Georg Waitz V, 399).

74. Karl Bosl in: Gebhardt's *Handbuch* I, 675. See also Gustav Köhler II 2, 71; Hans Delbrück III, 243, etc.

75. Jean-Pierre Ritter p. 115. As early as Jacob Falke we find: "Everybody, from the highest nobility to the lowest, from emperor to noble retainer had to become a knight; and that was the good thing about it, that in many respects it removed the differences within the nobility and made it into a single corporate body and its members . . . equal to one another in fellowship" (p. 32). Friedrich von Raumer called knighthood "a kind of democratic component of the aristocratic world" (VI, 554, note 6).

76. August von Fürth wrote long ago: "The knightly dignity of a retainer is very frequently explicitly stated" (p. 67). The instances he cites, however, are not evidence for the dignity of knighthood but once again only for the title *miles* for *ministeriales* and "lower unfree persons." On the understanding of the term *miles* as "a class designation for . . . free and unfree persons insofar as they have been dubbed knights" (Josef Bast p. 51), an opinion as widespread as it is unfounded, see above, pp. 62. "The attractively clear and comprehensible idea that it is possible to recognize and separate social classes in the Middle Ages according to classes of titles disappears without a trace as soon as one allows the documents to speak

on the subject of the use of titles without having first formed prejudices''
(Otto von Dungern, *Adelsherrschaft* pp. 23f.). In the special studies on the
initiation ceremony, only Ernst H. Massmann has posed the question "Who
could become a knight?" (pp. 63ff.); his answer is: a. those born as knights;
b. townsmen; c. peasants; d. craftsmen; e. the learned; f. the lower class.
Because of the mixing up of early and late evidence, the actual question
of who is meant by "those born as knights" is avoided and a very remarkable picture of the "class noble by birth" of the knights emerges.

77. Gustav Köhler III 2, 35f.

78. In the *Vita Ludewici comitis de Arnstein* (1139–1185) Johann F. Boehmer,
    ed., *Fontes rerum Germ.* III, Stuttgart, 1853, no. 23, 326–39), on which
    Gustav Köhler bases his argument, it is said of Graf Ludwig: *Sed ille primo
    manum misit ad fortia, et multis amicorum sumptibus et honore succinctus
    est baltheo militari, consuetisque secularium tirociniis, contubernii legalis
    anticipavit accessum* (p. 328). See on the subject Wilhelm Erben, ZfhWk.
    8, 121, n. 121.

79. In the *Martyrium Arnoldi archiepiscopi Moguntini* (1153–60), Johann F.
    Boehmer, ed., Fontes III, no. 22, 270–326, which was later issued under
    the title *Vita Arnoldi*, it is said of Archbishop Arnolt: *Unde quendam eorum
    Mengotum nomine, defuncti Mengoti* (a *ministerialis* of the archbishopric)
    *filium cingulo tandem militari accinxit, multisque beneficiis episcopatus
    ditavit* (p. 278). The authenticity of the source was disproved by the in-
    vestigation of Th. Ilgen, *Kritische Beiträge zur rheinisch–westfälischen
    Quellenkunde des Mittelalters, IV. Vita Arnoldi archiepiscopi Moguntini*,
    Westfäl. Zs. f. Gesch. u. Kunst 27 (1908), 38–97. Belief in it has not been
    restored by the attempts at rehabilitation by Peter Wackernagel, *Kritische
    Studien zur Vita Arnoldi archiepiscopi Moguntini*, Diss. Breslau 1921 and
    by P. Amandus G'sell O.S.B., *Die Vita des Erzbischofs Arnold von Mainz
    (1153–1160), auf ihre Echtheit geprüft*, Neues Arch. d. Ges. f. ältere dt.
    Geschichtskd. 43 (1922), 27–86; 317–79. "A new investigation is desir-
    able" (Karl Jacob, *Quellenkunde der dt. Geschichte in Mittelalter*, Vol.
    II, Sammlung Göschen 280, 4. ed. (Berlin, 1949), p. 87, n. 3.

80. Firstly the son of Der gute Gerhard (see above, n. 69) and secondly Ulrich
    von Lichtenstein (see above, p. 93).

81. In this connection a passage in the *Pöhlder Annalen*, which to my knowl-
    edge has never been noted, deserves attention. It is from the second half
    of the twelfth century. Under the year 1150 it is reported of the Markgraf
    Adelbert of Brandenburg that "a young man of the same name came to
    his court, born in Swabia and brought up to learning, who had been made
    deacon and excluded from a share in the inheritance by his brothers because
    of his clerical position. He concealed this decision and after three years
    took arms and became an efficient knight" (*Occultata igitur sententia post
    tres annos sumptis armis strenue militavit*); Georg H. Pertz, ed., MGH.
    SS. XVI, 1854, 48–98, quotation p. 85; Eduard Winkelmann, trans., Ges-
    chichtsschreiber der dt. Vorzeit, 2, Ges.-Ausgabe, 12. Jahrhundert, Vol.
    13 (Leipzig, 1894), p. 74. After this Adelbert had served the Markgraf
    conscientiously for some time, his real position was discovered, and the

Markgraf had him tonsured and returned to his clerical office. Unfortunately the terminology of knighthood used here is not unambiguous. It is true that the expression *arma sumere*, found in classical Latin, is sometimes used as a designation of the initiation ceremony (see Paul Guilhiermoz, pp. 393ff.) but it can also mean no more than the entry into a more definite service-relationship. There is the same uncertainty in regard to the document of Conrad III of 1145, frequently cited in research. It forbids the Abbot of the Allerheilige monastery in Schaffhausen to distribute benefices *aut milites aliquos creare* (see above p. 229, n. 41). Wilhelm Erben concludes from this that the abbot "had taken it upon himself to elevate people to knighthood" (ZfhWk. 8, 127); Roth von Schreckenstein, *Ritterwürde*, p. 117, and p. 207 expresses scepticism.

82. Wilhelm Erben, ZfhWk. 8, 120.
83. Fritz Pietzner, p. 26.
84. Erich von Guttenberg, DA. 3, 292.
85. Otto von Dungern, *Herrenstand*, p. 349; Franz von Löher: "It is clear from everything already stated that the dubbing ceremony did not confer any definite higher social rank. It was merely a symbolic ceremony . . ." (p. 411). Even Fritz Pietzner reluctantly concedes this: "It is to this extent true that initiation into knighthood did not mean acceptance into a higher class in that only nobles were admitted to knighthood" (p. 61). See also Leopold von Borch, *Beiträge zur Rechts-Geschichte des Mittelalters mit besonderer Rücksicht auf die Ritter und Dienstmannen fürstlicher und gräflicher Herkunft* (Innsbruck, 1881), p. 5.
86. This is well illustrated by the initiation of Count Raimond of Provence who, at the age of fifty, had himself "knighted at Hagenau in the winter of 1235/6 by the Emperor Friedrich II for the sake of his sons-in-law" (Wilhelm Erben, ZfhWk. 8, 111).
87. In Germany at least not until the middle of the thirteenth century. The fact that even in the highest aristocratic circles the initiation was not regularly carried out in the twelfth century is shown by a remark in Gislebert's *Chronicon Hanoniae* in regard to the initiation of Balduin V of Hennegau, whom his father, Graf Balduin IV made into a knight at Easter 1168 "and thus fulfilled an old wish of his father's, since it had not been granted to any of his forefathers for a long time to see their son as a knight" (Wilhelm Erben, ZfhWk. 8, 109).
88. Lists of the alleged laws of knighthood may be found in August von Fürth pp. 73ff.; Fritz Pietzner pp. 109f., etc. On the other hand Franz von Loher has already made it clear that "the dubbing ceremony in itself did not give any rights" (p. 393). See also Hans Delbrück: "The dubbing ceremony as such had no direct legal result" (III, 243). The most persistently held of these concepts is the one that states that a knight had the right to make knights himself, an idea that is obviously taken over from French research: "Every knight has the right to make other knights" (Léon Gautier p. 256; see Gustav Cohen p. 39); "Every knight was entitled to create other knights" (Ernst J. Massmann p. 202; see Hans Delbrück III, 244; Fritz Pietzner p. 80, etc.). Otto von Dungern has made it quite clear what is to

be understood by this "right": "The right to dub knights, by which many legal historians understood something like a privilege to ennoble, is in fact nothing more than an honorary entitlement to perform the ceremony of dedication to arms for young men who were of knightly birth" (in Dungern's terminology this means the sons of dynastic families) (*Herrenstand* p. 343).

89. Support has been given to a historical connection between the initiation ceremony and obligation to service by Léon Gautier pp. 15 ff.; Gustav Köhler III 2, 67; Ernst Mayer II, 161ff.; Paul Guilhiermoz pp. 403ff.; Wilhelm Erben, ZfhWk. 8, 119f.; Ulrich Stutz, ZRG. KA. 9, 313; Hans Naumann, *Deutsche Kultur* p. 60. Roth von Schreckenstein, *Ritterwürde* pp. 214f. and Hans Delbrück III, 243 and 275 do not express a definite opinion. The connection is denied by Franz von Löher pp. 389f.; Georg Kaufmann, *Wehrhaftmachung kein Ritterschlag*, Philologus 31 (1872), 490–510; Martin Baltzer pp. 7f.; Heinrich von Wedel p. 44 and most recently by Fritz Pietzner pp. 29ff., who bases his case chiefly on the *Kudrun*, where the facts given about the young Sigebant are in fact contradictory. On one occasion it says: *er wuochs unz an die stunde, daz er wâfen truoc* (4, 1), and later at his wedding it emerges that he was *dannoch kneht* (18, 2). From the remark: *vünf hundert recken nâmen bî im swert* (19, 1), it must be concluded that his initiation to knighthood was celebrated at the same time as his wedding. But that does not mean that here "obligation to service and initiation appear with an interval between them as completely separate ceremonies" (Pietzner p. 31), since there is no mention of a ceremony in either passage. The expression *wâfen tragen* in 4, 1 need not have the technical meaning of obligation to service but can mean merely that Sigebant had reached the age when he was capable of bearing arms.

90. Instances in Ernst H. Massmann pp. 43ff.; 116ff.: Fritz Pietzner pp. 36ff.

91. The evidence from poetry is evaluated by Ernst H. Massmann and Fritz Pietzner.

92. See Léon Gautier pp. 265ff.; Gustav Schnürer II, 271ff.; Wilhelm Erben, ZfhWk. 8, 121ff.; Marc Bloch II, 50ff.; Gustav Cohen pp. 17ff.; Jean-Pierre Ritter pp. 123ff.

93. Texts and evidence in Léon Gautier pp. 296ff.; Adolph Franz, *Die kirchlichen Benediktionen im Mittelalter*, 2 vols. (Freiburg i. Br., 1909), esp. II, 289ff.; Michel Andrieu, *Les Ordines Romani du haut moyen-âge*, 4 vols., Specilegium sacrum Lovaniense 11/23/24/28 (Louvain, 1931–56); Carl Erdmann, *Die Entstehung des Kreuzzugsgedankens*, (repr., Darmstadt, 1955), Exkurs I, pp. 326ff.; Marc Bloch II, 263; Gustav Cohen pp. 183ff.

94. *Quatinus defensio atque protectio possit esse ecclesiarum, viduarum, orphanorum, omniumque Deo servientium contra sevitiam paganorum, aliisque insidiantibus sit pavor, terror et formido* (quoted according to Carl Erdmann p. 330; trans. ibid., pp. 75f.)

95. Carl Erdmann p. 76.

96. See Fritz Pietzner p. 96. The pronouncements of John of Salisbury and Peter of Blois have all the more weight because, although not directly connected with Germany nevertheless give clear evidence of the widespread

distribution of the ceremony of blessing the sword in the twelfth century. John of Salisbury depicts it "as an old custom, now disused, that everyone who was girded with a knight's belt went to church on the same day, took his belt from the altar, and bound himself with a solemn oath to obey and serve the altar" (Wilhelm Erben, ZfhWk. 8, 127). Peter of Blois refers directly to contemporary times: *Sed et hodie tirones enses suos recipiunt de altari, ut profiteantur se filios Ecclesiae, atque ad honorem sacerdotii, ad tuitionem pauperum, ad vindicationem malefactorum et patriae liberationem gladium accepisse* (Epistola XCIV, Migne, *PL.* 207 (Paris, 1904), 293–97, quotation p. 294C.

97. Even from the thirteenth century we have only two pieces of historical evidence for the *consecratio ensis* in Germany and even these come from one and the same source, the *Annales Mellicenses*: on the initiation of the Austrian dukes Leopold VI in 1200 and Friedrich II in 1232, see Wilhelm Erben, ZfhWk. 8, 124. The other material which Fritz Pietzner (pp. 96f.) produces from the thirteenth century is either from later sources or refers only indirectly to the blessing of the sword.

98. The initiation ceremony of William of Holland falls right at the end of the period treated here, in 1247. Over a century later the Utrecht cleric Johann de Beka gave a very detailed account of it. This frequently quoted account (Friedrich von Raumer VI, 552; Jacob Falke pp. 34ff.; Alwin Schultz I, 146f.) has no value as testimony for the thirteenth century. See Roth von Schreckenstein, *Das angebliche Ceremonial bei der Ritterweihe des Königs Wilhelm 1247*, Forschungen zur deutschen Geschichte 22 (1882), 233–47; Julius Petersen p. 157; Wilhelm Erben, ZfhWk. 8, 159f.

99. Instances in Wilhelm Erben, ZfhWk. 8, 123; Fritz Pietzner pp. 41f.

100. See Roth von Schreckenstein, Ritterwürde, p. 208, n. 2.

101. Their significance can be seen from the fact that there are nine pieces of testimony in poetry for the blessing of the sword in Germany even before the middle of the thirteenth century as against one thirteenth-century historical text (see above, n. 97). They are: Wigalois 1645ff.; Gottfried 5011ff.; Willehalm 299, 13ff.; Walther 125, 1ff.; Flore 7512f.; Ems, Gerhard 3595ff.; Ems Willehalm 5759f.; Türheim Rennewart 2670ff. See Wilhelm Wackernagel, *Ritter-und Dichterleben Basels im Mittelalter*, in: Kleinere Schriften I, Leipzig 1872, 258–301, esp. p. 270, note 2 for evidence of the blessing of the sword in the later thirteenth and fourteenth century and also Alwin Schultz I, 142, n. 2; Julius Petersen pp. 158ff.; Ernst H. Massmann p. 39.

102. The works earlier than 1200 which give the most detailed accounts of an initiation, Lamprecht's *Alexander* and Veldeke's *Eneit*, are dealing with classical material and this excludes from the beginning any mention of a Christian blessing of the sword. The earliest description of a Christian initiation ceremony is in the *Nibelungenlied*, except for *König Rother*, where there is indeed a description of the accompanying framework, the *lantsprâche* and the *buhurt* but where the initiation procedure is dismissed in a sentence: *Do der koninc pippin. Vor rothere deme vatir sin. Das suert umbe gebant. Do reit her mit manicgeme uffe daz sant . . .* (5067–70). In

the *Nibelungenlied* there is in fact no expressed mention of the blessing of the sword, but it is made clear that a church feast is part of the ceremony of dedication to knighthood (Strophes 32f.), and the text does permit the interpretation that the girding on of the sword took place in church.

103. Carl Erdmann p. 66. There is a certain lack of clarity in Ermann's use of the word "ritter." "For the purposes of this study we use the term *ritter* in a general sense . . . as a unified category which comprises all those who were customarily obliged to undertake the profession of arms and we set these off as a whole against the king on the one hand and the church on the other" (p. 52). Such an interpretation of the knight-concept, which disregards the social differences between the upper nobility and the simple fighting men is perfectly understandable from the point of view of the reform church, since Christian ethics and a morality based on class are essentially incompatible and even in the Middle Ages were balanced out only superficially and with the greatest difficulty. Besides this, there is in the reform papacy an unmistakable feature of social revolution, which emerges quite clearly, for example, in the propaganda support of the Milanese Pataria and which brought on the pope the charge from the opposition, as Wido of Ferrara writes, that he had "stirred up the knights against their masters" (*Nunc autem versa vice milites armantur in dominos* from *De scismate Hildebrandi*, MGH Libelli I, 529–67, quote p. 539, p. 541f. See Carl Erdmann, p. 240). But if by any chance the Curia believed that it could make practical political capital in its struggle against the Salians from the distinction between kingship and knighthood—where "territorial princes and other knights are grouped together" under the term "knights" (Erdmann p. 52), then it was completely in error about the actual conditions in Germany. It was precisely the Salian kings who promoted the lesser knights, their *ministeriales*, by giving them political tasks and thus countered the determined opposition of the princes. And it was the great princes who gave the pope the most effective support in his struggle against the royal power. Any theory that puts princes and "other knights" on the same level obscures rather than clarifies the politico-social developments. Erdmann's conclusion that the form of procedure for the dedication to knighthood in the liturgical texts is modeled on the royal coronation ceremony and "showed a transference of ecclesiastical and ethical ideas which formally had been valid only for a ruler to an individual knight" is of particular importance (p. 76). Since the "ritter" who girded on the sword was always of princely rank, this transference makes it clear that after the reform period the princes were entering upon the heritage of royal power.

104. See Léon Gautier pp. 31ff. 47ff.; Marc Bloch II, 53ff., Gustav Cohen pp. 29ff.; Jean-Pierre Ritter pp. 136ff.; Friedrich Wentzlaff-Eggebert pp. 3ff.; Hermann Conrad, *Gottesfrieden und Heeresverfassung in der Zeit der Kreuzzüge, Ein Beitrag zur Geschichte des Heeresstrafrechts im Mittelalter*, ZRG. GA. 61, 1941, 71–126; Friedrich Heer, *Aufgang Europas. Eine Studie zu dem Zusammenhängen zwischen politischer Religiosität, Frömmigkeitsstil und dem Werden Europas im 12. Jahrhundert*, Wien-Zürich 1949, p. 157ff.; the most important source for the early spiritual

concept of knighthood is the *Liber de vita christiana* of Bonizo of Sutri (see Carl Erdmann pp. 233ff.; Wentzlaff-Eggebert pp. 5f.).

105. It remains a task of future research to investigate the tradition and development of the ecclesiastical ideal of knighthood in the twelfth and thirteenth centuries, in the famous *Liber ad milites Templi de laude novae militiae* or Bernard of Clairvaux, in the *Policraticus* of John of Salisbury, in the letters of Peter of Blois, in the *Sermones ad fratres ordinis militaris* of Jacob of Vitry, etc. There is an outline survey in Marc Bloch II, 53ff.; Sidney Painter pp. 65ff.; Hermann Conrad ZRG. GA. 61, 93ff.; Gustav Cohen pp. 173ff. On the crusading idea, see the section "L'idée de croisade" in: *Relazioni del X Congresso Internazionale di Scienze Storiche*, Vol. III, Biblioteca Storica Sansoni, Nuova Ser. XXIV (Firenze, 1955), 543–652. The history of the crusading idea in Germany, the continuation of Carl Erdmann's book into the thirteenth century, has not yet been written. Material and literature in Adolf Waas, *Kreuzzüge* and in Friedrich W. Wentzlaff-Eggebert. Waas sees the driving force of the crusading movement in a "pure knightly piety without any initiative on the part of the church or of the Cluniac movement" (I, 47); this kind of piety would be hard to prove from the sources.

106. See Adolf Harnack, *Militia Christi, Die christliche Religion und der Soldatenstand in den ersten drei Jahrhunderten*, Tübingen 1905. Paul Guilhiermoz has pointed out that even in the Latin classics the word *miles* is used metaphorically: *militia Veneris* (Propertius), etc. (p. 333 and n. 6).

107. See Carl Erdmann pp. 185ff.; Paul Guilhiermoz pp. 440ff.; Wentzlaff-Eggebert pp. 6f. Jean-Pierre Ritter (pp. 137f.) emphasizes that the old meaning of *miles Christi* persisted side by side with the new one.

108. In a sermon of Urban II on the first Crusade there is the statement: "The people who were once robbers have now become knights" (*Nunc fiant milites qui dudum exstiterunt raptores* from *Orationes in Concilio Claromontano* V, Migne, PL. 151 Paris, 1881, 574–76, quotation p. 576D); on this see Sidney Painter: "In other words the nobles who ignored the church's injunctions to abstain from rapine were not knights" (p. 67); Jean-Pierre Ritter is of a different opinion (pp. 136f, 248, n.108, 109.) Marbod of Rennes writes: "The only person who can rightly be called *ritter* is he who fights against the heathen" (*Debet enim plane, nisi nomen gestat inane, contra gentiles pugnare deicola miles*, quoted from Adolf Waas II, 58.)

109. In a Cologne manuscript of the eleventh century the most widely distributed versions of the blessings of the sword and standard are combined into an *ordo ad armandum ecclesiae defensorem vel alium militem* (see Carl Erdmann p. 332). In another manuscript of the eleventh century from the monastery at Einsiedeln the blessing of the sword is expanded into a knightly initiation, into a *benedictio militaris super ensem* (ibid.). The Roman *benedictio novi militis* is still in the *Pontificale Romanum* to this day (ibid. p. 333).

110. It is in the year 1086 that it is first called *insignia militiae accipiens*; there is testimony for the expressions *arma militiae* and *ad militiam promovere et ordinare* in 1098; the expression *militem facere* is used for the first time

in 1106; see the examples given by Wilhelm Erben pp. 113, 119f. and Fritz Pietzner pp. 27f.

111. In the sermons, St. Martin, who refuses to defend himself with the sword of this world, is celebrated as *gotes ritter* (Pr. Schönbach I, 355, 27; III, 239, 36; Pr. br. II Schönbach 249, 22). The martyrs Peter and Paul are called *gotes rittere* too (Pr. Schönbach I, 65, 28). The assemblies of saints are also *gotis rîter* (Specul. eccl. 47, 22) *meins trehtins ritter* (Pr. Schönbach II, 19, 26), *gotes ritterschaft* (ibid., I, 331, 22f.; Ems Weltchronik 6566). They fight against *dez lieden tievels . . . ritterschaft* (Ems Weltchronik 11346f.), against *die offinbare rittere des tîvils* and the *heimelichen rittere des tîvils* (Pr. Schönbach I, 332, 3/5; cf. ibid., 331, 26; Pr. br. I Schönbach 197, 25f.). See also the translations: *Michael prepositus paradysi .i. ecclesiae militantis. daz spricht: Mychahel ist vor gesazt der christenheit die noch ritteret* (Pr. Schönbach I, 77, 20–22); *militia est vita hominis. daz leben der mennischin ouf der erde ist ein ritterschaft, daz ist bicorunge und ein urliuge wider den tievel* (Pr. br. II Schönbach 225, 23–25).

112. The *Sächsische Weltchronik* writes about the nephew of the emperor Heinrich V: Conrad *lovede sin levent beteren unde dat he vore to Jherusalem unde worde goddes rittere* (197, 28f.). Knights in the service of God: *got nimt den dienest niht für vol, den ein ritter getuot, ern habe ouch ritterlichen muot* (Stricker Karl 4886–88); *ez ist ein ritterlîcher muot, daz man dem diene eteswaz, von dem man hât gar allez daz, guot, sêle und darzuo den lîp . . .* (Lichtenstein, Frauendienst 415, 4–7); cf. Ems Gerhard 574ff.

113. See also in *Erek: si kâmen da si messe vernâmen von dem heiligen geiste; des phlegent si aller meiste die ze ritterschefte sinnent und turnieren minnent* (662–66). In the Middle High German version of the statutes of the Deutscher Orden, which admittedly is not earlier than the second half of the thirteenth century, it is said: *sî sint rittere unde erwelte strîtere, die durch minne der ê unde des vaterlandes vertiligent die vîende des gelouben mit einer starken hant* (Max Perlbach, ed., Halle, 1890, Prolog, p. 25, lines 29–32).

114. On the significance of the crusading idea for the conception of knighthood in the classical period, see Friedrich W. Wentzlaff-Eggebert pp. 147ff.

115. See also Thomasin 7380ff.; 7445ff.; 8671ff.

116. I am quoting here from Albert Leitzmann's edition (3rd. ed. Halle, 1950), but I have taken from Lachmann's edition the quotation marks at the beginning of line 299, 16 and at the end of 299, 18. In the fifth edition, which I used, the punctuation is missing at the end of the blessing quotation; in the sixth ed. it is also missing at the beginning. The colon after 299, 15 is mine (Lachmann puts a comma, Leitzmann a period). *kernet* instead of *lernet* 299, 22 in Leitzmann is a printer's error.

117. Roth von Schreckenstein, *Ritterwürde* p. 229.

118. See Wilhelm Erben, ZfhWk. 8, 134ff.; Ernst H. Massmann pp. 53ff.; Fritz Pietzner pp. 70ff. The oldest historical evidence for Germany is in the *Reichersberger Chronik* for the year 1192, the oldest poetical evidence in Eilhart's *Tristrant*. Incidentally, the situation in regard to sources is similar to that in regard to the blessing of the sword: in German poetry after Eilhart

there is plenty of evidence for mass promotion—more than twenty instances up to the middle of the thirteenth century—but it is not until the second half of the thirteenth century that the evidence from historical sources becomes more frequent. The cases where two brothers or relations take the sword together are not to be counted here: the two sons of Barbarossa (Eneit 347, 22f.; Sächsische Weltchronik 232, 7ff.), the two sons of Rual (Gottfried 5728f.), the relatives of Fuckelinet, Elinant and Berant (Morant 5356ff.). Cases where a prince's son takes the sword with a noble friend and companion should be regarded as special: Graf Wentzel with the young Herzog Ernst (Hz. Ernst B 118ff.), and the *edelarme* father of Enite with Erck's father, King Lac (Erek 555f.). The view which was formerly held of the initiation ceremony as "always carried out with large numbers" is refuted by Erben p. 134; Massmann pp. 59f.

119. Other figures: 12 (Gottfried 5739; Ems Gerhard 3591f.; Ems Willehalm 5777f.); 20 (Holle Demant. 10568), 30 (Gottfried 4552ff.); 50 (Otte 2388); 60 (Eilhart 521f.; Ems Willehalm 5768): 100 (Klage 4371f.; Willehalm 63, 8f.; Flore 7510f.; Kudrun 171, 1f.; Wolfdietrich A 137, 2); 250 (Lichtenstein Frauendienst 40, 1f.); 400 (Nibelungenlied 30, 1f.); 500 (Kudrun 19, 1; 549, 1ff.).

120. Lichtenstein Frauendienst 40, 1ff. There is evidence from the *Nibelungenlied* on for mass initiation on the occasion of the wedding of a prince (see Fritz Pietzner p. 68): Nibelungenlied 646, 1ff.; Otte 2388ff.; Kudrun 549, 1ff.; Holle Darif. 54ff.

121. On the significance of the great Austrian families of *ministeriales* in the middle of the thirteenth century, see Paul Kluckhohn p. 110.

122. The relationship of the two other participants in mass promotion whom we know by name is less clear. Otte tells of the initiation of the young Eraclius, who received the sword with a group of fifty retainers at the wedding of the Emperor Focas (2388ff.). Eraclius began his career in the slave market at Rome and ended it on the imperial throne. Nevertheless he did come of a noble Roman family; his father was *ze Rôme ein vil rîcher man . . . ein edel burgaere* (165/167). The other instance is Tristan's friend and teacher Kurvenal, who was made a knight as one of twelve companions at the initiation of Rual's two sons (Gottfried 5740f.). Kurvenal is Tristan's *man* (10771); we know nothing about his origin. Gottfried says only: *daz knappe nie von höfscheit und von edeles herzen art baz noch gedelt wart* (2262–64).

123. In *Parzival, vil fürsten und ander kint* (348, 22) take ths sword with King Meljanz, if indeed a formal initiation is indicated in this passage. In Otte there are fifty retainers *die des den keiser dûhten wert* (2390). Berthold von Holle uses the same formulation: *knehte die des wâren wert in dar zô manich edel man* (Crane 1356f.). In Stricker's *Daniel* it is retainers, *der vetere alle wâren des künec Artûses gesellen* (6800f.).

124. See Fritz Pietzner p. 72.

125. See Wilhelm Erben, ZfhWk. 8, 118f.; Ernst H. Massmann pp. 134ff.; Fritz Pietzner pp. 38ff.; Léon Gautier (pp. 338f.) has worked out the cost of an initiation. From the thirteenth century on *filium in militem sublimare* was a legal ground for tax relief (see Pietzner p. 52, n. 14; Franz von Löher

p. 406). *See also* Achille Luchaire, *Social France at the Time of Philip Augustus*, Edward B. Krehbiel, trans. (New York, 1912; repr. 1929), pp. 340ff. (the French text was unobtainable).

126. A passage in *Wolfdietrich* A shows that, for the squire, the material outfitting was at least as important as the title "knight." Duke Berhtung goes to the king's court with a hundred *junchêrren* who are supposed to be made knights there. This does not happen, however, because the invitation was only a trick to entice Berhtung to court. Later, however, the queen determines to *ir schaden ergetzen* (239, 2) and equips the young men with everything they would have received at the initiation: *swaz ritter haben solden, des wurden si bereit. satel unde schilde und drîer hande kleit. Ieglîchem gegeben wurden driu kastellân starc, darzuo knehte kleider, ieglîchem vierzic marc* (239, 3–240, 2). See also Eneit 174, 8ff.; Gottfried 4550ff.; Flore 7527; Ems Willehalm 5344ff.; Kudrun 19, 1ff; 175, 1ff.; Stricker Daniel 6806ff.

127. *man gap in phärt und gewant. ez leite etelîcher an, daz sîn vater und sîn an sô guotes nie niht gewan* (Otte 2400–03).

128. See also in the *Nibelungenlied: vier hundert swertdegene die solden tragen kleit mit samt Sîvrîde* (30, 1f.); further Ems Gerhard 3591ff.; Ems Willehalm 5768ff.

129. This relationship also appears in the fact that Tristan, after Mark has girded the sword on him, himself puts the sword, spurs, and shield on his companions (Gottfried 5046ff.) and even explains to them the ethical idea of knighthood: *diemüete, triuwe, milte die leite er iegliches kür mit bescheidenlicher lere vür* (5050–52). Further instances in Ernst H. Massmann, pp. 201ff.; Fritz Pietzner pp. 74f.

130. Tristan too is accompanied by his fellow initiates on the journey to Parmenie (Gottfried 5129f.).

131. Only attributive adjectives are listed, with the exception of epithets indicating nationality and religion: *ritter britun* (Gottfried 5345, 5361); *diutscher ritter* (Ems Willehalm 6210); *ritter heiden* (Roland 4964); *heidenischer ritter* (Oswald M 2530); *ritter kristân* (Durne 1696). I have also omitted any adjectives which are due directly to the narrative: *durchstochener ritter* (Parzival 30, 26); *gebalsamter ritter* (Parzival 249, 16); *gekriuzter ritter* (Parzival 72, 13), but the distinction is not easy to make exactly. The order is alphabetical, without reference to the position of the adjective. I put the inflected form before the word *ritter*, the uninflected form after it. The spelling is normalized throughout.

132. I give here a list of words with which the word *ritterlich* is associated. No distinction is made between attributive and predicate position.

VI. The Social Position of the Knight

1. Helmut de Boor II, 4.
2. Hans-Friedrich Rosenfeld, *Humanistische Strömungen 1350–1600* in: *Deutsche Wortgeschichte* I, 329–438, quotation p. 415. The expression

stende des lands occurs in Lower Austrian sources as early as the first half of the fifteenth century. See Otto Brunner p. 404, n. 3.

3. See *Dt. Wb.* VIII, 1074f.

4. Instances in the appendix to this section.

5. See *Mittelhochdeutsches Wörterbuch* II 1, 305f. This periphrastic use of *ritters name* is not common at a later period: *da ez gieng an ein sheiden von den werden namen beiden, daz sint ritter und vrawen* (Türheim, Rennewart 7231–33); further Türlin Krone 8682, 8700, 8733.

6. In the early period only in *König Rother*; from the *notigen diet* (1313) taken in by Rother the knights are selected: *Svve dar hate ritaris namen. Die sundirte man dan. Vnde gach en gote rosse* . . . (1331–33). See above, p. 29f. The fact that they were called knights before they entered Rother's service may be connected with their training as cavalrymen; that at least is what the author stresses (1343f.). The *Sächsische Weltchronik* mentions *werliche rovere, der under ridderes namen alleswar vile was* (196, 41f.). In a sermon there appears a *ritter* . . . *der was ein ûppich man als leider noch vil maniger ist der ritters namen hat* (Pr. Schönbach I, 110, 13f.). I have not been able to find more than these three instances before the middle of the thirteenth century.

7. Gregorius 1665; Nibelungenlied 31, 4; Otte 2393; Ems Willehalm 5658. The use of the expressions *an ritters namen bringen* also refers to the initiation ceremony (Parzival 123, 9; this is the only instance of *ritters name* in Wolfram), *ritters namen nemen* (Türheim Rennewart 11655), *ritters namen gern* (Ems Willehalm 5260); see also Ems Gerhard 3609; Ems Willehalm 5591f.

8. Lanzelet 2221f.; 4651f.; Iwein 1455f.; 3037f.; Wigalois 995f.; 3921f.; Ems Willehalm 8215f.; 14365f.; Ems Alexander 43f.; in addition: *der schalkhafteste, der swacheste man, der ritters namen ie gewan* Stricker Daniel 145f.; 1165f.). Only rarely does *ritters name* refer to military capability only: *dô wart mit schild und mit sper gekoufet ritters name* (Ems Alexander 7344f.; similarly 17860f.).

9. Herbort 13041f.; Otte 2393f.; Erek 5468f.; Gregorius 1665f.; Iwein 3187f.; Lanzelet 2643f.; Parzival 123, 9f.; Gottfried 4409f.; Ems Willehalm 9203f.; Ems Alexander 17859f.; Türheim Rennewart 3037f.; 3281f.; 11655f.; Türheim Tristan 577, 17f.; Lichtenstein Frauendienst 1034, 7f.; Stricker Ehre D 495f.

10. See Herbort 13041ff.; Zw. Büchlein 69ff.; Lanzelet 2642ff.; Wigalois 9851f.; Stricker Karl 4876ff.; Türlin Krone 13154f.; Türheim Rennewart 3036ff.

11. See Ems Willehalm 9202f.; Ems Alexander 2472ff.; Türlin Krone 11762ff.; Türheim Tristan 577, 16ff.; Lichtenstein Frauendienst 1034, 6ff.

12. Even when it is stated in *Erek: hât dirre man ritters namen, sô möhtet ir iuch immer schamen daz er des niht geniuzet* (5468–70), there is no thought of social class or class law but rather of the ethical norms of aristocratic society; similarly Erek 4201; Wigalois 1940; Stricker Ehre D 495; Türheim Rennewart 2402; Holle Demant. 6155; Lichtenstein Frauendienst 1518, 5.

13. There is no evidence for *ritters ê* in our period. There is one occurrence

of *ritterlîchiu ê* with reference to the initiation ceremony: *dâ si ze ritter wurden nâh riterlîcher ê* (Nibelungenlied 33, 3).

14. The only other examples of *ritters ambet* are in Heinrich von dem Türlin: *als ez touc ritteramt* (Mantel 285) and in reference to Lanzelot: *Der der zweier ampte pflac, Daz er ritter unde pfaffe was* (Krone 2975f.). Ulrich von Lichtenstein, disguised as Venus, announces: *diu mînen ampt sint ritterlîch* (Frauendienst 757, 1). Wolfram's famous *schildes ambet*, obviously his own coinage, shifts in meaning. On a few occasions it refers concretely to the initiation: *"ine wil niht langer sîn ein kneht, ich sol schildes ambet hân"* (Parzival 154, 22f.; also 126, 14 and Willehalm 66, 9). It has the same function as *ritters name* is the expressions *der schoenste* or *der aller schadhafteste man, der schildes ambet ie gewan* (Parzival 209, 11f.; Willehalm 50, 5f.); *schildes ambet tragen, üeben, würken, zeigen* (Parzival 321, 24; 348, 20; 333, 27; 499, 9; 78, 15; 355, 1) means "to fight chivalrously." Otherwise the meaning extends from "military profession, military capability" (Parzival 414, 16; 461, 20; 534, 16; Titurel 8, 1; Willehalm 384, 17) to "membership in courtly society" (Parzival 108, 17; 280, 21). In an abstract sense *schildes ambet* means the ethical responsibilities of aristocratic knighthood or aristocratic knightly dignity (Parzival 97, 27; 269, 9; 524, 24; 612, 7; probably also 364, 12). The term deserves more thorough treatment than is possible here. The personal statement *schildes ambet ist mîn art* (Parzival 115, 11) is best translated as Hermann Schneider does: "My profession is the trade of weaponry" (p. 219). It is certainly not permissible to draw the conclusion that Wolfram had been formally initiated to knighthood.

15. *ritters leben* as aristocratic life style: Parzival 117, 25; Wigalois 2341; Gottfried 5967; Ems Willehalm 12210; Ems Alexander 1408; with reference to love service: *vröide, wunne, ritters leben daz hât sî ze lône mir umb mînen dienest geben* (Lichtenstein XLIV, 6, 5f.; also XXVII, 6, 4; Frauendienst 1178, 8; 1242, 7; Frb. 644, 25; Zw. Büchlein 67); *ritterlîchez leben* in contrast to *vita spiritualis* (Parzival 823, 19; Türheim Tristan 589, 13; as the soldier's trade: *diu vrouwe durch ir ruom wolde versuochen rîters leben* (Wigalois 9359f.; also 9154; Ems Alexander 1399).

16. *nâch ritters rehte rîten* (Kudrun 180, 3); *vehten* (Thomasin 7765); *den gevangen wider geben* (Türlin Krone 3094f.); *mit râte über ein komen* (Ems Willehalm 7869ff.); *ze man werden* (Ems Gerhard 3448f.); *ze kampfe gân* (Gottfried 6517ff.); *ze vehte bereit sîn* (ibid. 6683ff.); *daz gotes rîche koufen* (Stricker Karl 9732f.); *nâch ritterlîchem rehte die geste empfangen* (Ems Willehalm 3490f.); *wider ritter rehte under benken ligen* (Erek 6645ff.); *lestern und hoenen* (Lanzelet 6472f.); also Erek 5412; Türlin Krone 3881, 16099f., 16568, 22675f.; *ritters reht* always mean the code of conduct of aristocratic knighthood. In the same way *schildes reht* (Winsbecke 19, 1ff.), *rîters reht sprechen* (Parzival 78, 10) means to give official decisions at a tournament. The only passage which could possibly be interpreted as a reference to social standing is in Türlin's *Krone: Sô muoste er wandeln ritters reht Und muoste iemer als ein kneht Dem risen dienen* (5507–09); but this probably means no more than "he had to give up his aristocratic life-style."

17. In Wolfram the expression *von ritters art sîn* (Parzival 123, 11; 520, 17) means to be of distinguished birth and thus to be part of the social group of noble initiation. The expression refers to the two sons of kings, Parzival and Gawain. I have found this use elsewhere only in Berthold von Holle, where the King of England says: *"wen ich von art ein ritter bin"* (Demant. 6649). In addition to this, Wolfram twice says of people who were not part of this group: *von ritters art geborn, erborn sîn* (Parzival 544, 17; Willehalm 131, 1); Plippalinot is a *verje* (Parzival 548, 20, etc.), Wimar is a *koufman* (Willehalm 130, 17, etc.). Both keep up splendid households. As an explanation we might think of the rich merchant-knight in *König Rother* (see above, p. 55). Apart from this there is no parallel in courtly poetry for this use of the word. There is only one other instance of *von ritters art* up to the middle of the thirteenth century, in reference to military capability (Türlin Krone 17600). The other expressions are: *nâch ritters art komen* (ibid 24732), *tuon* (Holle Demant. 6160); *nâch ritters ritterlîcher art die wunde rechen* (Ems Alexander 21230f), *nâch ritterlîcher art ritter werden* (Ems Gerhard 4949f.); *bereit sin* (Ems Alexander 3424), *bewart sîn* (ibid 10811), *mit ritterlîcher art eine tjost vrumen* (Ems Willehalm 7495f.); act *als ez zimt ritters art* (Türlin Krone 21527), in all of which cases it is possible to translate "according to the commands of aristocratic knighthood." The only close connection with Wolfram's usage is in the *Sachsenspiegel* (Lnr 2 #1: Ldr I 20 #8; I 27 #2; II 21 #1). The title "knight" is here connected to birth, but the group of these knights shows little unity. See above p. 211, n. 16.

18. Other examples: Parzival 69, 4; Ems Willehalm 7361; 7803; Türlin Krone 827.

19. Other examples: Ems Willehalm 5210. Herzeloyde's question reaches beyond the initiation ceremony to the knightly-aristocratic life: *"sun, wer hât gesagt dir von ritters orden?"* (Parzival 126, 6f.), where the word is simply a substitute for *ritters leben* (117, 25).

20. Gustav Köhler III 2, 54.

21. Instances in August von Fürth pp. 70ff.; Georg Waitz V, 398f.; Gustav Köhler III 1, Breslau 1887, pp. xxf.; III 2, 29ff.; 54ff.; Martin Baltzer p. 12; Paul Guilhiermoz pp. 145f.; Hans Delbrück III, 240f. The following quotations are from these sources.

22. Hans Delbrück III, 240f. When *ordo equestris* is contrasted to *ordo pedestris* it has a pregnant sense: *fiscalini de equestre quam de pedestre ordine* (Strassburg UB., quoted from Ernst Mayer II, 187, n. 18). In a document from Berchtesgaden, two brothers testify that they *copiosam familiam tradiderunt sancto Petro in Perthersgadme sub tali conditione, ut qui eis militari et equestri ordine serviebant, eodem iure permaneant* (ibid.); from this it follows that *militari et equestri ordine servire* means only "to serve as a knight."

23. See Arthur Stein, *Der römische Ritterstand, Ein Beitrag zur Sozialund Personengeschichte des römischen Reiches*, Münchener Beiträge zur Papyrusforschung und antiker Rechtsgeschichte 10 (München, 1927), p. 5, n. 1. In Roman imperial times, as later in the Middle Ages, social strati-

fications within knighthood were designated by such expressions as *primi equestris ordinis, equites primores*, etc. See Stein pp. 96ff.

24. See Paul Kluckhohn p. 50; Du Cange III, 66a.

25. *"Urbis senatum equestremque ordinem instaurandum, quatinus huius consiliis, illius armis Romano imperio tuaeque personae antiqua redeat magnificentia"* (II, 29); trans. Horst Kohl, Geschichtsschreiber, 2. Ges. ausg., 12. Jh., Vol. 1 (Leipzig, 1894), p. 161.

26. *"Vis cognoscere antiquam tuae Romae gloriam? Senatoriae dignitatis gravitatem? Tabernaculorum dispositionem? Equestris ordinis virtutem et disciplinam, ad conflictum procedentis intemeratam ac indomitam audatiam? Nostram intuere rem publicam. Penes nos cuncta haec sunt . . . Nonne multo et forti stipatus milite inclitus sedeo?"* (II, 30); German trans. Horst Kohl, pp. 162/65.

27. See Paul Koschaker, *Europa und das römische Recht*, 3 ed. (München, 1958); in connection with the cultural movement of the twelfth century: Charles H. Haskins, *The Renaissance of the Twelfth Century*, (Cambridge, Mass., 1927; rptd. New York: Meridian Books 49, 1957), pp. 193ff. Wilhelm Erben sees in the "concept of knighthood as a closed social class determined by birth" the "result of a doctrine developed in Northern Italy in the Bologna law school" (ZfhWk. 8, 120). Ernst Mayer describes as a "reminiscence of Roman law" the idea for which the first evidence appears in Norman Sicily, that the king alone had the right to raise anyone to knighthood (II, 165). In this connection the term *cingulum militiae* is of some importance: "of whose Roman origin there can in fact be no doubt" (Léon Gautier p. 16); on this see Roth von Schreckenstein, *Ritterwürde* pp. 276ff.; Paul Guilhiermoz pp. 447ff. Perhaps there is a connection between the gold spurs by which a knight was recognized in the late Middle Ages (see Roth von Schreckenstein, *Ritterwürde* pp. 323ff) and the golden ring which was regarded as the "mark of membership of the knight-class" (Arthur Stein p. 43). Johannes Rothe also calls a *guldin fingerlin* a mark of knightly dignity (see Julius Petersen pp. 119ff.). A further extension of this is the theory, found first in Chrétien's *Cligès* and in *Moriz von Craun,* that knighthood originated in Greece, was taken over by Rome, and passed on by France; see Julius Petersen pp. 68f.; Erich Köhler pp. 40ff.; and on the Translatio doctrine Herbert Grundmann, *Sacerdotium—Regnum—Studium*, AKG. 34, 1951, 5–21; Walter Goetz, *Translatio imperii, Beiträge zur Geschichte des Geschichtsdenkens und der politischen Theorien im Mittelalter und in der frühen Neuzeit*, (Tübingen, 1958).

28. Quoted in Adolf Harnack p. 6, n. 1.

29. From a letter of Agobard to Ludwig the Pious of the year 833: *Jubet vestra prudentissima sollertia contra commotiones huius temporis paratum esse utrumque ordinem, militarem vero et ecclesiasticum, id est et eos qui saeculari militiae et illos qui sacris ministeriis inserviunt, et illos quidem ad certandum ferro, istos autem ad disceptandum verbo* (quoted from Paul Guilhiermoz p. 371); further instances, ibid., p. 371, n. 6; p. 440, n. 10; p. 445, n. 22; Georg Waitz V, 398, n. 4.

30. Otto Brunner p. 401.

31. Still basic: Hans Prutz, *Die geistlichen Ritterorden* (Berlin, 1908); most recently Adolf Waas, *Kreuzzüge* II, 1ff.

32. See Arno Borst, who speaks of "the one completed incorporation of knighthood into reality, in the spiritual knightly orders of the Holy Land (Saecul. 10, 219).

33. The oldest temple rule says nothing on the subject. It is not until the later version from the middle of the thirteenth century that it is demanded of each new brother in knighthood that he must first have received the accolade. See Marc Bloch, II, 58. On the conditions in the Deutscher Orden, see Manfred Hellmann, *Bemerkungen zur sozialgeschichtlichen Erforschung des Deutschen Ordens*, Hist. Jahrb. 80 (1961), 126–42. In the "acceptance ritual" of the Deutscher Orden which has survived it is demanded only that the knight be *dekeines hêrren eigen* (Max Perlbach 127, 17). Only three late manuscripts of the fourteenth-fifteenth centuries have the addition, which allegedly goes back to the "capitularies of 1264": *Der von ritteren nicht geborn ist, den sol man nicht zu ritterbrûder enpfaen ân des hômeisters urloube* (ibid., p. 136). If, in spite of this, the "social exclusivity" of the order is assumed even for the early period (Hans Prutz p. 43) and if it is emphasized that "its personal composition was basically aristocratic" (ibid., p. 530), then again a noble knightly class is a precondition: "The brother knights, like those in other knightly orders, had to be of the knightly class" (P. Marian Tumler, *Der Deutsche Orden im Werden, Wachsen und Wirken bis 1400 mit einem Abriss der Geschichte des Ordens bis zur neuesten Zeit*, Montreal-Wien, 1955, p. 378).

34. The first High Master of the Deutschherren, after their elevation to an order of knighthood in 1198 was Heinrich von Walpoto who, in the contemporary *Narratio de Primordiis Ordinis Teutonici*, is described as "knight" (*miles*) without any more exact description of his rank (see P. Marian Tumler pp. 579ff. and p. 581). The second High Master was of unknown origin (ibid., p. 31); the third, Heinrich Bart "seems to have come from Thüringen and to have been a *ministerialis* of the Landgraf" (ibid.). Hermann von Salza also seems to have come from a Thuringian family of *ministeriales* (ibid., p. 33).

35. Otto von Dungern, *Herrenstand*, p. 361.

36. This is true of the *rîterlîche bruoderschaft* of the Grail-guardians in Wolfram's *Parzival* (470, 19), about whose social composition the poet says nothing. But there is no evidence in any source that "the secular order of Christianity was constituted on the model of the spiritual knightly orders" (Gustav Köhler III 2, 8) and that "the introduction of the secular order of knighthood . . . became the basis for the formation of a new class of those born knights (ibid., p. 72).

37. Note the large numbers of secular court orders and orders of knighthood founded by princes in the late Middle Ages. See Roth von Schreckenstein, *Ritterwürde* pp. 669ff.; Johan Huizinga, *Herbst des Mittelalters, Studien über Lebens- und Geistesformen des 14. und 15. Jahrhunderts in Frank-*

reich und in den Niederlanden, T. Jolles Mönckeberg, trans. (München, 1924), pp. 107ff.

38. See the chapter "Kreuzzüge und Ritterkultur" in Adolf Waas, *Kreuzzüge* II, 57ff. "The Crusaders brought the new ideal of knighthood with them and France developed their forms" (Hans Planitz p. 90; see also Heinrich von Wedel p. 9; H. G. Atkins in: *Chivalry*, p. 88). This is a widespread conception for which there is little evidence. The "new ideal" is found in poetry; and the literary relationships do not run via Palestine but directly across the Rhine.

39. The German and the Latin texts from Friedrich Wilhelm, *Denkmäler* p. 119 and Commentary p. 229.

40. On the class division among the sons of Noah see Julius Petersen pp. 70ff.

41. Instances of such lists of ranks going beyond the middle of the thirteenth century: August von Fürth p. 94; Walther Kotzenberg pp. 11ff.; Paul Kluckhohn pp. 122ff.; Julius Petersen p. 83; see also Hans Fehr, *Vom Fürstenstand in der deutschen Dichtung des Mittelalters* in: Festschrift Th. Mayer I, 151–60. Similar lists of rankings in Latin in George Waitz V, 187f.

42. See also in Thomasin: *wir welln behalten niht unsern ordn noch unser leben . . . der gebûre wolt sîn kneht, . . . der kneht waere gerne gebûr, . . . der phaffe wolt gern rîter wesen, . . . vil gern der rîter phaffe waer, . . . der koufman, . . . der wercman . . . , etc; daz sich deheiner niht enschampt, ern well durch nît des andern ampt* (2634f.; 39/41/43/45/47/50/65f.)

43. Roth von Schreckenstein, *Ritterwürde* p. 398.

44. Otto Brunner p. 400; this is the most thorough investigation in more recent historical literature of the question of medieval class ideas. See ibid., pp. 395ff.

45. Wilhelm Schwer, *Stand und Ständeordnung im Weltbild des Mittelalters, Die geistes- und gesellschaftsgeschichtlichen Grundlagen der berufsständischen Idee*, Görres-Ges., Veröffentlichungen d. Sekt. f. Sozial- u. Wirtschaftswiss. 7 (Paderborn, 1934), p. 6; see also Theodor Steinbüchel, *Christliches Mittelalter*, Leipzig 1935, pp. 259ff.; Luise Manz, *Der Ordo-Gedanke, Ein Beitrag zur Frage des mittelalterlichen Ständegedankens*, Beiheft 33 zur VSWG. (Stuttgart-Berlin, 1937).

46. Wilhelm Schwer p. 42.

47. Otto Brunner p. 399.

48. See Ruth Mohl, *The Three Estates in Medieval and Renaissance Literature* (New York: Columbia U. Studies in English and Comparative Lit., 1933), pp. 9ff.; Paul Guilhiermoz p. 370ff. In Mohl, pp. 284ff., there is testimony to the fact that the authors of the Middle Ages were aware that this division goes back to the ancient philosophers. See also Nikolaus Paulus, *Die Wertung der weltlichen Berufe im Mittelalter* Hist. Jb. 32 (1911), 725–55.

49. Quoted from Hans Delbrück III, 262; see Paul Guilhiermoz p. 372.

50. Quoted from Georg Waitz V, 189, n. 1; see Paul Guilhiermoz pp. 372ff.; further instances ibid., p. 375, n. 20. Jacob de Vitry speaks of *diversis saecularium personarum ordinibus* and then lists: soldiers, peasants, mer-

chants, artisans, etc. (see Nikolaus Paulus, Hist. Jb. 32, 734).

51. For example, in the distinction between *imperantes, operantes* and *obtemperantes* in Alanus de Insulis (see Wilhelm Schwer p. 35).

52. See Luise Manz p. 49.

53. Nikolaus Monzel, *Geburtsstände und Leistungsgemeinschaften in der katholischen Soziallehre des Mittelalters und der Gegenwart*, Bonner Akad. Reden 10 (Bonn, 1953), p. 9; see also the epilogue in Monzel on the second edition of Wilhelm Schwer's book on *Stand und Ständeordnung* (Paderborn, 1952), pp. 87ff.; further Franz Steinbach, *Geburtsstand, Berufsstand und Leistungsgemeinschaft, Studien zur Geschichte des Bürgertums* II, Rhein. Vjbll. 14 (1949), 35–96. In spite of this, legal history still gives indications of its belief in the idea of professional class divisions: "The social classification of the Middle Ages originates in occupational divisions. The development moved from a social division by profession to a social division by birth" (Hermann Conrad, *Deutsche Rechtsgeschichte* I, 394).

54. Theodor Mayer, HZ 159, 463; see also Alfred von Martin, *Kultursoziologie des Mittelalters* in: *Handwörterbuch der Soziologie*, Alfred Vierkandt, ed. (Stuttgart, 1931), 370–90, esp. p. 377.

55. Theodor Steinbüchel p. 266; see also Wilhelm Schwer p. 41.

56. On the relationships between medieval concepts of class, see Gerhard Seeliger, *Ständische Bildungen im deutschen Volk*, Rektoratsrede, (Leipzig, 1905), esp. p. 15; Erich Molitor, *Ständerechtsverhältnisse als Geschichtsquelle*, HZ. 170, 1950, 23–39, esp. p. 26.

57. Otto Hintze, *Typologie der ständischen Verfassungen des Abendlandes,* HZ 141 (1930), 229–48, quotation pp. 229f.; on this see Otto Brunner, *Die Freiheitsrechte in der altständischen Gesellschaft*, in: Festschrift Theodor Mayer I, 293–303, esp. pp. 295f.

58. Heinz Markmann, *Sozialstruktur im allgemeinen*, in: *Einführung in die Soziologie*, Alfred Weber, ed. (München, 1955), 237–92, quote p. 249; on this see Otto Brunner, *Feudalismus* p. 6.

59. Dietrich Gerhard, *Regionalismus und ständisches Wesen als ein Grundthema europäischer Geschichte*, in: Wege der Forschung 2 (see above p. 186, n. 32), 332–64 (originally in: HZ. 174, 1952, 307–37), quotation p. 340.

60. Heinrich Mitteis, *Zur staufischen Verfassungsgeschichte*, in: *Die Rechtsidee* . . . , 481–500 (originally in: ZRG. GA. 65 1947, 316–37), quotation p. 500. See also Hans Freyer, *Soziologie als Wirklichkeitswissenschaft, Logische Grundlegung des Systems der Soziologie* (Leipzig-Berlin, 1930), p. 268.

61. See Theodor Mayer, HZ. 159, 482f.; Edmund E. Stengel, *Land- und Lehnrechtliche Grundlagen des Reichfürstenstandes*, in: E. St. *Abhandlungen und Untersuchungen zur mittelalterlichen Geschichte* (Köln-Graz, 1960), 133–73 (originally in: ZRG. GA. 66, 1948, 294–342).

62. Otto Hinze, HZ. 141, 242. Using the Schönburg domain as an example, Walter Schlesinger has observed that "the feeble development of the territorial class structure . . . is in agreement with the feeble development of the power of the territorial lords" (*Die Landesherrschaft der Herren von*

Schönburg, Eine Studie zur Geschichte des Staates in Deutschland, Quellen u. Stud. zur Verfassungsgeschichte des Deutschen Reiches in: MA u. Neuzeit IX, 1, Münster-Köln, 1954, p. 180).

63. Eberhard F. Otto, HZ. 162, 32; similarly Hermann Conrad, *Rechtsgesch.* I, 396. For an evaluation of the "fundamental laws of knighthood of Barbarossa" (Hans Naumann, *Deutsche Kultur* p. 13), see Otto pp. 19ff. and Jean-Pierre Ritter pp. 168ff.

64. The Empire had hardly any share in this development. The knightly class was a creation of the regions. The imperial knighthood which gradually developed in southwest Germany from the remains of the families of free noblemen and imperial *ministeriales*, "never reached the stage of becoming a politically effective independent class" (Karl S. Bader, *Reichsadel und Reichsstädte in Schwaben am Ende des alten Reiches*, in: Festschrift Theodor Mayer I, 247–63, quotation p. 252). It was not until 1671 that knighthood was "recognized in imperial law" where it was regarded "not indeed as a class within the Empire but rather as a fixed component of the Sacrum Imperium Romanum" (ibid., p. 261; see also Bader, *Der dt. Südwesten* pp. 160ff.).

65. See Hans Spangenberg, *Vom Lehnstaat zum Ständestaat, Ein Beitrag zur Entstehung der landständischen Verfassungen*, Hist. Bibl. 29 (München-Berlin, 1912), pp. 31f. "The change from the state of *ministerialis* to free knight has not yet been sufficiently investigated" ibid., p. 34, n. 4). See also W. Jappe Alberts, *Zur Entsstehung der Stände in den weltlichen Territorien am Niederrhein*, in: *Aus Geschichte und Landeskunde, Forschungen u. Darstellungen*, Franz Steinbach zum 65 Geburtstag, (Bonn, 1960), 333–49.

66. Herbert Helbig p. 351.

67. Gerd Tellenbach, *Zur Bedeutung der Personenforschung für die Erkenntnis des früheren Mittelalters*, Freiburger Univ. reden, N.F. 25 (Freiburg, 1957), p. 14.

68. Hans Hirsch, *Die hohe Gerichtsbarkeit im deutschen Mittelalter* (Prag, 1922), p. 234.

69. Karl Schmid, *Über die Struktur des Adels im früheren Mittelalter*, Jb. f. fränkische Landesforschung 19 (1959), 1–23, quotation p. 1.

70. I would like to call particular attention to the work of Gerd Tellenbach: *Vom karolingischen Reichsadel zum deutschen Reichsfürstenstand*, in: Wege der Forschung 2, 191–242 (originally in: *Adel und Bauern im deutschen Staat des Mittelalters*, Theodor Mayer, ed., Leipzig, 1943, 22–73); *Kritische Studien zur grossfränkischen und alemannischen Adelsgeschichte*, Zs. f. Württ. Landesgeschichte 15 (1956), 169–90; *Studien und Vorarbeiten zur Geschichte des grossfränkischen und frühdeutschen Adels*, ed. G.T., Forschungen zur oberrhein. Landesgesch. 4 (Freiburg, 1957); see also note 67 above. For France, see Karl F. Werner, *Untersuchungen zur Frühzeit des französischen Fürstentums (9. bis 10. Jahrhundert)*, Welt als Geschichte 18 (1958), 256–89; 19 (1959), 146–93; 20 (1960), 87–119. On the whole question, see the fine chapter "Ethos und Bildungswelt des europäischen Adels" in Otto Brunner, *Adeliges Landleben und europäischer*

Geist. Leben und Werk Wolf Helmhards von Hohberg, 1612–1688 (Salzburg 1949), pp. 61ff. For further information see the works listed above p. 203, n. 53.

71. Karl Schmid, *Zur Problematik von Familie, Sippe und Geschlecht, Haus und Dynastie beim mittelalterlichen Adel, Vorfragen zum Thema "Adel und Herrschaft im Mittelalter,"* Zs. f. d. Gesch. des Oberrheins 105 (1957), 1–62, quotation p. 42.

72. Gerd Tellenbach in: Wege d. Forschg. 2, 193.

73. Otto Brunner, *Neue Wege* p. 138. Marc Bloch characterizes German nobility as distinguished from that of the western lands "by a stratification pushed into the very interior of the nobility" (II, 71).

74. Heinrich Dannenbauer in: Wege d. Forschg. 2, 71, n. 7.

75. This meaning is found in first place in Kluge-Mitzka, *Etymologisches Wörterbuch*, but this surely does not mean that this was the original meaning but rather that which was predominant later.

76. Gustav Neckel, *Adel und Gefolgschaft, Ein Beitrag zur germanischen Altertumskunde*, in: G.N. *Vom Germanentum, Ausgew, Aufsätze und Vorträge* (Leipzig, 1944), 139–86 (originally in Beitr. 41 (1916), 385–436), quotation p. 142.

77. See Eberhard F. Otto: "Thus the position of the nobility rest upon the possession of hereditary property" (p. 36); in opposition to this Walter Schlesinger: "It is altogether remarkable that there is no visible connection in the sources between nobility and hereditary property whether this refers to the noblest of the noble or even the king" (*Entstehung der Landesherrschaft* p. 83, n. 306).

78. For a discussion of the etymology and original meaning of "Adel": Otto Behaghel, *Odal*, MSB., phil.-hist. Kl , Jg. 1935, Heft 8, (München, 1935); (on this the review by Wolfgang Krause, HZ. 154, 1936, 323–24); Willy Krogmann, *Adel und Udel*, ZfdPh. 63, 1938, 189–91); Oswald Szemerényi, *The Etymology of German Adel*, Word 8, 1952, 42–50; Friedrich Stroh, *Germanentum*, in: *Deutsche Wortgeschichte* I, 33–49, esp. p. 42.

79. Gustav Neckel, *Germanentum*, p. 178.

80. Otto von Dungern, *Adelsherrschaft*, p. 71.

81. Karl Bosl in: Gebhardt's *Handbuch* I, 593.

82. Otto von Dungern, *Adelsherrschaft*, p. 41. This dynastic nobility appears in the sources as *potentes, magnates, optimates, primores, principes*, etc. (see Georg Waitz V, 412ff.). The dynastic families were occasionally distinguished from the *Adel* even in the twelfth century: *principes, nobiles, ministeriales* (ibid., p. 422, n. 2).

83. On this see Karl F. Werner; "Constitutional historians do not hesitate even today to put minor 'Gentlemen' . . . on the same level as princes by some kind of senseless legal fiction, so that the latter have no category in state law assigned to them for their own. That is the view point of the gentry of the thirteenth to eighteenth centuries" (WaG. 18, 257).

84. This is also true of the separation made between "nobility by blood" and "nobility by service." See Karl Bosl in: Gebhardt's *Handbuch* I, 593. In research on the *ministeriales* especially, great importance is attributed to

service nobility: "Their nobility was the result of their service" (Paul Kluckhohn p. 47); "Service to a prince always ennobled even a retainer" (Karl Bosl in: Vortr. u. Forschg. 5, 65). The power of ennobling certainly did not come from the service itself but from the chances of advancement offered by service in the proximity of a prince: enrichment, increase in power, marriage into a noble family. In most cases it was the ability to marry that was the decisive factor. Jean-Pierre Ritter has some interesting material on "the idea of ennoblement by service" (pp. 206f.); but the statement "servitude, far from debasing, actually ennobled" is certainly not generally true (p. 210). *Ministeriales* were not counted among the nobility until they had shed the traces of their ancient condition of servitude. Heinrich Dannenbauer has emphasized that "service and nobility are a contradiction in terms" (in: Wege d. Forschg. 2, 71).

85. See Gerd Tellenbach in: Wege d. Forschg. 2, 195 and n. 18.
86. See Walter Schlesinger in: Wege d. Forsch. 2, 170.
87. Karl Bosl in: Gebhardt's Handbuch I, 593. "The exclusive nature of highly placed families does not need to be a class phenomenon based on constitutional law; it can be simply social" (Eberhard F. Otto p. 202).
88. Gerd Tellenbach, *Personenforschung* p. 18.
89. Karl Schmid, ZGO. 105, 34.
90. Gerd Tellenbach in: Wege d. Forschg. 2, 226.
91. "But what is nobility? The legal sources from the thirteenth century on designate as "noble" and "noblemen" the two levels of society . . . which had developed at that time . . . , the landed gentry and the knights and noble retainers" (Otto Brunner, Neue Wege p. 137; see also Brunner, *Land und Herrschaft* pp. 407f.). Even later than this there still existed a consciousness that this new concept of the term "nobility" had driven out an older meaning; Sebastian Münster writes in his cosmography: *es ist vor zeiten der titul des adels allein gegeben worden den fürsten und grossen herren,—der ander adel unter den fürsten hat vor zeiten andere namen gehabt* (quoted from Roth von Schreckenstein, *Ritterwürde* p. 186, n. 6). Later the word *Adel* was not infrequently used for knights only, and a sharp distinction was made between *Herren* and *Adel*: "The Swabian Freiherr von Zimmern in his chronicle which closes with the year 1566 distinguishes very sharply between his own social equals, the *Herren*, and the people who, as he puts it, are only of the *Adel* and whom he does not regard as his equals" (Heinrich Dannenbauer, in: Wege der Forschung 2, 71, n. 7; see also Roth von Schreckenstein, *Ritterwürde* p. 622). There are indeed social rankings in which the nobility is set below the knights, e.g., in the reformed city law of Augsburg (1548): "Herren Ritterschaft Adel" (quoted from Franz von Löher p. 373).
92. See Friedrich Vogt, *Der Bedeutungswandel des Wortes edel*, Rektoratsrede (Marburg, 1909); Ernst Benz, *Über den Adel in der deutschen* Mystik, DVj. 14 (1936), 505–36; Hans Schmitz, *Blutsadel und Geistesadel in der hochhöfischen Dichtung*, Bonner Beiträge zur deutsche Philologie 11 (Würzburg-Aumühle, 1941); Herman Kunisch, *Spätes Mittelalter (1250–1500)*, in: *Deutsche Wortgeschichte* I, 205–67, esp. pp. 222ff.,

where there is reference to further literature. I was not able to obtain the typewritten dissertation of Heta Zutt, *"Adel" und "edel,"* (Freiburg, 1956). On the differently structured conditions in French poetry, see Erich Köhler, *Zur Diskussion der Adelsfrage bei den Trobadors*, in: *Medium aevum vivum*, Festschrift für Walther Bulst (Heidelberg, 1960), 161–178.

93. Otto Brunner, *Adeliges Landleben* p. 77; see also Hans Schmitz p. 41.

94. Occurrences of the word *adel* in the poets are as follows: Walther von der Vogelweide once (102, 18); Hartmann von Aue twice in *Erek* (1837; 9349) [unadel]; Veldeke once in Servatius (334); once each in the *Strassburg Alexander* (3866), Herbort (17257) and *Kudrun* (1007, 4) twice in *König Rother* (39, 77); three times in the *Rolandslied* (3638; 6882; 7813) and in *Herzog Ernst B* (305; 685; 1169 [*edel* fem. noun]). The word is not common in postclassical epic either. Further examples in the literature given in n. 92. The instances from the *Wiener Genesis* in *Mittelhochdeutsches Wörterbuch 1*, 7f.; the instances in Old High German may now be found in full in the new *Althochdeutsches Wörterbuch* I. 27f.

95. "Nobility thus never existed as an actual class. Nobility is more a characteristic than a state in law" (Georg Waitz V, 405). "Nobility as a 'characteristic' is . . . the common basis of all noble associations of persons" (Karl Schmid, Jb. f. frk. Landesforschg. 19, 14). There was no word for nobility as an institution in medieval Latin either. There was only *nobilis* "that epithet of comparative quality which expressed only a characteristic of varying intensity" (Georges Duby p. 237); *nobilitas* was merely the abstract form of this personal characteristic.

96. *sîn adel* (Erek 1837; Salman 214, 4; 422, 3; Thomasin 3894; 3910; 4197; 4218; 4267; 4273); *mîn adel* (Salman 25, 1); *ir adel* (Rother 77; Salman 5, 5; Herzog Ernst B 305; Thomasin 3876; Kudrun 1007, 4), etc.

97. Even when it is stated *si is von adele geborn* (Strassburger Alexander 3866; similarly Servatius 334), this is not to be taken in the same abstract way as one would say in later times "er ist von Adel"; it means simply that her family possesses the quality "adel." The abstract sense of *Adel* is to be found in the passage from Herbort already cited: *Sie hette bosliche. Mit eime ritter getan. Den wolde sie zv adel han* (17255–57).

98. Gerd Tellenbach in: Wege d. Forschg. 2, 193; see on the subject the Latin instances in Georg Waitz: *magne nobilitatis homo, vir summae nobilitatis* (V, 387, n. 2); *principibus atque inferioris ordinis nobilibus* (ibid., n. 5); *femina nobilissima* (ibid., p. 388, n. 2), etc.

99. *swer niht enleistet sîn gebot, der hât daz adel daz im got gap von sînen schulden vlorn* (Thomasin 3887–89).

100. In *Lanzelet* it is stated: *es was im unbekant, wie er selbe was genant und welhes adels er waere* (31–33), where *adel* means nothing more than "family," "origin."

101. "Knights are clearly distinguished from the nobility in documents of the fourteenth century and even later" (Hans Spangenberg p. 89, n. 2, where further literature can be found). As late as the first half of the fifteenth century Johannes Rothe in his *Ritterspiegel* made "a distinction between nobility and knighthood" (Julius Petersen p. 62).

102. "A further step and one fraught with consequences took place because of the fact that knighthood was counted as part of the nation's nobility, as is clearly stated in the *Kaiserrechte*. From this time on and certainly from the fourteenth century there existed therefore a lower nobility" (Roth von Schreckenstein, *Reichsritterschaft* I, 200).

103. See *Deutsches Rechtswörterbuch* I, 429.

104. It has been observed and stated many times already that there are two different concepts behind the term "ritter;" by Roth von Schreckenstein: "Christian chivalry and Christian knightly class, concepts which by no means coincide, are nevertheless sometimes interchanged, a superficial usage which has produced many errors" (*Ritterwürde* p. 127); by Eberhard F. Otto: "Knightly class and chivalry are to some degree separate" (HZ. 162, 33); and particularly clearly by Herbert Klein: ". . . it could be assumed that the word 'knight' once had another meaning, that in earlier times it designated a man who performed knightly service as a cavalry soldier or even one like this who was in the service of or belonged to a particular lord; but later . . . only the man who had attained the dignity of knighthood by a ceremonial act. This would be supported by the fact that in later times both meanings are found side by side. There is a very instructive example of this in the list of 1319 from Mühldorf on creating knights: *Fridericus archiepiscopus . . . creavit milites sub notatos. Primo (1) Nicolaum de Tan, (2) Hainricum Öder, militem eiusdem Tannarii, . . . (4) Conradum Tumbshiren, militem . . .*" (MdGfSL. 80, 109).

105. Karl Bosl speaks cautiously of a "company with the same lifestyle" (Gebhardt's *Handbuch* I, 675). That is something different from a "class in which the emperor and king had the same standing as the lowest knight" (Hermann Conrad, *Deutsche Rechtsgeschichte* I, 396; similarly August von Fürth p. 80; Friedrich von Raumer VI, 554; Ludwig A. Winterswyl p. 18; Johannes Bühler, *Die Kultur des Mittelalters*, Kröners Taschenausgabe 79 (Stuttgart, 1931; repr. 1948), p. 177. As proof of the alleged class equality reference has frequently been made to the so-called *Kleines Kaiserrecht* of 1372, which does indeed equate retainers with the emperor: *Alsus wurden dinstlute gemachte von dem keiser, den er gab ritters namen, vn die er bestetigete mit dem schilde vn mit dem swerte, des riches gut erbeclich zu besitzin . . . vnd sal ein iglich man wiszen, wer ein dinstman ist des riches, daz er von den geborn ist, die der keiser also edelte, vn machte sie sin genozz an der wirde, vn als gesc. stet in der dinstlute rechte* (III, 1). *Eyn iglich man sal wiszen, daz der keiser ritter gemacht, durch daz sie ein schirmunge und ein mur sin, wider zu sten allen bosen dingen . . . vn hirvm hat der keiser den ritter gemacht sin genoz vnd hat im daz swert beuolhen . . . Auch stet anderswa gesc.: man sal den ritter kronen vn wirdigen mit des riches kronen* (III, 4). *Sint gesc. stet in des riches recht: dinstlute des riches sint des keisers genozzen . . . der keiser machte von erste fri des riches dinstman. Sint sie der keiser durch ir truwe geedelt hat von allen luten, vn machte sie sin genozz. Wan in des riches reht stet gesc.: das riche ist der dinstlute* (III, 5; Hermann E. Endemann, ed., Cassel, 1846, pp. 183ff.). This text is a fine testimony to the romanticizing of

chivalry in the late Middle Ages; as a source for the legal situation of the period it is virtually worthless. See Julius Ficker *Reichsfürstenstand* II 1, 210.

106. See above p. 88f.

107. See above p. 57.

108. An important aspect of this doctrine has been completely ignored in this work and will be dealt with elsewhere, namely the application of the concept of knighthood to the social conditions of Middle High German poets. Closely associated with this is the question of the share of the *ministeriales* in courtly culture, which is usually answered in a positive sense. Among historians, however, a clearcut warning is occasionally sounded. Erich von Guttenberg writes: "It is totally inappropriate to base the cultural phenomenon of the courtly period predominantly on social changes within the class of *ministeriales* and then to extrapolate these as indicators for the period" (DA. 3, 292); see also the observation by Karl Bosl that "the class of retainers grew only slowly . . . into the social and cultural world of dynastic knighthood and the legal class-distinctions . . . were not leveled out in the process" (I, 27). In the vast literature on the problem of the *ministeriales*, scarcely anything is to be found on this subject. The exception is Hans-Walter Klewitz, in whose area of research a series of great *ministeriales* families are to be found. According to his conclusions, "the tradition does not have a single detail which could throw light on the way of life or the intellectual culture of the *ministeriales*" (p. 59).

109. See Otto Brunner, *Adeliges Landleben* p. 88.

110. Johann F. Boehmer has put together a list of the murdered bishops which "is unlikely to be complete" (*Fontes* III, Preface p. xlvi, note 1). According to this, nine bishops were murdered in the classical period of literature (1150–1250) alone. In 1152 Graf Hermann von Winzenburg was murdered, in 1208 King Philip of Swabia, in 1231 Herzog Ludwig of Bavaria, before 1234 Konrad von Marburg, etc. A vivid glimpse of the brutality of the internecine wars is given by the chronicle of the little monastery of Stederburg near Wolfenbüttel (Eduard Winkelmann, trans., *Geschichtsschreiber der dt. Vorzeit*, 2. Gesamtausgabe, 12. Jh., Vol. 14, Leipzig, 1895). Not a great deal is said about this in the cultural histories. Justus Hashagen mentions "the frightful decline in moral standards among the French nobility about 1200" and asks "could it possibly have been otherwise in Germany? Research into the history of behavior is not sufficiently far advanced for us to be able to give a definite answer to this question" (*Kulturgeschichte des Mittelalters, Eine Einführung*, Hamburg, 1950, p. 364). See also Sidney Painter pp. 85ff.

111. Adolf Waas, *Kreuzzüge* II, 290. Opposed to this Julius Petersen: "Poetry was in decline, it is true; but the knightly class of the thirteenth and fourteenth centuries did not in actuality suffer the crass decline which one would have to deduce from the poetry" (p. 9).

112. "By the middle of the fourteenth century the noble class of France had accepted the ideas of feudal chivalry and was carrying them out in practice to a greater extent than at any earlier time" (Sidney Painter, p. 63). See

also Johan Huizinga: "How can there be any doubt about the serious nature of the knightly ideal in French society about 1400?" (p. 100 and frequently). Otto Brunner emphasizes "that chivalric-courtly culture, although subjected to considerable change lived on as the educational milieu of the nobility up to 1700" (*Adeliges Landleben* p. 86).

113. Otto von Dungern, *Herrenstand*, p. 389. Various views on the "Golden Age of Chivalry" in F.J.C. Hearnshaw, in: *Chivalry* pp. 18ff.

114. Only such instances have been included as show the knight-concept in absolute terms, that is, where it does not refer to a person (e.g., *des ritters hant, eines ritters swert*) or to a group of persons (e.g., *der ritter site, maneges ritters kraft*). No distinction is made between singular and plural.

VII. On the State of Research on Knighthood

1. Arno Borst, *Das Rittertum im Hochmittelalter. Idee und Wirklichkeit*. In: Saeculum 10 1959, pp. 213–231.

2. Johanna Maria van Winter, *Ridderschap. Ideal en werkelijkheid*, Bussum 1965. (= Fibulareeks 11) German version *Rittertum. Ideal und Wirklichkeit*, Axel Plantiko and Paul Schritt, trans., (München, 1969).

3. Johanna Maria van Winter, *Ministerialiteit en ridderschap in Gelre en Zutphen*, proefschrift Utrecht 1962 (Groningen, 1962). (= Bijdragen van het Instituut voor middeleeuwse geschiedenis der Rijksuniversiteit te Utrecht 31.)

4. Cf. Johanna Maria van Winter, *De middeleeuwse ridderschap als* "classe sociale", in: Tijdschrift voor geschiedenis 84 (1971), pp. 262–75.

5. Cf. Karl Bosl, *Kasten, Stände, Klassen im mittelalterlichen Deutschland. Zur Problematik soziologischer Begriffe und ihrer Anwendung auf die mittelalterliche Gesellschaft*, in: Zeitschrift für bayerische Landesgeschichte 32 (1969), pp. 477–94.

6. See the works of Duby, van Luyn, and Johrendt which are discussed later as well as *Histoire de la France*, publié sous la direction de Georges Duby, Vol. 1 (Paris, 1970), pp. 267ff.; Jean-Francois Lemarignier, *La France médiévale: Institutions et société* (Paris, 1970) (Collection "U", Série histoire médiévale), pp. 163ff.

7. Sidney Painter, *French Chivalry. Chivalric Idea and Practices in Mediaeval France* (Baltimore, Maryland 1940; repr. 1957), pp. 95ff.

8. Arnold Hauser, *Sozialgeschichte der Kunst und Literatur*, Vol. 1 (München, 1953), pp. 211ff.

9. Erich Köhler, *Observations historiques et sociologiques sur la poésie des troubadours*, in: Cahiers de civilisation médiévale 7 (1964), pp. 27–51; German version: *Die Rolle des niederen Rittertums bei der Entstehung der Trobadorlyrik*, in: E. Köhler, *Esprit und arkadische Freiheit, Aufsätze aus der Welt der Romania* (Frankfurt/M, Bonn, 1966), pp. 9–27.

10. Cf. below p. 157.

11. Hans Georg Reuter, *Die Lehre vom Ritterstand. Zum Ritterbegriff in His-*

toriographie und Dichtung vom 11. bis zum 13. Jahrhundert, Köln (Wien, 1971). (= Neue Wirtschaftsgeschichte 4) Cf. the review by Josef Fleckenstein in: Blätter für deutsche Landesgeschichte 108, 1972, pp. 524–8.

12. Georges Duby, *Les Origines de la chevalerie*, in: Ordinamenti militari in occidente nell'alto medioevo, 30 March–5 April 1967, Vol. 2 (Spoleto, 1968), (= Settimane di studio del Centro italiano di studi sull' alto medioevo 15), pp. 739–61. Again in: G. Duby, *Hommes et structures du moyen âge. Recueil d'articles* (Paris, The Hague, 1973). (= Le Savoir historique 1), pp. 325–41.

13. Cf. Karl Ferdinand Werner, *Untersuchungen zur Frühzeit des französischen Fürstentums (9.–10. Jahrhundert)* in: *Die Welt als Geschichte* 18 (1958), pp. 256–89; 19 (1959), pp. 146–93; 20 (1960), pp. 87–119. Also Georges Duby, *La Noblesse dans la France médiévale. Une enquête à poursuivre*, in *Revue historique* 226 (1961), pp. 1–22 and again G. Duby, *Hommes et structures* (see n. 12), pp. 145–66; this volume brings together several studies by Duby on the problem of French nobility. Also Léopold Genicot, *La Noblesse au moyen âge dans l'ancienne "Francie,"* in: Annales. Economies, sociétés, civilisations 17 (1962), pp. 1–22; See further the works listed by Genicot in his bibliography, especially his investigation, *L'économie rurale Namuroise au bas moyen âge*, Vol. 2, *Les Hommes, la noblesse* (Louvain, 1960) (= Université de Louvain, Recueil de travaux d'histoire et de philologie, Série 4, Fasc. 20). Cf. also Gerd Tellenbach, *Zur Erforschung des mittelalterlichen Adels (9.–12. Jahrhundert)*, in: Comité international des sciences historiques, XIIᵉ congrès international des sciences historiques, Vienne, 29 août–5 septembre 1965, Rapports Vol. 1, Grands Thèmes, Horn, Wien [1967], pp. 318–37.

14. Cf. the fundamental investigation by Georges Duby, *La Société aux XIᵉ et XIIᵉ siècles dans la région mâconnaise* (Paris, 1953) (= Bibliothèque générale de l'Ecole pratique des hautes études, Sect. 6).

15. Cf. George Duby, *Les Laics et la paix de Dieu*, in: *I laici nella societas christiana dei secoli XI e XII* (Milano, 1966), pp. 448–61. Also in: G. Duby, *Hommes et structures* (see n. 12), pp. 227–40.

16. Cf. the works of Johrendt and Fleckenstein above pp. 136ff.

17. Cf. on the subject Pérennec, above, p. 146.

18. P. van Luyn, *Les milites dans la France du XIᵉ siècle. Examen des sources narratives*, in: *Le Moyen Age* 77, 1971, pp. 5–51; 193–238.

19. Wilhelm Erben, *Schwertleite und Ritterschlag. Beiträge zu einer Rechtsgeschichte der Waffen*, in: *Zeitschrift für historische Waffenkunde* 8, 1918/1920, pp. 105–67.

20. Johann Johrendt, *Milites und Militia im 11. Jahrhundert. Untersuchung zur Frühgeschichte des Rittertums in Frankreich und Deutschland*. Diss. (Erlangen-Nürnberg, 1971).

21. Karl Bosl, *Die Reichsministerialität der Salier und Staufer. Ein Beitrag zur Geschichte des hochmittelalterlichen deutschen Volkes, Staates und Reiches*, Vol. 1 (Stuttgart, 1950) (= Schriften der Monumenta Germaniae historica [Deutsches Institut für Erforschung des Mittelalters], 10, 1), p. 27.

22. Cf. Josef Fleckenstein, *Bürgertum und Rittertum in der Geschichte des*

mittelalterlichen Freiburg, in: *Freiburg im Mittelalter. Vorträge zum Stadtjubiläum* 1970, Wolfgang Müller, ed. (Bühl/Baden, 1970) (= Veröffentlichungen des Alemannischen Instituts 29), pp. 77–95; idem, *Zur Frage der Abgrenzung von Bauer und Ritter*, in: *Wort und Begriff "Bauer". Zusammenfassender Bericht über die Kolloquien der Kommission für die Alter94tumskunde Mittel- und Nordeuropas*, Reinhard Wenskus, Herbert Jankuhn, and Klaus Grinda, eds. (Göttingen, 1975), (= Abhandlungen der Akademie der Wissenschaften in Göttingen, Phil.-hist. Klasse, Folge 3, Nr. 89), pp. 246–53; here p. 249, n. 19.

23. Josef Fleckenstein, *Friedrich Barbarossa und das Rittertum. Zur Bedeutung der grossen Mainzer Hoftage von 1184 und 1188*, in: *Festschrift für Hermann Heimpel zum 70. Geburtstag am 19. Sept. 1971*, hrsg. von den Mitarbeitern des Max-Planck-Instituts für Geschichte, Vol. 2 (Göttingen, 1972) (= Veröffentlichungen des Max-Planck-Instituts für Geschichte 36, 2), pp. 1023–41.

24. Josef Fleckenstein, *Zum Problem der Abschliessung des Ritterstandes*, in: *Historische Forschungen für Walter Schlesinger*, Helmut Beumann, ed. (Köln, Wien, 1974), pp. 252–71.

25. Cf., e.g., Hermann Conrad, *Deutsche Rechtsgeschichte. Ein Lehrbuch*, Vol. 1, 2 ed. (Karlsruhe, 1962), pp. 296ff.

26. Wilhelm Schwer, *Stand und Ständeordnung im Weltbild des Mittelalters. Die geistes- und gesellschaftsgeschichtlichen Grundlagen der berufsständischen Idee*, 2 ed. with preface and epilogue, Nikolaus Monzel, ed. (Paderborn, 1952) (= Görres-Gesellschaft zur Pflege der Wissenschaft. Veröffentlichung der Sektion für Wirtschafts- und Sozial-wissenschaft 7), p. 6. Cf. also Helmut Stahleder, *Zum Ständebegriff im Mittelalter*, in: *Zeitschrift für bayerische Landesgeschichte* 35 (1972), pp. 523–70; Gerd Tellenbach, *Irdischer Stand und Heilserwartung im Denken des Mittelalters*, in: *Festschrift für Hermann Heimpel* [see above, note 23], Vol. 2, pp. 1–16.

27. Cf. Otto Brunner, *Land und Herrschaft. Grundfragen der territorialen Verfassungsgeschichte Österreichs im Mittelalter*, 5 ed. (Wien, 1965), p. 400, n. 2; with reference to the satirical poem *Des Teufels Netz*, A. K. Barack, ed. (1863); cf. Barack's closing remarks, pp. 442ff. Also Horst Stuke, *La Signification du mot "Stand" dans les pays de langue allemande (Aperçu d'histoire des notions)*, in: *Problèmes de stratification sociale*, Actes du colloque international (1966), published by Roland Mousnier (Paris, 1968) (= Travaux du Centre de recherches sur la civilisation de l'Europe moderne 5), p. 37–49.

28. Otto Brunner [see n. 27], p. 399.

29. Cf. on the subject Jacques Le Goff, *Note sur société tripartie, idéologie monarchique et renouveau économique dans la chrétienté du IX*ᵉ*–XII*ᵉ *siècles* in: *L'Europe aux IX*ᵉ*–XI*ᵉ *siècles. Aux origines des états nationaux*. Actes du colloque international sur les origines des états européens aux IXᵉ–XIᵉ siècles, tenu à Varsovie et Poznań du 7 au 13 septembre 1965. Publiés sous la direction de Tadeusz Manteuffel et Aleksander Gieysztor (Warsaw, 1968) (Institut de l'histoire de l'Académie polonaise des sciences), pp. 63–71.

30. Johanna Maria van Winter, *Uxorem de militari ordine sibi imparem*, in:

Miscellanea mediaevalia in memoriam Jan Frederik Niermeyer (Groningen, 1967), pp. 113–124.

31. Cf. with further instances Edmund Wiessner, *Höfisches Rittertum (1200–1300)*, in: *Deutsche Wortgeschichte*, Friedrich Maurer and Friedrich Stroh, eds., 2 rev. ed., Vol. 1 (Berlin, 1959) (= Grundriss der germanischen Philologie 17, 1), pp. 149–203, esp. pp. 158f.

32. Daniel Rocher, *"Chevalerie" et littérature "chevaleresque,"* in: Etudes germaniques 21 (1966), pp. 165–79; 23 (1968), pp. 345–57.

33. René Pérennec, *Adaptation et société: l'adaptation par Hartmann d' Aue du roman de Chrétien de Troyes "Erec et Enide"*, in: Etudes germaniques 28 (1973), pp. 289–303.

34. Cf. Hans Naumann, *Verhältnis des deutschen zum westlichen Rittertum*, in: *Von deutscher Art in Sprache und Dichtung*, Vol. 2 (Stuttgart, Berlin, 1941), pp. 169–88.

35. Daniel Rocher, *Henric van Veldeke und das Problem der ritterlichen Kultur*, in: Heinric van Veldeken, Symposion Gent 23–24 oktober 1970. Verslag en lezingen uitgegeven door Gilbert A.R. de Smet, (Antwerpen, Utrecht, 1971), pp. 151–9.

36. Gert Kaiser, *Textauslegung und gesellschaftliche Selbstdeutung. Aspekte einer sozialgeschichtliche Interpretation von Hartmanns Artusepen* (Frankfurt/M 1973 (= Wissenschaftliche Paperbacks, Literaturwissenschaft).

37. Ursula Peters, *Artusroman und Fürstenhof. Darstellung und Kritik neuerer sozialgeschichtlicher Untersuchungen zu Hartmanns "Erec,"* in: Euphorion 69 (1975), pp. 175–96.

38. Werner Schroeder, *Zum ritter-bild der frühmittelhochdeutschen Dichter*, Germanisch-Romanische Monatsschrift 53 (1972), pp. 333–51.

39. Helmut de Boor, *Die deutsche Literatur von Karl dem Grossen bis zum Beginn der höfischen Dichtung, 770–1170*, 8 ed. (München, 1971) (= H. de Boor und Richard Newald, *Geschichte der deutschen Literatur von den Anfängen bis zur Gegenwart*, Vol. 1, p. 160.

40. Gustav Ehrismann, *Geschichte der deutschen Literatur bis zum Ausgang des Mittelalters*, Part 2, Vol. 1 (München, 1922) (= Handbuch des deutschen Unterrichts an höheren Schulen 6, 2, 1), p. 90. Dennis H. Green has acknowledged the central significance of this passage for his "Exodus" interpretation: *The Millstätter Exodus a Crusading Epic* (London, New York, 1966), pp. 273ff.

41. Konrad Zwierzina, *Mittelhochdeutsche Studien 13. Zur Textkritik des Erec*, in: ZfdA 45 (1901), pp. 317–66, esp. pp. 336f.

42. For the basis of the punctuation, see above p. 000, n. 10.

43. Cf. Johrendt (cf. n. 20), pp. 15f.

44. Karl Weinhold, *Die deutschen Frauen in dem Mittelalter*, Vols. 1–2, 3 ed. (Wien, 1897).

45. Felix Niedner, *Das deutsche Turnier im XII. und XIII. Jahrhundert* (Berlin, 1881).

46. Alwin Schultz, *Das höfische Leben zur Zeit der Minnesinger*, Vols. 1–2, 2 rev. ed. (Leipzig, 1889).

47. Julius Petersen, *Das Rittertum in der Darstellung des Johannes Rothe*

(Strassburg, 1909) (= Quellen und Forschungen zur Sprach- und Cultur-geschichte der germanischen Völker 106).

48. Paul Kluckhohn, *Die Ministerialität in Südostdeutschland vom zehnten bis zum Ende des dreizehnten Jahrhunderts* (Weimar, 1910) (= Quellen und Studien zur Verfassungsgeschichte des Deutschen Reiches in Mittelalter und Neuzeit, Vol. 4, No. 1).

49. Julius Schwietering, *Zur Geschichte von Speer und Schwert im 12. Jahrhundert* (Hamburg, 1912) (= Mitteilungen aus dem Museum für Hamburgische Geschichte 3). Repr. in: J. Schwietering, *Philologische Schriften*, Friedrich Ohly and Max Wehrli, eds. (München, 1969), pp. 59–117.

50. For a partial account, see Günter Siebel's dissertation (written under Werner Simon): *Harnisch und Helm in den epischen Dichtungen des 12. Jahrhunderts bis zu Hartmanns "Erek." Ein Beitrag zur Verwertbarkeit der Dichtung für die Realienforschung.* Diss. (Hamburg, 1968).

51. Werner Schröder (see n. 38), p. 334.

52. Paul Kluckhohn (see n. 48), p. 9.

53. Otto Brunner, *Moderner Verfassungsbegriff und mittelalterliche Verfassungsgeschichte*, in: Festschrift für Hans Hirsch (Wien, 1939) (= Mitteilungen des Österreichischen Instituts für Geschichtsforschung, Ergänzungsband 14), pp. 513–28. Revised version in: *Herrschaft und Staat im Mittelalter*, Hellmut Kämpf, ed. (Darmstadt, 1956) (= Wege der Forschung 2, pp. 1–19). Idem, *Neue Wege der Verfassungs- und Sozialgeschichte*, 2 ed. (Göttingen, 1968).

54. Eduard Schröder, *"Herzog" und "Fürst." Über Aufkommen und Bedeutung zweier Rechtswörter*, in: Zeitschrift für Rechtsgeschichte, Germanistische Abteilung 44 (1924), pp. 1–29.

55. Walter Schlesinger, *Burg und Stadt*, in: *Aus Verfassungs- und Landesgeschichte, Festschrift zum 70. Geburtstag von Theodor Mayer*, dargebracht von seinen Freunden und Schülern, Vol. 1 (Konstanz, 1954), pp. 97–150. Reprinted in W. Schlesinger, *Beiträge zur deutschen Verfassungsgeschichte des Mittelalters*, Vol. 2 (Göttingen, 1963), pp. 92–147.

56. Ruth Schmidt-Wiegand, *Historische Onomasiologie und Mittelalterforschung*, in: Frühmittelalterliche Studien 9 (1975), pp. 49–78. Idem., *Rechtswort und Rechtszeichen in der deutschen Dichtung der karolingischen Zeit*, in: Frühmittelalterliche Studien 5 (1971), pp. 268–83.

57. Gerhard Köbler, *Amtsbezeichnungen in den frühmittelalterlichen Übersetzungsgleichungen*, in: Historisches Jahrbuch der Görres-Gesellschaft 92 (1972), pp. 334–57. Idem., *Frühmittelalterliche Ortsbegriffe*, in: Blätter für deutsche Landesgeschichte 108, 1972, pp. 1–27.

58. *Wort und Begriff "Bauer"* (see n. 22).

59. Cf. Wilhelm Störmer, *Früher Adel. Studien zur politischen Führungsschicht im fränkisch-deutschen Reich vom 8. bis 11. Jahrhundert*, Vols. 1–2 (Stuttgart, 1973) (= Monographien zur Geschichte des Mittelalters 6, 1–2), esp. the important chapter "Adelige Lebensart im Spiegel literarischer Quellen," pp. 462–507. Idem., *König Artus als aristokratisches Leitbild während des späteren Mittelalters, gezeigt an Beispielen der Ministerialität und des Pa-*

triziats, in: Zeitschrift für bayerische Landesgeschichte 35 (1972), pp. 946–71, esp. p. 947.

60. On the class-ethic of the nobility see Wilhelm Berges, *Die Fürstenspiegel des hohen und späten Mittelalters* (Leipzig, 1938) (= Schriften des Reichsinstituts für ältere deutsche Geschichtskunde [Monumenta Germaniae historica] 2); Hatto Kallfelz, *Das Standesethos des Adels im 10. und 11. Jahrhundert*, Diss. (Würzburg, 1960); Gereon H. Hagspiel, *Die Führerpersönlichkeit im Kreuzzug* (Zürich, 1963) (= Geist und Werk der Zeiten 10); Ulrich Hoffmann, *König, Adel und Reich im Urteil fränkischer und deutscher Historiker des 9.–11. Jahrhunderts*. Diss. (Freiburg i. Br., 1968); H. Anton, *Fürstenspiegel und Herrscherethos in der Karolingerzeit* (Bonn, 1968) (= Bonner Historische Forschungen 32); Herwig Wolfram, *Mittelalterliche Politik und adelige Staatssprache*, in: Mitteilungen des Instituts für österreichische Geschichtsforschung 76 (1968), pp. 1 22; *Ritterliches Tugendsystem*, Günter Eisler, ed. (Darmstadt, 1970) (= Wege der Forschung 56); Hans Kloft, *Liberalitas principis, Herkunft und Bedeutung. Studien zur Prinzipatsideologie*, (Köln, Wien 1970) (= Kölner Historische Abhandlungen 18); Karl Bosl, *Die Grundlagen der modernen Gesellschaft im Mittelalter. Eine deutsche Gesellschaftsgeschichte des Mittelalters* (Stuttgart, 1972) (= Monographien zur Geschichte des Mittelalters 4), Vol. 1, pp. 137ff.; Vol. 2, pp. 266ff. Wilhelm Störmer, *König Artus als aristokratisches Leitbild* (see note 59); idem., *Früher Adel* (see n. 59); Erich Kleinschmidt, *Herrscher Darstellung. Zur Disposition mittelalterlichen Aussageverhaltens, untersucht an Texten über Rudolf I. von Habsburg. Mit einem Editionsanhang* (Bern, München, 1974) (= Bibliotheca Germanica 17).

61. Cf. Adolf von Harnack, *Militia Christi. Die christliche Religion und der Soldatenstand in den ersten drei Jahrhunderten* (Tübingen 1905; repr. Darmstadt 1963); Hilarius Emonds, *Geistlicher Kriegsdienst. Der Topos der militia spiritualis in der antiken Philosophie*, in: *Heilige Überlieferung. Ausschnitte aus der Geschichte des Mönchtums und des heiligen Kultes.* Eine Festgabe zum silbernen Abtsjubiläum des hochwürdigen Herrn Abtes von Maria Laach Dr. theol. et iur. h.c. Ildefonds Herwegen (Münster, 1938), pp. 21–50. Repr. in the appendix to the repr. of Harnack's *Militia Christi* already noted, pp. 131–62; Johannes Auer, *Militia Christi. Zur Geschichte eines christlichen Grundbildes*, in: Geist- und Leben. Zeitschrift für Aszese und Mystik 32 (1959), pp. 340–51; Andreas Wang, *Der Miles Christianus im 16. und 17. Jahrhundert und seine mittelalterliche Tradition. Ein Beitrag zun Verhältnis von sprachlicher und graphischer Bildlichkeit* (Bern, Frankfurt/M, 1975) (= Mikrokosmos 1).

62. Cf. Hartmut Hoffmann, *Gottesfriede und Treuga Dei* (Stuttgart, 1964) (= Schriften der Monumenta Germaniae historica 20); Albrecht Noth, *Heiliger Krieg und Heiliger Kampf in Islam und Christentum. Beiträge zur Vorgeschichte und Geschichte der Kreuzzüge* (Bonn, 1966) (= Bonner Historische Forschungen 28); Johannes Fechter, *Cluny, Adel und Volk. Studien über das Verhältnis des Klosters zu den Ständen (910–1156).* Diss.

(Tübingen, 1966); Hermann Jakobs, *Der Adel in der Klosterreform von St. Blasien* (Köln, Graz, 1968) (= Kölner Historische Abhandlungen 16); Friedrich Prinz, *Klerus und Krieg im früheren Mittelalter. Untersuchungen zur Rolle der Kirche beim Aufbau der Königsherrschaft*, (Stuttgart, 1971) (= Monographien zur Geschichte des Mittelalters 2).

63. Carl Erdmann, *Die Entstehung des Kreuzzugsgedankens* (Stuttgart, 1935; repr. Darmstadt, 1955) (= Forschungen zur Kirchen- und Geistesgeschichte 6).

64. Valmar Cramer, *Die Kreuzzugspredigt zur Befreiung des Heiligen Landes. 1095–1270. Studien zur Geschichte und Charakteristik der Kreuzzugspropaganda* (Köln, 1939). (Separate from *Das Heilige Land* Nos. 79–82, 1935–1938, and *Palästina-Hefte des Deutschen Vereins vom Heiligen Lande*, nos. 17–20, pp. 43–204), p. 6.

65. Cf. Ursula Schwerin, *Die Aufrufe der Päpste zur Befreiung des Heiligen Landes von den Anfängen bis zum Ausgang Innozenz' IV. Ein Beitrag zur Geschichte der kurialen Kreuzzugspropaganda und der päpstlichen Epistolographie*. Diss. (Berlin, 1936), p. 75.

66. Erich Köhler, *Observations historiques et sociologiques* (see n. 9); idem, *Vergleichende soziologische Betrachtungen zum romanischen und zum deutschen Minnesang*, in: *Der Berliner Germanistentag 1968, Vorträge und Berichte*, Karl H. Borck and Rudolf Henss, eds. (Heidelberg, 1970), pp. 61–76.

67. Eduard Wechssler, *Das Kulturproblem des Minnesangs. Studien zur Vorgeschichte der Renaissance*, Vol. 1, *Minnesang und Christentum* (Halle, 1909).

68. Gert Kaiser, *Textauslegung und gesellschaftliche Selbstdeutung* (see n. 36).

69. Cf. the reviews of research by Ursula Peters, *Niederes Rittertum oder hoher Adel? Zu Erich Köhlers historisch-soziologischer Deutung der altprovenzalischen und mittelhochdeutschen Minnelyrik*, in: *Euphorion* 67 (1973), pp. 244–60; idem, *Artusroman und Fürstenhof* (see n. 37): Ursula Liebertz-Grün, *Zur Soziologie des amour courtois. Die historisch-soziologischen Interpretationen des altprovenzalischen und des deutschen Minnesangs*. Diss. (Köln, 1976). On Kaiser's interpretation see also Volker Schupp, *Kritische Anmerkungen zur Rezeption des deutschen Artusromans anhand von Hartmanns "Iwein". Theorie-Text-Bildmaterial*, in: Frühmittelalterliche Studien 9 (1975), pp. 405–42.

70. Erich Köhler, *Die Rolle des niederen Rittertums* [see n. 9], pp. 24f.

71. Aloys Schulte, *Die Standesverhältnisse der Minnesänger*, in: Zeitschrift für deutsches Altertum 39 (1895), pp. 185–251.

72. Paul Kluckhohn, *Ministerialität und Ritterdichtung*, in: Zeitschrift für deutsches Altertum 52 (1910), pp. 135–68.

73. *Ministerialität und Ritterdichtung. Umrisse der Forschung* (München: Edition Beck, 1976).

74. Material on this from the documents of the Babenberg Dukes of Austria in Peter Feldbauer, *Rangprobleme und Konnubium österreichischer Landherrenfamilien. Zur sozialen Mobilität einer spätmittelalterlichen Führungsgruppe*, in: Zeitschrift für bayerische Landesgeschichte 35 (1972), pp. 571–90.

75. Cf. Eduard Schröder, *udolf von Ems und sein Literaturkreis*, in: Zeitschrift für deutsches Altertum 67 (1930), pp. 209–51, esp. pp. 219ff.; Karl Bosl, *Die Reichsministerialität der Salier und Staufer* [see note 21], Vol. 2, pp. 428ff.; Helmut Brackert, *Rudolf von Ems. Dichtung und Geschichte* (Heidelberg, 1968) (= Germanische Bibliothek, Series 3), pp. 26ff.; Günther Bradler, *Studien zur Geschichte der Ministerialität im Allgäu und in Oberschwaben*. (Diss. Berlin F.U., 1973), pp. 475ff.

76. *Des königlich fränkischen Kaplans Andreas 3 Bücher über die Liebe*, aus dem Lateinischen übertragen und hrsg. von Hanns Martin Elster, (Dresden, 1924) (= Opal-Bücherei).

77. Cf. Otto Brunner, *Adeliges Landleben und europäischer Geist. Leben und Werk Wolf Helmhards von Hohberg. 1612–1688* (Salzburg, 1949), esp. pp. 61ff.

Bibliography

1. In some cases the best editions were not available to me, e.g., for *Tnugdalus*, for Hartmann's *Rede vom Glauben*, etc. I have made grateful use of the specialized glossaries which are available, particularly the Indices of the University of Wisconsin Press: by R.-M. S. Heffner and Kathe Petersen for *Minnesangsfrühling* (1942); by R.-M. S. Heffner and W. P. Lehmann for Walter von der Vogelweide (2nd ed., 1950); by Alfred Senn and Winfred Lehman for *Parzival* (1938); by Melvin E. Valk for Gottfried's *Tristan* (1958). The two most recent works of R.-M. S. Heffner, *Collected Indexes to the Works of Wolfram von Eschenbach* and *A Word Index to the Texts of Steinmeyer "Die kleineren ahd. Sprachdenkmäler,"* both 1961, did not appear until after I had completed my collection. In addition I used Georg F. Benecke's classic glossary to *Iwein* (3rd ed. by Carl Borchling, Leipzig, 1901) and the glossaries of Karl Bartsch for the *Nibelungenlied* (Leipzig, 1880) and of Edmund Wiessner for Neidhart (Leipzig, 1954). All the information about the vocabulary of the works cited is taken from these glossaries unless a clear statement is made to the contrary.

2. For the volumes which did not appear in Halle the place of publication is noted below.

3. For the volumes which did not appear in Leipzig, the place of publication is noted below.

4. A superior "1" indicates the 1st edition, Heidelberg, 1912.

5. For the volumes which did not appear in Bonn, the place of publication is noted below.

6. Letters before the verse-number refer to the old Eilhart fragments Kurt Wagner ed., RBHP. 5 (Bonn-Leipzig, 1924).

7. M and S after the verse-number refer to the fragments which were printed later: M Marburg Fragment, Karl Bartsch ed., *Germ.* 19 (1874), 195–6; S Sagan Fragment, Willi Göber ed., *Festschrift Theodor Siebs*, GA. 67 (1933), 17–32.

8. The inserted brochure and letters are indicated separately: "Frd. 1. Büchl," etc. and the line-number, and "Frd. Br." according to volume, page, and line.

9. Only the pieces which are not printed in Schönbach's *Altdt. Predigten* are noted.

10. Only the sermons from the Zürich manuscript Wasserkirche 58/275 (Wackernagel No I–XIII, pp. 3–32) are noted.

11. A and D before the line-numbers designates the manuscript according to Wesle.

12. A and M before the line-numbers indicates the old fragments: A Amorbach Fragment, Eduard Schröder ed., ZfdA. 59 (1922), 161–2; M München Fragment, quoted according to Kluge I, 409ff. since the print by Friedrich Keinz is not available to me.

13. I later made a comparison with the edition of Gert Mellbourn, Lunder germanist. Forschungen 12, Lund-Kopenhagen, 1944.

14. D before the line-numbers refers to the manuscript ed. by K. F. Kummer, ZfdA. 25, 1881, 290–301.

15. The addition "Ep." refers to the epic fragments, ibid., pp. 10–18.

16. Only the few documents before 1250 are noted.

17. Only the Wien Fragments are of significance here, ibid., pp. 75–79.

Index

This index is a translation of that which appeared in the German edition of 1977 with the modifications made necessary by translation. Some of the technical expressions in German and other languages have been retained but they are translated when their meaning is not clear from their context.

The index contains the Middle High German sources named in the text only in so far as they are mentioned by title or name of author. No note has been taken of the appendices. Only the most important instances of supporting material given in the notes appear in the index.